SIR JOHN VANBRUGH

SIR JOHN VANBRUGH

Storyteller in Stone

VAUGHAN HART

Published for

THE PAUL MELLON CENTRE FOR STUDIES IN BRITISH ART

by

YALE UNIVERSITY PRESS

NEW HAVEN AND LONDON

Designed by Gillian Malpass

Printed in China

Library of Congress Cataloging-in-Publication Data

Hart, Vaughan, 1960–
Sir John Vanbrugh : storyteller in stone / Vaughan Hart.
p. cm.
Includes bibliographical references and index.
ISBN 978-0-300-11929-9 (cloth : alk. paper)
1. Vanbrugh, John, Sir, 1664–1726–Criticism and interpretation. 2. Architecture,
Domestic–England. 3. Architecture–England–18th century. I. Title.

NA997.V3H37 2008
720.92–dc22

2008006109

A catalogue record for this book is available from
The British Library

Page i
Stone cannon balls set in the outer, entrance gate to the kitchen court at Blenheim.

Frontispiece
Vanbrugh's Belvedere tower at Claremont, 1715.

To Charlotte and Christopher

Acknowledgements

I should like to thank the following for their help and support at various stages in the preparation of this book: Professor Joseph Rykwert, Professor David Watkin, Professor Andrew Ballantyne, Professor Robert Tavernor, Professor Peter Caroline, Dr Frank Salmon, Dr Peter Hicks, Dr Peter Clarkson, Mark Wilson Jones, Mary Courtman-Davies, Katharine Ridler, Ray Biggs, Marion Harney, Hannah South, and Gillian Malpass of Yale University Press. Professors Alan Day and Paul Richens together with Ben Garfitt and Robert Grover of the Centre for Advanced Studies in Architecture (CASA) at Bath University collaborated on the computer models which reconstruct Vanbrugh's lost houses, including those at Greenwich (of which only Vanbrugh Castle remains), his 'Goose-Pie' house in Whitehall, Chargate in Surrey and Eastbury House in Dorset. Paul Richens constructed the computer model of Vanbrugh's unrealised temple with four obelisks (c.1723) illustrated in Chapter Three.

The custodians of Seaton Delaval kindly gave permission to photograph the house. I should like to thank the librarians at the following institutions: the British Library, London, especially those in the Departments of Rare Books and Manuscripts; Bath University Library; Cambridge University Library; the Victoria and Albert Museum, London; The Paul Mellon Centre for Studies in British Art, both in London and New Haven; The National Monuments Record, both in Swindon and London; Lambeth Palace Library, London; Lincolnshire Archives Office; the Society of Antiquaries, London; the Canadian Centre for Architecture, Montreal; the National Archive, London; the Witt and Conway Libraries, Courtauld Institute, London; and the Bodleian, Oxford. Some of the research and writing of this book was carried out whilst a Senior Fellow at the Paul Mellon Centre in London during 2005 and the Centre generously funded travel associated with the work. In the summer of the same year I was a visiting scholar at St John's College in Oxford, which allowed full access to Oxford archives. The Arts and Humanities Research Council (AHRC) and the Department of Architecture and Civil Engineering at Bath University also funded visits to archives and buildings. Elisabeth Richmond of the Regional Building Record in Bath University Library assisted with research into Vanbrugh's Kings Weston. Coincidentally the Department of Architecture's first home was in Kings Weston, near Bristol, and so research for this book represented something of a home from home.

Finally I should like to thank my wife, Charlotte, for her encouragement, patience and support.

Vaughan Hart
University of Bath, 2008

Contents

Preface   Tory Mobs and Ignorant Priests   xi

Introduction   'A good-natured fellow': Vanbrugh's Character
and Works for the Crown   I
   'For Fools I own they are': Vanbrugh's Travels   I
   'She has heartily endeavour'd . . . to throw me into an English Bastile':
     Vanbrugh's Character and the 'Duchess Dispute'   9
   'Dark Stroaks in the Kings Closet': Vanbrugh, Wren and Hawksmoor at
     the Board of Works and Greenwich Hospital   14
   'Architecture has its political Use': Vanbrugh and Board Politics 18
   'An Image of Liberty': The Whig Golden Age   22

I   'BY ACHIEVEMENT, ARMS, DEVICE': DRAMATIST, HERALD AND
ARCHITECT   27

I   'Without thought or lecture': The Early Influences on Vanbrugh   29
   'People especially such, as are no Learnder than I am': Vanbrugh's Studies   29
   'To build by verse': From Heroic Literature to Heroic Architecture   36
   'Building Musick': From Opera to Architecture at the Haymarket Theatre   40

2   'The Historicall Argument': The Order of the Garter and
Vanbrugh's 'Castle Air'   45
   'The great houses in the North': Vanbrugh, Medievalism and British Liberty   45
   'Blew Garters' and 'Good houses': Vanbrugh and the 'Windsor point'   53
   'Arms, Emblems, Devices': The Orders of Knighthood and Architecture   70
   'Practic'd at Windsor': Vanbrugh's British Style and Castles to St George   73

3   'Agreable Objects': Vanbrugh on Architecture, Landscape and Mood   83
   'Lively and pleasing Reflections': Vanbrugh on Mood and Effect   83
   'Pd on a Subscription to Mr Addisons Works': Joseph Addison and the
     Pleasures of the Imagination   86
   'The Best of Landskip Painters can invent': Vanbrugh and the Landscape
     of the Imagination   89
   'Solemn and Awfull Appearance both without and within': Vanbrugh and
     the Architecture of Awe and Melancholy   91
   'An altar, on which the ancients made their offerings': Vanbrugh and the
     Architecture of Death   99
   'Different sensations from each point of view': Vanbrugh and the Architecture
     of Association   108

4 'The Reverend look of a Temple': Decorum and Vanbrugh's
London Church Proposals   III

    'Any thing of frost work or Rock work, may be more a propo': Vanbrugh on
       the Appropriate Use of Architectural Ornament and Form   III

    'The Reformation has reduc'd things to a tolerable Medium': Foppington's
       Pocket and Vanbrugh on Morality and Ornament   116

    'In a plain but Just and Noble Stile': Vanbrugh's London Church Proposals 121

II 'BUILDING HOUSES HERE T'OBLIGE THE PEERS':
LUXURIOUS PALACES AND SHAM CASTLES   127

5 'Wonder enough in the Story': Castle Howard and Blenheim   129

    'Paradise Regained': Vanbrugh at Castle Howard   129

    'Read the Duke of Marlborough in Story': Vanbrugh at Blenheim   136

6 'Something of the Castle Air': Characters in Stone at
Kimbolton and Seaton Delaval   147

    'A very Noble and Masculine Shew': Kimbolton and the 'Castle Air'   148

    'With a pretty Impudent countenance': Seaton Delaval and the Play of
       Oppositions   157

7 'Pleas'd to Storm my Castle': Englishmen's Homes and
Castles at Kings Weston, Eastbury, Grimsthorpe and Stowe   171

    'Your Chateau': Kings Weston for Edward Southwell   171

    'A New Design for a person of Quality in Dorsetshire': Eastbury House for
       George Doddington   186

    'The Seat of . . . the Hereditary Lord great Chamberlain of England':
       Grimsthorpe Castle for the First Duke of Ancaster   194

    'Much entertain'd with (besides his Wife) the Improvements of his House and
       Gardens': Stowe for the First Viscount Cobham   208

8 'A sort of Child of my Owne': Autobiography in Stone at
'Goose-Pie' House, Greenwich and Chargate   213

    'Pretty for a child': Jonathan Swift and 'Goose-Pie' House in Whitehall   213

    'A Tower of White Bricks . . . under the Cannon of this Castle': Vanbrugh
       at Greenwich   217

    'A few Shillings worth of distinction': Chargate into Claremont   232

Conclusion 'Starv'd London Rogues': Country Estates and
National Decay   243

    'The enemy approaches, we must set out our false colours': Masks and Façades 243

    'A good Estate, but it's a little aut at Elbows': English Homes and Castles 248

Appendix I Transcription of Vanbrugh's 'Reasons Offer'd for
Preserving some Part of the Old Manour' of 11 June 1709, sent
to the Duchess of Marlborough   253

Appendix II   Transcription of 'Mr Van-Brugg's Proposals about
Building ye New Churches', addressed to the Church Commissioners
around 1711   254

Notes   256

Bibliography   275

Photograph Credits   283

Index   284

1   Sir John Vanbrugh, portrait by Sir Godfrey Kneller, c. 1705, oil on canvas, 91.4 × 71.1 cm [National Portrait Gallery, London].

TORY MOBS AND IGNORANT PRIESTS

Sir John Vanbrugh (1664–1726) was by turns a business-man, soldier, playwright, herald and, most famously of all, the leading architect of his era (Fig. 1). As a prominent Whig and man of the world he was well placed in both court and town. Intellectually assured and nonconformist by inclination, albeit with strong Protestant sympathies, he moved easily amongst the Whig aristocrats who became his patrons, ridiculing in 1714 what he called 'the Meer Tory Mob, Ignorant, furious country Priests, and Stupid Justices'.[1] Having succeeded as a dramatist, Vanbrugh turned his attentions in 1699, on the eve of the new century, to architecture and a few years later to heraldry, despite lacking a formal apprenticeship in either. Nevertheless over two and a half decades his work as an architect ranged from influencing the austere façades produced by the Board of Ordnance to the layout of garden paradises, and from designing small pavilions to creating flamboyant national palaces.

Vanbrugh specialised in the design of the quintessential building type of his era, the country house, and he came to design its most important example, Blenheim Palace (Fig. 3). Although stylistically his houses are variations on a theme, they none the less form a coherent body of work in blending to a greater or lesser extent *all'antica* (that is, 'Palladian') decoration and forms with English castle motifs. Vanbrugh's eclectic style gave expression to his love affair with medieval military architecture and with Britain's history and traditions, whilst remaining grounded in the by then well-established classical canons of proportion, symmetry and order. As this book will show, Vanbrugh clearly identified this liberal mix as a quintessentially British style of architecture suited to national liberties and Whig ideals. Even at a superficial level, the freedom to apply a variety of architectural styles and a nonconformist attitude to classical canons might be seen to have suited the Whig mindset.[2] For the term 'Whig' generally connoted nonconformity in religious and state affairs, and particularly applied to those who championed limited constitutional monarchy – following the ideals of the Glorious Revo-lution of 1688 – rather than the Divine Right absolutism of Charles II and James II, favoured by the Tories.[3]

Following my earlier study of Nicholas Hawksmoor (Fig. 2), the principal aim of this book is to explain why each of Vanbrugh's buildings looks the way it does.[4] New interpretations are offered of two of his most famous works, Castle Howard (see Fig. 191) and Blenheim. In so doing the book examines the influence on Vanbrugh's architecture of his parallel interest in heraldry and of the completely neglected Garter Knights (since

2 Plaster bust of Nicholas Hawksmoor in the Buttery of All Souls College, Oxford, assumed to be by Henry Cheere, c. 1736.

3 Blenheim Palace, built to express the Duke of Marlborough's 'story', 1705–20.

he served as acting Garter King of Arms from 1715 to 1718); of Whig ideology and religious nonconformity; of Joseph Addison's theories as to architectural 'effect' and of British history as expressed in the country's medieval ruins, in creating one such stylistic effect – or, as he succinctly put it at Kimbolton (Fig. 4; see also Fig. 215), 'Something of the Castle Air'; and of exotic architecture, including the Mogul mausolea he saw in India (Fig. 5). The book does not attempt to describe Vanbrugh's life story independent of his activities as an architect, since he is one of the few great English architects to have been the subject of a biography, published by Kerry Downes in 1987.[5] As with my study of Hawksmoor, no attempt is made here to discuss at any length Vanbrugh's practical work for the Crown or Church – his inspection of foundations and his supervision of labour – work that more often than not owed little to theoretical matters and is covered by Downes.

Something of a tradition has grown up which presents Vanbrugh's architectural development as increasingly influenced by the rise of the Palladians Burlington, Campbell and Kent. This is evidenced by the supposed Palladian character of Vanbrugh's last designs, especially of Grimsthorpe Castle (1723; Fig. 6; see also Fig. 290)

where he is described by Tim Mowl as having made an 'ignominious capitulation to the Palladian'.[6] Yet Vanbrugh's work had been enthusiastically embraced by Colen Campbell much earlier, in his Palladian manifesto comprising the first volume of *Vitruvius Britannicus* published in 1715, and also featured in the later volumes (Grimsthorpe in volume three of 1725; see Figs 291, 297, 298). The 1715 volume included six views of Blenheim, six of Castle Howard and two of Kings Weston (see Figs 99, 164, 190, 201, 253, 263). In fact Vanbrugh's interest in Palladio's houses dates from his earliest days as an architect, Grimsthorpe is not particularly 'Palladian', and his shifts in style can be seen as less concerned with changing tastes than with circumstantial factors – using purely medieval forms for buildings constructed in a country location for his own pleasure (at Greenwich) and for follies (the Belvedere at Claremont), whilst blending *all'antica* and Palladian elements with medieval forms and motifs when building for noble patrons. Many of his patrons had a military past, like himself, and he gave particular expression to this characteristic through selective use of architectural elements drawn from both traditions, in blending Doric columns with crenellations and portholes. At Blenheim, for example, Campbell

4 The east, front façade of Kimbolton Castle, 1707–19.

observed that 'The Manner is Grand, the Parts noble, and the Air Majestick of this Palace, adapted to the Martial Genius of the Patron'.[7]

There are four principal sources for this study. Firstly, Vanbrugh's surviving drawings and those by his office record both built and unrealised schemes, and are held for the most part at the Victoria and Albert Museum in London (including those formally at Elton Hall),[8] whilst his important sketch of the English Cemetery at Surat in India is held at the Bodleian Library in Oxford (reproduced in Appendix Two). Secondly, Vanbrugh's letters provide an invaluable insight into his character and interests, and are mostly written to his Whig patrons – the Duke and Duchess of Marlborough (concerning Blenheim), the Earl of Manchester (concerning Kimbolton), the Duke of Newcastle (concerning alteration of Claremont House and Nottingham Castle, and Grimsthorpe for Robert Bertie) and Lord Carlisle (concern-

5 The tomb of Sir George Oxinden (d. 1669) in the English Cemetery at Surat, India, from the 'Album of architectural and topographical views, mostly in South Asia', taken by an unknown photographer in the 1890s [British Library, London].

6 The north, front façade of Grimsthorpe Castle, Lincolnshire, 1723–30.

ing Castle Howard). The most significant of these letters are probably those entitled 'Reasons Offer'd for Preserving some Part of the Old Manour' at Blenheim, sent to the Duchess of Marlborough in 1709, and what a copyist entitled 'Mr Van-Brugg's Proposals about Building ye New Churches', addressed to the Church Commissioners around 1711. These two are transcribed in the Appendices. In addition, important remarks by Vanbrugh on the 'Castle Air' appropriate for Kimbolton are contained in a letter of 1707 to the Earl of Manchester which is quoted in full in Chapters two and six. His letters are preserved in the British Library, the Bodleian and at Castle Howard, and were edited by Geoffrey Webb (1928) with further correspondence published by Whistler (1954), Rosenberg (1966), Huseboe (1974), Hopkins (1979), Milhous (1979), and Downes (1982 and 1987).[9] Thirdly, a journal of receipts and payments kept by Vanbrugh (from January 1715 until his death, and continued by Lady Vanbrugh) provides clues as to his book purchases and therefore his principal interests.[10]

Finally, when attempting to trace the interrelationship of Vanbrugh's diverse interests, an important source for any study of his architecture must be his plays.[11] Van-

brugh gained the distinction of being one of the most popular comic playwrights of his generation, alongside his friends John Dryden and William Congreve with whom he frequently collaborated.[12] His first stage success was at the age of thirty-two with *The Relapse, or Virtue in Danger* (1696), closely followed by *Aesop* (1697, adapted from a play by Edmé Boursault), *The Provok'd Wife* (1697), *The Pilgrim* (1700, adapted from a play by Fletcher), *The False Friend* (1701, adapted from a play by Francisco de Rojas Zorilla modified by Le Sage), *The Country House* (1703, adapted from a play by Florent Carton de Dancourt), *The Confederacy* (1705, again adapted from a play by Dancourt), *The Mistake* (1705, adapted from a play by Molière) and finally *A Journey to London* (an incomplete work published in 1728, after his death). Two of these, *The Relapse* and *The Provok'd Wife*, were defended by Vanbrugh in *A Short Vindication* (1698) from accusations of immorality and profanity; both plays are still performed to this day. It seems reasonable that the 'natural order' evident in these works for the stage – Vanbrugh's moral, political, and social themes – must also be traceable in his architectural works, that is in his choice of ornament, form and historical models.[13] In

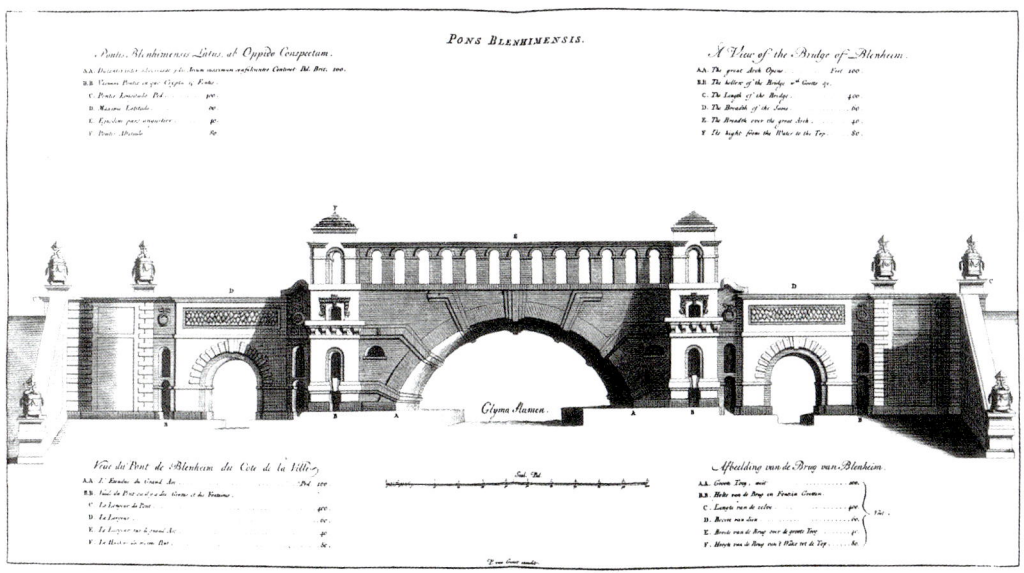

7   Vanbrugh's bridge at Blenheim, 1708–21.

8   Vanbrugh's bridge at Blenheim with intended arcade, engraving by Pieter van Gunst, 1709 [Bodleian Library, Oxford].

fact, architecture and literature have much in common, since architecture can be considered as a type of language comprised of a 'vocabulary' of medieval or classical forms. So when Vanbrugh turned from drama to architecture in 1699 at Castle Howard it was more a change in artistic medium than in intellectual outlook. After all, his observation in 1698 that 'The Stage is a Glass for the World to view itself in' suggests that one might indeed place his architecture before this stage 'glass' and see the reflection of these buildings in his dramas.[14] In their use of sources, Vanbrugh's plays and buildings betray a similar method of free adaptation of other, often historical – and particularly French – works. His theatrical sense of illusion, as well as dramatic conceits such as disguise and deceit, all have architectural expressions through visual surprise, distortion and concealment. Moreover, with their telling use of architectural metaphors, his plays can be seen to have been as much influenced by his buildings as the other way round, especially by those buildings designed around the same time, most notably Castle Howard from 1699 and Blenheim from 1705. For example, the 'Englishman's home is his castle' theme of *The Country House* (1703) is obviously related to – even closely indebted to – the fortified character and allusions fundamental to the conception of Castle Howard from about 1700. In other words Vanbrugh's plays and buildings should be considered as two sides of the same coin.

This interrelationship has been recognised in the case of garden design, where Vanbrugh's plays have been used to elucidate the meaning of the contemporary garden as a setting for assignations and intrigues.[15] With their winding paths and openings, Ray Wood and the Wilderness at Castle Howard, for example, were designed by Vanbrugh and his patron to be every bit as enigmatic as a disguised character in one of his plays.[16] Just as his plays spoke of the conceits, twists and turns of everyday life, so these garden elements were navigated through twisting paths with views both concealed and revealed, in strong contrast to the formal avenues and regular arrangement of earlier native gardens: it is as if life's journey was seen by Vanbrugh in the same terms of concealment and surprise, and was presented as such by him in the garden and on the stage. In Vanbrugh's *The Pilgrim* Alinda exclaims concerning the 'wild Woods', 'Did not I say these Woods had Wonder in 'em?'.[17]

Analogies can also be drawn between Vanbrugh's work as an architect and his role as a herald. For as with the display of family ancestry and marriage allegiances through the picture art of heraldry, so one of Vanbrugh's main aims with the related art of architecture was to use ornament and forms to represent the virtues of his Whig patrons, their achievements and character, and thus, as he put it concerning Blenheim, allow the observer to 'read the Duke of Marlborough in Story'.[18] This priority was the basis of his split with the Duchess, for his desire to emphasise the grandeur of the Duke's 'story' to Blenheim's visitors involved what she saw as unnecessary earthworks and ornamental bridges (Figs 7, 8).[19] Equally, just as Vanbrugh depicted the story of Carlisle and his ancestry at Castle Howard, so he can be seen to have told his own 'story' in the houses he built for himself at Whitehall and Greenwich through his choice of particular forms drawn from the 'language' of architecture. In this way he clearly designed his buildings not just for the enjoyment of his patrons but also for that of an audience, much as he wrote his plays for one. Similarly, just as his plays have common themes and specific plots, so too his buildings display not only common preoccupations – frequently with death and rebirth, the pairing of male and female characteristics, and what he termed the 'Castle Air' – but also specific identities unique to each, often to do with the particular character and 'story' of the patron and the building's location.

Following in the footsteps of the Renaissance architectural master Leon Battista Alberti, Vanbrugh identified with the archetypal wise and unpretentious ancient storyteller Aesop.[20] Vanbrugh chose to translate Edmé Boursault's *Les Fables d'Esope* despite the play's commercial unviability. Here, according to the Prologue, 'The stage turns Pulpit' and, as one of the characters, Learchus, puts it, Aesop 'often call's for Fable to his Aid, / Where under abject Names, of Beast and Birds, / Virtue shines out, and Vice is cloath'd in shame'.[21] Indeed it is clear from Vanbrugh's recommendations for the Queen Anne churches in London that his use of architectural ornament and forms had a similar moral dimension: they extolled the virtue of courage at Blenheim, of family honour at Castle Howard and Seaton Delaval and of humility at the 'awe-inspiring' churches.[22] One of the main purposes of this book is therefore to attempt to read Vanbrugh's buildings as edifying 'stories in stone'.

'A GOOD-NATURED FELLOW': VANBRUGH'S CHARACTER AND WORKS FOR THE CROWN

'FOR FOOLS I OWN THEY ARE': VANBRUGH'S TRAVELS

John Vanbrugh was born in London on 24 January 1664, or so it is thought. His father was Giles Vanbrook or 'Vanbrough' (1631–89), a London merchant of Flemish extraction, and his mother, Elizabeth (*c*.1637–1711), was the daughter of Sir Dudley Carleton and the widow of Thomas Barker. Vanbrugh's coat of arms contained a bridge (*brug* in Flemish) and this may have given expression to what had become the preferred family surname. Even in this small detail of Vanbrugh's background are aspects of his interests, in the association of meanings surrounding names and their heraldic make-up. John was

the fourth of nineteen children and assumed the responsibility of being the eldest surviving son. By October 1667 the family had settled in Chester (Fig. 9), refugees from the capital's dual calamities of the plague and the Great Fire. Chester's medieval architecture clearly left its mark on the young Vanbrugh, as a reference to the city's walls in a letter to the Earl of Carlisle on 21 November 1724 demonstrates: 'I think the Spire that Mr Etty sent will by no means do, a Cap is all that those sort of Towers shou'd have, and I have seen one upon a round Tower on the Walls of Chester, that I thought did extreamly well'.[23] Vanbrugh's education is unknown, although he probably had a private tutor. At some stage he was certainly taught French, a skill which facilitated his later

9   The city walls of Chester, drawn by William Smith and published in the third volume of Georg Braun and Franz Hogenberg's *Civitates Orbis Terrarum* (1581).

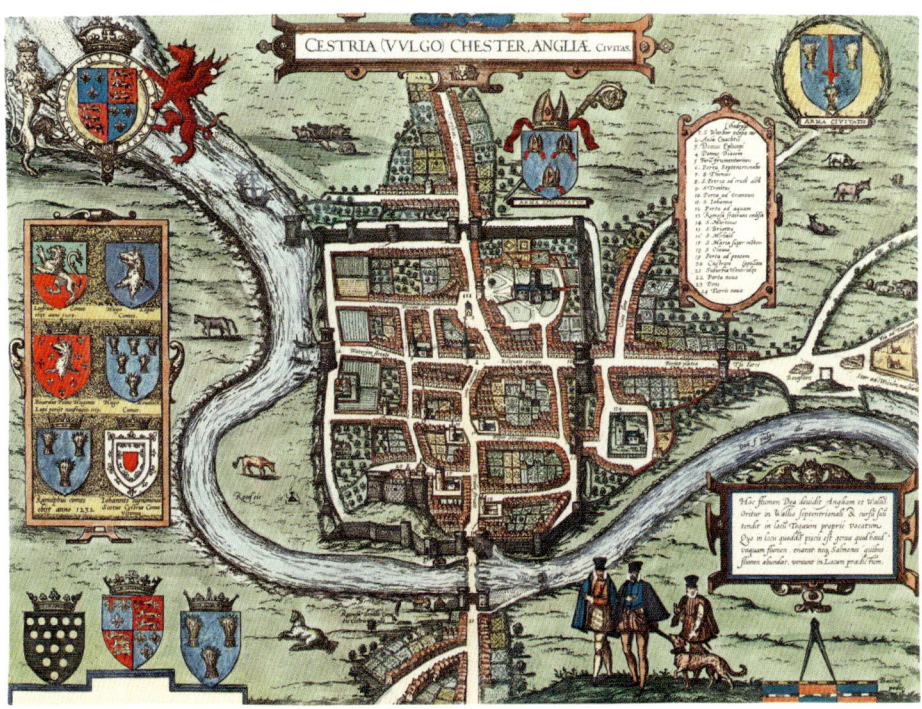

10   Jacob Tonson, portrait by Sir Godfrey Kneller, 1717, oil on canvas, 91.4 × 71.1 cm [National Portrait Gallery, London].

at Suwali, which is only four leagues distant from Surat, and but two from the mouth of the river, bearing from it northwards. Merchandise is conveyed from one place to the other either by cart or by boat, as large vessels cannot enter the river at Surat until after they are unloaded, on account of the sandbanks at the mouth. . . . Surat is a city of moderate size, with a poor fortress, close to which you must pass, whether you approach it by water or by land. It has towers at each of its four angles; and as the walls are not terraced, the guns are placed upon scaffoldings. The Governor of the fortress commands merely the soldiers of the garrison, and possesses no authority in the city, which has its own separate Governor to receive the customs and the other revenues of the King throughout the extent of his Province. The walls of the city

11   An encounter with indigenous peoples, from Jean-Baptiste Tavernier's *Les Six Voyages de Jean-Baptiste Tavernier* (1676).

travels, adaptation of plays and indeed his understanding of architectural theory, much of it in French. The edition of Palladio he eventually requested of his friend and publisher Jacob Tonson (*c.*1656–1736; Fig. 10), for example, was Roland Fréart de Chambray's French translation of 1650.[24]

In 1681, aged seventeen, Vanbrugh was working in London, at the wine business of his cousin William Matthews. After the failure of this venture, in the following year he was taken into service for five years as a 'Factor' in the East India Company and on 4 May 1683 he sailed in the *Scipio Africanus* with a cargo bound for Surat in India (Figs 12, 13). Vanbrugh may have been inspired to undertake this voyage by Jean-Baptiste Tavernier's *Les Six Voyages*, published in Paris in 1676 with vivid descriptions and illustrations of Indian peoples and natural resources, including diamonds, which were intended to encourage trade between the Mogul rulers and the French (Fig. 11). On arrival Vanbrugh would have witnessed Surat more or less as Tavernier had described it seven years earlier:

Vessels sailing for Surat, which is the sole port in the whole empire of the Great Mogul, steer for Diu and Point St. Jean [Sanjan], and then anchor in the roads

12 Surat in northern India viewed from the land, by Ludolf Bakhuizen, *c.*1680 [National Maritime Museum, Greenwich].

are built of earth, and the houses of private persons are like barns, being constructed of nothing but reeds, covered with cow-dung mixed with clay, to fill the interstices, and to prevent those outside from seeing between the reeds what goes on inside. In the whole of Surat there are only nine or ten well-built houses, and the Shah-bandar or chief of the merchants, owns two or three of them. The others belong to the Musalman merchants, and those of the English and Dutch are not the least fine, every President and Commander taking care to keep them in repair, the cost of which is charged against the accounts of their Companies. These dwellings are, nevertheless, only hired houses, as the King does not permit any Frank to possess a house of his own, fearing that he would thereby possess what he might convert into a fortress.[25]

Vanbrugh would certainly have been interested in Surat's fort, built by the Mogul rulers in 1546. His sojourn in Surat gave rise to a sketch of the 'Lofty and Noble Mausoleums' in the English Cemetery there, which was included as an example of enclosed cemeteries in his recommendations of about 1711 to the Church Commissioners charged with building the fifty new Queen Anne churches in London (reproduced in Appendix Two).[26] The exotic monuments of the Mogul rulers of Surat, in evident contrast to the ordinary dwellings of the town, can only have served to open Vanbrugh's mind to the architectural possibilities of the Near and Far East and helped foster a preference for a medley

13 Surat in northern India, detail from an engraving of 1723 published in Guillaume de Lisle's *Atlas de géographie* (1731).

14 Knights' Hall (the Ridderzaal) in The Hague built by William II from 1248.

15 'Noordeinde' Palace in The Hague built in 1533 and altered by Jacob van Campen and Pieter Post in 1639.

16 Drawing, c.1690, by Jan van Call of the Huis ten Bosch, The Hague, by Pieter Post, 1645 [Municipal Archives, The Hague].

of architectural styles which his chosen model, the English Cemetery, represented, with its 'classical' obelisks, symmetrical mausolea and Mogul-inspired domes (see Fig. 5). Here, surely, is the root of Vanbrugh's stylistic preference for the fusion of medieval and classical architectural details, and an important license for this inventive mix which characterises his work. Surat was, after all, at the forefront of his mind when advising the Church Commissioners twenty-eight years later.

Although clearly influential, Vanbrugh's stay in India was short-lived; he was back in London in August 1685. Perhaps the poor nature of Surat's domestic accommodation proved irksome. Through the agency of one of his mother's relations, Theophilus Hastings, who was the seventh Earl of Huntingdon and colonel of an infantry regiment, Vanbrugh was commissioned ensign in the Earl's regiment on 30 January 1686.[27] Both his colonel and captain were Roman Catholics, however, and Vanbrugh – a staunch Protestant throughout his life, like his father – quickly purchased his freedom. Nevertheless this equally short-lived experience of soldiering either inspired or informed Vanbrugh's lifelong interest in military matters which influenced everything from his later fascination with heraldry and coins to the militaristic metaphors, often concerning the protection of female chastity, in his plays and in his architecture, most famously expressed in his desire in refacing Kimbolton for 'Something of the Castle Air'.[28]

Judging from a letter Vanbrugh wrote to William Blathwayt in August 1692 from France, it is thought likely that he visited The Hague in 1688 with Robert Bertie (Lord Willoughby, later the first Duke of Ancaster), possibly to deliver a letter to William of Orange in order to help secure a Protestant succession.[29] Whilst there Vanbrugh would have witnessed fine examples of Dutch medieval architecture (the 'Knights' Hall', for example, built from 1248 by William II) as well as *all'antica* buildings of a much earlier date than any English examples (the Royal Palaces from the 1530s and the Old Town Hall of 1564; Figs 14, 15, 16).[30] What is certain is that in September 1688 Vanbrugh was in France with Willoughby, where he incautiously praised William who was then at war with France and preparing to invade England. Well-connected and possibly considered a valuable hostage, Vanbrugh was arrested and imprisoned in the citadel at Calais (Figs 17, 18). This was a rectangular structure, built largely by the leading fortification engineer Jean Errard de Bar-le-Duc (1554–1610), which incorporated the medieval castle. Although undoubtedly uncomfortable – his health deteriorated – the experience gave Vanbrugh first-hand experience of life in a castle.

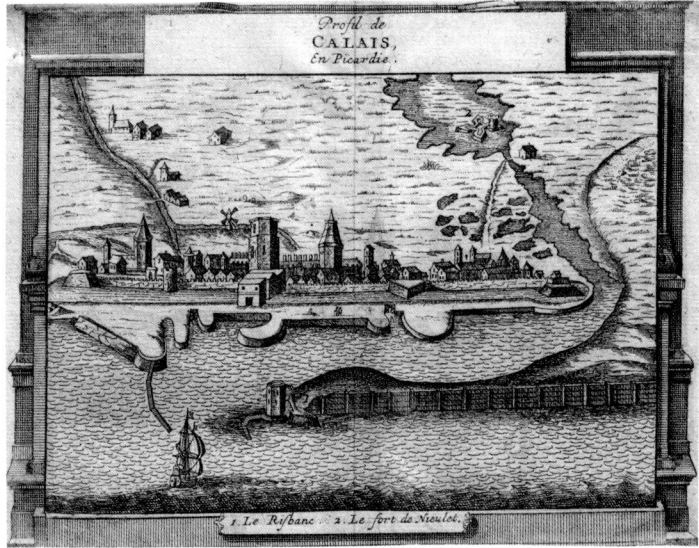

17 View of Calais and its fortifications, engraved by Pierre van Der Aa, c.1725.

18 Plan of the citadel at Calais, as altered by Vauban in the 1690s (destroyed), detail from César-François Cassini's *Carte de France* (1797).

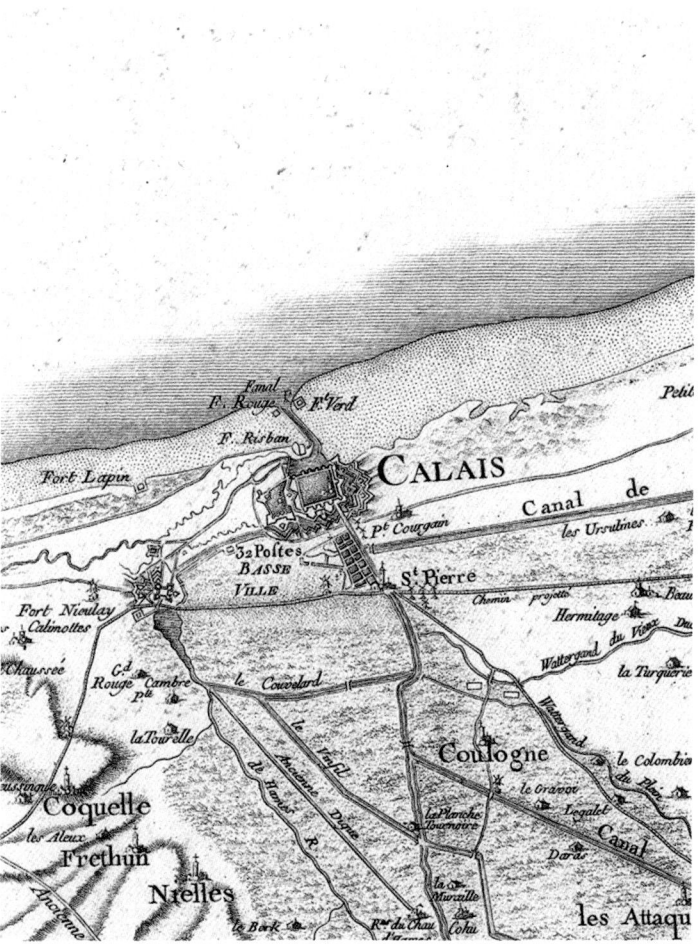

Vanbrugh remained in French custody for four years, from 1688 to 1692. After much negotiation involving his mother, he was transferred in April 1691 to improved quarters at Vincennes where, according to a report in October of that year, he was 'to have the liberty of the courtyard'.[31] Here at the royal residence Vanbrugh would have had plenty of opportunity to study its mix of medieval and *all'antica* buildings.[32] The great fortified walls and inner tower – the tallest medieval fortified structure in Europe – were combined with Louis Le Vau's ranges built in 1656–61 and as such formed a French rival to Windsor which can only have captivated Vanbrugh (Figs 19, 20). He was certainly influenced by

19 (*left*)   The inner tower of Vincennes château, Paris.

20 (*below*)   Louis Le Vau's King's Pavilion at Vincennes château, one of two ranges built in 1656–61 facing one another across a parterre.

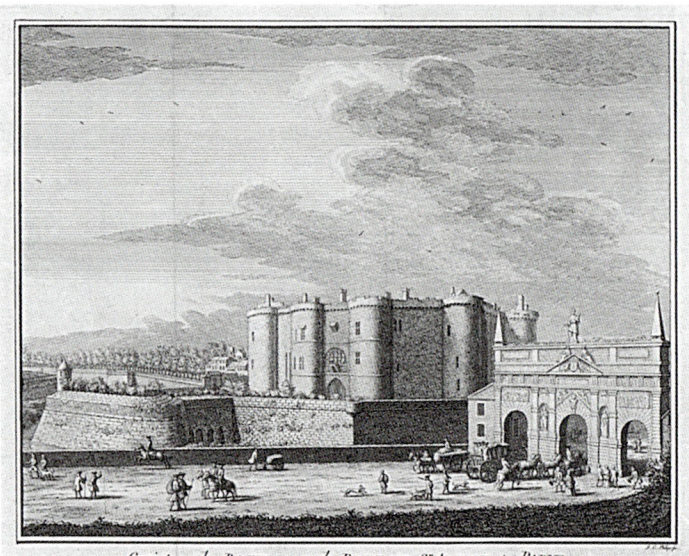

Gezigt op de BASTILLE en de POORT van St. ANTOINE te PARYS.

his experience of the planning of French châteaux, explaining to the Duchess of Marlborough on 10 July 1716 that 'The word Corridore Madam is foreign, and signifys in plain English, no more than a Passage'.[33] The *basecourt* of the French château clearly inspired his own front courts at Eastbury, Grimsthorpe, Seaton Delaval and (as planned) Kings Weston (Fig. 22; see Figs 227, 240, 275, 286, 290). In July 1691 Vanbrugh approached the exiled court of James II at St Germain, asking for help as a loyal follower (a claim which, given Vanbrugh's Protestant allegiance, was patently untrue). In January 1692 he was ordered to be transferred to the Bastille (Fig. 21), probably as a result of his complaints, and by

21   The Bastille and the St Antoine gate, Paris, engraved by J. G. Philips (1740).

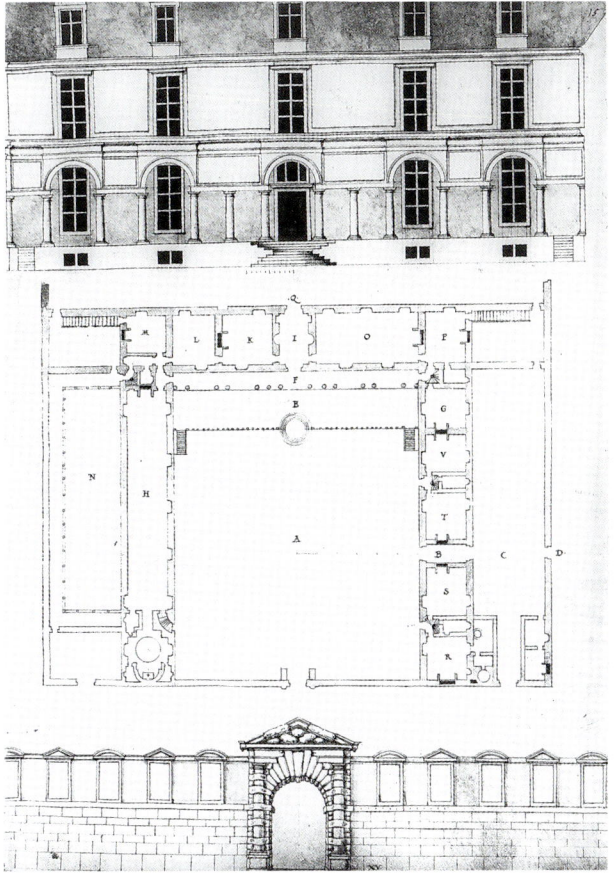

22 The *basecourt* in front of the Grand Ferrara at Fontainebleau (destroyed), designed by Sebastiano Serlio and illustrated in his unpublished *Libro Sesto* (*c.*1547–54), fol. 15r [Staatsbibliothek, Munich].

February it was reported that 'Mr Vanbrook, Mr Goddard, and Mr North . . . [are] clapt up in the Bastile, suspected to be spies'.[34] On 22 November he was released as part of an exchange of prisoners with the English authorities, and was able to spend some short time in Paris. Whilst there he would have seen Les Invalides, the prototype of the military hospitals at Chelsea and Greenwich, Le Vau's College of the Four Nations, as well as the grand palaces of the Louvre and Tuileries (Figs 23, 24, 25, 26). Perhaps the memory of the huge domes at Les Invalides and the College of the Four Nations influenced Vanbrugh at Castle Howard. In any event, he reached England at the end of March 1693.

This period of incarceration must have tried what Jonathan Swift observed was Vanbrugh's good nature, discussed below, and he was evidently left with a somewhat ambivalent attitude to his French hosts. In the Preface to *Aesop*, first performed some five years after his return, he predicted that the play would turn out to be less successful than it had been in France, 'The *French* having more *Mercury* in their Heads, and less Beef and Pudding in their Bellies. Our Solidity may set hard, what their Folly makes easy; for Fools I own they are, you know we have found 'em so, in the Conduct of the War: I wish we may do so, in the management of the Peace.'[35] Vanbrugh denied to the second Earl of Nottingham that he had ever been a spy and, no doubt in part to take revenge on the French, he obtained a captaincy in the marine regiment of Peregrine Osborne, the Marquess of Carmarthen (another kinsman). Carmarthen went on to praise Vanbrugh's courage during the ill-fated naval engagement at Camaret Bay, off Brest, on 7–8 June 1694, after which Vanbrugh saw no further action.[36] He retired on half-pay on 20 August 1698, following the end of that particular conflict with France and having by now become a successful dramatist on the London stage.

23 The Dome of the Hôtel des Invalides, Paris, by Jules Hardouin Mansart, 1679–91.

24   The College of the Four Nations (Collège Mazarin), Paris, by Louis Le Vau, 1662.

25   East front of the Louvre, Paris, by Claude Perrault, 1667–74.

Yet Vanbrugh's travels were not quite over. In May–June 1706 he and Lord Halifax led a delegation to Hanover to confer the Order of the Garter on Prince George, the future George II. During his stay he must have had time to see the impressive formal garden at Herrenhausen, the Elector of Hanover's summer palace, as well as Hanover's medieval architecture, with its romantic high-pitched roofs and half-timber houses (Figs 27, 28). With sojourns in India, France, The Hague

26   Tuileries, Paris (1564–1680; destroyed), engravings by the Perelle family, early eighteenth century.

and Hanover, Vanbrugh was thus well travelled by contrast with his colleagues in the Board of Works, given that Hawksmoor never went abroad, as far as is known, and Wren limited his foreign travels to a period in France and, it has been speculated, the German territories.[37]

⋆   ⋆   ⋆

However, Vanbrugh returned once again to soldiering, possibly out of a need for a more steady income, and was commissioned on 10 March 1702 as a captain in the new foot regiment of George Hastings, eighth Earl of Huntingdon (the son of his original colonel). Queen Anne's declaration of war on France two months later and Vanbrugh's pending architectural appointment as Comptroller of Her Majesty's Works in place of William Talman, confirmed on 20 May, prompted him to find a substitute and resign his commission.

27   Market Church in Hanover, built in the fourteenth century (rebuilt as a replica in 1952).

'SHE HAS HEARTILY ENDEAVOUR'D . . . TO THROW ME INTO AN ENGLISH BASTILE': VANBRUGH'S CHARACTER AND THE 'DUCHESS DISPUTE'

In the famous portrait of Vanbrugh painted by Sir Godfrey Kneller around 1705 as part of a series of pictures of Kit Cat members, the architect poses with a good-humoured expression (see Fig. 1). One might expect this, perhaps, from the writer of comedies. Writing on New Year's Day 1706 to Edmund (or William) Boulter, the Blenheim Comptroller at the time, Vanbrugh observes, 'You never had in your Life to do with any body more easy than you'll find me, & I beg nothing may ever happen to make any dispute between us'.[38] Even Jonathan Swift was forced to concede that 'he be a good-natured fellow', despite the fact that both writers came from opposite political camps and that following Swift's verses mocking Vanbrugh's house in Whitehall, nicknamed 'Goose-Pie' (Fig. 29; see Figs 316, 317), the architect had 'had a long quarrel with me about those verses on his house; but we were very civil and cold. Lady Marlborough used to tease him with them, which had made him angry'.[39] This is not to say that Vanbrugh was without enemies: he fell out with John Anstis over the role of Garter Herald and with the Duchess of Marlborough over Blenheim (Fig. 30). However, he appears to have remained sanguine, commenting to the Duke of Newcastle in 1719 that 'I am

28   Garden theatre designed by Peter Wachter and Martin Charbonnier between 1689 and 1693 in the Herrenhausen, the Elector of Hanover's summer palace in Hanover, engraving from J. Müller and J. van Sasse, *Gartenhäuser und Gartenansichten aus dem Königl. Lustgarten zu Herrenhausen bei Hannover* (1751).

29   Vanbrugh's 'Goose-Pie' House, Whitehall, built in 1700 (destroyed), watercolour drawing from the Soane office, *c*.1803 [Sir John Soane's Museum, London].

not one of those, who drop their Spirits, on every Rebuff: if I had, I had been under ground long ago'.[40] To Lord Carlisle he observed in 1721 that 'I . . . have every day of my Life Since twenty years old, grown more and more of opinion, that the less one has to do, with what is call'd the World, the more Quiet of mind; and the more Quiet of mind, the more Happyness'.[41] Vanbrugh seems even to have agreed with his detractors concerning the light-weight nature of his early works. In his prologue to *The Confederacy*, first performed in 1705, he mocks his achievements to date. A 'shabby poet', in thanking the gods, observes regarding the play's author:

> He'as thank'd you, first, for all his Decent Plays,
> Where he so nick'd it, when he Writ for Praise . . .
> For building Houses here t'oblige the Peers,
> And fetching all their House about his Ears;

> For a new Play, he'as now thought fit to write,
> To sooth the Town – which they – will damn to Night.[42]

This modesty extended, for the most part, to the ornamentation of Vanbrugh's domestic residences which he designed for himself and his family at Esher (Chargate) and Greenwich, in that these are sham castles with austere façades rather than grandiose houses with porticoes and decorative embellishments. Something of this distinction is reflected in Vanbrugh's observation to Tonson concerning Blenheim: 'one may find a great deal of Pleasure, in building a Palace for another; when one shou'd find very little, in living in't ones Self'.[43] The only exception might be said to be Vanbrugh's residence in Whitehall, 'Goose-Pie', which Swift mocked for its trying to look larger than it was, in the verses already mentioned.

30   Sarah Churchill, Duchess of Marlborough, portrait after Sir Godfrey Kneller, *c.*1700, oil on canvas, 105.5 × 88.9 cm [National Portrait Gallery, London].

Vanbrugh was a confirmed bachelor in his youth; indeed he was even hostile to the matrimonial state, as his early comedies such as *The Relapse* and *The Provok'd Wife* make perfectly clear. Nevertheless his marriage to Henrietta Maria Yarburgh in January 1719, when he was fifty-four, brought much contentment.[44] Although at first observing to the Duke of Newcastle in that month that ''tis better however to make a Blunder towards the end of ones Life, than at the beginning of it', by July of that year Vanbrugh was writing to Tonson that 'I have taken this great Leap in the Dark, Marriage . . . if there be any truth in Married Man, (who I own I have ever esteem'd a very lying creature) I have not yet repented'.[45] He became a devoted husband and father, commenting to Tonson in June 1722 that 'I am now two Boys Strong in the Nursery but am forbid getting any more this Season for fear of killing my Wife. A Reason; that in Kit Cat days, wou'd have been stronger for it, than against it: But let her live, for she's Special good, as far as I know of the Matter'.[46] To Carlisle a month later he observed that 'I fancy your Lordships Godson will be a Professor that way, for he knows Pillars, & Arches and Round Windows & Square Windows already, whether he finds them in a Book or in the Streets, and is much pleas'd

with a House I am building him in the Field at Greenh: it being a Tower of White Bricks, only one Room and a Closet on a floor. He talks every thing, is much given to Rhyming, and has a Great turn to dry joking'.[47] Charles was evidently following in his father's footsteps in combining the pleasures of rhyming and building, just as Vanbrugh was following his son's in building miniature castles at Greenwich, as will be seen in Chapter Eight.

Perhaps in line with his religious leanings as a Protestant with nonconformist tendencies, Vanbrugh was plainly not overly superstitious and, unlike with Hawksmoor, there is no evidence that he was interested, for example, in what were by tradition the superstitious practices of the Masons.[48] In a letter to the Lord Treasurer, Sidney Godolphin, on 9 November 1704, on the subject of the Kensington Orangery (Fig. 31), he comments concerning a stonemason (called Thomas Hill):

> But a few days after finding he had not begun, and enquiring into the reason; I found he had been frighten'd with some hints of what shou'd befall him if he durst meddle with the Master Masons business. And this had been put so home to him that he sent to me to desire I would excuse him. I went to Sr. Chr: Wren and tould him what had past. He said the Man was a Whimsicall Man, and a piece of an Astrologer, and would Venture upon nothing till he had consulted the Starrs, which probably he had not found favourably enclin'd upon this Occasion and therefore had refus'd the Work. I desir'd he would employ Somebody that was less Superstitious which he said he wou'd.[49]

Whereas Hawksmoor can be seen to have expressed his Masonic interests through his use of particular *all'antica*

31   Orangery, Kensington Palace, London, designed by Nicholas Hawksmoor, 1704–5.

32   St Luke, Old Street, London, by Nicholas Hawksmoor and John James, 1727–33, engraving by T. Lester (before damage during the Second World War) [British Library, London].

33   St John, Horselydown in Bermondsey, London (destroyed), by Nicholas Hawksmoor and John James, 1727–33 [London Metropolitan Archives].

forms associated with that tradition, most strikingly perhaps with his obelisk steeples at St Luke and St John in London (Figs 32, 33),[50] Vanbrugh was much more concerned with the integration of medieval elements and regular *all'antica* forms such as pediments and columns, and there is no discernable trace of Masonic imagery in his work. Nevertheless, as will be seen, he certainly valued the theatrical aspect of traditional building rituals such as the laying of foundation stones, which had strong Masonic overtones.

The accusation by the French that Vanbrugh had acted as a spy was probably false but he clearly had a secretive side to his character and became a keeper of court secrets. In a letter to Carlisle in February 1721 he notes concerning correspondence with the Duke of Marlborough that 'The Kings writing this Letter, I have only known as a Secret, not yet to be Spoken of'.[51] As a fashionable member of society, he belonged to a number of secretive Whig clubs such as the Kit Cat, the Hanover and the Tate a Tate (an offshoot of the Kit Cat) where he socialised with many of his architectural patrons.[52] Writing to the Duke of Marlborough on 29 May 1714 he praises 'Those warm honest Gentlemen of the Hanover club'[53] and he observes to the Duke of Newcastle in August 1718 that 'the Tate a Tate Club reviv'd last night, at the Hercules Pillars Alehouse, in high Holborn There was Stinking fish, and Stale cold Lamb for Supper with divers Liquours made of Malt in an execrable Manner'.[54] Near the end of his life, in August 1725, Vanbrugh recalled to Tonson that 'our former Kit Cat days, were remembered with pleasure. We were one night reckoning who was left, and both Ld Carlisle & Cobham exprest a great desire of having one meeting next Winter, if you come to Towne, Not as a Club, but old Friends that have been of a Club, and the best Club, that ever met.'[55] Vanbrugh's dramatic plots frequently hinged on the comedy of errors ensuing from intrigues, most obviously in *The Mistake* where Camillo's 'secret' identity as a boy lies at the play's heart. He was undoubtedly regarded as secretive by some of his compatriots, especially the Duchess of Marlborough. In a letter to her of 3 August 1716, concerning the causeway to the bridge at Blenheim (see Figs 7, 8), Vanbrugh observes: 'I neither did intend to promote that work by any trick or indirect means: Or that I ever do intend to conceal any thing from you relating to the works in general. If you do not believe me in this I hope you will Madam when I declare (which I now do) very truly and positively that I will make no secret to you of any thing, and by consequence, if I do must be (what by God I am not) a very Lying Rascal.'[56] The letter is endorsed by the Duchess: 'A letter of Sir Johns to excuse his having done anything about the Causeway, pretending it was the signed Orders for every thing else, but that was kept a secret.'[57] Later in August Vanbrugh writes to the Duchess that 'I desire your Grace will believe me that I have no underhand projects or fancys of my own to execute . . . for I have resolv'd, never to give you any disturbance of that kind'.[58] Ever suspicious of her architect's intentions, again the Duchess endorses the letter: 'Sir Johns letter assuring me, that he will give me no more trouble about the Manor House at the same time he was making Walls Slopes and Gardens.'[59] Evidently there was some foundation for her suspicions. As far as the Duchess was concerned, Vanbrugh had made a secret of living in Old Woodstock Manor (Fig. 34), which he re-roofed in 1708, as well as of the true, inhabitable nature of the bridge at Blenheim.[60] He kept secret funds: for example, he wrote to Henry Joynes, his Clerk of Works at Blenheim, in October 1710, 'I desire you will make such a demand for the Country People in Generall, that you may be Able to keep two or three hundred pounds in private Bank for Exigencys which She [the Duchess] can't forsee. but make no Mention of this to any body'.[61]

The correspondence between Vanbrugh and the Duchess charts their deteriorating relationship at Blenheim. Things evidently started well enough, for in November 1709 she writes concerning her architect that

> though you have vext me extreamly, in forcing me to things against my Inclination; yet I shall always think myself oblig'd to you, and will always be endeavouring to be out of your Debt; because I know, that what I did not like, as well as what I did approve of, you intended for the best, and tho' it is said that in this World there is no perfection, you are not the only Architect that thinks 'tis impossible they can err.[62]

After their dispute about Woodstock Manor and the bridge and causeway, however, Vanbrugh's tone of conciliation changed markedly and by 3 August 1716 his style to the Duchess had become much more direct: 'as I have very often seen you *heated* by wrong informations or misconceptions; and not make any difficulty at owning your *mistake* when you have found it So I shall be much disappointed, if when I wait upon you at Blenheim, I do not find you very well satisfied with my defence about the Causeway.'[63] On 8 November of that year he wrote that

> you had resolv'd to use me so ill in respect of Blenheim . . . These Papers Madam are so full of Far-fetched, Labour'd Accusations, Mistaken Facts, Wrong Inferences, Groundless Jealousies and strain'd Constructions: That I shou'd put a very great affront upon your understanding if I suppos'd it possible you cou'd

34   Woodstock Manor, Oxfordshire, watercolour by anonymous artist, 1714 [British Museum, London].

mean any thing in earnest by them; but to put a Stop to my troubling you any more. You have your end Madam, for I will never trouble you more.[64]

Vanbrugh withdrew from Blenheim, leaving behind perhaps his greatest achievement (see Fig. 3). On 10 November he commented to the Duke of Newcastle on the 'Abominable Womans proceeding' and on the 'Wicked Womans Temper', adding on 15 November that 'she is not a Fool, tho' she's a – Worse thing'.[65] During his subsequent protracted legal dispute with the Duchess over his and his workmen's unpaid fees, which occupied the years following, Vanbrugh elaborated by calling her a 'Vile Woman' and a 'Wicked Dutchess'[66] and, having listed the Duke's considerable assets in a letter to Tonson in June 1722, he adds 'And yet, this Man wou'd neither pay his Workmen their bills nor his Architect his Salary.'[67]

The final insult came when, years after his effective dismissal from the works at Blenheim, Vanbrugh was denied access to the site and was reduced to peering over the wall to check on progress.[68] He wrote to Tonson on 12 August 1725 that

> We Stay'd Two Nights in Woodstock, My Lord and the Ladys, having a mind to View Blenheim in every part with leisure. But for my own Share, There was an order to the Servants, under her Graces own hand, not to let me enter any where. And lest that shou'd not mortify me enough, She having some how learn'd, that my Wife was of the Company sent an Express the Night before we came there with orders, if she came with the Castle Howard Ladys, the Ser-

vants shou'd not Suffer her to see either House, Garden, or even to enter the Park, which was obey'd accordingly, and She was forc'd to Sit all day and keep me Company at the Inn.[69]

Nevertheless Vanbrugh never lost his sense of humour over the affair. On winning his legal case for unpaid fees two months later, near the end of his life, he again wrote to Tonson noting that 'My carrying this point enrages her much, and the more, because it is of considerable weight in my Small Fortune, which She has heartily endeavour'd so to destroy, as to throw me into an English Bastile to finish my days, as I begun them, in a French one.'[70]

In fact Vanbrugh was neither poor when compared to many of his contemporaries, nor rich when compared with the assets of his noble friends and patrons. He became involved in the financial disaster of his age, the South Sea Bubble of late 1720. Initially he had observed to Tonson, in February 1720, 'Our South Sea, is become a Sort of a Young Messissippy, by the stocks rising so vastly; I am however only a looker on, and a Rejoycer, not an Envyer, of other peoples good Fortune'.[71] The reference to Mississippi was to Tonson's investment in the ill-fated Mississippi scheme, which was similar to the South Sea idea but based on French investments made in Virginia.[72] However, Vanbrugh went on to invest in the South Sea scheme, as his accounts record,[73] and by March 1721 he was writing to Carlisle in reference to the infamous 'Bubble' of the year before: 'The South Sea is so hatefull a Subject one do's not Love to name it; And yet it do's so interfere with almost every bodys Affairs more or less, that all they have to do, is in some degree govern'd by it. Even I, who have not gain'd at all, Shall probably be a Loser near £2000.'[74] In order to improve his finances, on occasion Vanbrugh even acted as a property developer in his own right.[75]

In the end Vanbrugh became resigned to his fate at Blenheim and his lack of recognition and financial reward there and elsewhere. This resignation was perhaps due to his keen awareness of the uncertainties of human affairs, as demonstrated by his relative financial caution and, most clearly of all, by the content of his plays. In the second part of *Aesop*, written by Vanbrugh (and not present in Boursault's original version), the ancient storyteller is made to observe:

> You'd see perhaps, a Venerable Statesman, sit fast asleep in a great Downy Chair; whilst in that soft Vacation of his thought, Blind Chance (or what at least we blindly call so) shall so dispose a thousand secret Wheels, that when he wakes, he needs but write his Name, to publish to the World some blest Event, for

which his Statue shall be rais'd in Brass. Perhaps a moment thence, you shall behold him torturing his Brain: His thoughts all stretcht upon the Rack for Publick Service. The live-long Night, when all the World's at rest, consum'd in Care, and watching for their safety, when by a Whirlwind in his Fate, in spight of him, some mischief shall befall 'em, for which a furious Sentence straight shall pass, and they shall Vote him to the Scaffold. Even thus uncertain are Rewards and Punishments; and even thus little do the People know when 'tis the Statesman merits one or t'other.[76]

These words, written in 1697, might be taken as a perfect reflection of Vanbrugh's own attitude to earthly achievements and as prophetic for his fortunes at Blenheim.

'DARK STROAKS IN THE KINGS CLOSET': VANBRUGH, WREN AND HAWKSMOOR AT THE BOARD OF WORKS AND GREENWICH HOSPITAL

Throughout Vanbrugh's working life as an architect, with the exception of a short break from 1713 to 1715, he served in the Board of Works, that body which administered the building and repair of Crown properties. Much as at Blenheim, his time at the Board was coloured by disputes and rivalries with other officers. These disputes are again recorded in his correspondence, which throws light on the Board's workings and on the role of political patronage in them. Vanbrugh replaced his rival William Talman as Comptroller of the Board – the second highest office – on 20 May 1702 at the age of thirty-nine. He then served until he too was dismissed, under Tory pressure, in April 1713, only to be reinstated two years later under the new Whig administration.[77] He remained in this post until his death in 1726 and from 1715 he also served as Surveyor of Royal Gardens and Waters. As Comptroller Vanbrugh was expected to attend daily morning meetings of the Board's officers, to fix building rates, to examine the work books which recorded the monthly expenditure, to check stores and to make frequent site visits. During this time he worked under the master architect of his age, Sir Christopher Wren (Fig. 35), who served as the Board's Surveyor-General from 1669 until his own dismissal in 1718, followed briefly by service under Wren's replacement William Benson (also dismissed, in 1719) and then Sir Thomas Hewett. Vanbrugh also worked alongside his friend and colleague at Castle Howard and Blenheim, Hawksmoor, who served at first as Secretary to the Board – from 1715 until 1718 – and then from 1721 as

Vanbrugh's deputy. It was Vanbrugh who loyally secured the newly created post of Secretary for Hawksmoor and from 1719 he made persistent pleas on behalf of 'poor Hawksmoor' for his re-appointment to the Board and, in 1725, for his re-instatement as Secretary (eventually confirmed in 1726).[78]

The Board of Works thus brought together three of England's leading baroque architects during the period of the style's greatest popularity, and its work would have served as a valuable training for Vanbrugh following his appointment only three years after the commencement of Castle Howard (see Fig. 191). None the less, the three were different in temperament and approach. Indeed Vanbrugh's support for Hawksmoor in the Board is all the more commendable since in their various collaborations here and elsewhere the two architects evidently had not always seen eye to eye. Anonymous remarks concerning Blenheim written at the end of a letter by Vanbrugh to Lord Carlisle in 1717, record that 'M^r. Hawkesmoor protested . . . that it had given him a great deal of trouble very often to see the unreasonable proceedings of Sir John'.[79] Moreover Vanbrugh was also an occasional rival to Wren at Blenheim, whilst serving under him at the Board. For Vanbrugh notes to the Duchess on 3 August 1716 regarding the design for the causeway to the bridge that, 'the Modells were inspected, and that of Sir Christopher Wren, Stuck full of pins, by which he pretended to lessen the charge, was quite rejected, and that I propos'd was resolv'd on.'[80]

Vanbrugh's correspondence on the subject of his duties at the Board confirms the essential honesty of his character. He had in fact been critical of Wren's management of the Board almost from the outset of his service, writing to the Lord Treasurer, the first Earl Godolphin, on 9 November 1704 on what he terms the 'shamefull abuse in the Board of Works'. This concerned an important rule that officers were not to undertake Crown building works themselves, a practice in which they gained a financial advantage, but were rather to oversee those works entrusted to their care. Vanbrugh continues to Godolphin that when

> I made severall attempts upon Sr Chr. Wren to perswade him to redress it himself without troubling yr Lordship; putting him in mind; that besides its being utterly against common Sense, it was contrary to an Express Direction to the Board upon the Establishment after the Restoration. He always own'd what I urg'd him to was right and often promis'd to join with me in Overruling so bad a practice; but when I press'd him to the Execution, he still evaded it, and that so many times, that at last I saw he never intended it, and so I gave your L'dship the trouble of a Complaint.[81]

35   Sir Christopher Wren, portrait by Sir Godfrey Kneller, 1711, oil on canvas, 124.5 × 100 cm [National Portrait Gallery, London].

Later, in 1714 Vanbrugh proposed reforming the Board by abolishing the office of Master Mason and Carpenter in order to 'Save the King, a very great Sum of Money, in unnecessary and unreasonable Works; and lessen his expence considerably in many Useless or Mischievous Officers.'[82]

Following Wren's dismissal, Vanbrugh plainly coveted the Surveyorship.[83] On reports that Sir James Thornhill was to be made Surveyor, Vanbrugh wrote to the Duke of Newcastle on 15 August 1719 that

> Twou'd be a pleasant Joke to the World, to See a Painter made Surveyor of the Works, in Order to Save money; When all the Small knowledge or taste they ever have of it, is only in the Great expensive part, As Collumns, Arches, Bass reliefs &c which they just learn enough of, to help fill up their Pictures. But to think, that Such a Volatile Gentleman as Thornhill, Shou'd turn his thoughts & Application to the duty of a Surveyors business, is a Monstruous project.[84]

Despite his initial lack of training, clearly by now Vanbrugh saw himself as a 'professional' architect, in contrast

36   Greenwich Hospital for Seamen.

to the 'amateur' Thornhill. A few months later, on 29 November 1719, he commented to his friend Tonson that he had 'had a very hard Disappointment of not being made Surveyour of the Works; Which I believe you remember, I might have had formerly, but refus'd it, out of Tenderness to Sr Chr: Wren.'[85] Vanbrugh's loyalty turns out to have been somewhat ironic, for it appears Wren had tried to engineer the Surveyorship for his son, also called Christopher.[86] Nevertheless Vanbrugh's good character is once again perfectly apparent.

Perhaps not surprisingly, Vanbrugh failed to get on with Wren's replacement as Surveyor, William Benson. In fact, Benson actively campaigned against him, and Vanbrugh reported to the Duke of Newcastle in 1718 that

> I have reason to believe, the King has had such an unfair Account given him secretly of my Management, both of his Houses and Gardens; As must make me Appear a very bad Officer in the Employments he has been pleas'd to intrust me with. And I am infor-

m'd, This Representation has been follow'd, with an Attempt to have me remov'd from his Service: And that this Attempt, is in a way of Succeeding.[87]

Later, when writing to the Duke on the same subject in 1719 he adds, 'I have a wild strange Acc^t: of the rout my Friend and Superior Officer, Benson, makes at the Treasury . . . Let me be but protected from any dark Stroaks in the Kings Closet, and I have nothing to fear.'[88] Vanbrugh's honesty in executing his duties is attested once more by his public opposition to a corrupt scheme of Benson's to receive additional payment for the execution of Crown works – a scheme which contributed to the swiftness of the new Surveyor's downfall.[89] Unfortunately Vanbrugh's relationship with Benson's replacement, Hewett, was equally awkward. A letter to the Duke of Newcastle of 1718 has the postscript: 'I Apprehend being put more out of humour at this Rascally Board of Works, than ever.'[90] Writing again to Tonson, on 31 December 1719, Vanbrugh's exasperation is obvious: 'I wish I may find means to change my Place in the Board of Works for something else, being very uneasy in it, from the Unparralel'd Ingratitude of the present Survey[r], Hewet: who owes his coming in, entirely to me, and that, in so known a manner that he has not the Confidence to deny it to anybody, But he's a Son of a Whore, and I'll trouble you no more about him.'[91] Destined never to be made Surveyor himself, Vanbrugh's time at the Board was inevitably problematic yet he remained good-humoured and at all times honest.

Vanbrugh had better luck elsewhere, for from 1703 he had served as a member of the Board of Directors of Greenwich Hospital (Fig. 36). He attended meetings but was unable to approve specific designs until after Wren's death in 1716, when he became the Surveyor. He served in this capacity until his own death in 1726 when he was succeeded by Colen Campbell.[92] Wren should, in fairness, have been replaced by Hawksmoor, who had served as Assistant Surveyor from 1705, but it was Vanbrugh who got the salary of £200 per year. Subsequently Hawksmoor somewhat bitterly made out that the post of Surveyor was unnecessary, commenting to Lord Carlisle following Campbell's appointment in 1726 that

> Sr John Vanb – had obtained, of Mr Dorrington (when in y[e] Admiralty), to be Surveyour of Greenwich hospitall, and an allowance of 200 £ p annm. This place I desired the Lords of y[e] Admiralty to sink, (as useless) and soe did all that were concernd for they all knew that I had carried on, and finished so much as was done of that fabrick; for little more than one hundred pds p annm. But Mr Colin Campell Author of a book calld Vitruius Britanicus. Smelling this out, in spite of all y[e] Lords of y[e] Admiralty could doe; got y[e] place Sr John, had made at Greenwich hotel. with all y[e] allowances therof. So that in that place we are hansomly saddled – however thank God and y[e] Lp, for what we have got.[93]

Certainly Vanbrugh was not responsible for the sole design of any one range at Greenwich. Rather, from the time of his taking up the Surveyor's duties until his death, he had a hand in all the building activity – from the fitting up of a library cum exhibition room at the south end of the King Charles building to the supply of a pulpit from Hampton Court in 1716.[94] In this way he was closely involved in perhaps the greatest collaborative building project of his age and here again he must have learnt valuable lessons in the art of building. Indeed as with other buildings with which Vanbrugh was connected, Greenwich Hospital had a military association – this time through the treatment of sailors from the Royal Navy. The buildings expressed this association through the sea monsters and four cherubs blowing winds on the

37   Sea monsters and four cherubs on the west façade of the Painted Hall, Greenwich Hospital.

38   Shellfish on the four Ionic capitals on the east façade of the King William building, Greenwich Hospital, 1702.

west façade of the Painted Hall, and the festoons with shellfish on the four Ionic capitals on the east front of the King William building of 1702 (Figs 37, 38). This adaptation of ornament – possibly led by Hawksmoor – may well have informed Vanbrugh's own emerging architectural tastes and principles in the early 1700s for, as will be seen, his preference for the appropriate use of ornament was articulated elsewhere in order to reflect both his patron's mythology, or 'story', and his building's function.

★   ★   ★

39   Drawing by Thomas Fort (Clerk of Works at Hampton Court, 1714–45) representing a version of Vanbrugh's scheme for remodelling the north side of Hampton Court, probably a copy of a now lost drawing held by the Office of Works [Historical Royal Palaces].

'ARCHITECTURE HAS ITS POLITICAL USE': VANBRUGH AND BOARD POLITICS

It was noted earlier that Vanbrugh's tenure as Comptroller was interrupted when his patent was revoked
under the Tory administration of Queen Anne's last
years, that is between April 1713 and when the Whigs
returned to power in January 1715. Evidently his dismissal was politically motivated, since he had taken too
active a part in Oxfordshire politics in the defence of the
Whig Duke of Marlborough. By then the Duke and his
wife had fallen from grace at Court, in part due to their
financial requests and in part to the bickering between
Anne and the Duchess. In a letter to a relation on 2 April
1713 Vanbrugh explained:

> I don't Know whether you have heard, that I am
> turn'd out of my place in the Works, for writing a
> Letter to the Mayor of Woodstock in which I say the
> Duke of Marlborough has been bitterly and bar-
> barously persecuted, for these two Years past, in which
> I only meant the Continuall and Daily Libels and
> Pamphlets which pelted him, but some High-Church
> Members of Parliament wou'd needs have it, I meant
> the House of Commons and so have push't the Matter
> to my being turn'd out, I believe I cou'd have pre-
> vented it, if I wou'd have made my Submission to
> those High-Church Blockheads, but that I wou'd on
> no terms do. However, I wou'd not have you Con-
> cerned at it, for if the Pretender comes in, I shall gett
> more by it then they that made it their buisness, or
> were imploy'd to turn me out.[95]

An anonymous letter to the Earl of Oxford in June of
that year denounced Vanbrugh for harbouring 'trecher-
ous Principles', in that 'altho' being rais'd to such Honor,
under her Majesty' at the Board 'yet [he] makes no
scruple of railing against the Church's Upholders, and
Owns his chief Interest lies, in the coming in of the
Pretender'.[96] Resentments lingered despite his eventual
re-instatement, for in a letter to the Duchess in July 1716
Vanbrugh refers to 'the impertinent storys those Oxford
beasts, are ready to send round the country and are nib-
bling at already'.[97]

The circumstances of Vanbrugh's dismissal and subsequent re-instatement to the Board clearly underline its
political importance. As a leading Whig, Vanbrugh was
obviously fully aware of the political significance of
architecture to the State, not least through connections
made when working at the Board and at Blenheim in
the celebration of national glory. As a key ambition
behind his work for the Board, Wren had written that
'ARCHITECTURE has its political Use; public Buildings
being the Ornament of a Country; it establishes a
Nation, draws People and Commerce; makes the people
love their native Country, which Passion is the Original
of all great Actions in a Common-wealth.'[98] These links
had been brought home to Wren when visiting Paris
at the outset of the Restoration, and Vanbrugh too
acknowledged links between politics and public buildings which were especially pertinent in the context
of the French architecture of his day. For in a letter
to Brigadier William Watkins in 1721 concerning
Hawksmoor's need for Board preferment, Vanbrugh
observed: 'What wou'd Mons.r: Colbert in France have

40 Proposal for remodelling the entrance (north) court at Hampton Court, by
an unknown draughtsman working for Vanbrugh, winter 1717. [National Archives,
Kew]. The new works, including two vast assembly rooms, are shown in yellow.

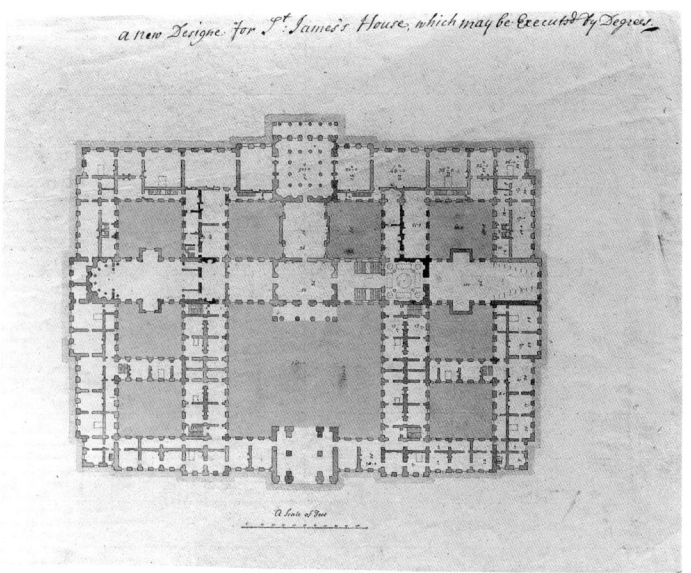

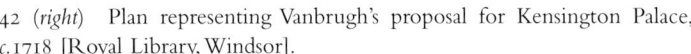

41   Plan representing Vanbrugh's proposal for St James's Palace, 1714 [Royal Library, Windsor].

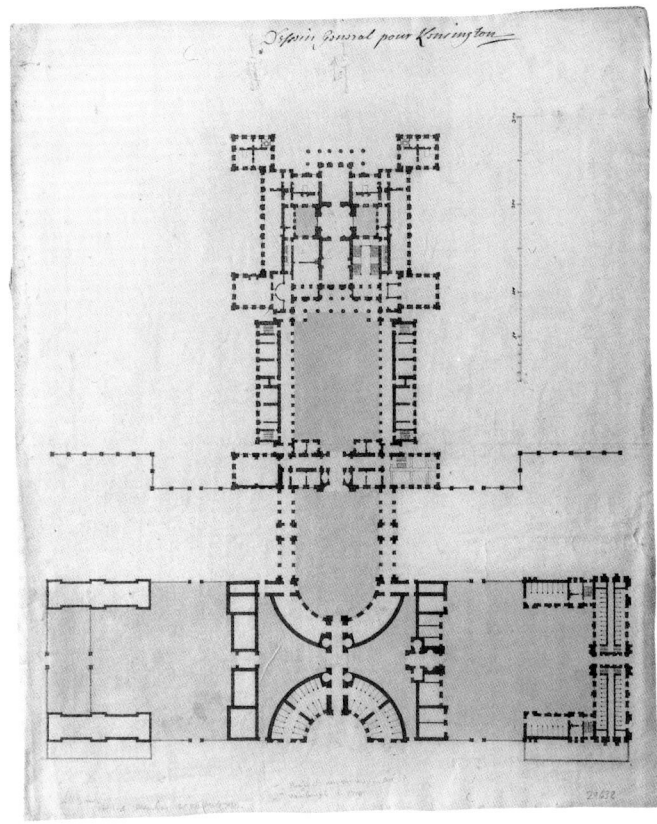

42 (*right*)   Plan representing Vanbrugh's proposal for Kensington Palace, *c.*1718 [Royal Library, Windsor].

given for Such a Man? I don't Speak as to his Architecture alone, but the Aids he cou'd have given him, in almost all his brave Designs for the Police'.[99] By 'police' Vanbrugh meant the general organisation of the State, which included public architecture. Colbert was Louis XIV's Chief Minister, and one result from their public policy (or 'police') had been the sponsorship of Claude Perrault's *Ordonnance des cinq espèces de colonnes selon la méthode des Anciens* (1683), as well as his 1673 French edition of the Roman author Vitruvius's treatise on architecture, both of which works had attempted to regulate French architectural production along the lines of Colbert's legal *Ordonnances* (the *Ordonnance civile* of 1667 and the *Ordonnance criminelle* of 1670).[100] During his time in Paris Vanbrugh must have seen Perrault's Louvre colonnade designed for Colbert, with its paired columns (see Fig. 25), and he was a subscriber to John James's translation of the *Ordonnance* of 1708.[101] As a herald and keen monarchist, albeit of the constitutional variety, Vanbrugh's time at the Board is notable for three grand plans for rebuilding royal palaces which might be seen through their porticoes, assembly rooms and courts to represent his own 'brave designs for the Police' – one at St James's Palace (1714), one at Hampton Court (*c.*1717) and one at Kensington Palace (*c.*1718) (Figs 39, 40, 41, 42).[102] In

the event only minor building works were realised by him, most notably the Prince of Wales's rooms in the north-east corner of Wren's Hampton Court and most likely the kitchen in St James's Palace (Figs 43, 44 and 45).[103]

As a Whig, however, Vanbrugh was not in favour of absolutism on the French model. In one of the lines he added to his translation of *The False Friend*, as but one example, Lopez remarks on the Spanish branch of Louis XIV's family: 'There's neither Liberty nor Property in this Land, since the Blood of the *Bourbon's* came amongst us.'[104] When looking at Vanbrugh's palace designs one should remember that although they were for a new form of monarchy initiated by the events of 1688, the available European palace models were for the most part built for absolutist rulers. Vanbrugh's designs somewhat inevitably reflect these, but nevertheless in his outlook there seems to have been a persistent and perhaps equally inevitable conflict between his constitutional preferences and his celebration of the architectural and militaristic achievements of absolutist monarchy. I shall show that given the problem of how to represent the constitutional freedoms of his countrymen, Vanbrugh found the solution in a selective use of medieval details and in his attempt to formulate a language of architecture based on

43 The Great Kitchen in St James's Palace, 1716–17, attributed to Vanbrugh, from William Pyne's *The History of the Royal Residences of Windsor Castle, St. James's Palace, Carlton House and Frogmore* (1819).

both a medieval and a classical vocabulary of forms which spoke equally of national glory and classical virtue. Vanbrugh's yeomen-herms on the fireplace in the Queen's Guard Room at Hampton Court (1716; Fig. 46), for example, illustrate perfectly his inventive adaptation and blending of *all'antica* and medieval forms to reflect national traditions, costumes and architectural styles.

The desire to represent constitutional freedoms certainly found expression elsewhere in the Board's work.

For not only were the appointments to the Board politically influenced, but its work can also on occasions be seen to express the Whig political beliefs of its officers, especially at times when these beliefs prevailed, and the constitutional freedoms enjoyed by the English nation. For example, by February 1702 Antonio Verrio was working on the King's great staircase at Hampton Court. Here the ceiling and walls are devoted to the central theme of Julian the Apostate's satire called *The Caesars*, in which work Alexander the Great is preferred to

44 and 45   Vanbrugh's chimneypieces in the Prince of Wales's rooms, 1716, in the north-east corner of Wren's Hampton Court [National Monuments Record, Swindon].

Romulus and all the Caesars (Fig. 47). Alexander represents the Protestant William III, who is introduced to the banqueting gods by his patron Hercules, whilst the Roman emperors are equated with Roman Catholics. According to Whig philosophers such as Locke, Somers and the third Earl of Shaftesbury, Julian the Apostate was a symbol of toleration and freedom, which, as Howard Colvin has pointed out, helps to explain this choice of subject at this particular time.[105]

★   ★   ★

'AN IMAGE OF LIBERTY': THE WHIG GOLDEN AGE

Many Englishmen at the turn of the eighteenth century saw their era as having renewed – indeed as having surpassed – the Golden Age of antiquity. This belief in a reborn Golden Age appeared to be supported by the new knowledge flowing from the Royal Society, the increase in trade facilitated by peace and exploration, the advantages of constitutional monarchy and the revived Church of England (ultimately symbolised by Hawksmoor's London churches).[106] The Treaty of Ryswick of

46 Vanbrugh's chimneypiece in the Queen's Guard Room at Hampton Court (1716), in the form of yeomen herms.

47 Antonio Verrio's depiction of Alexander the Great in the King's great staircase at Hampton Court, 1702 [National Monuments Record, Swindon].

48   French almanac for the year 1698 entitled *La Paix de Ryswyk*
[Bibliothèque Nationale de France, Paris].

September 1697 had marked the albeit temporary end
of hostilities between France and England, and increasingly liberal conditions of trade enhanced the wealth of
the new Whig aristocracy (Fig. 48).[107] Vanbrugh celebrated this theme in his plays.[108] In *The Mistake*, for
example, the error of the title – Camillo's disguise – is
corrected and the play closes with the lines 'From this
good Day, then let all Discord cease;/Let those to come
be Harmony and Peace.'[109] The return of the age of
Peace and Plenty (symbolised by Venus and Diana) introduced under James i but interrupted by the Civil War
(symbolised by Mars) is also the central theme of
Dryden's masque at the close of *The Pilgrim*, a play
adapted by Vanbrugh and first performed at the dawn of
the new century, in 1700. The play ends with the lines
''Tis well an Old Age is out,/And time to begin a
New.'[110]

John Sturt's dedication to Queen Anne of John James's
1707 English translation of Pozzo's *Perspectiva pictorum et
architectorum* (1693) celebrated an expected artistic supremacy under Anne which would match the military
glories under Marlborough. Together with Wren and
Hawksmoor, Vanbrugh endorsed the book. Sturt's dedication expressed a hope that 'Whitehall is to be Raised
from its ruins', having noted 'The Great Dispatch lately
given to those Noble Fabricks of St Pauls, Greenwich-
Hospital, and Blenheim'. Of these, Blenheim was
perhaps the most provocative symbol of Whig ambitions,
built as it was at vast expense by the State to glorify the
recently ennobled Whig Duke. With its crowning statue
of Pallas Athene – the embodiment of the warrior-artist
– the house openly proclaimed the harmony between
military and artistic glory, whilst in his column project
at Blenheim, Hawksmoor idealised the Duke of Marlborough as a worthy successor to none other than Trajan,
whose column he copied, and described the Duke as 'a
British Starr, the brightest Europe has yet at any time,
ever Seen'.[111] At Castle Howard too the Whig vision of
enlightened rule found expression under its patron, Lord
Carlisle. Carlisle was an ardent campaigning Whig[112] and,
as seen, like Vanbrugh he was a prominent member of
the Kit Cat Club that flourished during the time the
house was being built, around 1705.[113] Vanbrugh was
chosen as architect precisely because of his Whig affiliations and evidently discussed the design of the house
with fellow Kit Cat members.[114] The internal decoration of the house can be understood to celebrate the
Whig triumph in classical, emblematic terms: the dome
of the hall was painted by Gianantonio Pellegrini with
a scene depicting the 'Fall of Phaeton' which had followed Apollo's permission to drive the chariot of the sun
(Fig. 50). Contemporary observers could not fail to
identify the replacement of French ambitions towards
absolutism with Whig ones towards liberty.[115] Moreover,
the Whig's confidence in their age might equally be seen
reflected in the garden monuments – the Temple by
Vanbrugh, the Pyramid and Mausoleum by Hawksmoor
(see Figs 175, 189, 195) – recalling as they do the great
eras of history, here, as it were, revived and renewed.
Following Lady Irwin's description of these monuments
as '*Grecian*, *Roman* and *Egyptian*', she proudly heralded
the modernity of her father's Mausoleum through its
having emulated, and even rivalled, its ancient Halicarnassus namesake: 'Tho' that a Wonder was by Ancients
deem'd,/ This by the Moderns is not less esteem'd.'[116]

Ornamentation and landscaping also played their part
in the expression of the Whig cause.[117] Whig country
houses such as Blenheim and Castle Howard, Chatsworth and Lowther Castle ostentatiously sought to cel-

ebrate through their ornament and decoration the possibility of men born in a free society (that is, ruled by a constitutional monarchy) to surpass in grandeur the established Tory nobility.[118] Whilst by tradition the country house had represented the quintessential Tory means to express political power, Tory landowners had sought to build unpretentious houses in harmony with their formalised gardens, not ones dominating their landscape as at Blenheim and Castle Howard.[119] This traditional restraint had been famously celebrated in Ben Jonson's 'To Penshurst' (1616): 'Thou art not, Penshurst, built to envious show/Of touch, or marble; nor canst boast a row/Of polish'd Pillars, or a Roof of Gold'. Some contemporaries reacted negatively to the new Whig houses by recalling the traditional links between ornamental and moral licentiousness debated since the Elizabethan architectural treatise of John Shute.[120] Roger North, for example, in his 'Notes of Building' (1698) wrote that 'Pomp and ornament are but fancy and chimera of the imagination, and lean on pride, ambition, and envyous comparison'.[121] Most famously of all, the Tory poets Swift and Pope, both on the side of the

49 Joseph Addison, portrait by Sir Godfrey Kneller, *c.*1703–12, oil on canvas, 91.4 × 71.1 cm [National Portrait Gallery, London].

50 Dome of the hall at Castle Howard painted by Gianantonio Pellegrini, depicting the Fall of Phaeton (1712; destroyed) [National Monuments Record, Swindon].

'Ancients', clearly identified Vanbrugh's domestic architecture with the over-scaled, vulgar claims of the 'Moderns' and, by implication, of the Whigs.[122]

In comparison to the formal restraint characterising the gardens of Tory landowners, the Whigs favoured a more natural, that is, more open, style of garden. This ideal has often been compared with the more natural, post-Glorious Revolution form of constitutional gov-

51 Engraving of Robert Walpole's garden at Houghton in Norfolk, from Colen Campbell's *Vitruvius Britannicus*, vol. III (1725), pls 27 and 28.

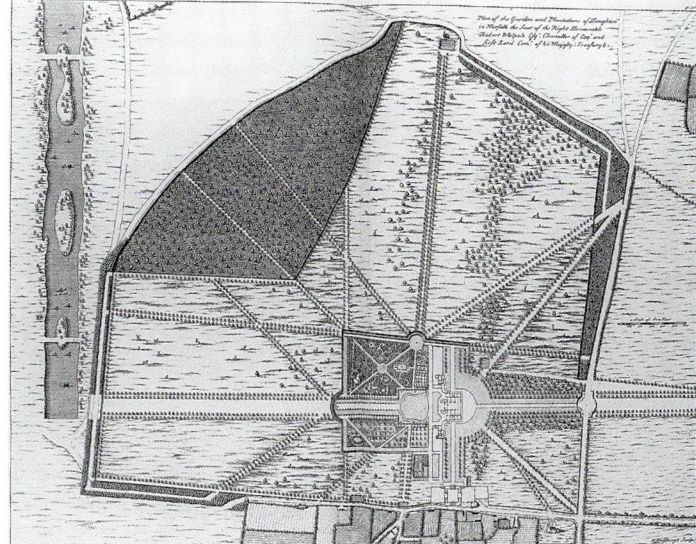

ernment under the Whigs.[123] For the promotion of
simple, or 'natural', nature over the highly formal and
geometric 'artifice' of gardens such as Versailles was seen
as a distinctly English invention, one that parallelled and
even legitimised the search for a society of liberty,
tolerance and natural law.[124] Shaftesbury used the wilderness as a symbol of nature in its primitive state and
as such as a symbol of universal order. In 1712 the
Whig writer Joseph Addison (1672–1719; Fig. 49)
applied his ideas on the pleasures of an open landscape
to concepts of infinity promoted by contemporary
science and, by allusion, to political ideals of liberty. He
observed that

> The Mind of Man naturally hates every thing that
> looks like a Restraint upon it, and is apt to fancy it
> self under a sort of Confinement, when the Sight is
> pent up in a narrow Compass, and shortned on every
> side by the Neighbourhood of Walls or Mountains.
> On the contrary, a spacious Horison is an Image of
> Liberty, where the Eye has Room to range abroad, to
> expatiate at large on the Immensity of its Views, and
> to lose it self amidst the Variety of Objects that offer
> themselves to its Observation. Such wide and unde-
> termined Prospects are as pleasing to the Fancy, as the
> Speculations of Eternity or Infinitude are to the
> Understanding.[125]

The great Whig Prime Minister Sir Robert Walpole,
with whom Vanbrugh had frequent enough business
(including alterations of Walpole House in Chelsea in
1715–16),[126] advised that 'Loose groves' should be planted
to crown 'an easy eminence' with 'happy ornament' and
statues and buildings should be positioned to decorate
the horizon.[127] As Vanbrugh was well aware, during the
1720s Walpole had sought to put these ideas into practice at Houghton in Norfolk (Fig. 51): in a letter to the
Duke of Newcastle on 30 July 1723 Vanbrugh reports 'I
din'd with Mr Walpole at Chelsea on Wednesday last, and
find him much content with what is doing in Norfolk.
I desire your Grace will not let any body hinder you
from being so at Claremont.'[128] The siting of Vanbrugh's
Belvedere on the hill overlooking Claremont in Surrey
reflects perfectly Walpole's vision (see Fig. 70). As will be
seen in this book, in this way the estates of Blenheim,
Castle Howard and Claremont were idealised in their
architect's mind as semi-fortified havens of Golden Age
prosperity ushered in under Whig rule.

I

'BY ACHIEVEMENT, ARMS, DEVICE': DRAMATIST, HERALD AND ARCHITECT

52   Watercolour drawing, c. 1770, by William Capon of the main entrance façade, on the north-east arm, of Vanbrugh's Queen's Theatre, Haymarket (destroyed) [Guildhall Library, London].

Chapter 1

'WITHOUT THOUGHT OR LECTURE': THE EARLY INFLUENCES ON VANBRUGH

Vanbrugh's recommendations to his patrons show him to have had a sophisticated understanding of *all'antica* architectural theory, the particular application of which was clearly articulated in statements such as his emphasis to the Earl of Manchester at Kimbolton in 1707 that 'tis certainly the Figure and Proportions that make the most pleasing Fabrick, And not the delicacy of the Ornaments'.[1] He has often been presented as ill-prepared for his career as an architect, having had no apprenticeship before his apparent baptism of fire with the commission to design Castle Howard in 1699. Swift had sown the seeds of this assumption in his poem 'The History of Vanbrug's House' (1710) with the lines 'Van's genius, without thought or lecture,/Is hugely turned to architecture'.[2] Yet Vanbrugh's youthful studies and experiences abroad, as well as the range of his early influences and interests, belie this assumption. His journal of financial accounts demonstrate an eagerness to collect the latest publications, often facilitated through his friend and publisher Jacob Tonson, and his early interest in drama and opera – as well as in heraldry, as will be seen in Chapter Two – would have provided a grounding in principles which were perfectly compatible with the classical, or 'Vitruvian', architectural thinking of his age.

'PEOPLE ESPECIALLY SUCH, AS ARE NO LEARNDER THAN I AM': VANBRUGH'S STUDIES

If a passing remark in one of his letters to Lord Carlisle is to be taken at face value, Vanbrugh was modest concerning his scholarly achievements. In reference to Alexander Pope's involvement with Lord Cobham's gardens at Stowe, he observes to Carlisle in September 1725:

> I am glad your Ldp likes Mr Popes Inscription My Lord Cobham (who I take to be a very good Judge

in such matters,) thinks it as well, as it cou'd possibly be. Every thing proper to be said on the Occasion being express'd in the shortest Compass, and quite in the antique Style and manner. I don't know whether it cou'd have been put into any other English, that wou'd have done better, (He thinks not) but the Expression will not be very familiar to many People especially such, as are no Learnder than I am.[3]

It is worth noting from this just how important clarity of expression was to Vanbrugh and how he evidently carefully considered the audience's reaction to his work.

Vanbrugh here undoubtedly downplays his learning. Evidence of his architectural studies and interests can be gleaned from a number of sources, most notably his letters, plays and accounts. In the absence of any formal apprenticeship in architecture, of the type served by Hawksmoor with Wren, Vanbrugh relied on the Renaissance architectural treatises to provide *all'antica* design patterns and codes. He purchased Roland Fréart de Chambray's French translation of Andrea Palladio's *Quattro Libri* of 1650, as noted in the Introduction, choosing this edition because of its illustration of the plans of Palladio's houses (and in acknowledging to Tonson that 'there is one without the Plans', he shows that he was at least aware of Le Muet's 1645 edition of Palladio's Book I).[4] The accounts record his consistent subscription to James Leoni's English translation of Palladio's work: an entry on 12 July 1717 has 'pd Seigr: Leoni in part of five Guineas Subscrib'd for Palladio's Architecture £3 4s 6d'; on 30 May 1718 'pd Seigr: Lioni on the delivery of the 3d book of Palladio, he having recd 3 Gs. before'; on 18 May 1719 'To Monsr: Lioni, for ye 4th Book of Palladio'; and on 23 February 1720 'Given Seigr: Lioni, on the Delivery of his last Book, being over and above my Subscription'. In January 1721 he also paid Leoni on subscription for a copy of his translation of Leon Battista Alberti.[5] Although not published until

1726 (after Vanbrugh's death), he was thus at least well aware of the Italian architectural master, as one might expect, and some have speculated that Alberti's principles informed Vanbrugh's own architectural thinking.[6] It was noted in the Introduction that he was also a subscriber to John James's translation of Claude Perrault's *Ordonnance* (published in English in 1708 as *A Treatise of the Five Orders of Columns in Architecture*), a work which was a landmark in the breakdown of the universal validity of the classical rules of proportion, in stimulating a plurality in architectural tastes. James's translation of Andrea Pozzo's *Perspectiva* published in 1707 was also endorsed by Vanbrugh, together with Wren and Hawksmoor, as 'a Work that deserves Encouragement, and very proper for Instruction in the Art'.[7] This was a leading baroque painter's manual concerned with how to merge real and painted space in a continuum. Colen Campbell thanked Vanbrugh in *Vitruvius Britannicus* (1715) for his supply of original drawings for engraving and he is listed amongst the subscribers. His close study of this prominent work on the English architecture of

his era was in any case inevitable. Campbell illustrates Vanbrugh's projects for Blenheim, Castle Howard, Grimsthorpe Castle, Cholmondeley Hall, Kings Weston, Eastbury and Seaton Delaval (Fig. 53; see also Figs 99, 151, 164, 190, 201, 228, 240, 242, 253, 263, 280, 282, 287, 288, 291, 297, 298). Given Vanbrugh's involvement at Greenwich Hospital, the clear use of Vignola's plate illustrating the entrance to the Palazzo Farnese at Caprarola in the design of the archway between the two riverside pavilions of the King Charles Building in 1714–15 (Figs 54, 55) suggests his full knowledge of the Italian's famous work, either in the form of the original *Regola delli cinque ordini d'architettura* (first published in 1562 but with the Palazzo Farnese door added to later editions) or in the popular English translation dedicated to Wren in 1655 by Joseph Moxon.[8] Vanbrugh also endorsed the proposal to publish an English edition of Augustin Charles d'Aviler's *Cours d'Architecture* (1691) based on the *Orders* of Vignola, a fact which indicates his knowledge of the French original and of the plates produced for the English edition (the work was eventually published in

53   Engraving of an unrealised design attributed to Vanbrugh for the north façade of Cholmondeley Hall, Cheshire, c.1713, from Colen Campbell's *Vitruvius Britannicus*, vol. II (1725), pl. 32.

55   The archway between the two riverside pavilions of the King Charles Building of 1714–15, Greenwich Hospital.

54   Giacomo Barozzi da Vignola's plate illustrating the entrance to the Palazzo Farnese at Caprarola, from the *Regola delli cinque ordini d'architettura* (1635 edition).

1761).[9] Thus, far from being untutored in architectural theory, Vanbrugh was evidently keenly aware and supportive of the canonical works on *all'antica* architectural theory and models published from the Renaissance onwards.

Many of these antique models, such as the Pantheon, were to be found in one city in particular, Rome. Although Vanbrugh never visited Rome, as far as is known, he was familiar enough with its marvels, both ancient and modern. In a letter of 28 April 1710 he comments to the Duke of Marlborough:

And I am glad that I can now assure Your Grace, the Model of the Fountain of piazza Navona, is of Bernini's doing. I shewed it before it went to Blenheim to Mr Gibbons, and the best connoisseurs here who at first sight owned it to be what was pretended, and think it scarce to be valued. The four figures make the most valuable part of it and there is but one of them that has received any damage worth naming.[10]

Bernini's fountain, with its statues of four river gods symbolising Rome's dominance over the continents of the known world, would have appealed to Vanbrugh's fundamental desire to use architecture to tell his patron's 'story', or more accurately mythology, and the fountain eventually formed the model for Hawksmoor's design of

56   Detail of Bernini's fountain of the Four Rivers, 1648–51, in the Piazza Navona, Rome.

'Temple of the Four Winds' at Castle Howard which was based via Palladio's Villa Rotonda on the Italian's reconstruction of the Temple of Fortuna Primigenia at Praeneste (Figs 60, 61). This temple was also used as the model for Vanbrugh and Bridgeman's terraces and temple at Eastbury (Fig. 63).[15] His accounts journal notes having 'pd: Mr Valliant . . . on a Subscription to the Collosseum £1 1s', probably referring to Carlo Fontana's *Anfiteatro Flavio* published in The Hague in 1725.[16] Vanbrugh's construction of the Queen's Theatre in the Haymarket, London, complete with its amphitheatrical pit, gave him first-hand experience of theatre design ultimately derived from such ancient models (see Figs 52, 66). The study of antiquity might even have supplied him with the authority for his use of a mixed style of ancient and medieval architectural forms. For Fischer von Erlach's famous fanciful reconstructions of the Wonders of the

57   Hawksmoor's design for the Blenheim obelisk celebrating Marlborough's dominance of Europe, of *c.*1724 [Bodleian Library, Oxford].

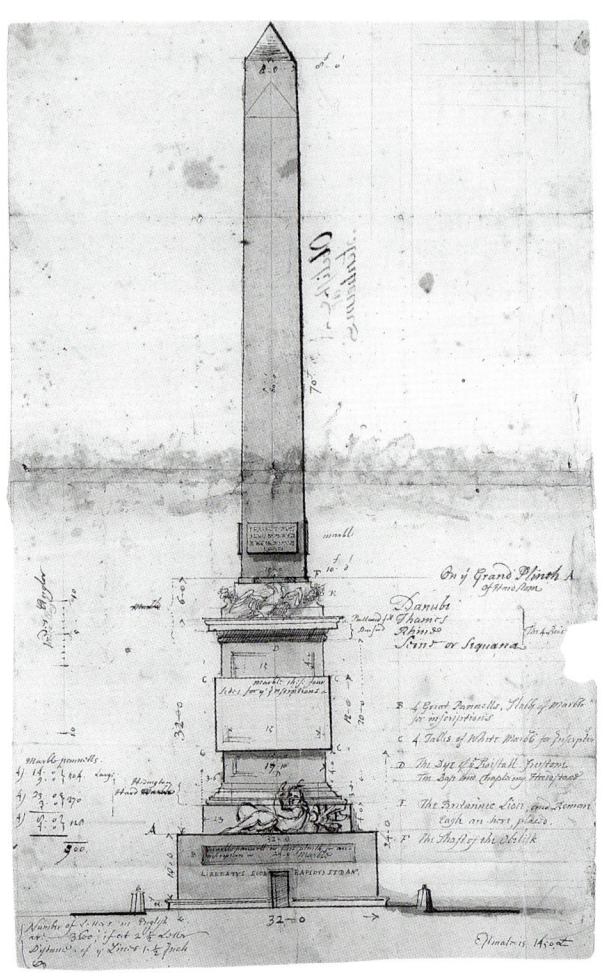

about 1724 for the Blenheim obelisk celebrating Marlborough's similar dominance (Figs 56, 57).[11] Equally, Vanbrugh drew on the work of Michelangelo when designing the doorcases at the stair-heads at Grimsthorpe (1723–6), adapting those designed by the Italian master for the side palaces of the Capitol in Rome (known through Alessandro Specchi's engraving of 1702; Figs 58, 59).[12]

Vanbrugh was also a keen student of ancient buildings, as testified by his reference to 'the Remains of distant Times' when arguing to preserve Woodstock Manor and, concerning the covered walkways at Blenheim, what had been 'practis'd in Ancient buildings'.[13] He was interested in all aspects of these ancient works, from the social to the tectonic, for in his letter regarding the preservation of Woodstock he cites their 'Magnificence' and 'Curious Workmanship', their ability to evoke 'pleasing Reflections . . . on the Persons who have Inhabited them', 'the Remarkable things which have been transacted in them' and 'the extraordinary Occasions of Erecting them'.[14] He used ancient works as the model for a number of his buildings, such as the

58 Michelangelo's doorcase for the side palaces of the Capitol in Rome, detail from Alessandro Specchi's engraving in Domenico de Rossi's *Studio d'Architettura Civile*, vol. 1 (1702), pl. 5.

59 Vanbrugh's doorcase at the stair-head at Grimsthorpe, 1723–6.

antique world (which were known to Hawksmoor), first issued around 1700 and published in one volume in 1721, on occasions combined *all'antica* and medieval details in a somewhat Vanbrugian manner, as with the illustration of the fortified Pharos lighthouse in Alexandria (280 BC) with its pedimented door and corbel-tables (Fig. 62).[17]

Nevertheless, these ancient works had limited efficacy amongst contemporaries since antiquity no longer provided the sole touchstone for architectural canons – as it had, say, for Inigo Jones. In an article published in the collected, 1721 edition of Addison's works (owned by Vanbrugh), the writer notes that 'Musick, Architecture and Painting, as well as Poetry and Oratory, are to deduce their Laws and Rules from the general Sense and Taste of Mankind, and not from the Principles of those Arts themselves; or in other words, the Taste is not to conform to the Art, but the Art to the Taste.'[18] Later he added:

Those who have surveyed the noblest Pieces of Architecture and Statuary both ancient and modern, know

very well that there are frequent Deviations from Art in the Works of the great Masters, which have produced a much nobler Effect than a more accurate and exact way of Proceeding could have done. This often arises from what the *Italians* call the *Gusto Grande* in these Arts, which is what we call the Sublime in Writing.[19]

This breakdown in the universal validity of classical rules during the latter half of the seventeenth century – rules demoted by Addison in favour of visual 'effect' – was balanced by the new plurality in architectural tastes, from exotic to medieval styles, to which Vanbrugh's work gave expression. As but one case in point, his highly original use of the pyramid form, in placing it over a gateway to Castle Howard, is a graphic example of this freedom from classical canons (see Fig. 156). Increased travel, for one, had opened up new architectural horizons. Vanbrugh was fully aware of these, having travelled further afield than most, including his Board compatriots Hawksmoor and Wren. As already seen, Vanbrugh trav-

60   Andrea Palladio's Villa Rotonda, near Vicenza, *c.*1569.

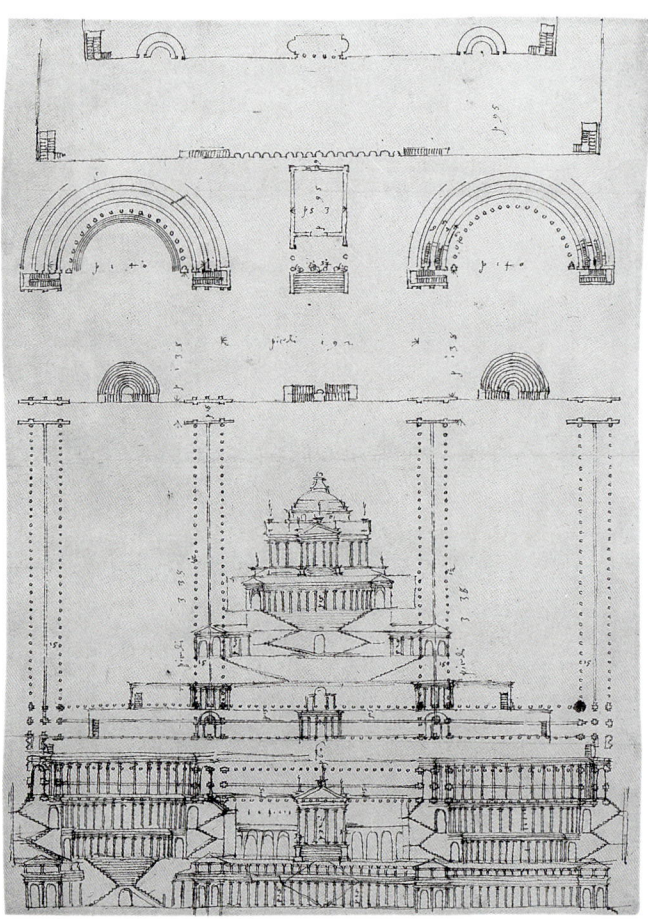

61 (*right*)   Andrea Palladio's fanciful reconstruction of the Temple of Fortuna Primigenia at Praeneste (Palestrina) [RIBA, London].

62 (*below*)   The fortified Pharos lighthouse in Alexandria, 280 BC, with its pedimented door and corbel-tables, copper engraving after Johann Bernhard Fischer von Erlach, *c.*1700.

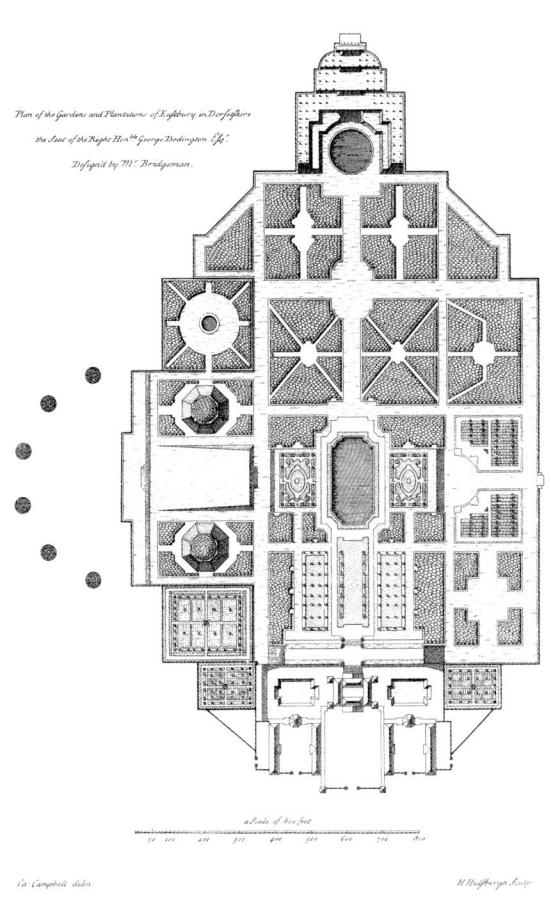

Plan of the Gardens and Plantations of Eastbury in Dorsetshire
the Seat of the Right Hon.ble George Dodington Esq.
Design'd by M.r Bridgeman.

a Scale of 800 feet

Co. Campbell delin.   H. Hulsbergh Sculp.

63 Vanbrugh and Charles Bridgeman's terraces and temple at
Eastbury, from Colen Campbell's *Vitruvius Britannicus*, vol. III
(1725), pl. 15.

his proposals for out-of-town cemeteries made to the
Church Commissioners many years later he was influenced not by antique practices but by his youthful study
of the English cemetery there.[21] He had knowledge of,
and interest in, other places abroad: he refers to the
topography of Constantinople in a letter to Carlisle,[22]
for example, whilst *The False Friend* is set in Valencia.[23]
In May 1718 he paid Tonson for 'Binding Bleaus Atlas',
a reference to Joan Blaeu's *Atlas Major* which was a large
work published in Amsterdam in the 1660s.[24]

Vanbrugh was certainly well travelled in England, and
gained special knowledge of the towns and monuments
on or near the Great North Road to Castle Howard.
His travels would have been informed in later years by
his copy of John Stevens's *The History of the Antient
Abbeys, etc.* (1722–3), an extension of William Dugdale's
Monasticon Anglicanum (1655–73), and less directly informed by his purchase of Laurence Eachard's *The
History of England, from the First Entrance of Julius Caesar*
(1707–18; see Figs 73, 74, 75, 87, 88).[25] Vanbrugh's
accounts for January 1716 record payment of £4, 4s and
9d 'for horses meat on ye Road, in the Bath Journey'.[26]
Such trips were often made under difficult circumstances. Writing to the Duke of Newcastle from Castle
Howard on Christmas Day 1718, Vanbrugh observes:

> Your Graces Letter to meet you at Nott[m]: tomorrow,
> I found here yesterday. And had been three days,
> getting from thence to York; through such difficultys
> as the Stage Coach cou'd not pass, which I left over
> set and quite disabled upon the way. There has now
> fallen a Snow up to ones Neck, to mend it, w[ch] may
> possibly fix me here as long as it did at the Bath this
> time two Years: w[ch] was no less than five Weeks. In
> short, tis so bloody Cold, I have almost a mind to
> Marry to keep myself warm.[27]

Hence, it is worth noting in passing, Vanbrugh often
chose to direct work from London using sketches and
models, for example writing to Henry Joynes in 1708 on
the four pinnacles for one of the towers at Blenheim that
'the Moddell in Wood will Show what is design'd'.[28]

Vanbrugh had a wide range of interests. He plainly
gleaned aesthetic and compositional principles from the
study of painting, as demonstrated by his now famous
remark that Woodstock Manor was 'One of the Most
Agreable Objects that the Best of Landskip Painters can
invent'.[29] He owned a copy of the celebrated prints by
Nicolas Dorigny of the Raphael Cartoons of the Acts
of the Apostles, bought in July 1719.[30] Indeed he studied
scripture: for in his *A Short Vindication of The Relapse and
The Provok'd Wife, from Immorality and Profaneness* (1698),
he points out that 'The Scripture is made up of History,

elled to India when employed by the East India
Company between 1683 and 1685, as well as to France
and Hanover, and these travels made a lasting impression
by introducing different vistas of available architectural
styles and heritages. His experiences in France together
with those as a soldier and his brief imprisonment in the
Bastille, for example, were probably early inspirations for
the romantic military imagery employed by him
throughout his subsequent buildings. Vanbrugh wrote to
Tonson, who was himself in Paris, in July 1719: 'as to the
Place you are in: I am so far from being disgusted to it,
by the treatment I once met with That I think that very
thing (at least the Occasion of it) has doubled a
Romantick desire, of Seeing it again'.[20] When stationed
at Surat in India he had witnessed the Mogul architecture of the region (see Fig. 5) and it was noted that in

Prophecy, and Precept' and goes on to cite from the Gospels of St Luke and St Paul.[31] Vanbrugh would also have been perfectly aware of the breakdown of traditional, biblical explanations of origins in the wake of the new sciences advanced in the Royal Society by his eminent colleague at the Board of Works, Christopher Wren. He showed interest in the new experimental techniques, for on 10 June 1725 he 'pd for a Microscope',[32] as well as in the theological response, outlined in works such as Thomas Burnet's *The Sacred Theory of the Earth* (1684), to the questions which the new sciences posed (Burnet is referred to in *The Relapse*).[33] This interest extended to works by contemporary philosophers, such as François de la Pillonnière's *Défense des principes de la tolérance*, published in London in 1718 and subscribed to by Vanbrugh in the same year (implying that he read it),[34] Joseph Addison's *Works* of 1721,[35] John Dennis's *Original Letters, Familiar, Moral and Critical* of the same year,[36] and an unidentified work by the natural philosopher J. T. Desaguliers.[37] Vanbrugh's accounts record his likely purchase of Ovid for his son Charles (probably Tonson's folio edition of the *Metamorphoses* of 1717, translated by Dryden, Addison, Congreve and others) and Charles is also known to have had copies of Juvenal and Persius, possibly Dryden's collected edition of 1693 published by Tonson.[38] The influence of Ovid will be shown in Vanbrugh's architecture. Clearly as a playwright and garden designer he was well enough versed in the works of the classical authors. The poem by Carlisle's daughter Lady Irwin which celebrates the Castle Howard landscape explicitly refers to Hesiod and Virgil, and underlines the common links between classical literature and the gardens of this period.[39] As but one literary example of Vanbrugh's education in the classics, he makes a passing reference in a letter to Tonson to 'Clitus at the Banquet'.[40] Clitus was murdered by Alexander the Great in a drunken brawl, as related in Plutarch's 'Life of Alexander' from his *Lives* (a work which had been published by Tonson in 1683–6 and prefixed with the 'Life of Plutarch' by Dryden). Vanbrugh's knowledge of the life of Alexander might well have been prompted by his interest in military matters and the use of the legendary general as a symbol for William III at Hampton Court.[41] Blenheim, after all, was built for a general of Alexandrian proportions. Not surprisingly, perhaps, Vanbrugh's accounts also record his purchase of the near contemporary poetical works of John Milton, Matthew Prior, Elkanah Settle and Charles Gildon.[42]

The fourth main occupation of Vanbrugh – other than as a soldier, dramatist and architect – was as a herald and this too was represented in his accounts. Here in April 1719 one finds him paying £1 10s for John Guillim's *A*

Display of Heraldrie (first published in 1610, with a fifth edition in 1678–9; see Fig. 108).[43] Heraldry fitted perfectly with Vanbrugh's concern to represent the 'story' of the nobility of England through building grand country houses, as well as his interest in the military and its insignia. Indeed the accounts also record in June 1716 'pd Subscription to Browns book of Medals'.[44] He also purchased in the year of its issue Nicola Haym's *Del Tesoro Britannico . . . overo il Museo Nummario*, published in London in 1719 by Tonson, and bought the English translation (*The British Treasury*) the following year.[45] Of related interest was John Arbuthnot's *Tables of the Grecian, Roman and Jewish Measures, Weights and Coins, reduc'd to the English Standard* which was first published around 1705, with a second edition in 1727 for which Vanbrugh paid a subscription in December 1725; unfortunately he died before receiving it. Unsurprisingly for a writer of comedies, not all Vanbrugh's reading matter was serious. He also took a keen interest in the more frivolous gossips of the time, his letters referring to the *Weekly London Journal*, the *Gazette* and 'other papers'.[46] Thus despite his own modesty, intellectually he was evidently a well-rounded man of his time.

'TO BUILD BY VERSE': FROM HEROIC LITERATURE TO HEROIC ARCHITECTURE

Vanbrugh's training as a dramatist and man of letters was vital to his transition into an architect. Swift made associations – albeit sarcastic and at a general level – between Vanbrugh's work as both dramatist and architect in his poem 'Vanbrug's House' (1709 version), which concerned 'Goose-Pie' in Whitehall (see Figs 29, 316, 317), when he observed:

> And as a poet, he has skill
> To build in speculation still.
> 'Great Jove!' he cried, 'the art restore
> To build by verse as heretofore;
> And make my muse the architect;
> What palaces shall we erect![47]

Sir Richard Steele had implied the interchangeability of Vanbrugh's work as a playwright, architect and herald in his prologue to *The Mistake* when introducing the play to the audience:

> Yet, as your Taste now stands, our Author draws
> Some Hope of your Indulgence and Applause.
> For that great End this Edifice he made,
> Where humble Swain at Lady's Feet is laid;
> . . .
> Thus all must own, our Author has done more,

For your Delight, than ever Bard before.
His Thoughts are still to raise your Pleasures fill'd;
To Write, Translate, to Blazon, or to Build.[48]

In examining Vanbrugh's interests and studies, and their possible influence on him as an architect, it is worth considering the traditional links between literary and architectural theory which, with his friends Dryden and Congreve, he would have been exposed to as a dramatist and translator.

Since antiquity the art of *all'antica* architectural design and the composition of ancient literature had been understood to share an underlying pattern in their use of language and form (*Ut architectura poesis*).[49] These connections between architecture and literature, and in particular between Vitruvius and the new age of literary achievements under Charles II, had been underlined by Dryden in his poem 'To my dear Friend Mr Congreve on His Comedy Call'd The Double Dealer' (1694). In alluding to the two biblical temples in Jerusalem as precursors to the two cathedrals in London dedicated to St Paul – the old building by Inigo Jones and the new and incomplete one by Christopher Wren – Dryden criticises the architecture of the modern era; but, as Vanbrugh would have been well aware, he praises Congreve as a new Vitruvius bringing an ideal poetic balance between vigour and beauty, with his poetry 'built', in effect, using the Roman's principles:

> Our Age was cultivated thus at length;
> But what we gain'd in skill we lost in strength.
> Our Builders were, with want of genius, curst;
> The second Temple was not like the first;
> Till you, the best *Vitruvius*, come at length;
> Our Beauties equal; but excel our strength.
> Firm *Dorique* Pillars found your solid Base;
> The Fair *Corinthian* Crowns the higher Space;
> Thus all below is Strength, and all above is
>   Grace.[50]

A number of influential writers, including Jonson and Pope, had extended the Vitruvian aesthetic – perfect harmonies, proportions and symmetries – to poetry, such that these 'classical' principles became a model for the composition of poetry and orations as well as for buildings.[51] Wren too had made a theoretical link between the composition of poetry and buildings in the first of his theoretical writings, or 'Tracts', on architecture when he noted that 'Variety of Uniformities makes compleat Beauty: Uniformities are best tempered, as Rhimes in Poetry, alternately, or sometimes with more Variety, as in Stanza's'.[52] Around 1695 Roger North had explained the virtue of unity in architecture by an analogy with dramatic writing: 'If a play be double, that is 2 storys without dependance on each other, the audience is distracted which to attend, and when one comes, it breaks off the attention to the other, and hath the same disturbance at every transition'.[53] In 'The Pleasures of the Imagination' (1712), Addison noted that the study of 'the great Works of Architecture which are in their present Glory, or in the Ruins of those which flourished in former Ages . . . have their Influence on all Kinds of Writing, if the Author knows how to make right use of them . . . *Paradise Lost* . . . is like a stately Palace built of Brick'.[54] Not surprisingly given what has already been seen of Addison's approach, his link between writing and architecture was on the basis of sensory effect rather than on shared canonic rules.

With these contemporary literary and architectural associations in mind, Vanbrugh might be understood to have taken the skills and principles he had learned as a dramatist – his sense of drama, intrigue, rhetoric, effect, symmetry and narrative – and, in the absence of a formal architectural training, to have applied them to his architecture, which might in turn be 'read' as a form of visual language with a consistent vocabulary of emblematic forms.[55] After all, he clearly drew on his genius as a comic writer in designing the iconography at Blenheim, where a verbal pun is translated into the decoration (see Fig. 203): Addison, in the course of explaining the rules for wit, observes disapprovingly that

> I shall conclude this Topic with a *Rebus*, which has been lately hewn out in Free stone, and erected over two of the Portals of *Blenheim* House, being the Figure of a Monstrous Lion tearing to pieces a little Cock. For the better understanding of which Device, I must acquaint my English Reader that a Cock has the Misfortune to be called in *Latin* by the same word that signifies a *French*-man, as a Lion is the Emblem of the *English* Nation. Such a Device in so noble a Pile of Building looks like a Pun in an Heroic Poem, and I am very sorry the truly ingenious Architect would suffer the statuary to blemish his excellent Plan with so poor a Conceit; But I hope what I have said will gain Quarter for the Cock, and deliver him out of the Lion's Paw.[56]

If the literary analogy of Blenheim as a form of heroic poem is taken further, then Vanbrugh's work on less grand compositions like Kimbolton (see Fig. 4), with its robust 'Castle Air', might be seen to reflect the more stoic sentiments of Juvenal and Persius recommended to his son.

Moreover, as Steele hints at in the lines 'His Thoughts are still to raise your Pleasures fill'd;/To Write, Translate, to Blazon, or to Build', Vanbrugh's skill as a translator and adapter of stage works – by Boursault, Fletcher, Le Sage, Dancourt, and Molière – also finds a ready parallel in his attitude to house design, where he was a keen adapter of 'existing formulas' such as those provided by the English and French castle, and the houses of Palladio.[57] Just as Vanbrugh sought a simple, direct style when translating and writing, in reaction to the affectation of much contemporary drama,[58] so he sought a parallel simplicity, when merited, in ornament and dress (as demonstrated by his attitude to the 'beau' Lord Foppington in *The Relapse*, for example, as will be seen in Chapter Four). He makes Aesop comment to the pretentious Hortentia: 'Pray speak that you may be understood; Language was design'd for it.'[59] In *The Mistake* Don Alvarez admonishes the tutor Metaphrastus for his reliance on Latin quotations (from Virgil), following Molière's original text.[60] Don Alvarez protests at what he regards as the inappropriate use of ancient sources to explain modern circumstances: 'my Father was a wise Man, but he taught me nothing beyond common Sense; I know but one Tongue in the World, which luckily being understood by you as well as me, I fancy whatever Thoughts we have to Communicate to one another, may reasonably be convey'd in that, without having Recourse to the Language of *Julius Cæsar*'; Don Alvarez has 'no need of a better Phrase than my own to tell you my Meaning'.[61] As with Vanbrugh's use of language in drama, so in architecture he followed Don Alvarez's advice and avoided the application of (ancient) architectural forms and decoration for their own sake – as a 'Modern' he was no slave to antiquity as an absolute basis for all designs. His aim was to speak, or 'communicate', in a style relevant and understandable to his contemporaries, often by using the native vocabulary of medieval architecture.

Addison, whose taste was for antique simplicity, had made the analogy between plain styles of writing and building:

> Poets who want this Strength of Genius to give that Majestic simplicity to Nature, which we so much admire in the Works of the Ancients, are forced to hunt after foreign ornaments, and not to let any Piece of Wit of what kind soever escape them. I look upon these writers as *Goths* in Poetry, who, like those in Architecture, not being able to come up to the beautiful Simplicity of the old *Greeks* and *Romans*, have endeavoured to supply its Place with all the Extravagancies of an Irregular Fancy.[62]

It was an 'irregular fancy' in composition, both poetic and built, which Vanbrugh also sought to avoid. He

dropped into blank verse only for a purpose, in emotional passages for example,[63] just as he sought for the most part to respect the rules of classical design – stressing the use of proportion and symmetry at Kimbolton and of canonically proportioned columns at Blenheim and Castle Howard. On 26 March 1724 he observed to Carlisle concerning a garden obelisk at Castle Howard:

> I keep to the Proportions of a Dorick Column, which is eight diameters and that is the usual proportion of those in Italy, and succeeds mighty well in two pretty large ones in Mr Dodingtons Garden. I have plac'd one of the present Obelisks by it, drawn to the Same Scale, that your Ldship may See the Great Difference, by adding one foot more to the Diameter.[64]

When Vanbrugh broke these rules, such as in the banded Doric columns at Seaton Delaval (which might be seen as a form of blank verse), he did so for dramatic effect – in this case to emphasise 'strength' (Fig. 64). He comments to Lord Carlisle that the canonic Doric pillar 'is the Shortest in proportion to its height, & in that regard is best to Stand alone', later adding 'I have made the Piedestal Spread a little more than the Rule, which I think is quite reasonable, and will have a right effect, where a Pillar Stands Single, The Rule being Calculated for Pillars that stand in lines, which alters the Case much.'[65]

It appears that Vanbrugh had a considerable understanding of the classical rules of speech and drama.[66] The formal rules of rhetorical composition, for example, emphasised the use of the artifice of concealment, as well as of variety and contrast through quotation and imagery, to aid the orator or preacher to stimulate and persuade the audience, and these rules may well have informed Vanbrugh's own approach to the manipulation of mood in his drama and indeed in his architecture whose perception is varied via similar means.[67] Vanbrugh's aim, after all, was to produce an 'eloquent' architecture, as his comment on telling stories at Blenheim makes clear. Daniel Barbaro had famously compared the architect to the orator in his 1567 'Vitruvius',[68] and contemporary evidence for the interrelationship between architectural and rhetorical composition, as outlined by Marcus Tullius Cicero ('Tully'), can be found in the work of Isaac Browne (1705–60) who wrote in 1734 on design:

> Design, that Particle of heavenly Flame,
> Soul of all Beauty, thro' all Arts the same.
> This to the stately Dome its Grandeur gives,
> Strikes in the Picture, in the Statue lives;
> Persuades in Tully's, or in Talbot's Tongue;
> And tunes the Lyre, and builds the lofty Song.[69]

Whilst Vanbrugh cannot be linked to any particular rhetorical treatise, he was certainly aware of the principal antique authors on the subject. Encircling the dome at Castle Howard are busts of antique philosophers including the rhetoricians Seneca and Cicero,[70] whilst Lopez's remark in *The Mistake* that he had been 'as eloquent as *Cicero*' confirms not only Vanbrugh's understanding of the rhetorician's reputation but the popular one as well.[71] Cicero had opposed the tyranny of Caesar, making him an attractive figure to Whigs. Amongst the many books produced by Tonson were Cicero's *De Finibus* in 1702, with its discussion of the moral purpose of rhetoric, and Longinus's *On the Sublime* in 1724, with its discussion of rhetorical composition. Through the use of often suppressed details in the form of barely formed pediments (as on the 'Nunnery' at Greenwich) and concealed staircases (as viewed through arcades at Grimsthorpe), and a contrasting mix of *all'antica* and medieval details and forms (as on Seaton Delaval), the arrangement of Vanbrugh's architecture appears to reflect the rules of rhetorical composition with which he may well have been familiar (see Figs 227, 324, 326, 361).

If one bears in mind these analogies and Vanbrugh's wish to tell 'stories' through his choice of particular architectural forms and ornament, it is tempting to interpret his grand country houses as similar in spirit to classical heroic drama as revived by his friends and collaborators Dryden and Congreve. In other words one might see Vanbrugh as having attempted to formulate an architectural expression for Dryden's 'Discourse on Epic Poetry', given their friendship and collaborations on the stage.[72] Dryden's discourse was appended to his 1693 translation of Juvenal and Persius, published by Tonson and possibly owned, as has been seen, by Vanbrugh's son Charles. In any case, as a leading playwright of his generation, Vanbrugh would have been familiar with heroic poetry as a form of narrative verse which is elevated in mood and uses a dignified, dramatic and formal style to describe the deeds of aristocratic warriors and rulers. Dryden opens by observing that

> An heroic poem (truly such) is undoubtedly the greatest work which the soul of man is capable to perform. The design of it is to form the mind to heroic virtue by example; it is conveyed in verse that it may delight while it instructs. The action of it is always one, entire, and great. The least and most trivial episodes or under-actions which are interwoven in it are parts either necessary or convenient to carry on the main design – either so necessary that without them the poem must be imperfect, or so convenient that no others

64 Vanbrugh's banded Doric columns at Seaton Delaval, Northumberland, 1720–8.

> can be imagined more suitable to the place in which they are. There is nothing to be left void in a firm building; even the cavities ought not to be filled with rubbish which is of a perishable kind – destructive to the strength – but with brick or stone (though of less pieces, yet of the same nature), and fitted to the crannies. Even the least portion of them must be of the epic kind; all things must be grave, majestical, and sublime . . . Who, then, can pass for an inventor if Homer as well as Virgil must be deprived of that glory! Is Versailles the less a new building because the archi-

tect of that palace hath imitated others which were built before it? Walls, doors and windows, apartments, offices, rooms of convenience and magnificence, are in all great houses. So descriptions, figures, fables, and the rest, must be in all heroic poems; they are the common material of poetry, furnished from the magazine of nature . . . But the argument of the work (that is to say, its principal action), the economy and disposition of it – these are the things which distinguish copies from originals.[73]

Analogies such as these between heroic architecture and verse cannot have escaped Vanbrugh's attention, and surely the definition of heroic poetry offered here by his friend and stage-colleague helped inspire the emblematic role which Vanbrugh assigned to his architecture in the telling of stories or fables – and often heroic ones at that. After all, Dryden's definition would have been especially pertinent at Blenheim when designing the 'grave' and 'majestical' great house for the warrior Duke, with its episodic revelation of the Duke's 'story' through major parts such as the portico and dependent parts such as the flanking wings (see Fig. 209). As a building consciously designed to raise the visitor's thoughts to virtuous actions, Blenheim clearly ranks alongside Versailles and other heroic, rhetorical buildings. Indeed Vanbrugh seems to be paraphrasing Dryden's desire to lift the 'mind to heroic virtue by example' when expressing the wish at Blenheim that *'tho' they may not find art enough in the* Builder, to make them *admire the Beauty of the Fabrick* they will find Wonder enough in the Story, to make 'em pleas'd with the Sight of it'.[74]

'BUILDING MUSICK': FROM OPERA TO ARCHITECTURE AT THE HAYMARKET THEATRE

Just as Vanbrugh was thus introduced to the principles of *all'antica* architecture through his occupations as a dramatist and, as will be seen in Chapter Two, as a herald, so too his sensitivity to architectural harmony and proportion, as reflected in his correspondence to patrons and his buildings, would naturally have stemmed from his interest in music. Wren had compared architectural composition to that of music in his report on Salisbury Cathedral of 1668, when noting 'the Mouldings are decently mixed with large planes, without an affectation of filling every corner with ornaments, which (unlesse they are admirably good) glut the eye, as much as in Musick too much division cloyes the eare'.[75] Vanbrugh's life-long interest in music is attested by the fact that in

1719 and again in 1720 he paid an annual subscription to the Royal Academy of Music, founded in the middle of 1719 for staging Italian opera at the Haymarket Theatre in London, and in December 1725 he paid its then musical director, Attilio Ariosti, 'for a Musick Book'.[76] The Royal Academy was founded in imitation of, and as a rival to, the Académie Royale de Musique in Paris. It had twenty-one directors and subscribers included leading aristocrats headed by George I. Not only would the Academy have instructed Vanbrugh in the principles of musical harmony, it would also have served as a valuable forum for understanding history and its lessons, since the aim was to educate as well as to entertain. The plots of the Academy's operas drew heavily on stories from major passages in world history: in Handel's *Giulio Cesare in Egitto* (1724), for example, the libretto warned of the pitfalls in the destruction of liberty, in accord with the best Whig sentiments of the day.[77] Here Vanbrugh would have received full confirmation of his political beliefs through art.

Moreover, Vanbrugh was even more directly involved in the emergence of opera in England through his role in sponsoring, designing and building a new theatre in the Haymarket.[78] The inter-connections between Vanbrugh's interests in opera and architecture have been either ignored or rejected by commentators, yet connections can be made.[79] Opera was a new form of drama in eighteenth-century England. Defoe in his *A Tour Through the Whole Island of Great Britain* (1725) explained that

> Advancing hence to the Hay-Market, we see, first, the great new theatre, a very magnificent building, and perfectly accommodated for the end for which it was built, tho' the entertainment there of late, has been chiefly operas and balls. These meetings are called balls, the word *masquerade* not being so well relished by the English, who, tho' at first fond of the novelty, began to be sick of the thing on many accounts; however, as I cannot in justice say any thing to recommend them, and am by no means, to make this work by a satyr upon any thing; I choose to say no more; but go on.[80]

In designing and building the new playhouse, to be called the Queen's Theatre, Vanbrugh would have found the perfect vehicle for the interplay of his interests. He reports to Tonson on 15 June 1703 that 'I have finished my purchase for the Playhouse, and all the tenants will be out by Midsummer-day; so then I lay the corner stone; and tho' the season be thus far advanced, have pretty good assurance I shall be ready for business at Christmas'.[81] The foundation stone of the theatre was

O how refin'd how elegant we're grown! | *Or to the Opera's, or to the Masques,*
What noble Entertainments Charm the Town! | *To eat up Ortelans, and empty Flasques,*
Whether to hear the Dragon's roar we go, | *And rifle Pies from Shakespear' clinging Page;*
Or gaze surpriz'd on Fawks's matchless Show, | *Good Gods, how great's the gusto of the Age.*
Price 1 shill. 1724.

65   William Hogarth, *The Bad Taste of the Town ('Masquerades and Operas')*, 1724, etching and engraving, 13 × 17.5 cm, in which the opera is satirised as an ephemeral and alien pleasure. The theatre bears a strong resemblance to Vanbrugh's Haymarket [British Museum, London].

laid in 1704, a contemporary account by Charles Leslie noting that 'The Foundation was laid with great Solemnity, by a Noble Babe of Grace. And over or under the Foundation Stone is a Plate of Silver, on which is Graven Kit Cat on the one side, and Little Whigg on the other'.[82] The 'Noble Babe of Grace' or 'Little Whigg' has been identified as Anne, Countess of Sunderland, second daughter of the Duke of Marlborough.[83] However, when the walls of the theatre were being repaired in 1825, by report a stone was discovered with the inscription 'April 18th, 1704. This corner-stone of the Queen's Theatre was laid by his Grace Charles Duke of Somerset'.[84] Either way, the playhouse was evidently conceived of as a Whig venture (since Somerset was also a strong Whig). On 14 December 1704 Vanbrugh and William Congreve were granted authority by the Queen to form 'a Company of Comedians' and the theatre was opened on 9 April 1705 with a performance of an Italian opera, *The Loves of Ergasto*.

The site cost Vanbrugh £2000 and here he designed a building half as big again as Drury Lane, which was the first purpose-built Restoration playhouse. He drew attention to the unprecedented nature of his own scheme on 13 July 1703, when commenting again to Tonson: 'I have drawn a design for the whole disposition of the inside, very different from any Other House in being',[85] and Defoe disapprovingly described the finished building as resembling 'a French Church, or a Hall, or a Meeting-House', clearly deploring the transformation of the building's sacred model to a profane use.[86] The original theatre was destroyed by fire in 1789, but judging from a watercolour by William Capon of the 1770s depicting the main entrance front, on the northeast arm, its façades were astylar (Figs 52, 65).[87] Whilst the outside façades were plain, the inside was much more opulent, a dichotomy in keeping with Defoe's ecclesiastical analogy. One gets a glimpse of this opulence in Colley Cibber's critical description of 1740:

66   Drawing (undated) of the stage of Vanbrugh's Queen's Theatre (destroyed) [Burney Collection of Theatrical Portraits, British Museum, London].

every proper Quality and Convenience of a good Theatre had been sacrificed or neglected to shew the Spectator a vast triumphal Piece of Architecture! . . . For what could their vast Columns, their gilded Cornices, their immoderate high Roofs avail, when scarce one Word in ten could be distinctly heard in it? Nor had it then the Form it now stands in, which Necessity, two or three Years after, reduced it to: At the first opening it, the flat Ceiling that is now over the Orchestre was then a Semi-oval Arch that sprung fifteen Feet higher from above the Cornice; the Ceiling over the Pit, too, was still more raised, being one level Line from the highest back part of the upper Gallery to the Front of the Stage: The Front-boxes were a continued Semicircle to the bare walls of the House on each Side: This extraordinary and superfluous Space occasion'd such an Undulation from the Voice of every Actor, that generally what they said sounded like the Gabbling of so many People in the lofty Isles in a Cathedral.[88]

Indeed a drawing in the Burney Collection of Theatrical Portraits in the British Museum thought to represent the proscenium shows a 'semi-oval' arch springing from concave pedestals above the entablatures of widely spaced pairs of Corinthian columns (Fig. 66).[89] Here at the Haymarket, much as at Blenheim slightly later, is an early example of Vanbrugian architectural excess, in which the sense of the theatrical triumphs over the practical. Whilst restraint was evidently required externally, perhaps in the wake of popular Puritan associations between licentiousness and the stage, internally Vanbrugh felt free to bedeck his playhouse in a style befitting its function as a veritable temple to music and the arts.

Although these acoustical and other difficulties – the auditorium was hard to fill and was modified in 1708 – led Vanbrugh's theatre to be something of a failure financially, it did help in establishing opera in England despite Defoe's scepticism. Vanbrugh notes to the Earl of Manchester on 24 February 1708 that, 'the Operas are Establish'd at the Haymarket, to the generall liking of the whole Towne; . . . people are now eager to See Operas carry'd to a greater perfection, And in Order to it the Towne crys out for A Man and Woman of the First Rate to be got against Next Winter from Italy'.[90] And he adds on 27 July of that year that 'I lost so Much Money by the Opera this Last Winter, that I was glad to get quit of it; And yet I don't doubt but Operas will Settle and thrive in London.'[91] They had proved expensive to stage and on 14 August 1706 Vanbrugh leased the theatre to

Owen Swiney for seven years, only to buy Swiney out in early 1708. However, the financial implications of Vanbrugh's involvement in the building continued to haunt him for most of his life. On 20 November 1713 he notes regarding an inventory of the stock at the Haymarket: 'it was the Richest and compleatest Stock, that ever any Company had in England . . . there can be no doubt left, of the Stock being far beyond what ever had been known before upon the Stage'.[92] And on 29 November 1719 he comments to Tonson: 'I have been many years at hard Labour, to work thorough the Cruel Difficultys, that HayMarket undertaking involv'd me in . . . Nor are those difficultys, quite at an end yet. Tho' within (I think) a tolerable View'.[93] He eventually sold the building to his brother Charles in 1720, and the wardrobe to Drury Lane.

Vanbrugh's concern for the dramatic potential of both real and staged architecture came together in his 1707 production at the Haymarket of fellow Kit Cat member George Granville's opera *The British Enchanters*, which included a scene of 'the intire front prospect of Blenheim Castle'.[94] Thus, as Inigo Jones had done before him when using an image of the Banqueting House in the masque 'Time Vindicated to Himself and to His Honours' (1623), a 'real' building is presented by its architect as scenography. This is a sure indication, if one were needed, of how Vanbrugh intended his architecture to be viewed by the spectator, that is as a stage-managed experience of visual effects. Hence although his production of opera was unprofitable financially, it clearly informed his conception of architecture as a related dramatic art and one dependent on proportions and the harmony of forms, as emphasised to the Earl of Manchester in 1707 at Kimbolton. For at the end of his letter to the Earl a year later concerning opera, Vanbrugh echoed Wren's concept of architecture as 'visual music' – and harmonious music at that – in noting that he must postpone any further discussions of what he termed 'Building Musick'.[95]

Chapter 2

'THE HISTORICALL ARGUMENT': THE ORDER OF THE GARTER AND VANBRUGH'S 'CASTLE AIR'

In Vanbrugh's famous letter to the Duchess of Marlborough written in 1709 to advocate the preservation of Woodstock Manor (see Figs 34, 125), he makes two arguments. The first, what he calls the 'Historicall Argument', concerns the representational power of the medieval building as a symbol of its owner's noble character, advanced when noting that the Manor was 'rais'd by One of the Bravest and most Warlike of the English Kings'. The second argument concerns the emotional effect on the viewer of the Manor's forms and setting, advanced when observing that such 'Buildings . . . move more lively and pleasing Reflections (than History without their aid can do) on the Persons who have Inhabited them'.[1] In this way the Manor was presented by Vanbrugh as appealing to both the intellect and the emotion of an observer. These arguments accord with his other principal interests, namely heraldry, which uses symbols to express nobility, and drama, which uses scenic effects to manipulate an audience's emotions. Both aspects came together in his work as an architect, in which he aspired to impress on the viewer aspects of the character and achievements of his patrons. The next two chapters examine each of Vanbrugh's 'arguments' in turn, outlining their sources and implications for understanding the meaning behind his buildings.

'THE GREAT HOUSES IN THE NORTH': VANBRUGH, MEDIEVALISM AND BRITISH LIBERTY

Following the Glorious Revolution of 1688, the theory of a constitutional monarchy became closely associated with the administration of Republican Rome, a relationship which can only have served to legitimise, as it were, the use of the antique architectural Orders by Whig patrons.[2] This view of Roman artistic and political supremacy was apparently undermined, however, by the increasing interest in gothic buildings and remains (due in part to the Goths having defeated Rome). In the context of the necessary justification of the constitutional agreement of 1688, gothic structures set within the British landscape came increasingly to be viewed by Whigs as carrying compatible libertarian associations with those of the classical era.[3] For since the Whig aristocracy saw themselves as the guardians of public liberties, their ancestry had to be stressed through championing not only their heraldry but also their medieval buildings set in the landscape (such as Woodstock Manor), a land from which their power derived. Indeed, the monastic ruins of England often signified the beginnings of independent landed power for families who received Church lands from Henry VIII. There were also historical precedents associating a modern English political settlement with a non-Roman – that is, medieval – past. According to this myth of gothic freedom, King Alfred was the founding father of a system of civic liberties lost at the Norman invasion and re-established by Magna Carta. Thus both the Roman Republican era and the medieval period came to be widely used in Whig circles to justify Britain's major claim to contemporary political achievement, namely the events of 1688. It has been noted that, perhaps significantly in this context, Vanbrugh frequently mixed elements drawn from the architectural styles associated with both periods – at Claremont for the Whig Duke of Newcastle (Thomas Pelham-Holles), for example, where a 'gothic' Belvedere tower looked down on what appears to have been a largely astylar, symmetrical and ostensibly classical house (which incorporated Vanbrugh's earlier house called

facing page Vanbrugh Castle, Greenwich.

68   James Gibbs's Temple of Liberty at Stowe, 1741.

69   Vanbrugh's 'Robin Hood's Well', Skelbrooke, Yorkshire, *c.*1720.

Chargate, with its battlements removed; Fig. 70; see Figs 346, 348, 349, 350).[4] At Vanbrugh Castle he mixed gothic crenellations with openings arranged in that most classical of forms, the Serlian or 'Venician' window (see Fig. 315; an *all'antica* form of which Vanbrugh was particularly fond, using it at Seaton Delaval and Grimsthorpe and which may well have carried Republican connotations in the Whig mind given its association with Venice).[5] At Stowe these styles were powerfully combined to celebrate Lord Cobham's Whig ideals, expressed particularly through Vanbrugh's *all'antica* work on the main house and James Gibbs's triangular gothic Temple of Liberty (1741) in the garden (Fig. 68).[6] A celebration of native freedoms and chivalrous yeomanry found expression, no doubt, in the rustic arches of 'Robin Hood's Well', designed by Vanbrugh in about 1720 for Lord Carlisle in Skelbrooke, Yorkshire, at a significant changing-post on the Great North Road (Fig. 69).[7]

Vanbrugh's active working life as both playwright and architect coincided with the growing interest amongst contemporaries in all things medieval – the period's architecture, myths and legends – fuelled in large part by the antiquarian and archaeological preoccupations of institutions such as the Royal Society and of individuals such as William Stukeley. The Society of Antiquaries was re-founded in 1717 with the express purpose of studying British ruins pre-dating the reign of James I.[8] Purcell's 'King Arthur, or, The British Worthy' had been presented in June 1691 at the Dorset Garden Theatre by Vanbrugh's theatrical patron Sir Thomas Skipwith.[9] Influenced by his desire for contextualism, Hawksmoor was equally concerned to understand medieval architecture and considered it as amongst the legitimate styles of building. He later used the style not for freestanding structures – as Vanbrugh used it – but rather for additions to existing gothic works. His drawing for a gothic west gate at All Souls is labelled 'after yᵉ Monastick Maner' (Fig. 71), for example, whilst in a letter regarding Westminster Abbey to Dean Wilcocks of 1734/5, he described gothic as the 'Monastic style'.[10] This expression seems to have been coined to convey the style's associative, rather than its physical, qualities. Wren too advocated the use of medieval forms for contextual reasons, justifying his gothic Tom Tower at Christ Church, Oxford (Fig. 72), in a letter of 1681 by noting that 'I resolved it ought to be gothic to agree with the Founders worke'.[11]

Indeed Vanbrugh was an enthusiastic medievalist. It was noted in Chapter One that on 9 June 1720 he paid the first instalment of a subscription for John Stevens's *The History of the Antient Abbeys, Monasteries, Hospitals, Cathedrals and Collegiate Churches. Being two additional volumes to Sir William Dugdale's Monasticon Anglicanum*

70 (*facing page*)   Vanbrugh's Belvedere tower at Claremont, Surrey, 1715.

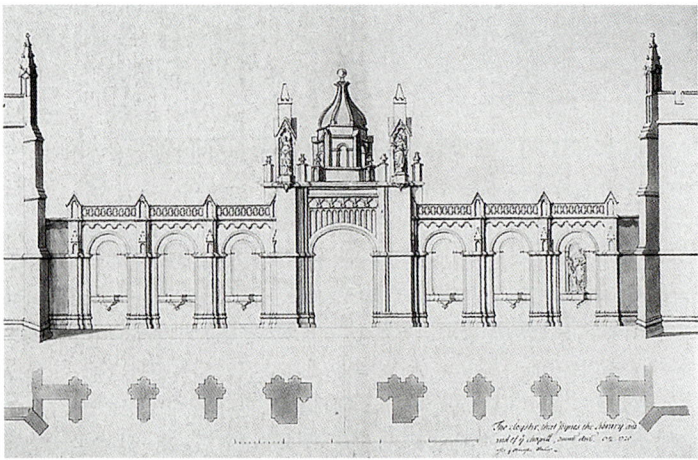

71   Hawksmoor's drawing for a gothic west gate to All Souls, Oxford, 1720 [Worcester College, Oxford].

72   Wren's Tom Tower, at Christ Church, Oxford, 1681–2.

(1722–3).[12] In this, one of the early studies of England's medieval architectural heritage, Vanbrugh would have seen plates of such austere edifices as 'the abbey church of Holmcoltram in Cumberland' with its round-headed windows and 'the Church of Radford, by Worksop' with its crenellations (Figs 73, 74).[13] Studying Stevens's illustrations of the ruined Glastonbury Abbey (Fig. 75), Vanbrugh would have read of its legendary foundation by Joseph of Arimathea and of the burial there of King Arthur.[14] Here Vanbrugh's heraldic interest in religious Orders of knighthood, such as the Garter (to be examined shortly), merged with his architectural concerns with the antiquity of monastic foundations which Stevens, following Dugdale, is careful to emphasise.

As part of his early architectural education, Vanbrugh made a northern tour in the summer of 1699, explaining to the Earl of Manchester on Christmas Day of that year: 'I have been this Summer at my Ld Carlisle's, and Seen most of the great houses in the North, as Ld Nottings: Duke of Leeds Chattesworth &c.'[15] This itinerary must have taken him past all of the most prominent medieval and Elizabethan structures, including Burghley House, Wollaton Hall, Hardwick Hall, Little Castle at Bolsover, Welbeck Abbey, Worksop Manor and Kiveton Hall (Figs 76–9).[16] Vanbrugh was preoccupied in his house designs with elements drawn from such Elizabethan and Jacobean country houses. These elements included the clerestory (as at Wollaton Hall), corner towers and rooftop sentry-boxes (as at Worksop Manor), the long gallery (as at Hardwick Hall), the Bow Window (as at Burghley House), walled entrance courts and corner pavilions (as at Syon House), freestanding towers (as at old Chatsworth House) and the 'H' plan (as at old Charlton House).[17] In his use of these forms Vanbrugh expressed not only his abstract interest in architectural form and massing, in common with the continental baroque masters such as Bernini (whose Piazza Navona fountain, it has been noted, he studied), but also his desire to find a truly national basis for an architectural vocabulary of forms which were distinct from foreign influence. This followed in the wake of attempts by Philibert de l'Orme in the 1560s to establish an architectural style befitting French traditions and sentiments, for example, and rivalled more contemporary efforts to express French grandeur made by Colbert, Louis xiv's minister, of which Vanbrugh was well aware. With similar nationalistic motives in mind, Hawksmoor too admired the great Elizabethan 'prodigy houses': he described Wollaton Hall as 'an admirable piece of Masonry', adding that there were 'some true Stroaks of Architecture'.[18] In this quest for a national style, the architecture of the Elizabethan era – the age of great playwrights such as Shake-

The North side of the Abby Church of Holmcoltram in Cumberland.

73 The abbey church of
Holmcoltram in Cumbria,
from John Stevens's
*The History of the Antient
Abbeys, Monasteries,
Hospitals, Cathedrals and
Collegiate Churches. Being
two additional volumes to
Sir William Dugdale's
Monasticon Anglicanum*,
vol. II (1722–3), p. 55.

A SOUTH WEST PROSPECT OF THE CHURCH OF RADFORD, BY WORKSOP.

74 The Church of
Radford, Worksop, from
John Stevens's *The History
of the Antient Abbeys,
Monasteries, Hospitals,
Cathedrals and Collegiate
Churches*, vol. II (1722–3),
p. 134.

The South Prospect of the Ruins of Glastonbury Abby.

75 Glastonbury Abbey,
from John Stevens's
*The History of the Antient
Abbeys, Monasteries,
Hospitals, Cathedrals and
Collegiate Churches*, vol. I
(1722–3), p. 452.

76 (*above left*)
Burghley House,
Lincolnshire,
1555–87.

77 (*above right*)
Hardwick (New)
Hall, Derbyshire,
1590–97.

78 (*right*)   Little
Castle at Bolsover,
Derbyshire, 1621.

79   Wollaton Hall, Nottinghamshire. Detail of a view by Jan Siberechts, 1695, oil on canvas, 191.8 × 138.2 cm
[Lord Middleton Collection, Birdsall, Yorkshire].

speare and of chivalrous knights such as Drake – must
have particularly appealed to Vanbrugh the playwright-
soldier and knight of the realm whose kinsmen included
the Earls of Berkshire, Carlisle, Dorset and Suffolk.[19]

Vanbrugh's correspondence with his Whig patrons
also makes clear his respect for English medieval buildings. Writing to the Duke of Newcastle on 6 August
1719, for example, concerning the threatened Holbein
Gate in Whitehall (Fig. 80), he comments, 'I find many
people Surpris'd there shou'd be no other Expedient

found to make way for Coaches &c, than destroying
One of the Greatest Curiositys there is in London as
that Gate has ever been esteem'd'.[20] Most famously, it
was noted earlier that Vanbrugh's admiration for old
Woodstock Manor and Rosamond's Well (Fig. 81, 82)[21]
was expressed in his letter to the Duchess of Marlborough of 11 June 1709 entitled 'Reasons Offer'd for
Preserving some Part of the Old Manour'. Having
praised Blenheim as a monument to the Duke's services,
he continues:

80   The Holbein Gate in Whitehall (destroyed), watercolour by anonymous artist, 1725 [Guildhall Library, London].

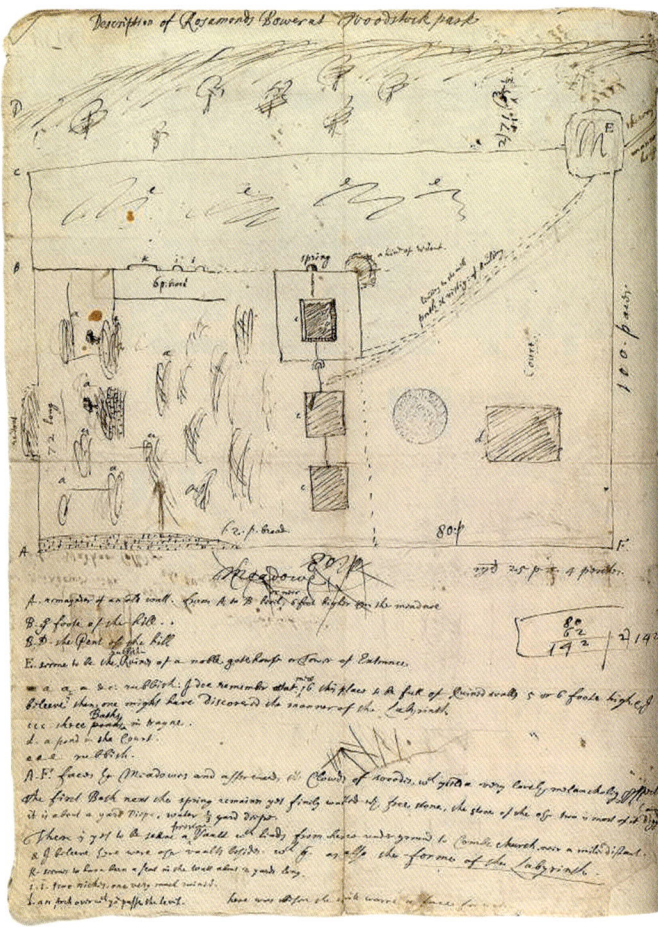

81   Rosamond's Bower and Well in Woodstock Park, drawn in the late seventeenth century by John Aubrey [Bodleian Library, Oxford].

I hope I may be forgiven, if I make some faint application of what I say of Blenheim, to the Small Remains of ancient Woodstock Manour. It can't indeed be said, it was Erected on so Noble, nor on So justifiable an Occasion; But it was rais'd by One of the Bravest and most Warlike of the English Kings; And tho' it has not been Fam'd, as a Monument of his arms, *it has been tenderly regarded as the Scene of his Affections. Nor amongst the Multitude of People, who come daily to View what is raising to the Memory of the Great Battle of Blenheim; are there any that do not run eagerly to See what Ancient Remains are to be found of Rosamonds Bower. It may perhaps be worth some Little Reflection Upon what may be said, if the Very footsteps of it are no more to be found.*[22]

82   The remains of Rosamond's Well in the gardens at Blenheim.

83 The kitchen court at Blenheim.

The 'Bravest and most Warlike of the English Kings' was Henry II (1133–89), whose achievements included the building of stone defences at Windsor, and the 'Rosamond' was Jane Clifford, his mistress. In this Vanbrugh emphasises the themes of medieval chivalry and knighthood, expressed by such medieval sites as Woodstock, as models for his own time; implied in what he calls his 'Historicall Argument' is a 'greatness by association' with this particular British royal monument. Vanbrugh is encouraging the Duchess to recognise a national inheritance that the Duke can assume as his own through the Manor's preservation and use as a model. Indeed he later assured the Duchess that 'the homely simplicity of the Antient Manor' was in his 'constant thoughts for a guide in what remains to be done, in all the inferior Buildings' at Blenheim.[23] The astylar, crenellated arcade and simple monumentality of the kitchen court are the result (Fig. 83). As will be seen, such explicit reference to historical forms, especially martial ones, must have been natural for a herald.

'BLEW GARTERS' AND 'GOOD HOUSES': VANBRUGH AND THE 'WINDSOR POINT'

In Kneller's famous portrait of Vanbrugh, the architect holds a pair of dividers whilst proudly wearing his badge of office as a herald (see Fig. 1). Thus the portrait unites, symbolically, two of Vanbrugh's main concerns. Given that his emerging interests in both arts closely coincided and were intertwined, it seems natural to trace the influence of the principles and medieval mythology of heraldry on Vanbrugh's architecture. For he held high office in the College of Heralds, serving as both Clarenceux King of Arms and as Garter King of Arms.[24] Despite a lack of previous experience, he was first installed in the revived office of Carlisle Herald in March 1703 by the Earl of Carlisle, who served as Deputy Earl Marshal (1701–6).[25] This was as a reward for the architect's early work at Castle Howard and as a prelude to his becoming Clarenceux King of Arms. On 15 June 1703 Vanbrugh wrote to Tonson concerning this ambition: 'Lord

Carlisle went homeward yesterday, with wife and children, and has made Ld Essex Deputy Earl Marshall; to crown that, Harry St George Garter, and me Herald Extraordinary (if the Queen pleases), in order to be Clarencieux at his return to towne; but whether we shall carry either point at Court, is not yet sure, tho' it stands home prest at this moment, and will I believe be known tonight'.[26] Writing to Tonson near the end of his life, in October 1725, he was the first to admit his lack of heraldic experience, commenting: 'I got leave to dispose in earnest, of a Place I got in jest, Clar[x] King of Arms'.[27] The most damaging ridicule came from the pen of Swift, who in implying the interconnection between the arts of architecture and heraldry observed 'Now Van will be able to build houses'; and in 'Vanbrug's House' (1709), on the specific subject of Vanbrugh's new house in Whitehall which Swift nicknamed 'Goose-Pie' (see Figs 29, 316, 317), he added:

> Van (for 'tis fit the reader know it)
> Is both a herald and a poet;
> No wonder then, if nicely skilled
> In both capacities to build.
> As herald, he can in a day
> Repair a house gone to decay;
> Or by achievement, arms, device,
> Erect a new one in a trice.
> And as a poet, he has skill
> To build in speculation still.[28]

What made matters worse for Vanbrugh was the fact that he had even appeared to attack the heraldic profession in one of his plays, *Aesop*, through the character of a sycophantic genealogist called Jacob Quaint, although as will be seen the object of his satire for the most part lay elsewhere. Naturally enough, there was much opposition from the College of Heralds to his appointment. On 13 July 1703 Vanbrugh reported to Tonson that Carlisle 'stay'd in Towne a good while about our Heralds business; there was a great deal of Saucy Opposition, but my Ld Treasurer set the Queen right, and I have accordingly been Souc'd a Herald Extraordinary, in order to be a King at Winter. Ld Essex was left Deputy to do the feat which he did with a whole Bowle of wine about my ears instead of half a Spoonfull. He at the same time crown'd Old Sr Harry, Garter'.[29]

In fact Vanbrugh went on to take his various roles as a herald, including the design of heraldry, very seriously and in the twenty-two years as Clarenceux he was a frequent attendant at the College of Heralds.[30] As his accounts reveal, these duties were certainly lucrative. On 14 October 1715 he received £66, 3s and 11$^1/_4$d 'from the Heralds Colledge for Coronation Fees and Largess

for Peers'.[31] Attending Garter ceremonies, investitures and State occasions such as the coronation of George I clearly had the effect of further stimulating Vanbrugh's patriotic sensibility towards the history of England, of which its heraldry and sombre medieval buildings such as Woodstock Manor were a joint legacy. Links between the two had famously been emphasised in the seventeenth century by William Dugdale, Garter King of Arms and antiquarian, and by Elias Ashmole, Windsor Herald and early Freemason. The importance of this ceremonial role to Vanbrugh's Whig political vision and, in turn, to his work as an architect – that is, to its meaning and purpose – has never received the recognition it deserves. The stylistic term 'baroque', often used to describe Vanbrugh's architecture, has served only to obscure the meaning behind his frequent use of medieval ornament and architectural forms, most notably those derived from fortifications, which should instead be seen as a kind of heraldic celebration of the nation's chivalrous history.

Vanbrugh is likely to have been influenced in his admiration of medieval architecture by one heraldic role above all, that of Garter King of Arms. He temporarily occupied the position in 1706–7 and was again acting Garter King between 1715 and 1718. In this role he was placed at the heart of court ceremonial. For example, he carried out the degradation of the Duke of Ormond at Windsor on 12 July 1716 (the Duke having become a fugitive after siding with the Jacobite Pretender, the Catholic James II).[32] According to the account of George Beltz, Vanbrugh as 'Clarenceux king of arms, exercising the office of Garter, read the Sovereign's warrant at the brazen desk. The achievements of the degraded knight were then severally thrown down by the heralds, and spurned out of the choir and the west door of the chapel, where the soldiers of the garrison were under arms. Clarenceux concluded the ceremony by pulling the plate of the arms from the stall'.[33] Here is a vivid account of Vanbrugh's ceremonial role, which combined his interests in public theatre and military show. As either Garter King or Clarenceux he would also have played a central part in the annual convocation in St George's Hall to elect new knights, held on the feast day of St George (23 April), and in the ceremonial procession and dinner on its eve in celebration of the Garter's patron, St George (Fig. 84).[34] Ashmole makes clear that the Officers of Arms were to assemble at the lower end of the Hall, 'and there make themselves ready to proceed up in the following Order: *Garter, Clarenceux* and *Norroy, Heralds*, two and two, *Pursuivants*, two and two'.[35] Vanbrugh's accounts indicate something of his Garter duties, recording for 23 May 1716 that £50 was 'Recd from the Wardrobe by

84   The annual convocation in St George's Hall at Windsor Castle, from Elias Ashmole's *The Institution, Laws and Ceremonies of the Most Noble Order of the Garter* (1672), pp. 592–3.

Composition for Sr Henry St George's Coat, wch he gave me for having officiated for him', for example, and for 15 July 1718 that he was paid £3, 17s and 4d for a Garter installation.[36]

The Noble Order of the Garter was the most senior of Orders at the British court and consisted of the Sovereign and Prince of Wales as well as twenty-four knights, or Knights Companion, with the monarch as its supreme head and St George as its patron.[37] The closed nature of its fraternity and its military character, its outwardly Protestant mission and the theatricality of its ceremonies carried out on what Vanbrugh termed the 'public stage',[38] must all have held a special appeal for him. With the symbolic duty to protect London as the 'New Jerusalem' on English soil, following in spirit the

crusading ancestors, the Order had been founded by Edward III but was seen to embody an unbroken link, past the Crusades, to the chivalry of Arthur's court and, through Roman occupation, back to Troy.[39] The fairy scenes in Shakespeare's *The Merry Wives of Windsor* had referred to the Order and to its chapel at Windsor as the embodiment of the Arthurian ideal, and Michael Drayton in *Poly-Olbion* (1613–22) noted the Garter's 'ancient rites' centred on Windsor's 'Temple of Saint George'.[40] From the outset of James I's reign, the Stuarts used the Order as a public sign of the continuity of British history under their rule. Prince Henry had been made a Garter knight in 1603 and an antique scene drawn by Inigo Jones which centred on 'St George's Portico' in the masque 'Prince Henry's Barriers' (1610)

85   Inigo Jones's drawing entitled 'St George's Portico', a backdrop in the masque 'Prince Henry's Barriers' (1610) [Devonshire Collection, Chatsworth].

represented a clear celebration of the Garter's antiquity (Fig. 85).[41] Of special significance for Vanbrugh, the architectural Orders were thus proclaimed from the outset of Stuart rule as a specific backdrop to Garter ceremonial. Dryden echoed this theatrical tradition in his *Albion and Albanius* (1685) which closed with 'that part of Windsor, which faces Eton', focussing on the Terrace Walk with the King's Lodgings, St George's Chapel, the Keep and the Upper Ward, while 'In the Air is a Vision of the Honours of the Garter; the Knights in Procession and the King under a Canopy'.[42] Given his background and interests one might expect Vanbrugh to have been well aware of this theatrical tradition linking the ancient Orders of chivalry and architecture in the context of medieval Windsor. The most important Garter historian of the late seventeenth century was Ashmole, who in *The Institution, Laws & Ceremonies of the Most Noble Order of the Garter* (1672) refers to 'Roman Knights' and concerning 'The Order of Knights of the Round Table' notes: 'The *Founder* of this most ancient Order, was *Arthur* King of *Britain*, Crowned in the year of our Lord

516 . . . King *Edward* the Third having designed to restore the Honor of the *Round Table*, held a Juste at *Windsor*, in the 18. Year of his Reign . . . and this meeting in truth occasioned the *Foundation* of the most noble *Order* of the *Garter*'.[43] Published with Hollar's beautiful illustrations recording Windsor Castle's medieval splendour (before the remodelling by Hugh May for Charles II), Ashmole's work praised the 'elegant and beauteous Structure' of the medieval chapel (Fig. 86).[44] His historical study would have had an obvious appeal to Vanbrugh in his joint role as herald and architect, given how mindful both roles would have made him of the appropriate use of historical precedent. Indeed as the embodiment of a lost, chivalrous world necessarily centred on the king, Windsor became one of Vanbrugh's main architectural models, thus clearly uniting his heraldic and architectural interests.

Vanbrugh was certainly keenly interested in the English national story. As was noted in Chapter One, his accounts for 22 May 1718 record the payment for 'Echards 3 Volls: of the English History', that is, Laurence

W. Hollar delin. et sculp.

86   The medieval chapel at Windsor Castle, engraving by Wenceslaus Hollar from Elias Ashmole's *The Institution, Laws and Ceremonies of the Most Noble Order of the Garter* (1672), p. 139.

87   Queen Anne, engraved by George Vertue after Kneller, from
Laurence Eachard's *The History of England, from the first Entrance of
Julius Caesar and the Romans (to the conclusion of the reign of King
James the Second, and establishment of King William and Queen Mary)*
(1707–18).

88   George I, engraved by George Vertue after Kneller, from
Laurence Eachard's *The History of England* (1707–18).

Eachard's *The History of England, from the first Entrance of
Julius Caesar* (1707–18). Published by Tonson, the first
volume opened with a dedicatory engraving by George
Vertue of Anne and the second with one of George I,
both monarchs wearing their Garter insignia of St
George (Figs 87, 88). Eachard thus stressed the lineage of
British monarchy back to the Romans represented by
Caesar and, following Ashmole, included Edward III's
foundation of the Garter and the story of King Arthur.[45]
Judging from his plays Vanbrugh was scornful of other,
more fanciful versions of the nation's history. In *Aesop*
(written in 1696 and performed in January 1697) he
satirises the popular Welsh claim to have descended from
the chosen, the children of Israel. Here the character
called Jacob Quaint, a Herald, exclaims: 'Why, Sir, I'm a
Herald by Nature, my Mother was a *Welch Woman*'.
Aesop replies: 'A *Welch Woman*? Prithee of what
Country's that?' Quaint responds:

> That, Sir, is a Country in the World's back-side, where
> every Man is born a Gentleman, and a Genealogist.

Sir, I cou'd tell my Mothers Pedigree before I cou'd
speak plain: which, to shew you the depth of my Art,
and the strength of my Memory, I'll trundle you down
in an instant. Noah had three Sons, *Shem*, *Ham* and
Japhet; *Shem*–.[46]

At which point Aesop interrupts, impatient at this affectation. Vanbrugh was consistent in his attack on the
pretentiousness of this national Welsh genealogy. For in
the first scene of the fourth act of *The Provok'd Wife*, as
rewritten in 1725 for performance in that year, Sir John
Brute appears disguised in his wife's cloak and gown
(rather than, as in the first version, more controversially
as a clergyman). In this guise he is introduced as the
model female warrior: 'Sirrah, I am *Bonduca*, queen of
the *Welshmen*, and with a Leek as long as my Pedigree,
I will destroy your *Roman* Legions in an instant – *Britons*,
strike home'.[47] Vanbrugh took the character of Bonduca,
better known as Boadicea, from Henry Purcell's opera
'The Tragedy of Bonduca' (1695), in which the words of
the chief Druid's song are, '*Britains*, Strike Home:

Ana A: M: Delin.   *The Chief Druid*   *from a Statue*

89   A Druid chief, from Henry Rowlands's *Mona Antiqua Restaurata* (1723), p. 64.

with an ancient divinely inspired theology which had excelled the culture that the Romans imposed. The counter, more rational view of a superior Romano-British race under Roman rule was outlined in Eachard's history and in Samuel Clarke's 1712 edition of Caesar's commentaries, to which Vanbrugh contributed: plate 62 was sponsored by him and includes, as with the other subscribers, his coat of arms (Fig. 91).[51] As an Imperial governor, Caesar was an ambiguous figure for the Whigs, both despotic and glorious, as indicated by his treatment in Handel's opera *Giulio Cesare in Egitto* of 1724.[52] In Clarke's *Caesaris* the notion of modern supremacy over ancient culture, at least politically, was indicated by his opening plate engraved by Vertue of the Whig Duke of Marlborough complete with his Garter insignia (followed by one of Caesar with his Roman insignia), whilst the idea that the commentaries should also be seen as a warning against absolute power was indicated by the Whig affiliations of the book's subscribers and of its publisher, Tonson.[53] Nevertheless the fact that Vanbrugh's plate included his family coat of arms and a legend celebrating his twin roles as royal Comptroller and herald had the effect of linking these with the glorious military achievements of Caesar which the book clearly also

90   Detail from Andrea Mantegna's *The Triumphs of Caesar*, as engraved in Samuel Clarke's *C. Julii Caesaris, Quae Extant . . .* (1712), pl. 79.

Revenge your Country's Wrongs: Fight and Record your selves in *Druids* Songs'.[48] The object of this satire is clear enough. Following Pliny's discussion of Druid magic and Geoffrey of Monmouth's description of Wales as the refuge of the last of the descendants of the Trojan prince Brute, Drayton had represented Welsh priests or Druids as the native heirs of biblical and antique sages initiated in Nature's secrets.[49] There was a resurgence of Druid writing around 1700. A new edition of *Britannia* in 1695 contained some of John Aubrey's theories concerning Druid prehistory and Vanbrugh's rewritten scenes in *The Provok'd Wife* came just after Henry Rowlands's *Mona Antiqua Restaurata* (1723), with its illustration of a Druid chief (Fig. 89). John Toland's unflattering view of the Druids had been published around 1702 as *A Critical History of the Celtic Religion and Learning: Containing an Account of the Druids; or, the Priests and Judges, . . . of the Bards, or the Poets and Heralds*[50] and Vanbrugh is likely to have taken to heart Toland's argument that the Druids were an oppressive oligarchy whom the Romans were right to suppress.

Thus Vanbrugh evidently regarded as fanciful the mythic history of a native, pre-Roman Celtic civilisation

91   Engraving sponsored by Vanbrugh from Samuel Clarke's *C. Julii Caesaris, Quae Extant . . .* (1712), pl. 62.

celebrated (Fig. 90). Elsewhere his approval of Caesar's military achievements is indicated by the copy by Pellegrini of Mantegna's epic *Triumphs of Caesar* painted in Kimbolton Castle around 1711 (Fig. 92). Vanbrugh's use of Roman military insignia – trophies and shields, eagles and arrows – in the metopes at Castle Howard and Seaton Delaval follow Jones's designs at Whitehall (Figs 93, 94; see Fig. 231) and, as there, might be understood to celebrate the Golden Age of the Romano-British under Caesar's Roman rule – whose passing the Castle

Howard urns have been seen as 'mourning'.[54] In this understanding Vanbrugh was consistent with the Garter historians who had emphasised not only the medieval but also the Roman origins of knighthood; this can surely only have served to legitimise further the mixed style of his architectural vocabulary, in uniting both medieval and Roman elements.

Indeed this very mix of architectural elements drawn from medieval and classical traditions was to be found at Windsor as remodelled by Hugh May under Charles II,

92   Copy by Giovanni Antonio Pellegrini of Mantegna's *Triumphs of Caesar*, painted in Kimbolton
Castle, *c*.1711 [Country Life Picture Library].

with its combination of crenellations and round-headed
windows (instead of the instantly recognisable gothic
pointed arch; Figs 95, 96).[55] The main theme of the decorative scheme of the rebuilt medieval Hall, which had
been painted by Verrio and completed in 1683, was the
glorification of the Garter (Fig. 97). St George and the
dragon were pictured on the west wall, above the throne.
The achievements of Edward III were pictured in classical terms through, as Defoe reported, 'the representation

of Prince Edward's triumph, in imitation of Caesar's glorious entry into Rome, and which was drawn marching
from the lower end of the room, to the upper'.[56] Charles
II was enthroned amongst clouds in the central oval of
the ceiling, whilst the two octagonal fields occupying the
remainder of the ceiling featured the Garter collar and
the Muses surrounding the Garter Star.[57] The message
that artistic inspiration – at least regarding work for the
Crown – was ultimately illuminated by the Order and

93   Military insignia carved into the entablature on the north, front façade of Castle Howard (1706).

94   Trophies of arms in the Doric metopes, part of the Jones and Webb designs for Whitehall Palace. Engraved by Henry Flitcroft from William Kent's *The Designs of Inigo Jones* (1727).

thrived, as it were, under its star cannot have escaped Vanbrugh's attention on the occasions when he took part in Garter ceremonies in this gilt room. For here the architectural Orders became literally part of Garter her-

aldry, with pairs of fictive Corinthian columns supporting putti, each holding Garter mantles, and framing upper circular windows in the south wall, each surrounded by the Garter motto. Concern with the chapel's fabric continued during the reign of George I whilst Vanbrugh was Comptroller at the Board of Works. The *Weekly Journal* of 1724 reported: 'When his Majesty went to offer in St. George's chapple at Windsor last Sunday . . . he took Notice of a Chappel at the East End thereof, which was built by Cardinal Woolsey. The Ceiling was very beautifully painted in King Charles the second's Time, and intended for a Chapter House and Robeing Room upon all Installations, Ec. but never finished. His Majesty ordered it to be fitted up for that purpose.'[58]

Vanbrugh's long involvement with the Garter and its ceremonies coincided, not surprisingly, with much of his built work. Many of his most prominent patrons were either Garter knights or were connected with the Order. Obviously the most important of these were the monarchs Anne (whose coronation had been on St George's day in 1702) and George I (who was made a Garter knight in 1701 and installed in 1703 whilst Elector of

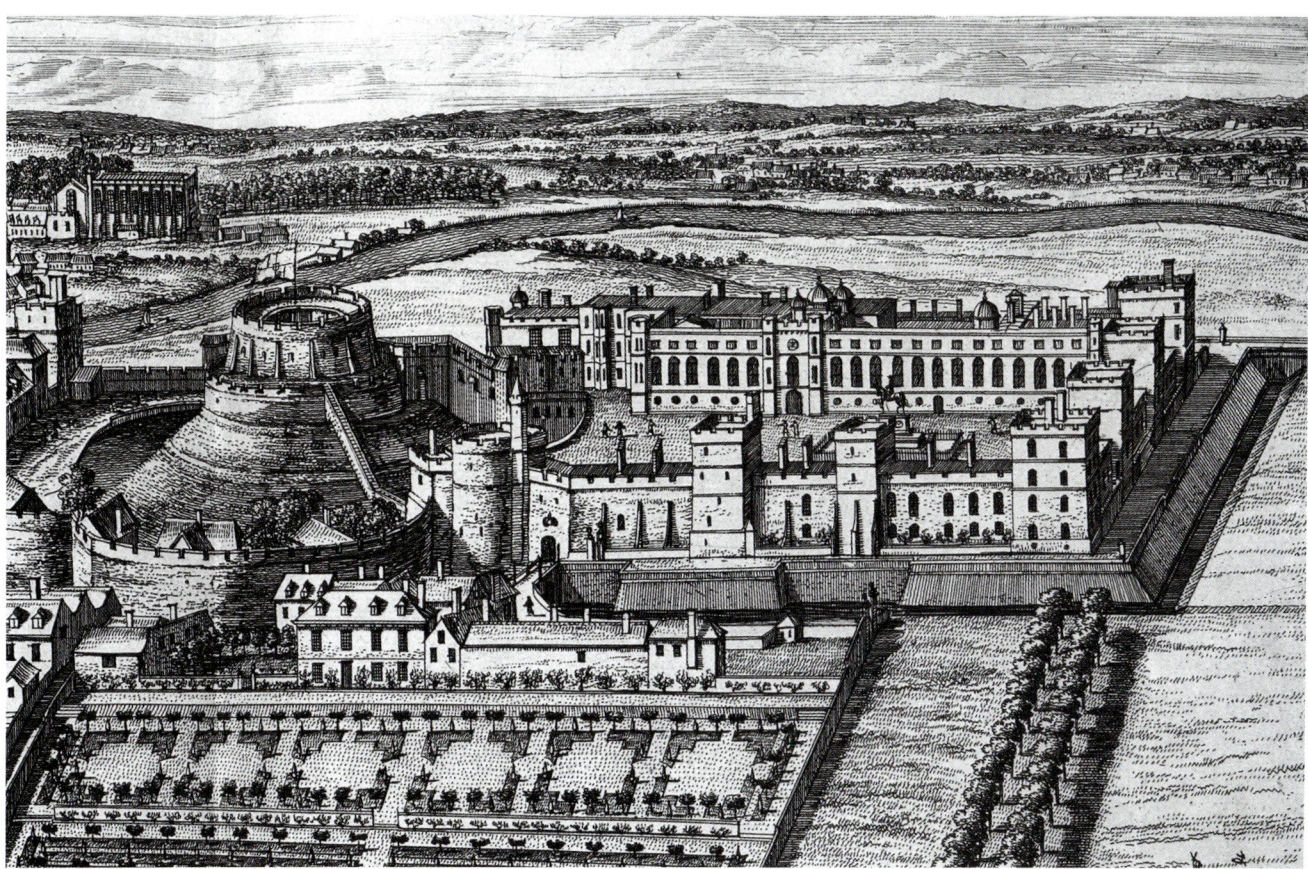

95   The Upper Court of Windsor Castle as remodelled by Hugh May for Charles II (altered in the early nineteenth century), engraved by Leonard Knyff from Johannes Kip's *Britannia Illustrata* (1707), pl. 14.

Hanover), for whom Vanbrugh worked in the Board. Of great prominence was also the Duke of Marlborough, who was installed in March 1703, two years before work at Blenheim began (Marlborough's crest included the cross of St George, as represented on the pediment at Blenheim, Fig. 98, and a dragon-like beast featured in one of Hawksmoor's column designs there).[59] The inscription on the engraving of the south, garden façade of Blenheim in the first volume of Campbell's *Vitruvius Britannicus* (1715) makes explicit the conception of the house as a celebration of the Duke's status as a 'Knight of the most noble Order of the Garter' (Fig. 99). Vanbrugh was himself knighted at the Queen's House on Marlborough's instruction, on 19 September 1714. Sidney Godolphin, who as Lord Treasurer (until 1710) was deeply involved in the work at Blenheim as well as in projects for the Office of Works, was made a Garter knight in 1704. John Holles (the Earl of Clare and later

96   The surviving round-headed windows designed by Hugh May in Henry III's tower at Windsor Castle.

Drawn by C. Wild.   Engraved by W.I. Bennett.

St George's Hall
WINDSOR CASTLE

97   St George's Hall at Windsor Castle completed in 1683 with paintings by Verrio (destroyed), from William Pyne's *The History of the Royal Residences of Windsor Castle, St James's Palace, Carlton House and Frogmore* (1819).

the Duke of Newcastle) had been made a Garter knight in 1698. He helped sponsor Vanbrugh's new Haymarket theatre and commissioned his (unbuilt) designs for Welbeck. Vanbrugh wrote to Holles in June 1703 (having only recently been made Carlisle Herald) citing the Garter and architecture as joint expressions of pedigree: 'I believe if your Grace will please to consider of the Intrinsique vallew of Tytles and Blew Garters, and Jewells and Great Tables and Numbers of Servants & in a word all those things that distinguish Great Men from small ones, you will confess to me, that a Good house is at least upon the Levell with the best of 'em.'[60] Between 1715 and 1720 Vanbrugh designed Claremont House and

Belvedere (see Figs 70, 346, 348, 349, 350) and, between 1718 and 1719, altered internally the 'Noble Dwelling'[61] of Nottingham Castle for the Duke's nephew and heir, Thomas Pelham-Holles. He in turn was made a Garter knight during this time, in 1718, on which occasion Vanbrugh wrote 'I hope all past at Windsor, as it Shoul'd do. And most heartily wish you joy, of your Installation' (Vanbrugh was evidently suffering from 'Blisters' and missed the ceremony).[62] Although not a Garter knight himself, Charles Montague as the Earl of Manchester traced his lineage to the knight-founders of the Order;[63] Vanbrugh remodelled Kimbolton Castle for him in 1707 (see Figs 4, 215). The first Earl of Bindon, subsequently

98 Marlborough's crest, including the cross of St George (top-left quarter), on the pediment at Blenheim.

the sixth Earl of Suffolk and a distant relation of Van-brugh,[64] served as Deputy Earl Marshal (to whom the Garter King answered); Vanbrugh carried out work at Audley End in Essex for him in 1708 (although it cannot be absolutely proved that he designed the screen – in a Jacobean style – often attributed to him; Fig. 100).[65] Finally, Lord Carlisle, although not a Garter Knight, had

also served as Deputy Earl Marshal and was Constable of Windsor Castle.[66]

In this involvement with the Garter and its knights Vanbrugh followed in the footsteps of his master at the Board of Works, Christopher Wren. For Wren also had a lifelong devotion to the Order in succession to his father and uncle who both served in turn as Dean of

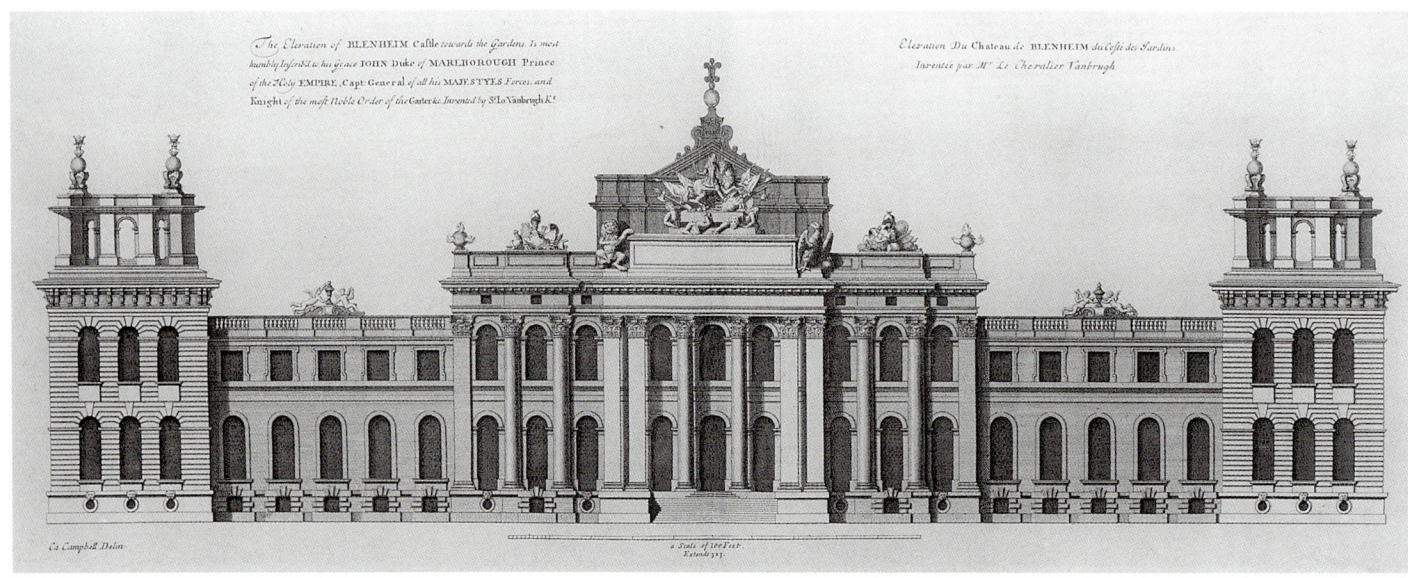

99   Engraving of the south, garden façade of Blenheim, from Colen Campbell's *Vitruvius Britannicus*, vol. 1 (1715), pls 59 and 60.

100   The Jacobean-style screen at Audley End in Essex, *c.*1708, lower section attributed to Vanbrugh [English Heritage Photo Library].

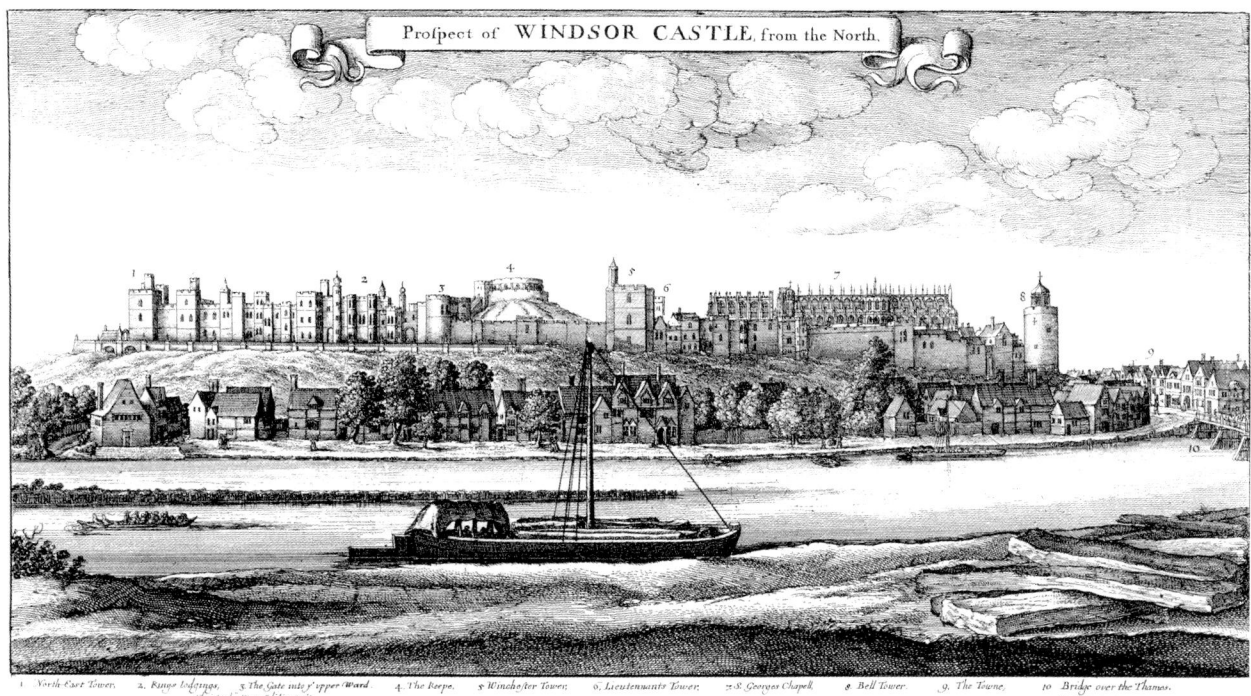

101   Windsor Castle from the north, as drawn by Wren and engraved by Wenceslaus Hollar for Elias Ashmole's *The Institution, Laws and Ceremonies of the Most Noble Order of the Garter* (1672), p. 134.

Windsor and chief protector, or Register, of Garter monuments and records.[67] When aged twenty-seven, Wren drew one of the plates illustrating Windsor Castle (from the north) engraved by Hollar for Ashmole's Garter history (Fig. 101) and a year later (in 1660) restored the Garter records to Charles II on behalf of his father.[68] As Surveyor General, Wren went on to repair the fabric and produce a number of schemes for Windsor.[69] Given the intertwined story of survival of the Wren family and the Garter – through the perils of the Civil War – his use of dragons in his Fire Monument in London, reflecting the City's coat of arms (two dragons either side of the cross of St George), must surely have given him particular satisfaction (Fig. 102). (The legend of St George was a perfect one for the monument's theme of rescue from the dangers of fire.) Drawings by Hawksmoor for fireplaces at Hampton Court, as part of work supervised by Wren, incorporate Garter insignia (Fig. 103).[70] Furthermore two of the six churches completed by Hawksmoor in his own right had St George as their patron saint, one in Bloomsbury and the other in the East End (St George's-in-the-East) (Figs 104, 105).

The seriousness with which Vanbrugh regarded his ceremonial duties for the Order is evident from the correspondence concerning his long-running campaign to be appointed the permanent Garter King following the death of Sir Henry St George in 1715, a matter he termed the 'Windsor point'. This ambition was equal to, and went hand in hand with, his much better-known one to be appointed Surveyor-General at the Board of Works. He observed to the Duke of Marlborough on 18 March 1713 that he had given up 'all hopes of succeeding either to Sʳ Chr. Wren, or Sʳ Harry St. George, which were two things, I once thought I could not fail of.'[71] His failure to get appointed was bound up in the deteriorating relationship at Blenheim and rivalry with the herald John Anstis. Writing to the Duke on 29 May 1714 he reported that 'The Queen has at last pass'd a Patent (even without my Lord Suffolks concurrence in it) to Mʳ Anstis for the reversion of Garter. She said she had been under an obligation to me not to consent to it; but my behaviour had been such in writing that Letter to Woodstock, that now she had done with me – That was her expression.'[72] However Anstis was put in prison on a charge of complicity in the Jacobite rebellion of 1715 and so for the time being Vanbrugh was allowed to perform the office of Garter. When Anstis was released following his acquittal, he inevitably claimed the post. Vanbrugh fought it, on the grounds that the Queen could not appoint Garter, Charles II having relinquished the right. Anstis took his stand (successfully as it turned out) on the grounds that Charles had done no such

102　Playful dragons on Wren's Monument to the Great Fire of London, 1671–77, part of the coat of arms of the City of London.

thing, only waved it in a particular instance. On 14 October 1717 Vanbrugh wrote to the Treasury Commissioners regarding their

> Commands signified to me by Mr Kelsall, relating to ye Attorney Gen^{lls}. report, on Mr Anstis's Petition for a Salary belonging to him as Garter King of Arms . . . upon an Application to his Maj^{ty}. in Councill from ye Earl of Suffolk [the Deputy Marshal], the Lords of ye Cabinet sent for ye Attorney Gen^{ll}. before them, to know why he had not (in pursuance of his Majestys Commands . . .) prepared a Bill for his Royall Signature, to pass ye Great Seal, containing his Majestys Grant of ye Office of Garter Principall King of Arms to me.[73]

A hearing before the Attorney General was deemed necessary but, much to Vanbrugh's annoyance, delays ensued. He took the whole matter extremely seriously, noting that

> I do Assure your L^{d}ships no manner of delay, will be practis'd from my side, it being my most earnest desire to have this dispute determin'd, as soon as possible.

But till it is so, and that ye delay lys entirely on ye opposite side I humbly hope Your Lordships will think it Just & reasonable for ye King to keep his Money in his hands, till he sees whether a Patent granted by himselfe or his Predecessour, determins who is to have ye honour of being his Officer.[74]

Slightly later in the same year he wrote to the Duke of Newcastle, mentioning his preoccupation with the 'two Accursed things of determining the Windsor point, and My Friend Bensons' (the latter concerning the Office of Works).[75] Vanbrugh held his opponent Anstis in low esteem, calling him 'a sad thief' in his next letter to the Duke, adding on the subject of Anstis's fees and licence to officiate at Garter ceremonies that 'if his Patent be Void he has no more pretence to these Fees than your Coachman has.'[76] Some time after April 1718, when Anstis was finally granted the position, Vanbrugh wrote to Lord Stanhope to urge him to 'Speak to Our new Earl Marshall, Not to let Anstis put any tricks upon me; which he has Already Attempted; in a very Benson like Manner. I have dam'd luck to have two Such Fellows get over me.'[77]

103   Drawing by Hawksmoor for a fireplace at Hampton Court incorporate Garter insignia [Sir John Soane's Museum, London].

Despite this setback, Vanbrugh maintained a lifelong interest in Garter affairs. He reported to Lord Carlisle on 20 February 1721 with regard to their shared interest in Garter proceedings:

I think all are Safe at Court, and My Ld Carteret's (as 'tis taken for Granted) to be Secretary; and Lord Lincolns having the Duke of Rutlands Garter; shows my Lord Sund. Stands on firmer Ground, than people in general fancy'd. Those who are esteem'd the Duke of

104 (*top right*)   Hawksmoor's St George, Bloomsbury, 1716–31.

105 (*bottom right*)   Hawksmoor's St George-in-the-East, Wapping Stepney, 1714–29 (gutted in 1941).

Graftons chief Friends, I believe were not a little disturb'd he had not that Garter, but the Duke of Buckingham dying, that matter is pretty well made up, he
being to Succeed him. Upon the whole, I hope they
will Agree enough to Act pretty well together for the
publick Service.[78]

Vanbrugh was well aware of the political power of
heraldic appointments. On the death of the Deputy Earl
Marshal, the Earl of Suffolk, he wrote to the Duke of
Newcastle in September 1718 concerning his preferred
candidate, the Earl's son Lord Walden, that 'there is not
a more zealous and Determin'd Whig in England'. He
added tellingly that 'there is in that office, opportunitys
daily, of Obliging Numbers of People which power one
wou'd wish, in the hands of One, who will be sure to
oblige the Right Sort'.[79] Moreover, it was noted in the
Introduction that in 1706 Vanbrugh had travelled to
Hanover as acting Garter King to invest the future King
George II with the Order of the Garter, taking the place
of Sir Henry St George whose age prevented him from
travelling. In so doing he played his part in the use of
the British chivalric order to underpin the Whig vision
of a Protestant – that is, Hanoverian – succession and
paved the way for his own knighthood in 1714. As an
architect Vanbrugh would have been particularly sensitive to the requirement to find a suitable setting in
Hanover for the investiture and used the interiors at
Windsor as the model. The 'Instructions to invest ye
Electoral Prince of Brunswick' of 23 April 1706 made
clear the importance of the decoration at Windsor for
what it termed 'election into that our most noble
Society': 'Concerning the Place and Mannor to perform
it in, the most proper for it would be that wch comes
nearest to our Installations at Windsor'.[80] In this context
it would have been perfectly natural for Vanbrugh to
have seen Windsor as a model not just for the all-important settings of Garter rituals but for more general 'architectural' ones provided by him for his Garter patrons.
Indeed the hall at Windsor, with its painting of Phaeton
taking the chariot of the sun, seems to have served as a
model for the hall at Castle Howard, with its depiction
of the fall of Phaeton (see Fig. 50).[81]

A letter written by Samuel Stebbing to Henry St
George on 19 June 1706 regarding the Hanover investiture provides a unique glimpse into Vanbrugh's part
in the solemnities of the occasion.[82] The 'Solemn Investiture' was fixed for Sunday, 13 June, and Vanbrugh, as
acting Garter King, played a leading role. The ceremony
reached its climax – centred on the George – at which
point

> Mr Vanbrugh delivered the Diamond Garter to my
> Lord Halifax, they together buckled it about His H^s

left leg, Mr Vanbrugh reading the accustomd Admonition. Then the Prince arose, and the Comm^rs taking
off his H^s Blew Ribbon George, they first Invested
him with the Mantle of the Order, then the Hood,
and afterwards with the Great Collar and George, M^r
Vanbrugh reading the Admonition upon putting on
each Ensign.

Consistent with his sense of theatre, Vanbrugh's preoccupation with ritual, court hierarchy and the Garter
ensigns is perfectly demonstrated by this vivid report. It
again underlines what seems to have been his preoccupation elsewhere in his work, and most notably in his
buildings, with the meaningful use of medieval forms
and symbols which were drawn from British traditions
centred in particular on Windsor Castle.

'ARMS, EMBLEMS, DEVICES': THE ORDERS OF KNIGHTHOOD AND ARCHITECTURE

In his role as one of the Kings of Arms, Vanbrugh was
directly responsible for the design of one particular set
of symbols, royal heraldry. In a letter of 25 November
1707 to the Deputy Earl Marshal, he and his fellow
heralds requested the making of 'copies of the Droughts
of such Alterations in the Queen's Arms, Emblems,
Devices, Ec. as were agreed to by the Lords of the
Council upon the Union . . . We humbly conceive yor
Lop (as Lord Marshal) is the proper Person to transmit
such Orders (as to yor Office appertaineth) for avoiding
Mistakes in matters of so nice a Nature.'[83] Not surprisingly Vanbrugh was proud of his own coat of arms.[84]
Naturally enough, as Deputy Earl Marshal Lord Carlisle
also had an interest in heraldry, for among his private
papers is a manuscript title-page by him of 'A Book of
Coates & Crests', dated 1699.[85] This shared interest of
patron and architect in the design of heraldry and
ciphers, as badges of identity, found expression at Castle
Howard: Carlisle had his cipher – 'CCC' for 'Carolus
Comes Carleolensis' – carved into the central keystone
of the front façade and his arms sculpted into the pediment to the rear (Figs 106, 107). Indeed, heraldry and
architecture had much in common. Since antiquity, the
display of heraldry and the use of the *all'antica* architectural language, particularly the column, were both signs
of status on a façade. Architecture and heraldry were
ancient arts governed by principles of decorum and
order, and Swift's lines, albeit sarcastically, play on the
ancient etymological links between the two centred on
the word 'House'. Vanbrugh had himself made this link
when remarking in the prologue to *The Confederacy* that
he was famed 'For building Houses here t'oblige the

107 (*above*) The Howard arms in the pediment of the rear, garden façade of Castle Howard, from 1699.

106 (*left*) Carlisle's cipher on the front façade of Castle Howard.

108 (*below*) Arms between Corinthian columns forming a heraldic triumphal arch, engraved frontispiece to John Guillim's *A Display of Heraldrie* (1610 edition).

Peers,/And fetching all their House about his Ears'.[86] Swift implied that 'Goose-Pie' house (see Figs 29, 316, 317) was not only a pretentious failure as architecture but also as heraldry, that is, as an expression of Vanbrugh's claims to a dynastic 'house' otherwise expressed by his coat of arms.

As a playwright interested in word associations Vanbrugh would surely have been particularly aware of the similarity in heraldic and architectural terminology, at least from the time of his installation as Carlisle Herald in 1703. Chapter One noted that on 18 April 1719 his accounts record the purchase of John Guillim's *A Display of Heraldrie* (1610, with a fifth edition in 1678–9), a work that underlined these similarities (Fig. 108).[87] The book's opening remarks and frontispiece would have had an instant appeal to Vanbrugh the herald-architect:

The noble *Pindare* doth compare somewhere,
Writing with Building, and instructs us there,
That every great and goodly *Edifice*,
Doth ask to have a comely *Frontispiece*.
Where (*Guillim*) better can the curious looke,
T'have this observ'd, then in they present *Booke*?[88]

109   Paired antique columns in the heraldry of Elizabeth I, engraving by Crispin van de Passe Senior, published by Hans Woutneel in London in 1596 [British Library, London].

In addition, Guillim endeavoured '*to give unto this erst unshapely and disproportionable profession of* Heraldry, *a true* Symmetria *and proportionable correspondence of each part to other*'.[89] Vanbrugh's method of design – his combination of medieval with *all'antica* elements and, on occasions such as Kimbolton (see Figs 4, 215), his 'making regular' essentially medieval façades – was very similar to the process he must have used in heraldic design, where traditional forms (castles and gates amongst them) were combined using Vitruvian principles, as Guillim thus makes clear. Just as various human characteristics were attributed to the different Orders and these columns were then deployed on a façade according to the ancient principles of architectural decorum, so similar characteristics were assigned particular devices and then marshalled in a shield or coat of arms according to the principles of heraldry. As Blenheim and Castle Howard in particular indicate, column and shield were used by Vanbrugh to serve the same purpose, to tell the story of his patron's character and achievements.

Perhaps of some significance to Vanbrugh's preference for more sombre, Doric architecture was the fact that Guillim termed antique columns 'the *Hieroglyphicks* of *fortitude*'.[90] That Vanbrugh and the Tate a Tate Club met at the Hercules Pillars Alehouse in High Holborn in 1717 can only have reminded the herald-architect of the traditional role of paired antique columns (such as the Doric pilasters used on the Blenheim inner gates; see Fig. 203) in the heraldry of European monarchy and in contemporary Freemasonry as a symbol of Herculean strength and of a boundary or gateway (Fig. 109).[91] In fact the Doric column in particular had been 'introduced' and explained in Stuart England in the context of the native art of heraldry.[92] Henry Wotton in his *Elements of Architecture* (1624), when outlining the 'masculine Aspect' of the Order, commented: 'His ranke or degree, is the lowest by all Congruity, as being more massie then the other three, and consequently abler to support . . . To descerne him, will bee a peece rather of good *Heraldry*, than of *Architecture*: For he is best knowne by his place, when he is in company, and by the peculiar ornament of his Frize . . . when he is alone'.[93]

Vanbrugh adapted the Doric Order to include heraldic details in a number of his house designs. For example it has been noted that he carved Roman military insignia including arrows, shields and eagles into the metopes on the north façades of Castle Howard (1706) and Seaton Delaval (1720–28; see Figs 93, 231). Not surprisingly, as a herald and a former soldier, Vanbrugh was especially interested in military insignia. Chapter One noted that an entry in his accounts on 9 June 1716 records 'pd Subscription to Browns book of Medals', whilst on 8 April 1719 it records 'pd Sigr: Haym on a Subscription of 5. Gs. for a book of medals' and on 25 February 1720 a payment for 'ye 2d. Vo'.[94] Haym's *Del Tesoro Britannico*, together with the subsequent English translation (*The British Treasury*), was published in London in 1719–20, once again by Vanbrugh's friend Tonson. This comprised a catalogue, with illustrations, of the antique Greek, Syrian and Roman medals in prominent British collections, most notably those of the Earl of Pembroke, Hans Sloane and Christopher Wren junior (see Fig. 232). Through his use of these chivalrous insignia, as perhaps through Doric columns, Vanbrugh's buildings might be seen to be 'decorated' both architecturally and militarily.

Moreover when identifying the Doric in preference to the other four architectural Orders as especially suited to military figures, Sebastiano Serlio in his treatise on the Orders of 1537 had made particular mention of 'St George or other similar Saints', adding that 'since they not only professed to be soldiers, but were also manly and strong in leading out their lives in the faith of Christ, the Doric type is suitable for Saints of this sort'.[95] This Order would thus have carried explicit associations with the Garter to Serlio's English readers and, in combination with Wotton's explanation of the Doric as a form of heraldry, might easily have been identified as a form of Garter heraldry signifying the story of St George on houses such as Seaton Delaval designed by the Garter King.

'PRACTIC'D AT WINDSOR':
VANBRUGH'S BRITISH STYLE AND
CASTLES TO ST GEORGE

As early as 1712 the third Earl of Shaftesbury, in his *Letter concerning the art or science of design* addressed to the Whig Lord Somers (which was first circulated in manuscript and eventually published in 1732), had argued that since Britain had been successfully unified and had tempered the monarch's power through the will of Parliament, it was high time for the nation to take a lead in promoting the arts. Shaftesbury went on to predict the emergence from the 'national taste' of a new British architectural style. He did not define this style – except negatively as anti-French, anti-Wren and anti-Baroque – but it was destined to be supplied by the Palladian designs illustrated in Campbell's *Vitruvius Britannicus* (1715–25). The influence which Campbell's Palladian models enjoyed rendered the so-called baroque period in England an interlude between the era of Inigo Jones and that of his emulation by Burlington and Kent. In his own search for an architectural vocabulary based on national historical models, it has been seen that Vanbrugh turned to Britain's medieval buildings and to her country houses and castles in particular.[96] After all, the castle was the nation's principal secular architectural legacy and symbol of its medieval history; as such it represented the quintessentially British architectural form (a fact graphically underlined by its absence from the Renaissance treatises with their Italian-based models). Vanbrugh was well aware of the archetypal image of the castle in the medieval myths and legends which the Garter cultivated: one of his characters in *The Relapse*, Lory, remarks, 'Igad, Sir, this will prove some Inchanted Castle; we shall have the Gyant come out by and by with his Club, and beat our Brains out.'[97]

Just as Vanbrugh's involvement with the Garter knights clearly informed his attitude to medieval history, so the Garter's home at Windsor Castle must have influenced both his desire to preserve ancient structures and his architectural vocabulary of forms. It was noted earlier that Hugh May's remodelling of the medieval castle had united crenellations with round-headed windows and thereby mixed elements drawn from both medieval and classical traditions (see Fig. 95). Amongst Vanbrugh's favourite motifs were the round-headed window and the corbel-table or machicolation (Figs 110, 111). He certainly considered May's work a model for his own practice. Writing to the Earl of Manchester on 18 July 1707 concerning Kimbolton he notes:

> As to the Outside, I thought 'twas absolutely best, to give it Something of the Castle Air, tho' at the Same time to make it regular. And by this means too, all the Old Stone is Serviceable again; which to have had new wou'd have run to a very great Expence; This method was practic'd at Windsor in King Charles's time, And has been universally Approv'd, So I hope your L^{d}ship won't be discourag'd, if any Italians you may Shew it to, shou'd find fault that 'tis not Roman, for to have built a Front with Pillasters, and what the Orders require cou'd never have been born with the Rest of the Castle: I'm sure this will make a very Noble and Masculine Shew; and is of as Warrantable a kind of building as Any.[98]

Vanbrugh here emphasises the British, that is the essentially un-Italian, nature of what became his 'castle' style, whilst it is simultaneously put on an equal footing with classical architectural forms. It was noted that Manchester's ancestors were founding members of the Garter, for which a 'noble' and masculine 'Castle Air' signified by crenellations reflecting May's work at Windsor would have been an especially appropriate form of architectural heraldry. On 9 September 1707 Vanbrugh again observed to Manchester: 'I shall be much deceiv'd if People don't See a Manly Beauty in it when tis up, that they did not conceive cou'd be produced out of such rough Materialls; But tis certainly the Figure and Proportions that make the most pleasing Fabrick, And not the delicacy of the Ornaments: A proof of wch I am in great hopes to Shew y^r L^{d}ship at Kimbolton.'[99] In thus prioritising symmetry and proportion over classical ornament, Vanbrugh renders these principles perfectly compatible with British medieval forms such as towers and crenellations.

All of which helps to explain Vanbrugh's frequent use of castle forms – battlements and turrets, corbel-tables and rustication – in both direct and indirect ways in his work. In the case of the group of houses he built for himself and his family at Greenwich from 1718 (where in acting as the patron he had an unlimited brief), the castle is obviously his chosen model. Vanbrugh Castle and House have their turrets and machicolations, the 'Nunnery' has its slit windows and tower and the White

110   Round-headed windows at Vanbrugh Castle, Greenwich, 1718–19.

111   Corbel-table, or machicolation, at Vanbrugh Castle, Greenwich.

Towers have their turrets (see Figs 111, 324, 332). Van-brugh Castle in particular was clearly intended to evoke the image of a medieval castle, or more accurately a French château, in the observer's mind (see Fig. 334). Elsewhere, Chargate had its crenellations (see Figs 342, 343, 344). At Castle Howard and Blenheim, although neither house closely resembles a castle (Blenheim, for example, has massive pavilion blocks), crenellations and corbel-tables are used – in the fortified estate walls and Pyramid Gate to the former and in the kitchen court to the latter (see Figs 83, 128, 156). (Vanbrugh seems also to have toyed with crenellated garden buildings at Castle Howard.[100]) At Seaton Delaval the castle archetype is more directly alluded to in the bastion-like rustication and overall form of the house (see Fig. 227), and even

more explicitly at Kimbolton, as seen, through its crenel-lations and 'Castle Air'. The Belvedere at Claremont with its tower crenellations is overtly castle-like (although strictly symmetrical; see Figs 70, 346), whilst corbel-tables were also used by Vanbrugh on the gateway at Eastbury House and in influencing the brew-house at Kings Weston with its portholes (see Figs 261, 279). Actual military buildings erected by the Board of Ord-nance in the design of which Vanbrugh may well have assisted (given that Marlborough was Master of the Ord-nance) – such as at Chatham Dockyard with the great store and gate, at Woolwich Arsenal with the Old Board of Ordnance, at Devonport with the Gun Wharf and at the barracks at Berwick – presented ideal opportunities for his functional and astylar 'castle style' (Figs 112–17).[101]

112 Great store at Chatham Dockyard (destroyed), possibly designed by Vanbrugh [National Monuments Record, Swindon].

113 Gate at Chatham Dockyard, possibly designed by Vanbrugh [National Monuments Record, Swindon].

114   Front façade of the Old Board of Ordnance, 1718–20, at Woolwich Arsenal, possibly designed by Vanbrugh and Hawksmoor.

115   The Gun Wharf at Devonport, possibly designed by Vanbrugh (destroyed) [National Archives, Kew].

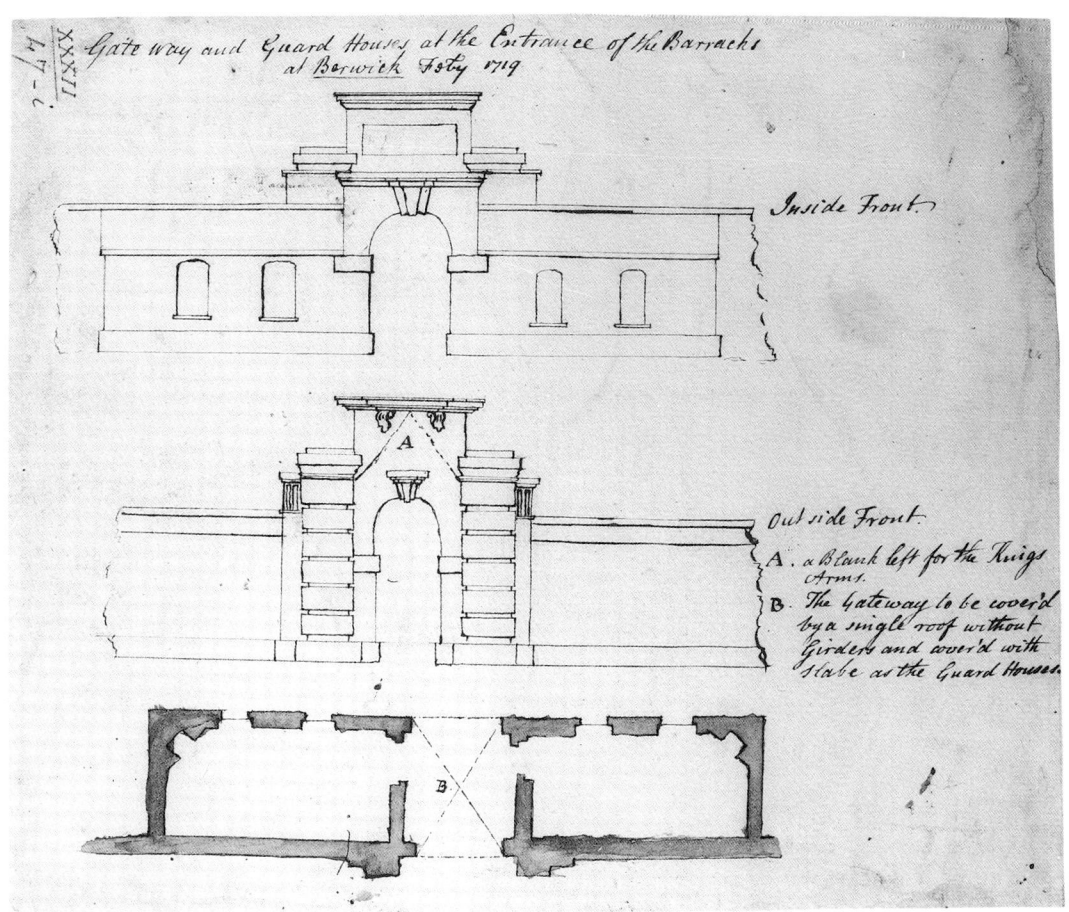

116   Design for the gateway and guardhouse of the Ravensdowne Barracks at Berwick-upon-Tweed, attributed to Vanbrugh (possibly with Hawksmoor), 1719 [British Library, London].

117   Hawksmoor's proposal for Ravensdowne Barracks at Berwick-upon-Tweed, 1717 [Wiltshire Records Office, Trowbridge].

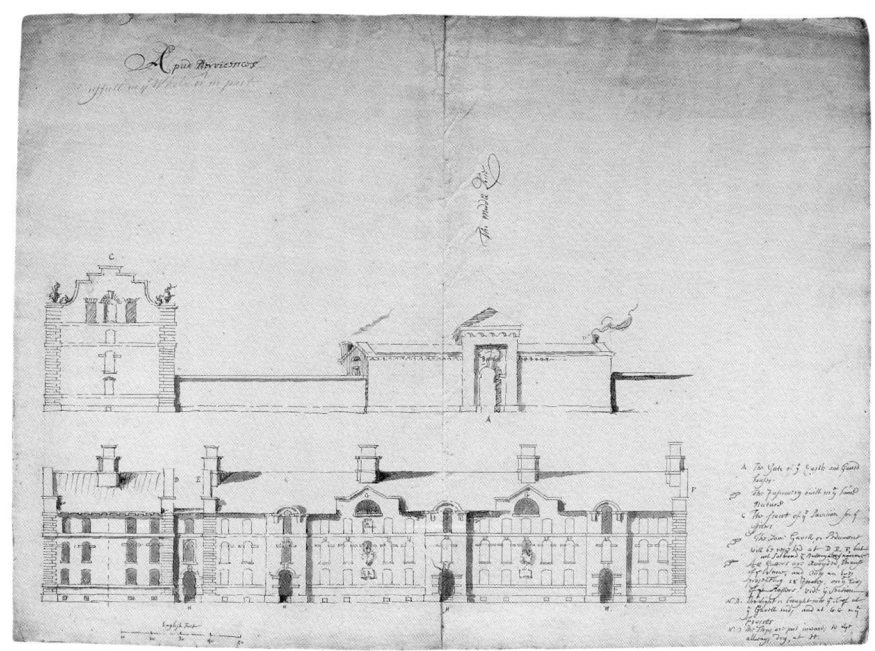

118   Vanbrugh's unbuilt design for the south entrance façade at Welbeck Abbey, drawn by Hawksmoor (1703) [RIBA, London].

Moreover when Vanbrugh used an architectural Order on the front façade of one of his houses, it was invariably the Doric: this is so at Castle Howard, and on the north fronts of Grimsthorpe Castle and Seaton Delaval (where the masculine effect is enhanced by the banded column shafts; see Figs 191, 227, 290).[102] At Welbeck Abbey Vanbrugh's unbuilt design for remodelling the south entrance façade had smooth Doric pilasters, revising the fluted Corinthian pilasters of Talman's design (whilst Vanbrugh's round-headed windows, without

119   William Talman's design for Welbeck Abbey (1703) [Sir John Soane's Museum, London].

121 (*above*)   Wren's Doric colonnades at Chelsea Hospital for retired soldiers, London, 1682–91.

120 (*left*)   Wren's Doric colonnades at Greenwich Hospital for retired seamen, 1696–1710.

architraves, replaced Talman's pedimented openings; Figs 118, 119).[103] Furthermore, as will be seen, at Blenheim the original intention was for a Doric portico, altered only by expediency.[104] As the masculine Order suitable to men of arms according to Serlio and to heraldry according to Wotton, the Doric was therefore most appropriate to the castle theme – especially as intended in the case of Blenheim, where the patron was a soldier, and as realised at Seaton Delaval, where he was a sailor. At Seaton Delaval this association between the Doric Order and the patron's military career is made explicit in the metopes with their trophies and anchors (interlocked with an admiral's cap) and in the pediment with its trident (the symbol of Neptune; see Figs 233, 234).[105] In this case the Doric Order and 'Castle Air' join forces to tell the story of the patron's military chivalry. Appropriately enough, Wren chose the Doric for his colonnades at Greenwich Hospital for retired seamen,[106] the drawings for which were prepared by Hawksmoor in 1696–7, as well as at Chelsea Hospital for retired soldiers (Figs 120, 121), the façades of which were intended to carry reliefs of trophies of arms, making the military theme even more explicit.[107]

This preference for either astylar or male, Doric façades – albeit modified in various ways to suite the particular patron and location – was in strong contrast to the fashion for more female decorative forms prevalent in Britain's great rival, France. Wren wrote from Paris concerning Varsailles that

> the Mixtures of Brick, Stone, blue Tile and Gold make it look like a rich Livery: Not an Inch within but is crouded with little Curiosities of Ornament: the Women, as they make here the Language and Fashions, and meddle with Politicks and Philosophy, so they sway also in Architecture; Works of Filgrand, and little Knacks are in great Vogue; but Building certainly ought to have the Attribute of eternal, and therefore the only Thing uncapable of new Fashions. The masculine Furniture of *Palais Mazarine* pleas'd me much better.[108]

In response Vanbrugh sought to evoke through his work the timeless image of the medieval castle, as the most quintessentially British (and masculine) form. He also sought to express through brick and stone the essential quality of permanence which the castle embodied, made

122   William Kent's Temple of British Worthies at Stowe, *c.*1735.

manifest through the massive quality of his ubiquitous outworks and bastion walls (see Fig. 128). He warned the Duke of Newcastle concerning the new masonry outworks of the Duke of Rutland's castle, Belvoir (viewed by Vanbrugh on his way to Nottingham), 'for want of

123   Engraved view by Antoine Benoist (*c.*1760) of Merlin's Cave, built by William Kent in the Royal Park at Richmond, 1735 (destroyed).

being rightly understood, the whole grace of them is lost: it looks all like pastboard work'.[109] Indeed a sense of permanence was one of his most consistent architectural aims, commenting on the London churches that only a small amount of money stood between whether a church 'be crippled in a hundred Years, or stand like a Rock a Thousand'.[110] On his houses and military structures Vanbrugh manipulated the elemental forms of fortification to convey the effect of such virtues as 'strength' and 'British history', a symbolic and psychological role underlined by the fact that these forms had lost any practical purpose long ago. Given that the most important of Vanbrugh's houses was born from a victory in battle, namely Blenheim, his preference for the patriotic masculine 'Castle Air' at Kimbolton and elsewhere should also be understood in the context of, and as a response to, a period in which the national character was shaped by conflict on land and at sea. After all, domestic anxiety caused by foreign conflict is perfectly evident in Vanbrugh's plays: for example *The Relapse* closes with the lines 'Nay, shou'd the War at length such Havock make,/That Lovers shou'd grow scarce, yet for your sake,/Kind Heaven always will preserve a Beau–'.[111]

Vanbrugh paved the way for the expression of British medieval legends by the next generation of Office of

Works officials, particularly William Kent (Deputy Surveyor from 1735). Kent built the Temple of British Worthies at Stowe around 1735, with its busts of medieval heroes, and designed Merlin's Cave in the Royal Park at Richmond, a thatched gothic cottage built, after Vanbrugh's death, again in 1735 (Figs 122, 123).[112] (Merlin was supposed to have prophesied the accession of the Hanoverian dynasty to the English throne.[113]) In drawing details and forms from medieval and subsequent Elizabethan buildings, united using the timeless principles of the classical language, Vanbrugh sought to create an architecture which reflected and told the story of past and present British martial glory. The source and home for Vanbrugh of this style, as for his beloved Garter, was Windsor Castle.

Chapter 3

'AGREABLE OBJECTS':
VANBRUGH ON ARCHITECTURE, LANDSCAPE
AND MOOD

In Vanbrugh's plea to save Woodstock Manor he distinguishes his 'Historicall Argument' from what he calls 'Other Considerations'. Evidently the preservation of medieval buildings and their landscape could be justified in a number of ways. Having outlined how the Manor appealed to the intellect, he proceeds with a second, more emotional argument for the old Manor's preservation involving the importance of visual effect in influencing the mood of the onlooker.

'LIVELY AND PLEASING REFLECTIONS':
VANBRUGH ON MOOD AND EFFECT

Vanbrugh would have been familiar with the stimulation of visual effects in the minds of an audience through the staging of his dramas, and this was a sensibility he clearly considered when designing buildings and their landscapes.[1] On 31 May 1709 he wrote to Lord Godolphin regarding the landscape around Woodstock Manor:

> I am very doubtfull whether Your Lordship (or indeed My Lord Duke) has yet rightly taken the design of forming that side of the Valley; where several irregular things are to have such a regard to one another, that I much fear the effects of so quick a sentence as has happen'd to pass Upon the remain of the Manour I have however taken a good deal of it down, but before tis gone too far I will desire your Lordship will give yourself the trouble of looking upon a picture, I have made of it, which will at one view explain the whole design, much better than A thousand words.[2]

The sketch is lost but Robert Plot illustrated the Manor in his *The Natural History of Oxford-shire* of 1677, and a watercolour and a related engraving of 1714 also survive (Fig. 125; see Fig. 34).[3] Vanbrugh's concerns led to his now famous 'Reasons Offer'd for Preserving some Part of the Old Manour', addressed to the Duchess of Marlborough on 11 June 1709:

> But if the Historicall Argument Stands in need of Assistance; there is Still much to be said on Other Considerations.
>
> That Part of the Park which is Seen from the North Front of the New Building, has Little Variety of Objects Nor dos the Country beyond it Afford any of Vallue. It therefore Stands in Need of all the helps that can be given, which are only Two; Buildings, And Plantations[.] These rightly dispos'd will indeed Supply all the wants of Nature in that Place. And the Most Agreable Disposition is to Mix them: which this Old Manour *gives so happy an Occasion* for, That were the inclosure fill'd with Trees (principally Fine Yews and Hollys) Promiscuously set to grow up in a Wild Thicket. So that all the Building left, (which is only the Habitable Part and the Chappel) might Appear in two Risings amongst 'em; it wou'd make One of the Most Agreable Objects that the Best of Landskip Painters can invent. And if on the Contrary this Building is taken away; there then remains nothing but an Irregular, Ragged Ungovernable Hill, the deformitys of which are not to be cured *but by a Vast Expence. And that at last will only Remove an Ill Object* but not produce a good One.[4]

Here a marked emphasis is placed on emotions such as 'agreable' and 'happy' which are to be aroused in the onlooker through the effect of 'picturesque' composition, that is, a landscape self-consciously arranged like a picture to maximise optical effects from particular aspects.[5]

Vanbrugh's enthusiasm for the beneficial effects on the onlooker of certain architectural forms, especially those

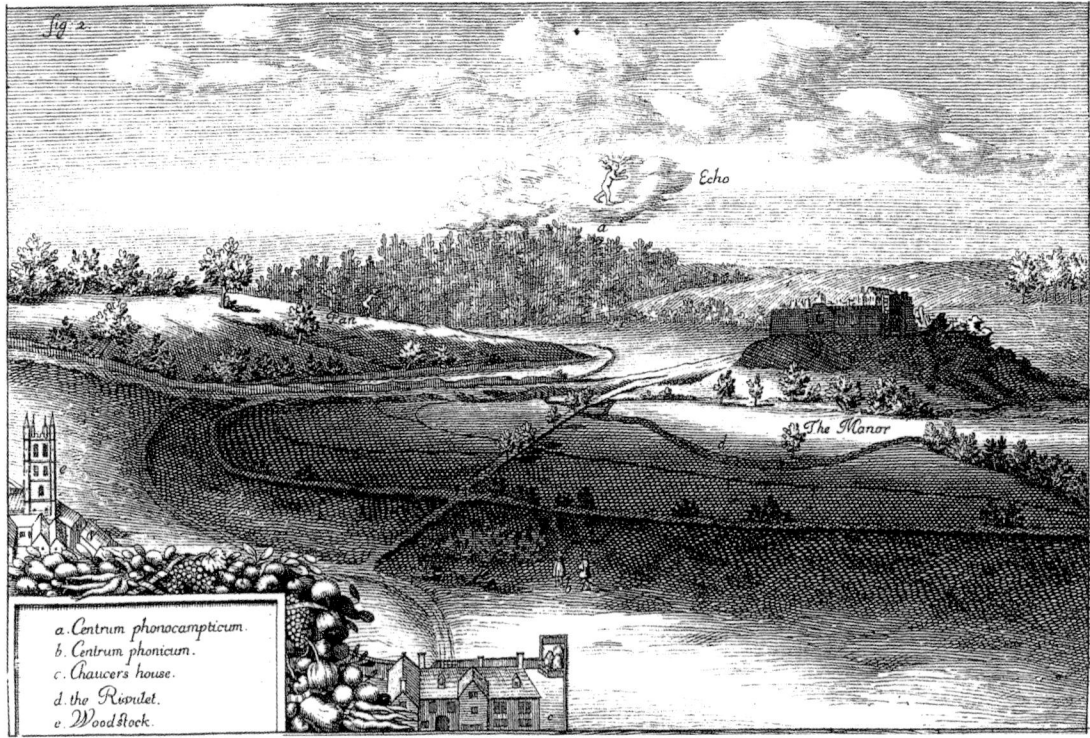

125 Woodstock Manor and its setting in the Oxfordshire countryside, detail from Robert Plot's *The Natural History of Oxford-shire* (1677), p. 16.

derived from Britain's medieval ruins, is equally reflected in this letter, which he opened by observing:

> There is perhaps no One thing, which the most Polite part of Mankind have more universally agreed in; than the Vallue they have ever set upon the Remains of distant Times. Nor amongst the Severall kinds of those Antiquitys, are there any so much regarded, as those of Buildings; Some for their Magnificence, or Curious Workmanship; And others; as they move more lively and pleasing Reflections (than History without their aid can do) on the Persons who have Inhabited them . . .

Vanbrugh thus spells out how architecture, in this case medieval ruins, can stimulate positive emotions in moving 'lively and pleasing Reflections'. Given that he starts this letter by discussing Blenheim, plainly his own architecture – and especially medieval fantasies reminiscent of Woodstock such as Vanbrugh Castle (Fig. 126) – must equally have been designed by him with this way of 'seeing' objects and landscapes in mind. After all, having witnessed Blenheim the visitor was also expected to experience 'Wonder' and thereby be 'pleas'd with the Sight of it'. These positive emotional associations clearly helped visitors reflect on the virtues of Blenheim's

inhabitants – or as he puts it, to 'read the Duke of Marlborough in Story' – just as elsewhere it will be seen that Vanbrugh relied on similar visual effects evoked through form and iconography to assist his buildings in the representation of 'stories' particular to their locations and patrons.

The castellated forms such as those on Vanbrugh's own house called Chargate (see Figs 342–4) were novel in contemporary works. At Kimbolton (see Figs 4, 214, 215) he reported to his patron, the Earl of Manchester, that the works' supervisor, William Coleman, 'Own'd he begun to discover a Gusto in it, that he had no Notion of before'.[6] Vanbrugh's forms were neither re-creations of medieval details solely for the sake of continuity with respect to neighbouring buildings, as, say, with Wren's Tom Tower in Oxford (see Fig. 72), nor were they fanciful creations such as later characterised the garden buildings of the early gothic revival. Instead, they were used to create what might be termed an 'associational' style. Vanbrugh's wish was to 'move a lively reflection' in the mind of the onlooker through this style, that is, to suggest an association with the nation's medieval heritage as principally represented by its castles, forts and walls. Since castle forms were charged with popular, national associations, it follows that in so doing Vanbrugh intended his architectural language to become legible to a wider audience than would have been the case if he had restricted himself to the exclusive use of more alien, antique forms. This can be seen to echo his ambition for popular legibility in the language of his plays, and his mockery in *The Mistake* of the use by contemporaries of antique quotations for their own sake (discussed in Chapter One). Indeed, much like the associational quality of his forms, Vanbrugh used rules of word association in his plays when following the conventions of Restoration drama by giving his *dramatis personae* and their buildings descriptive names signifying their character – Beast Hall, Headpiece Hall, Wagonrut-Lane, Smoke-dunghil Farm and so on.[7] An 'architecture of association' is fully exploited on the stage, where the stimulation of mood and effect are vital. Of all the arts, opera most exploits such effects through its unity of music, drama and setting. As seen in Chapter One, Vanbrugh used the phrase 'Building Musick' – a phrase resonant of the unity of the arts – to describe his involvement in the emergence of opera in England through his role in sponsoring, designing and building the Haymarket theatre (see Figs 52, 66).

It was noted in the previous chapter that as well as using crenellations and towers in his domestic architecture, Vanbrugh evidently saw medieval castle forms as particularly suited to buildings of a military or functional typology. An example of this is his or Hawksmoor's now demolished water-tower on Kensington Palace Green, which was in the form of a medieval tower with a projecting corbel-table common in Florentine palazzi (Fig. 127). As was also observed, Vanbrugh possibly influenced the use of defensive forms at Chatham Dockyard on the great store and gate, and at Woolwich Arsenal on the Old Board of Ordnance with its appropriately undecorated, astylar façade, and used them at Eastbury on the west arch of the north court, and at Blenheim on functional buildings such as the kitchen court (see Figs 83, 112, 113, 114, 279). On these buildings the elemental forms of fortification were manipulated to evoke ideas in the onlooker of 'strength' and 'functionality' or commodity, an associative role underlined by the fact that these forms had long before lost any practical purpose. Given the military function of the Ordnance buildings at Chatham, their fortification style and details would have had particular significance to contemporary onlookers as evocative of Britain's newly acquired martial strength, on both land and sea, under the Master of the Ordnance, Marlborough.[8]

In practice Vanbrugh switched between, and sometimes mixed, forms drawn from medieval and classical architecture in order to evoke a variety of moods in the

126   Vanbrugh Castle, Greenwich.

spectator, much as an orator might combine various images in order to persuade an audience. A range of customary emblems and architectural styles were combined at Castle Howard, for example, each attempting to remind the observer of distinct virtues such as 'strength' (Doric Order), 'British history' (crenellated walls), 'classical mythology' (statues), 'philosophy' (busts), 'luxury' (fruit), 'naturalness' (sea horses), 'victory' (trophies of arms), 'nobility' (heraldry) and so on (see Figs 188, 191,

127   Water tower on Kensington Palace Green (destroyed), from the *Gentleman's Magazine* (1821).

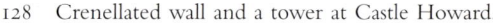

128   Crenellated wall and a tower at Castle Howard.

199, 200). Vanbrugh's outworks have the appearance of medieval fortifications to most observers, although they were possibly also conceived of as Roman in spirit and are obviously intended to lend the required air of architectural permanence to the landscape (Fig. 128).[9] However, rather than serving any actual function, that of protection against imminent attack, they helped in the more peaceful, psychological purpose of linking the new estate in the observer's mind with the noble traditions of British history – also recalled by its 'castle' name and heraldic character – especially in the wake of the destruction of the parish church and old house.[10] Elsewhere, Vanbrugh's description of his scheme for Kimbolton as having 'Something of the Castle Air' is in the same semantic spirit of association (see Fig. 4). As has been seen, the 'Castle Air' was not only masculine but necessarily astylar. It derived its character not from antique columns but rather from evoking associations with the English domestic archetype – the castle – through using once functional, but now associational, elements such as crenellations and portholes. As the house within which Henry VIII imprisoned his wife Katherine of Aragon, Kimbolton carried rich historical associations which Vanbrugh's dramatic crenellated motifs sought to evoke.

'PD ON A SUBSCRIPTION TO MR ADDISONS WORKS': JOSEPH ADDISON AND THE PLEASURES OF THE IMAGINATION

Beyond their subjective appreciation of visual beauty, Vanbrugh's architectural explanations recorded in his correspondence with his patrons reflected more objective seventeenth-century theories of perception in that he made clear his aim of evoking a range of moods, including those of solemnity and even fear, through the visual effects created by certain settings and architectural forms. He lived in the period of the rise of the Natural Sciences and, following the work of René Descartes and John Locke, the growing awareness of the psychological power of various architectural effects. Descartes, for example, had stressed the effects produced in the mind through the apprehension of colour and light.[11] In Locke's *An Essay Concerning Human Understanding* (1690), various forms, objects and settings were seen as capable of triggering particular memories and moods in the onlooker. One of the leading contemporary proponents of Locke's ideas in England was Joseph Addison (see Fig. 49), whose application of the theory of association to landscape and architecture did not escape Vanbrugh's attention.[12] He was on familiar terms with Addison, since

N° 411.   *The* SPECTATOR.   83

With Care direct their Steps, nor turn astray
To tread the Paths of her deceitful Way;
Least they too late of Her fell Power complain,
And fall, where many mightier have been Slain.
                                                        T

N° 411.   *Saturday, June* 21.

Avia Pieridum peragro loca, nullius ante
Trita solo; juvat integros accedere fonteis;
Atque haurire:——   Lucr.

OUR Sight is the most perfect and most delightful of all our Senses. It fills the Mind with the largest Variety of Ideas, converses with its Objects at the greatest Distance, and continues the longest in Action without being tired or satiated with its proper Enjoyments. The Sense of Feeling can indeed give us a Notion of Extention, Shape, and all other Ideas that enter at the Eye, except Colours; but at the same time it is very much streightned and confined in its Operations, to the Number, Bulk, and Distance of its particular Objects. Our Sight seems designed to supply all these Defects, and may be considered as a more delicate and diffusive Kind of Touch, that spreads its self over an infinite Multitude of Bodies, comprehends the largest Figures, and brings into
          G 2   our

129 Joseph Addison's 'The Pleasures of the Imagination' as published in *The Spectator* (21 June 1712), p. 83.

both were Kit Cat members and also writers.[13] Vanbrugh was Addison's senior by only eight years and the architect's accounts for December 1716 show that he let a house in Kensington to a 'Mr Addison', thought to be Joseph.[14] Perhaps both men discussed the stimulating effects of their surroundings when Addison served as secretary to Lord Halifax on the Garter trip to Hanover undertaken with Vanbrugh in 1706.[15] Indeed, the architect's interest in, and even his support for, Addison's ideas (an interest which has for the most part been neglected by commentators) can be proved by the fact that he subscribed not only to the original 1712 octavo edition of the writer's daily essay called *The Spectator* but also to the republication of Addison's essays in a collected quarto edition in 1721 (Fig. 129).[16] Both these editions were published by Vanbrugh's friend, Tonson (see Fig. 10).[17] On receipt of these publications Vanbrugh must have read, and by 1721 probably have re-read, Addison's influential essays 'The Pleasures of the Imagination' first pub-

lished in 1712 (nos 411–21), with their discussion of architecture and indebtedness to Locke on the association of pleasure with certain forms and colours.[18]

According to the associational view of art, beauty and pleasure lay not only in intrinsic, objective properties such as symmetry and proportion, but also in the power of artworks, monuments and settings to evoke a train of associations, memories and emotions in the onlooker or 'spectator'.[19] For example, in 1711 Addison referred to Locke when discussing the emotional effect of monastic ruins, echoes and graves, noting that

> These Objects naturally raise Seriousness and Attention; and when Night heightens the Awfulness of the Place, and pours out her supernumerary Horrours upon every thing in it, I do not at all wonder that weak Minds fill it with Spectres and Apparitions. Mr. *Lock*, in his Chapter of the Association of Ideas, has very curious Remarks to show how by the Prejudice of Education one Idea often introduces into the Mind a whole Set that bear no Resemblance to one another in the Nature of things.[20]

Addison referred to Locke again when discussing 'The Pleasures of the Imagination', this time concerning the nature of colour:

> that great Modern Discovery . . . Namely, that Light and Colours, as apprehended by the Imagination, are only Ideas in the Mind, and not Qualities that have any Existance in Matter. As this is a Truth which has been proved incontestably by many Modern Philosophers, and is indeed one of the finest Speculations in that Science, if the *English* Reader would see the Notion explained at large, he may find it in the Eighth Chapter of the Second Book of Mr. *Lock's* Essay on Human Understanding.[21]

As one such 'English reader', Vanbrugh might be pictured taking up his friend's invitation and consulting Locke directly in one of the many English editions of the *Essay* published from the early 1690s (especially since Locke was a leading proponent of the ideal of constitutional liberty). Addison also drew on Locke's *Essay* when distinguishing between the primary and secondary 'pleasures', 'as arise originally from Sight'. The primary proceeded 'from such Objects as are before our Eyes'; the secondary, following the theory of association, derived 'from the Ideas of visible Objects'.[22] Vanbrugh's letter to the Duchess of Marlborough about Woodstock Manor gives examples of both: the primary are the 'Ancient Remains' of Rosamond's Bower and Woodstock Manor and Chapel – described as 'Agreable Objects' – as well as their landscape, and the secondary are the 'lively and pleasing Reflections' suggested by them, recalling British monarchy, courage, landscape painting and romantic legend.

Addison makes clear the influence of setting on mood. Drawing on the genre of medieval romance, with which Vanbrugh was certainly familiar, he notes regarding the stimulation of 'agreeable Ideas' that

> In short, our Souls are at present delightfully lost and bewildered in a pleasing Delusion, and we walk about like the Enchanted Hero of a Romance, who sees beautiful Castles, Woods and Meadows; and at the same time hears the warbling of Birds, and the purling of Streams; but upon the finishing of some secret Spell, the fantastick Scene breaks up, and the disconsolate Knight finds himself on a barren Heath, or in a solitary Desart.[23]

Much like these 'beautiful Castles', Vanbrugh's Kimbolton and his own Greenwich buildings (see Figs 4, 126) were not intended to be actual castles built to survive attack but were instead to represent the Platonic 'Idea' of the castle in the imagination, thereby giving a secondary pleasure to the onlooker by calling the generic castle to mind – 'Our Imagination takes the Hint', as Addison puts it.[24] This consideration represents a departure from the norms of Renaissance architectural design, wherein form and iconography were replicated, albeit with modifications, from a set of classical models, as illustrated in the third book of Serlio's treatise for example. Rather, a building was to be designed somewhat like sculpture to evoke the 'Idea' of historic forms held in the popular imagination. In Vanbrugh's case at Kimbolton this was through reflecting what he termed the 'Castle Air'. Addison notes concerning 'secondary pleasures' that 'Among the different Kinds of Representation, *Statuary* is the most natural, and shews us something *likest* the Object that is represented'. For the association to be successful, he added, 'it is in the Power of the Imagination, when it is once Stocked with particular Ideas, to enlarge, compound, and vary them at her own Pleasure'.[25]

One might expect Vanbrugh to have paid especial attention to Addison's description of architecture, outlined in 1712 in essay no. 415, as an art 'which has a more immediate Tendency, than any other, to produce those primary Pleasures of the Imagination'. Addison notes that '*Greatness*, in the Works of Architecture, may be considered as relating to the Bulk and Body of the Structure, or to the *Manner* in which it is built. As for the first, we find the Antients, especially among the Eastern Nations of the World, infinitely superior to the Moderns'. Vanbrugh would have witnessed such 'Eastern monumentality' at first hand during his time in India,

and Addison's sentiments would have accorded with the architect's fondness for massiveness in bastion outworks and in castle details to achieve what he termed 'Manly Beauty' at Kimbolton.[26] Amongst the ancient structures admired by Addison, 'what could be more noble than the Walls of Babylon'. Addison also emphasises what he terms the '*Greatness of Manner* in Architecture, which has such force upon the Imagination, that a small Building, where *it* appears, shall give the Mind nobler Ideas than one of twenty times the Bulk, where the Manner is ordinary or little'.[27] Vanbrugh's tiny 'Goose-Pie' house, with its urns and rusticated loggias, certainly sought to achieve just such a 'greatness of manner', since it was for this very pretension that Swift, ever conscious of issues of scale, ridiculed the building (see Figs 29, 316, 317).[28] When discussing traditional optical concerns stemming from the Renaissance, Addison notes that 'We are struck, we know not how, with the Symmetry of any thing we see', and that a form of beauty was derived from 'the Symmetry and Proportion of Parts, in the Arrangement and Disposition of Bodies'.[29] This was much as Vanbrugh had emphasised at Kimbolton in his observation that 'tis certainly the Figure and Proportions that make the most pleasing Fabrick'.[30] Vanbrugh's and Addison's optical priorities serve to underline the process whereby the visual had been privileged over other, more ontological factors, a development traceable to the invention of linear perspective in the early Renaissance.[31]

In Addison's essay on the 'primary pleasures' of architecture, as no doubt elsewhere, Vanbrugh would have read of the marvels of antiquity, with a pluralistic emphasis on the wonders of the Bible and those outside the classical canon discovered through increased trade and travel. Addison lists the Great Wall of China, the Egyptian pyramids, the Tower of Babel and the hanging gardens of Babylon. Having witnessed the Mogul architecture of India (see Fig. 5), Vanbrugh had equally broadened his own tastes beyond admiration for the antique. In an age which increasingly aspired to rival antiquity, in learning, conquest and the arts, readers of Addison's 'Pleasures of the Imagination' – and especially those involved in the arts, like Vanbrugh – must have been inspired by the enthusiastic endorsement of these diverse structures as wonders of lost, ancient civilisations. Vanbrugh certainly sought to evoke their magnificence in his own work, in common with his assistant and collaborator Hawksmoor: witness the Pyramid Gate at Castle Howard, designed by Vanbrugh and completed in 1717, which directly refers to one such lost civilisation (see Fig. 156). This is also true of the pyramid corner towers at Eastbury and proposed gate at Kings Weston, and the pyramid at Stowe of 1724 built to his design (Fig. 130;

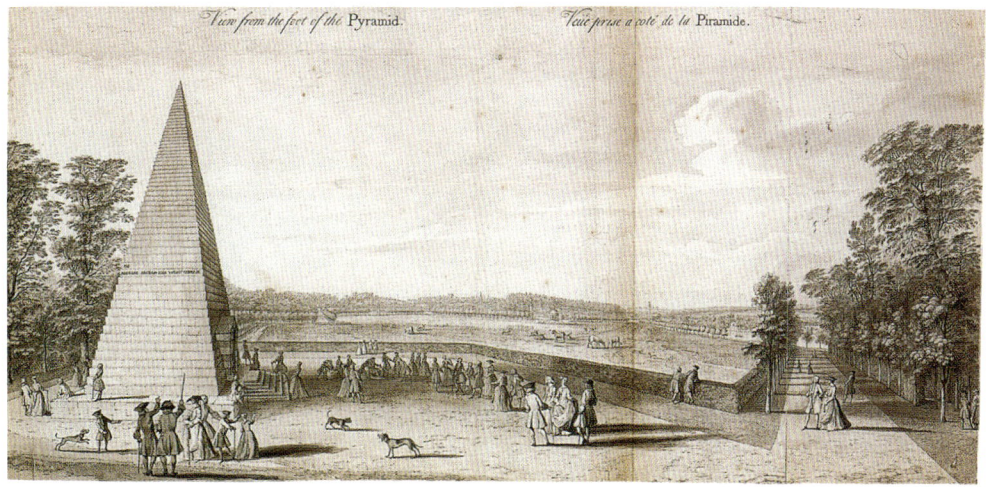

130 View of Vanbrugh's Pyramid at Stowe (erected in 1724 and turned into a memorial to the architect, now destroyed), engraving by Jacques Rigaud (c.1733–4) [The Metropolitan Museum of Art, New York].

see Figs 275, 286). Like Hawksmoor, however, Vanbrugh would not have shared Addison's wholesale rejection of gothic architecture as 'mean' and his exclusive preference for classical architectural forms following the French theorist Roland Fréart, whom he quotes.[32] To a greater degree than Hawksmoor, Vanbrugh sought to integrate into this vision of a lost ancient grandeur the medieval ruins such as Woodstock Manor that had so inspired his own imagination and which distinguished the English countryside. Nevertheless the 'castle style' evident at Vanbrugh Castle and House in Greenwich, for example, did not include the pointed arch. As noted in the previous chapter, Vanbrugh's arches are circular-headed, following Hugh May at Windsor and in line with Addison's preference for the concave and convex (see Figs 95, 110). For Addison warned that in forms other than the circular, such as the pointed arch, 'the Sight must split upon several Angles, it does not take in one uniform Idea, but several Ideas of the same kind. Look upon the Outside of a Dome, your Eye half surrounds it; look up into the Inside, and at one Glance you have all the Prospect of it; the entire Concavity falls into your Eye at once, the Sight being as the Centre that collects and gathers into it the Lines of the whole Circumference'.[33] Vanbrugh may even have had Addison's ideas on such 'primary pleasures' in his thoughts when he designed the dome at Castle Howard.

★   ★   ★

'THE BEST OF LANDSKIP PAINTERS CAN INVENT': VANBRUGH AND THE LANDSCAPE OF THE IMAGINATION

These ideas on the pleasures of the imagination were expressed by Vanbrugh most obviously in his understanding of landscape. His notion that architecture and its setting should be designed to tell a story owed much to contemporary ideas concerning garden design advanced by, amongst others, Alexander Pope.[34] Pope chose to emphasise scenery that could be read as much as seen. Garden design was both a visual and a literary exercise, with Pope and Addison stressing the appreciation of landscape for its poetical and philosophical associations and its capacity, like poetry, to evoke moods in the onlooker. Commentators have noted the influence of Addison's ideas on Vanbrugh as a landscape designer, although not the possibility that, given their friendship, the influence might well have been reciprocal.[35] For example the architect's recommendation for a 'Variety of Objects' and a 'Mix' of buildings and plantations at Woodstock in 1709 clearly mirrors Addison's call in 1712 for 'a spacious Landskip cut out into Rivers, Woods, Rocks, and Meadows', which increased the primary pleasure of the onlooker since 'it arises from more than a single Principle'.[36] Judging from a computer model recreating Vanbrugh's lost buildings at Greenwich, these buildings were self-consciously arranged much as in a painting to take full advantage of the natural rise in ground towards Vanbrugh Castle and the long vistas across the meadows, creating views full of such visual 'variety' and 'mix' (Fig. 131; see Fig. 341). This emphasis

131   Computer model of the view towards Vanbrugh Castle, Greenwich [author].

by both men on the use of visual 'variety' to evoke pleasing reflections may well have been inspired by literary
models, for it echoes the ancient rhetorical arts through
which an orator would stimulate and persuade via a
variety of contrasting examples, as both writers would
have recognised.[37] It reflected also the early eighteenth-
century fashion for the landscapes of Salvator Rosa
(1615–73) who, in contrast to the order implicit in the
allegorical scenes of classical antiquity, had captured the
pleasure that could be had from wildernesses, decay and
ruin (Fig. 132).[38]

In rejecting the formalised gardens of geometric
regularity which surrounded the traditional English
country house, Addison went on once again to associate
an open landscape with liberty in noting that 'The Beauties of the most stately Garden or Palace lie in a narrow
Compass, the Imagination immediately runs them over,
and requires something else to gratifie her; but, in the
wide Fields of Nature, the Sight wanders up and down
without Confinement, and is fed with an infinite variety
of Images, without any certain Stint or Number'.[39] In
stressing a similar need for natural variety, Vanbrugh had

132   Salvator Rosa, *The Finding of Moses*, c.1660–5, oil on canvas, 123 × 202.5 cm [Detroit Institute of Arts].

recommended to the Duchess the Woodstock trees which were 'Promiscuously set to grow up in a Wild Thicket'. With the varied and irregular landscape round Woodstock Manor, together with the formal avenue and lake giving way to woods and wilderness as recorded on a plan of 1709 by Vanbrugh and Charles Bridgeman and the engraving in *Vitruvius Britannicus* (1725) which closely follows it (Fig. 133), the landscape at Blenheim particularly springs to mind as reflecting Addison's point that

> we take Delight in a Prospect which is well laid out, and diversified with Fields and Meadows, Woods and Rivers, in those accidental Landskips of Trees, Clouds and Cities, that are sometimes found in the Veins of Marble, in the curious Fret-work of Rocks and Grottos, and, in a Word, in any thing that hath such a Variety or Regularity as may seem the Effect of Design, in what we call the Works of Chance.[40]

Although the gardens were eventually planted by Henry Wise, Vanbrugh was clearly involved given the Duchess's reference to him 'making Walls Slopes and Gardens' round Woodstock Manor.[41] With its wildernesses and woods, the landscape at Castle Howard as devised by Lord Carlisle with designers including Vanbrugh can also be seen as the natural expression of these ideas concerning what might be termed the 'landscape of the imagination'.[42] Addison commends the landscapes of France and Italy, with their 'agreeable mixture of Garden and Forest, which represent every where an artificial Rudeness, much more charming than that Neatness and

Elegancy which we meet with in those of our own Country', where 'Our Trees rise in Cones, Globes, and Pyramids'. In contrast to this norm, here again Castle Howard's 'agreeable mixtures' and 'artificial rudenesses' spring to mind. At Stowe, too, Vanbrugh and Bridgeman implemented these ideas of natural landscape by the early 1720s (see Fig. 311).[43] When considering garden buildings Vanbrugh frequently played with visual contrast, that is between order and regularity centred on the house and the contrived chaos of the outer regions of the garden. At Castle Howard for example he recommended to Carlisle a freestanding fluted pillar of the Doric Order and commented that 'I rec'd the Designs Mr Etty sent me, wch are very well; But I think any thing of frost work or Rock work, may be more a propo, in some other parts of the Garden, more retir'd and Solomn; or where there is Water'.[44] The solemnity here is obviously the intended mood of the onlooker as much as that of the setting.

'SOLEMN AND AWFULL APPEARANCE BOTH WITHOUT AND WITHIN': VANBRUGH AND THE ARCHITECTURE OF AWE AND MELANCHOLY

Addison's mood-orientated ideas on visual contrast can be seen to have been reflected not only in Vanbrugh's landscapes but also in aspects of his architecture, as the opening of this chapter outlined, and in particular in his attitude to a building's situation, ornament and form.

133   Plan of the Blenheim landscape, from Colen Campbell's *Vitruvius Britannicus*, vol III (1725), pls 71 and 72.

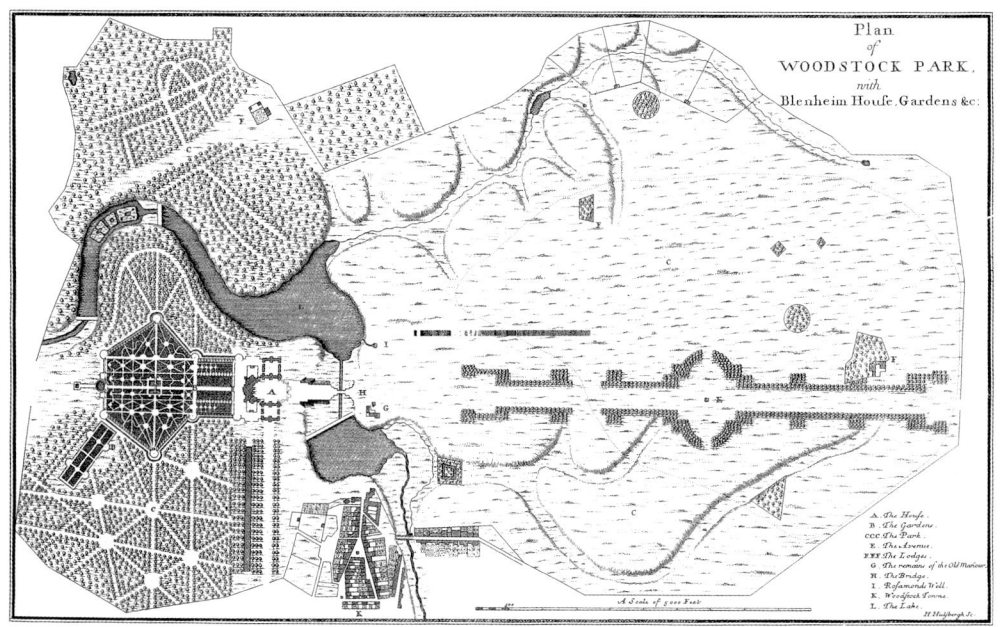

After all, by convention the signification of the character and mood of a play, whether comic, satiric or tragic, and the manipulation of the audience's mood accordingly, was related to the stage setting.[45] Wren in the second of his architectural 'Tracts' had commented on the effect on the onlooker's mood of the siting of ancient temples, noting that 'a Grove was necessary not only to shade the Devout, but, from the Darkness of the Place, to strike some Terror and Recollection in their Approachers'.[46] Following this, Vanbrugh made his own comments on the mood-inspired design of new temples in his famous recommendation to the Commission for building the fifty Queen Anne churches in London, in which he notes that 'the Reverend look of a Temple . . . shou'd ever have the most Solemn and Awfull Appearance both without and within, that is possible'.[47] Curiously enough, these remarks were made at about

134 (*above*) The west façade of Blenheim.

135 (*left*) Caryatids on the west façade of Blenheim.

136   Hawksmoor's Carrmire Gate at Castle Howard, *c.*1730.

the same time as Addison wrote (in June 1712) that 'Temples and Publick Places of Worship' must 'open the Mind to vast Conceptions, and fit it to converse with the Divinity of the Place. For every thing that is Majestick, imprints an Awfullness and Reverence on the Mind of the Beholder, and strikes in with the Natural Greatness of the Soul'.[48] Vanbrugh went on to contrast the evocation of awe through 'a plain, but Just and Noble Stile' with its opposite manner, described by him as buildings with a 'Gayety of Ornaments as may be proper to a Luxurious palace' and 'the Air of a Gay Lanthorn'. In so doing he equated gaiety with light and lightness of structure and, by implication, solemnity with darkness and structural heaviness. Such a contrast between 'solemn', dark window-less walls and 'gay', light-filled lanterns might easily be related to Addison's observation in *The Spectator* in 1711 that 'As the shadows in Picture represent the serious or melancholy, so the Lights do the bright and lively Thoughts'.[49] This all suggests that Vanbrugh was particularly sensitive to the uplifting effect of an architectural sequence which moved form dark-

ness to light, implicit in most church sections which rise from crypt to lantern as an aspect of their expression of resurrection. Moreover, the light-filled long galleries, orangeries and colonnades in Vanbrugh's country houses seem, at the very least, to have been attempts by him to uplift their visitor's mood much in the spirit of the 'gay lantern'. At Blenheim Vanbrugh observed on 18 July 1709, 'Nor will there be so pleasant a Room for View Nor so cool (yet all the same Gay and light) in the Whole house, as that Greenhouse or Detach'd Gallery'.[50]

Following Vanbrugh's advice, a 'Gayety of Ornaments' is indeed to be found on the 'Luxurious Palace' of Castle Howard, especially facing the garden and in the landscape with the 'Temple of the Four Winds', as well as at Blenheim on the garden façade and on the west front with its caryatids (Figs 134, 135). In contrast, the crenellated walls, towers and fortress-style Carrmire Gate encountered on approaching Castle Howard can be seen as an exercise in effecting just such feelings of awe and wonder in the visitor (Fig. 136). Vanbrugh boasted to the Duke of Newcastle concerning these walls that 'I think

137 The chimneys at Kings Weston in Gloucestershire, turned into fictive arcades and
crenellations, 1713–14 [Regional Building Record, Bath University].

all that come here, are Supris'd at their Magnificent
Effect', and later that Lords Bathurst, Binny and Stairs
'are vastly Surprised and taken with the Walls and their
Towers, which they talk much of. I always thought we
were sure of that Card'.[51] Here, incidentally, is a rare
account of how actual observers responded to Vanbrugh's
work and it underlines the importance of the observer's
reaction to the work's conception. As noted earlier, these
fortifications were built much more for effect than for
any actual defence: Vanbrugh himself described to Lord
Carlisle the 'round bastions' at the southernmost angles
as 'Considerable ornaments and distinguish'd termina-
tions of the Garden', and cited what he called 'an
Admirable good effect, the plain Wall in the Front
looking with a bolder air of Defence than if there had
been a Gate through it'.[52] Rather like the dramatic function of stage scenery, the landscape buildings at Castle
Howard can thus be seen as intended to evoke distinct
moods in the onlooker through their various ornamental styles and features.

Vanbrugh was obviously especially aware of the
opportunity for dramatic effect presented by the skyline
of his country houses, given the frequency of their urns
and monumental chimneys, crenellations and altars, and
towers and statues (see Figs 161, 165). These forms were
for the most part embellishments and can be seen as a
powerful example of his inventive use of ornament and
form to create an effect. At Kimbolton for example he

added what he refers to as 'battlements' along the
roofline as part of his novel works there, in order to
convey the desired 'Noble and Masculine Shew' and
'Castle Air'.[53] His use elsewhere of urns on the skyline
was evidently seen as particularly novel, and therefore
visually striking, since in a letter of Christmas Day 1699
to the Earl of Manchester Vanbrugh notes that on being
shown his Castle Howard designs the Duke of Devonshire 'absolutely approved the whole design, particularly
the low Wings, which he said wou'd have an admirable
effect without doors as well as within, being adorn'd
with those Ornaments of Pillasters and Urns, wch he
never thought of'.[54] Even the architectural elements on
Vanbrugh's houses which do have a function were often
disguised by being transformed into monumental forms
– most notably, chimneys into fictive arcades and crenellations as at Kings Weston (Fig. 137; see Fig. 264), a transformation which only seems to underline the primary
role of these forms in the manipulation of the onlooker's
mood. The skyline was certainly conceived in this way
at Blenheim, with its statues and other elements fittingly
described by Hawksmoor as 'eminencies',[55] as well as at
Castle Howard with its domed pantheon of antique
philosophers (see Figs 107, 209). At both houses the roofscape was clearly intended to inspire noble thoughts in
the mere mortals below. On Grimsthorpe Castle the
statues representing Neptune's rape of Medusa and
Pluto's rape of Proserpine (see Figs 305, 306) again

138 Drawing for an abortive church, design attributed to Vanbrugh, c.1712–14 [Victoria and Albert Museum, London].

139 Hawksmoor's St Anne, Limehouse, 1714–30.

suggest that the skyline above the parapet was conceived by Vanbrugh as the proper, heroic realm of the gods and consequently of human mortality symbolised by its ubiquitous urns. After all, country houses were invariably viewed from a distance, a fact which Vanbrugh took into consideration when praising the figure and proportions of Kimbolton in 1707 or the view of Woodstock Manor in 1709 and a cap to the towers at Castle Howard in 1724 which would 'make the best figure' when viewed as a whole.[56] Vanbrugh's recommendations for the London churches had included that 'they may be so

plac'd, to be fairly View'd at such proper distance, as is necessary to shew their Exterior Form', and that they have 'High and Bold' towers 'to shew at a distance what regard there is . . . to Religious Worship'.[57]

A surviving pair of drawings for an abortive church design attributed to Vanbrugh illustrates just such a tower (Fig. 138; see Fig. 167).[58] Here the quoins and keystones together with the urns are no doubt directly related to his recommendation for solemnity and awe and set the tone for Hawksmoor's later buildings (Fig. 139). In a near-contemporary passage in 'The Pleasures of the

140   A basement keystone on Hawksmoor's St Mary Woolnoth, London.

141   A basement keystone on Hawksmoor's St George, Bloomsbury, London.

Imagination' of 1712 which one might apply to help understand these forms, Addison asked, regarding descriptions aimed to terrify, 'how comes it to pass, that we should take delight in being terrified?' and speculated that 'When we look on such hideous Objects, we are not a little pleased to think we are in no Danger of them . . . so that the more frightful Appearance they make, the greater is the Pleasure we receive from the Sense of our own Safety'.[59] He added: 'Such Representations teach us to set a just Value upon our own Condition, and make us prize our good Fortune which exempts us from the like Calamities'. In this one is reminded further of Hawksmoor's ponderous, oversized keystones on his London churches (Figs 140, 141), especially those to his crypts which suggest to the observer the presence of an 'underworld' and reflect a Michelangeloesque sense of *terribilità* popularised by Serlio's rustic gates (Figs 142–4).

Vanbrugh's early design for Eastbury of about 1713, the sketch of which depicts smoking chimney monuments which are heavily shaded (Figs 145, 146), conveys a similar air of 'the serious or melancholy' to that which Addison had observed when describing such drawn shadows.[60] As this drawing indicates, one of the principal purposes of Vanbrugh's (and Hawksmoor's) heavily profiled rooftop elements may well have been the casting of long shadows for just such a melancholic effect (given that the art of shadow-casting had become a highly developed science through the design of sundials).[61] The capacity of architecture to dispel or evoke melancholy through light or shade and through uplifting or brooding forms was actively discussed by Vanbrugh's contemporaries. John Locke had observed that 'We have the ideas of figures and colours by the operation of exterior objects on our senses, when the sun shows them us'.[62] In 1707 John Evelyn described gothic buildings as 'Congestions of Heavy, Dark, Melancholy and *Monkish Piles*'.[63] John Breval in his *Remarks on several Parts of Europe* (1726) observed on Roman mausoleums that 'Most of the considerable Avenues to Rome . . . are cover'd with the Vestiges of these Tombs; which, in their entire State must have spread an Air of Horrour and Melancholy over the Places they took in'.[64] Vanbrugh himself refers to the power of architecture – and of castles in particular – to dispel melancholy in his version of *The Pilgrim* when a 'Gentleman' comments to Pedro that 'I wou'd divert your melancholy if I cou'd. Will ye view our Castle?'.[65] Indeed, Addison further notes in 'The Pleasures of the Imagination' that 'Delightful Scenes, whether in Nature, Painting, or Poetry, have a kindly Influence on the Body, as well as the Mind, and not only serve to clear and brighten the Imagination, but are able to disperse Grief and Melancholly'.[66]

The dispelling of melancholy had been famously outlined in Robert Burton's *The Anatomy of Melancholy*, which first appeared in 1621 and subsequently included a title page illustrating the link between mood and shadowy garden settings (Fig. 147).[67] Burton spelt out the benign effect of gardens and of noble buildings by citing various architectural exemplars, both ancient and modern. Concerning the legendary Temple of Solomon he observes: 'The Temple of *Jerusalem* was so fairly built of white marble, with so many pyramids covered with

142 (*above left*) Sebastiano Serlio's
Rustic gate IIII, with its pulvinate frieze,
from the *Extraordinario Libro* (1551),
fol 4*v*.

143 (*above right*) Serlio's Rustic gate
VIII, with its satyrs, from the
Extraordinario Libro (1551), fol 6*v*.

144 (*left*) Serlio's Rustic gate XXIX,
with its monsters, from the *Extraordinario
Libro* (1551), fol 17*r*.

145 and 146 (*above and below*)   Vanbrugh's early design for the front façade of Eastbury, *c.*1713, with matching plan [Victoria and Albert Museum, London].

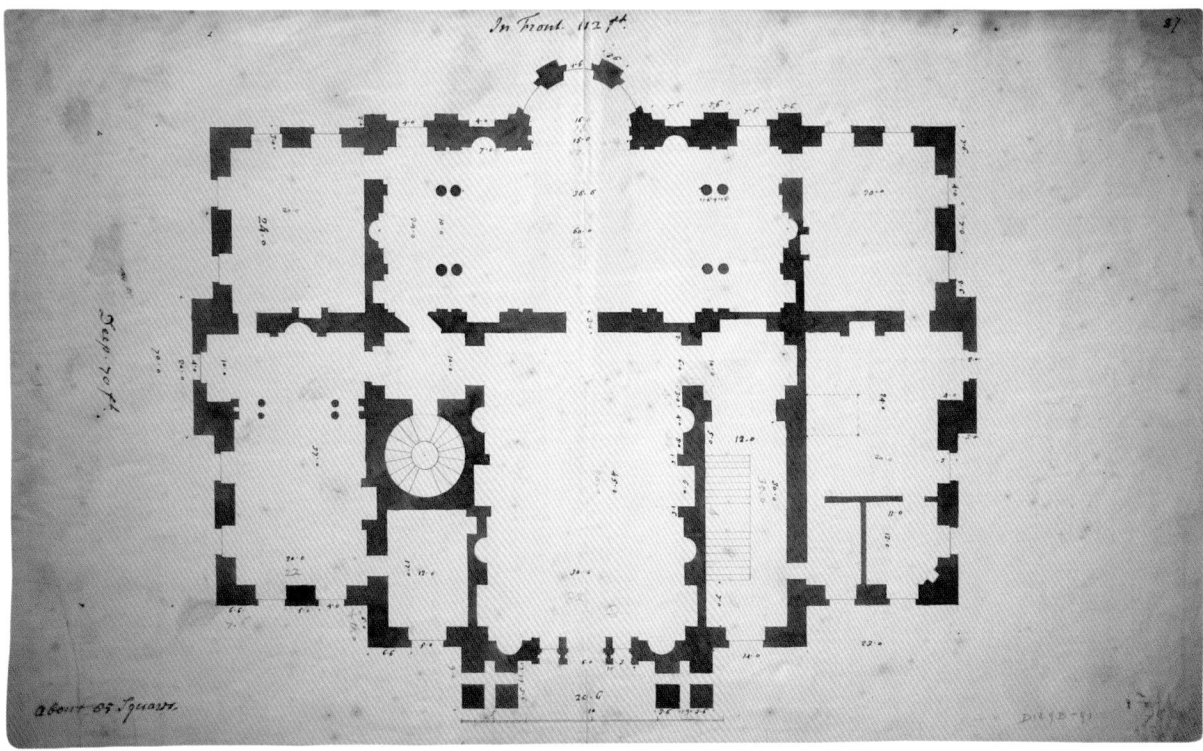

Demoeritus Abderites.

THE
ANATOMY OF
MELANCHOLY.
What it is, With all the kinds, causes,
Symptomes, Prognostickes, & seuerall cures of it.

147 Detail from the title page by Christof le Blon to Robert Burton's *The Anatomy of Melancholy* (first published in the edition of 1628), in which Democritus of Abdera seeks the shade of a greenwood tree and illustrates the link between mood and shadowy garden settings.

between architecture and the state of mind of the inhabitant or onlooker (Fig. 148). The grotesque masks on the four corner urns of this temple clearly evoked the idea of entering the mutually untamed worlds of sleep and landscape (Figs 149, 150; see Fig. 124).[72]

'AN ALTAR, ON WHICH THE ANCIENTS MADE THEIR OFFERINGS': VANBRUGH AND THE ARCHITECTURE OF DEATH

A mood of melancholy and solemnity in the onlooker was encouraged by Vanbrugh through his use not just of urns but of the full vocabulary of funereal forms. Following his youthful study of what he called the visual 'effect' of the cemetery at Surat in India (illustrated in

148 Vanbrugh's Temple of Sleep (Sleeping Parlour) of 1725 in the wilderness at Stowe (destroyed), illustrated top left in Benton Seeley's *Stowe: a description of the magnificent house and gardens* (1750), pl. V [Stowe School Photographic Archives].

gold . . . was so glorious, and so glistered afar off, that the spectatours might not well abide the sight of it'.[68] Perhaps these uplifting golden pyramids inspired the mysterious pyramid that Hawksmoor proposed in 1732, in either copper or silver, at Castle Howard?[69] For as seen, this was a landscape consciously conceived to affect the mood of the onlooker, in which Vanbrugh recommended balls on the masonry obelisks to make them look 'Gay, without being Tawdry'.[70] When outlining the role of gardens as an antidote to melancholy, Burton observes that 'To walk amongst Orchards, Gardens, Bowers, Mounts and Arbours, artificial wildernesses, green thickets, Arches, Groves, Lawns, Rivulets, Fountains and such like pleasant places . . . must needs be a delectable recreation'.[71] It was noted that such contrasts were evident at Castle Howard with its wilderness and groves, whilst Vanbrugh's Temple of Sleep of 1725 in the wilderness at Stowe made a somewhat obvious link

149a–d   Four urns with their grotesque masks originally on the Temple of Sleep but now on the Oxford Bridge at Stowe.

150 Drawing of urns with masks, probably by Vanbrugh's Office and bound in the Elton Hall volume, undated [Victoria and Albert Museum, London].

Appendix Two), he had a lifelong preoccupation with the commemoration of death and rebirth, a duality played out most fully in the iconography of Castle Howard where, as will be seen in Chapter Five, trophies of arms and symbols of death give way to flora and other symbols of rebirth (see Figs 188, 191). This interest should be understood in the context of his Protestant beliefs, and the parallel theme of sin and redemption articulated in his plays and more obviously still in his copy of the works of John Milton.[73] (In *The False Friend*, for example, death is used to reveal the truth through Don John's closing repentance.[74]) The Pyramid Gate at Castle Howard evokes the idea of death at the very entrance to the estate, just as the unbuilt forecourt obelisk gate

would have done which was sketched by Vanbrugh and illustrated in *Vitruvius Britannicus* (Fig. 151).[75] At Stowe he designed the freestanding 'Egyptian pyramid' in a clear effort to recall in the mind's eye of onlookers the ancient funereal prototype (see Fig. 130). Much as these ancient forms traditionally symbolised the spiritual boundary between one world and the next, so Vanbrugh appears to have used pyramids and obelisks to mark symbolically the transitional point between one realm and another, as with the gates and obelisk at Castle Howard, the pyramids proposed at Kings Weston and built at Eastbury based on those at Surat and the four corner obelisks on an unidentified temple or mausoleum design of about 1723 (Figs 153–5).[76]

Like Hawksmoor, Vanbrugh frequently placed these objects drawn from the traditional iconography of death on the all-important rooftop of his buildings, no doubt in order to maximise their melancholic effect from a distance and, as previously noted, remind everyone of their own mortality. In this position these elements also once again mark the physical boundary between two distinct realms. The monumental freestanding rooftop arches and pavilions which dominate the skyline at Eastbury and elsewhere, for example, are strongly reminiscent of the pavilions used in the same positions on the mausoleums of the Mogul emperors and English traders witnessed by Vanbrugh in India (Fig. 152; see Figs 5, 145, 280). Clearly the appropriation of these Mogul forms by the English at Surat would have provided Vanbrugh with a valuable precedent for his own adaptation of these forms. Even less ambiguous were the obelisks which he placed on the roof in a design for a small house (Fig. 159).[77] Obelisks were customarily used as funereal monuments, Serlio having recorded in his third book that the obelisk placed by Domenico Fontana in front of St Peter's (Fig. 158) 'is of Egyptian stone and in its apex are said to be the ashes of Gaius Caesar'.[78] However Vanbrugh used them in unusual, elevated locations. Perhaps in so doing he was influenced by the pyramid-obelisk twin towers on Philibert de l'Orme's Chapelle Royale at the Château d'Anet of 1552 (Figs 156, 157), given his time in France and the fact that the chapel's towers, together with the inventive use of sarcophagus forms as chimneys on the gatehouse at Anet (Fig. 160), were illustrated in de l'Orme's *Le Premier tome de l'architecture* of 1567 which Vanbrugh must surely have seen following his interest in French châteaux. After all, as a storyteller Vanbrugh's adaptation of these French country-house forms into the vocabulary of English architecture might be understood as somewhat equivalent to his translation and adaptation of Dancourt's play *La Maison de campagne* into that entitled *The Country House*.

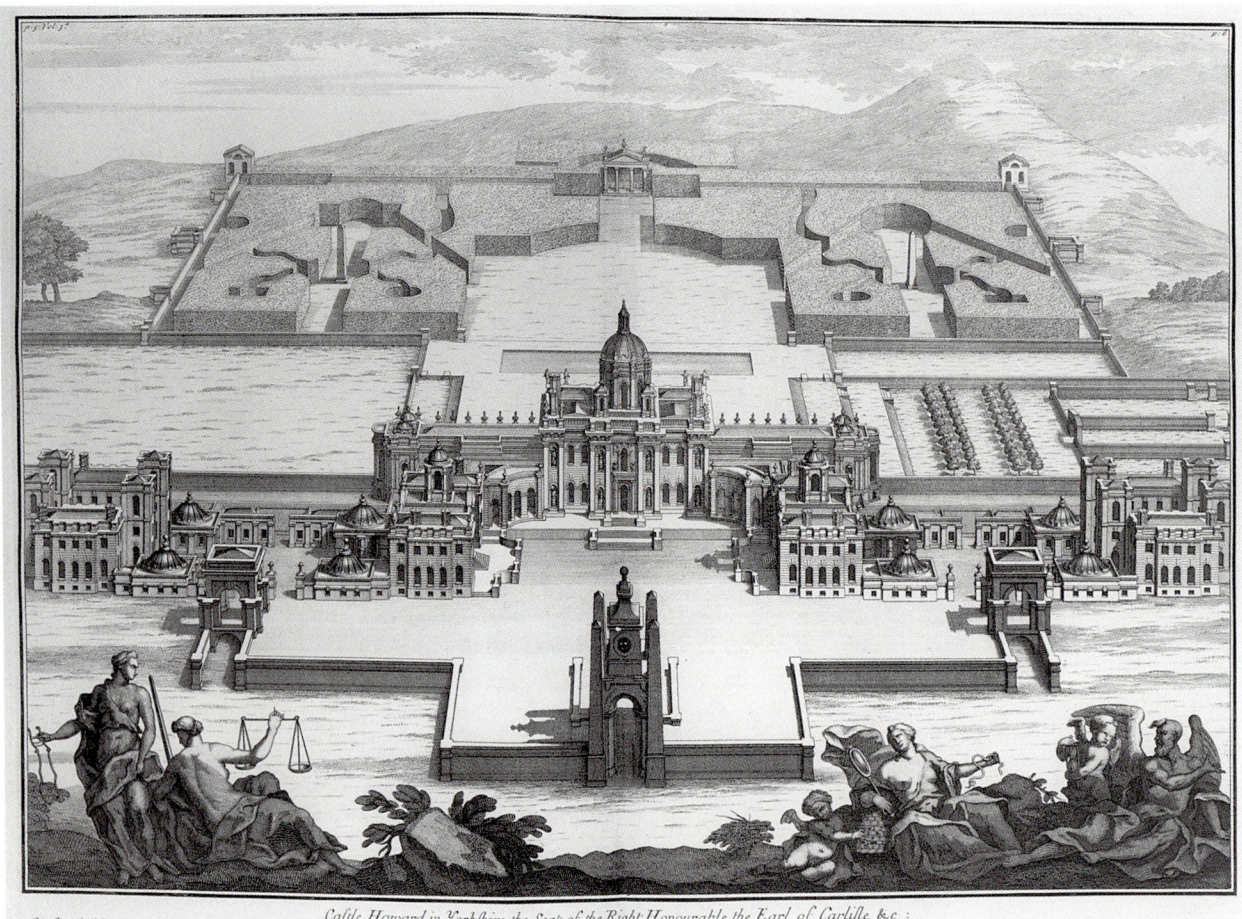

Ca: Campbell Delin: Castle Howard in Yorkshire the Seat of the Right Honourable the Earl of Carlisle &c: H:Hulsbergh Sculp:

151 Engraving of an idealised view of Castle Howard, with the unbuilt obelisk gate, from Colen Campbell's *Vitruvius Britannicus*, vol III (1725), pls 5 and 6.

152 The gate to the Taj Mahal, India, 1648, with it pavilions on the skyline similar to Vanbrugh's forms.

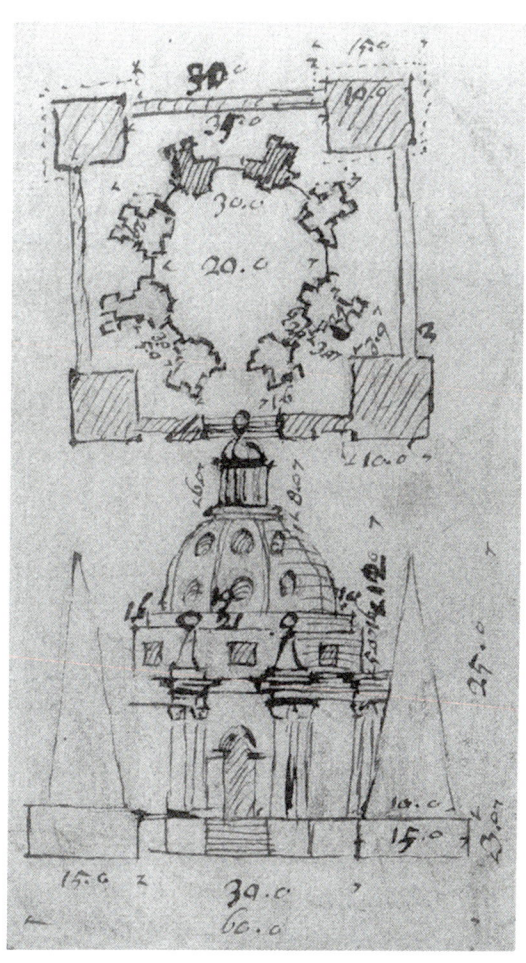

153 Vanbrugh's obelisk at Castle Howard celebrating Marlborough's victories, designed in 1714.

154 An unidentified temple or mausoleum design by Vanbrugh, c.1723, drawing in the hand of Vanbrugh, bound in the Elton Hall volume [Victoria and Albert Museum, London].

155 Computer model of the temple or mausoleum design by Vanbrugh [Paul Richens].

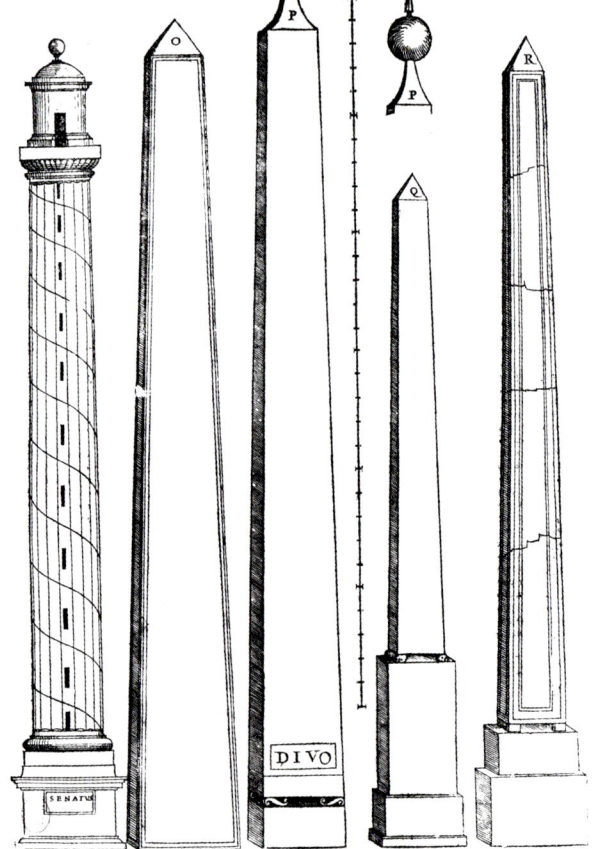

156 (*above left*)   Vanbrugh's Pyramid Gate at Castle Howard, completed in 1717.

157 (*above right*)   Philibert de l'Orme's Chapelle Royale at the Château d'Anet, France, 1552.

158 (*right*)   Obelisk placed by Domenico Fontana in front of St Peter's, Rome, illustrated by Sebastiano Serlio in *Terzo Libro* (1540), obelisk 'P', p. LXII.

159　Design for an unidentified small house, drawing from Vanbrugh's Office [Victoria and Albert Museum, London].

In the same spirit, Vanbrugh placed urns with flaming lids on the parapet at Kings Weston. These are illustrated in a surviving drawing of the façade, possibly executed by Vanbrugh, and in the plates approved by him for *Vitruvius Britannicus* published in 1715, whilst of the urns themselves, two were carved by Thomas Sumsion in 1717 (Figs 161, 163, 164).[79] Urns with flames traditionally symbolised life after death – witness Hawksmoor's use of them at St George-in-the-East, along with Roman altars (Fig. 162).[80] Vanbrugh proposed using identical Roman altars on the skyline at Kings Weston and Seaton Delaval and actually used them at Grimsthorpe Castle as chimneys whose smoke adds to the sacrificial effect (Fig. 165; see Fig. 228).[81] Such altars were well enough understood by contemporaries as bound up in ancient rituals of death and resurrection. Wren observed concerning the Romans that 'not only their Altars and Sacrifices were mystical, but the very Forms of their Temples'.[82] Batty Langley, in describing Hawksmoor's altars atop proto-

160   Sarcophagus forms used as chimneys on the gatehouse at Anet.

161   Urn on the front façade at Kings Weston, *c.*1717.

162   Urns and Roman altars at Hawksmoor's St George-in-the-East, London.

163   The front façade of Kings Weston in Gloucestershire, drawing attributed to Vanbrugh or his Office [Yale Centre for Studies in British Art, New Haven].

164   Proof before lettering of an engraved plate of Kings Weston for Colen Campbell's *Vitruvius Britannicus*, eventually published in vol. I (1715), pl. 48, from 'The Kings Weston Book of Drawings' (see also Fig. 263) [Bristol Civic Trust].

165   Chimneys as Roman altars at Grimsthorpe Castle in Lincolnshire.

Doric pilasters (the Order traditionally most associated with sacrifice[83]) at St George–in–the–East, noted that the 'tower is of more solemn aspect than that of *Lime-house*, being crown'd with a group of square columns affix'd to a cylinder, each supporting an ornament in manner of an altar, on which the ancients made their offerings'.[84] The use of these forms on Hawksmoor's London churches from 1712 no doubt helped establish them in Vanbrugh's mind as appropriate Protestant iconography. Moreover François Blondel had added authenticity to such funereal forms by illustrating them as the origin of architectural order in his *Cours d'architecture* (1683; Fig. 166; this illustration included a pyramidal form very similar to Vanbrugh's gate at Castle Howard, and he may have been familiar with the work through his time in France and association with Hawksmoor, who owned a copy).[85] It is as if Vanbrugh conceived the skyline of his houses as the proper place to remind everyone of their fate, in striking a sense of humility in the onlooker, a conception wholly compatible with the moral purpose of his plays and his admiration for the fables of Aesop.

More specifically, these forms were perhaps intended to lend a commemorative meaning to Vanbrugh's houses, as memorials to his various patrons. After all, the use of funereal iconography would have been especially poignant in situations where the patron had died before or during the building work, as with George Dodding-ton at Eastbury and George Delaval at Seaton Delaval. Hawksmoor used these same forms on his churches to evoke the memory of their benefactor, Queen Anne, as well as to stimulate the required mood of solemnity in the onlooker.[86] Vanbrugh was certainly fully aware of the potential of domestic buildings to serve as a memorial to their builders, as evidenced by the Woodstock ruins. When writing to Lord Carlisle on 19 July 1722 he once again underlines his priority to achieve the effect of architectural permanence by emphasising the impor-tance of physical, funereal monuments over more tran-sient ones:

> I believe my Lord Godolphin would have likt very well to have had the Duke of Marlbh: buryed in the Park, with a Very good Monument over him; but the Duke directs in his Will that they shou'd bury him in the Chappell at Blenheim. Here is a Pompous funeral preparing, but curb'd and Crippl'd by her Grace; who will govern it by her fancys, amongst which, there is but one good one, and that is that She'll pay for it. I don't know whether it won't cost her Ten Thousand pounds. What a Noble monument wou'd that have made, whereas this Idle Show, will be gone in half an hour, and forgot in Two days. The other, wou'd have been a Show, and a Noble one, to many future Ages.[87]

Vanbrugh would surely have intended the memorial forms placed on the skyline of his houses to have pro-voked a similar emotional reaction in the viewer to that evoked when studying the ruins of Woodstock, namely to 'move more lively and pleasing Reflections (than History without their aid can do) on the Persons who have Inhabited them'.[88]

'DIFFERENT SENSATIONS FROM EACH POINT OF VIEW': VANBRUGH AND THE ARCHITECTURE OF ASSOCIATION

The writings of Addison and, indirectly, of Locke and Burton thus emerge as a major, if somewhat neglected, source for Vanbrugh's understanding of architectural theory and ideas regarding the intellectual and emotional power of architecture. Given the friendship between Addison and Vanbrugh, it is perfectly possible that the former's essays may even have given expression

L'Origine des Chapiteaux des Colonnes.

166 'L'Origine des chapiteaux des colonnes', from François Blondel's *Cours d'architecture* (1683).

to the latter's design principles. In the absence of a formal architectural apprenticeship, Vanbrugh has all too often been presented by historians as a novice reliant on others – Hawksmoor in particular – in matters not only of architectural practice but also of theory.[89] This has perhaps arisen because his theoretical precepts can in fact be traced, not surprisingly, as much to the relatively neglected works of literary associates (and to heraldry) as they can to formal architectural sources such as the Renaissance treatises. These alternative sources led Vanbrugh to formulate an architecture, and a vocabulary of architectural theory, aimed not only at the emotional effect on the onlooker of certain forms but, more specifically, at the stage-like ability of forms to tell moving stories such that these onlookers would, as he put it at Blenheim, 'find Wonder enough in the Story, to make 'em pleas'd with the Sight of it'.

It is true that Palladio had emphasised what he called 'the first impression that the temple makes on the person who approaches it'.[90] However Vanbrugh's essentially theatrical experience of 'wonder-working' through his frequently novel use of ornament and architectural forms clearly departed from the more abstract Vitruvian norms of beauty based on Platonic harmonies advanced by Palladio. Moreover in the context of Addison's 'associational' theory, Vanbrugh's architecture can be seen as more a matter of allusion than of illusion in the baroque manner.[91] Of course whereas Palladio aimed at influencing the potential noble patron, with educated tastes, when writing his treatise on architecture, Addison like Vanbrugh aimed at a much more general audience, with more universal emotions, when writing in *The Spectator*. Given their popularity, Addison's writings on architecture can also be understood as a valuable record as to how contemporaries appreciated Vanbrugh's buildings, especially since they emphasise qualities which his architecture exemplified, such as massiveness.

Locke's theory outlining the association of ideas came to underlie the 'Gothick' movement, initiated to some extent by Vanbrugh's letter concerning Woodstock Manor, and the prevailing sentimentalist and nationalistic attitude to gothic forms.[92] Later still, Vanbrugh's buildings – and his chimneys in particular – were presented by John Soane in his lectures to students of 1809–15 as exemplars of the principle that 'A building to please must produce different sensations from each point of view'.[93] In the standard histories of the English baroque, Vanbrugh's architecture is seen alongside the work of Hawksmoor and Wren as a stylistic termination, in the wake of the triumph of Palladianism. However, it is clear that in its associational intentions his work should be viewed as a forerunner of the picturesque ideas of Richard Payne Knight and 'Capability' Brown.[94]

167   Drawing for an abortive church, design attributed to Vanbrugh, c.1712–14 [Victoria and Albert Museum, London].

Chapter 4

'THE REVEREND LOOK OF A TEMPLE': DECORUM AND VANBRUGH'S LONDON CHURCH PROPOSALS

Vanbrugh's recommendations of about 1711 to the Commission charged with building the London churches contain all the basic elements of his architectural principles – a preference for clear views and vistas, for grand porticoes and towers, for architectural effect and for the appropriate expression of a patron's wealth, a building's purpose and the spirit of the age. For, as seen in the previous chapter, here he made the moral and ornamental distinction between 'a plain, but Just and Noble Stile' appropriate for the new church buildings and what he called 'such Gayety of Ornaments as may be proper to a Luxurious Palace'.[1] In a direct link between theory and practice, the surviving drawings of an unidentified church the design for which is attributed to Vanbrugh indicate that he followed his recommendations to the Commission in his own unrealised London church designs (Fig. 167; see Fig. 138), where he attempted to find an appropriate architectural style for his Protestant beliefs following classical ideals of decorum and more modern associational ones of architectural effect. One might expect the classical principles of architectural decorum to have had particular appeal to Vanbrugh since architecture was understood as an expressive language whose vocabulary of forms was capable of representing, or narrating, the patron's virtues and character.

'ANY THING OF FROST WORK OR ROCK WORK, MAY BE MORE A PROPO': VANBRUGH ON THE APPROPRIATE USE OF ARCHITECTURAL ORNAMENT AND FORM

Having specified the gender of the three Greek columns – which ranged from the 'masculine' Doric and 'matronly' Ionic to the 'maidenly' Corinthian – Vitruvius had related these human types to the character, or decorum, of temples dedicated to particular gods. Hence the Doric was appropriate for Minerva, Mars and Hercules because 'of their might'; Ionic for Juno, Diana and Bacchus taking account 'of their middle quality'; and Corinthian for Venus, Proserpine and Flora 'on account of their gentleness'. In this way, as but one example, the 'matronly' caryatids on the west front of Blenheim are appropriately matched with Ionic capitals (see Figs 134, 135).[2] Vanbrugh would have been well versed in the mythic characters of the classical gods through his dramatic work. Don Guzman refers in *The False Friend* to '*Diana, by her borrow'd Light*',[3] for example, whilst it has been seen in the Introduction that Dryden's masque at the close of *The Pilgrim* brings together the huntress Diana (representing the reign of James I), the warrior Mars (representing the Civil War) and the passionate Venus (representing the courtly debauchery of the Restoration). In his fourth book of 1537 Serlio had developed Vitruvius's ornamental range to include the two Roman Orders – Tuscan and Composite – and to take account of modern building functions, patrons and Christian dedications.[4] A particular Order might be matched to the social rank or character of a patron, as already seen in the case of the Doric, to his or her building's type, from 'robust' fortress to 'delicate' convent, or to a building's location. Location particularly affected the ornamentation on a given building type. For whilst ornament must always be appropriate to the rank of the patron, in the centre of towns this decoration should, for Serlio, be 'solemn and modest', whereas in more open places in the city and in the country 'a certain license can be taken'.[5]

The buildings of Inigo Jones bear witness to the fact that he saw the five antique column types as a language capable of expressing the shifting ambitions of his Stuart masters, from Protestant imperialism and decorative temperance on the one hand, to Catholic toleration and decorative luxury on the other.[6] By the turn of the eighteenth century the individual characteristics of these architectural Orders were widely understood in England. Defoe's *Tour* of 1725 praises St Paul's Cathedral by (slightly mis-) quoting the lines from Dryden cited in Chapter One: 'Strong Dorick Pillars form the Base, / Corinthian fills the upper Space; / So all below is Strength, and all above is Grace'.[7] John Evelyn, in both editions of his 'Account' (1664 and 1707) appended to his translation of Fréart, defined decorum as 'where a *Building*, and particularly the *Ornaments* thereof, become the *station*, and *occasion*, as *Vitruvius* expresly shews in appropriating the several *Orders* to their natural affections; so as he would not have set a *Corinthian Column* at the Entrance of a *Prison*, nor a *Tuscan* before the *Portico* of a *Church*, as some have done among us with no great regard to the *decorum*'.[8] The principles of decorum, amongst other Vitruvian virtues, were even presented as of importance to national wellbeing. For in his dedication to Sir John Denham (Surveyor of the King's Works), Evelyn had lamented that 'it is from the *asymmetrie* of our *Buildings*, want of *decorum* and proportion in our *Houses*, that the irregularity of our *humors* and *affections* may be shrewdly discern'd'.[9]

Vanbrugh's attempt to use ornament appropriately, in line with the classical principles of decorum, necessarily dictated the stylistic range which his houses display. The very possibility for such a range in ornamental display, matched to building type and location, has been linked by Christian Norberg-Schulz to a native freedom of artistic and political expression which contrasted with continental shows of absolutism and dogmatic religion that tended towards stylistic uniformity. Norberg-Schulz goes on to suggest that the 'aim of Vanbrugh, instead, must have been to achieve a "democratic" architecture wherein every building is given a character appropriate to its use'.[10] As a dramatist Vanbrugh may well have been aware of the literary and rhetorical origins of architectural decorum as a means to express qualities. After all, Vitruvius had been inspired by the classical rules of rhetorical writing and the three styles of oratory – grand, middle and plain – as outlined in particular by Cicero.[11] Rhetorical handbooks emphasised that for maximum effect the orator should always take account of the particular circumstances of the speech or sermon in selecting figures, or styles, of speech. Indeed, as with Hawksmoor, many of Vanbrugh's statements on architecture relate to these time-honoured principles. It was noted that on matching ornament – or the lack of it – to building status and type, Vanbrugh observed concerning Blenheim on 27 July 1716 that 'the homely sim-

plicity of the Antient Manor' was in his 'constant thoughts for a guide in what remains to be done, in all the inferior Buildings'[12] and that the crenellated arcade and simple monumentality of the kitchen court were the result (see Fig. 83). He further observed that '''twas necessary the Inside of this Court should be Regular Decent and clean, which is all it pretends to; it being impossible to make any thing in nature plainer'. He defended the covered walkways, adding that they 'may make some little shew, being opened towards the Court in Arches; But when 'tis considered, that the making it close[d] would have cost much more money, I hope it won't be reckond a fault, but otherwise'.[13] When also deciding against the use of the Orders at Kimbolton (see Fig. 4), I have shown that he related his decision to the Vitruvian norms of context and gender-specific ornamental effect when noting that 'to have built a Front with Pillasters, and what the Orders require cou'd never have been born with the Rest of the Castle: I'm sure this will make a very Noble and Masculine Shew', adding that 'I shall be much deceiv'd if People don't See a Manly Beauty in it when tis up, that they did not conceive cou'd be produced out of such rough Materialls'.[14] Vanbrugh certainly seems eager here to reassure Manchester that the astylar, castle style gave appropriate expression to the Earl's (masculine) character and status – and also, perhaps following Wren's distinction, to British 'permanence' in contrast to French 'fashion'.

Again much like Hawksmoor, Vanbrugh was also sensitive to the match between a building's setting and its ornamental style and mood. As seen in the previous chapter, he observed to Lord Carlisle at Castle Howard that 'I think any thing of frost work or Rock work, may be more a propo, in some other parts of the Garden, more retir'd and Solomn; or where there is Water'.[15] His concern here was the appropriateness of ornament for its setting ('a propo'). He added that 'I am very much afraid of Venturing to Flute the Obelisks: But the Balls upon them, I think will make them Gay, without being Tawdry. The Venturing at one fluted, in a Flower Garden, might be well enough, but I doubt going farther wou'd not be lik'd which I think the Whole Decorations of the Parterre will be extreamly, if rightly and Properly hit off'.[16] Alternatively, when it came to his more refined 'Temple of the Four Winds' at Castle Howard (Fig. 168) he notes, 'As to husbanding the Stone by Rusticks, it might be done; but tho' I am a very great Lover of Rusticks, I do not think they wou'd by any means do in this Case the whole turn of the Design being of the more delicate kind; but another expedient will husband the Stone, better than Rusticks, and be but what ought to be in this Design, and that is to flute the Pillars'.[17]

Vanbrugh's sensitivity extended to his choice of certain architectural forms for particular locations and functions. It was noted in the Introduction that the buildings at Greenwich Hospital with which Vanbrugh was associated expressed their naval function in their ornament, through the sea monsters and winds on the west façade of the Painted Hall and festoons with shell-fish on the four Ionic capitals on the east front of the King William building of 1702 (see Figs 37, 38). Medieval details were chosen by Vanbrugh on the same basis. Concerning the appropriate manner of roofing the wall towers at Castle Howard (see Fig. 128), and William Etty's proposal for a spire form set against his for a 'cap', Vanbrugh advised Carlisle on 10 December 1724 that

> The Spires upon Steeples, are not meant for covering to the Towers they stand upon, but are ornaments rais'd upon them, to be seen a great way off. But Towers upon Walls, are Suited to them as part of the Fortifications, and are Suppos'd to be lodgings or Storehouses, and as Such only require a Covering, which may however be in a degree ornamental, but shou'd not look too light and trifling; I am therefore much inclin'd to think, that the First Design, rais'd so high as to show the Whole Cap above the Battlements would be much the Properest covering in this Case, and make the best figure, with regard to what it belongs considering the whole thing, from the ground to the Ball on the Top.[18]

In his priority to match form and function Vanbrugh emphasises tradition ('not meant' and 'Suppos'd'), suitability ('are Suited to them') and propriety ('much the Properest covering'). This particular concern with propriety, in matching a building's 'name' or 'type' with its situation and character (following the common role of names in Restoration drama), is emphasised when he further notes on his 'Temple' at Castle Howard that 'I have some doubts about the Name of Belvedere, which is generally given to some high Tower; and such a thing will certainly be right to have some time and in Some Place, tho' I can't say I do at present think of one about the Seat, where the View is better than this, But this Building I fancy wou'd more naturally take the Name of Temple which the Situation likewise is very proper for'.[19] Here again, true to the principles of decorum, situation clearly influences Vanbrugh in the choice of building type.

The French translation of Palladio's *Quattro Libri* by Fréart de Chambray, published in 1650, was one source for Vanbrugh's ideas on propriety that it is known he owned and used in his work.[20] As noted above, he had been keen to get his hands on a copy of this particular

168 Vanbrugh's 'Temple of the Four Winds' (Belvedere), 1723–38, at Castle Howard.

edition, writing to Tonson on 13 July 1703 that 'Tis Palladio in French, wth the Plans of most of the Houses he built. There is one without the Plans, but 'tis that with 'em I would have'.[21] In this Vanbrugh would have seen Palladio quoting Vitruvius on the appropriate ornamentation of temples dedicated to particular gods at the outset of Book Four, and his definition of decorum as 'one of the most beautiful aspects of architecture'.[22] Fréart's edition included an explanation of Greek and Roman architectural terms in the last two books. Other, less obvious sources may also have informed Vanbrugh's ideas on propriety and decorum in ornament and, by extension, in stage costume and dress. For he would have been introduced to the idea of using ornamental styles and historical forms to symbolise particular virtues and

169 (*above left*)   Comic scene, from Sebastiano Serlio's *Secondo Libro* (1545), fol. 67v.

170 (*above right*)   Tragic scene, from Serlio's *Secondo Libro* (1545), fol. 69r.

171 (*left*)   Satiric scene, from Serlio's *Secondo Libro* (1545), fol. 70v.

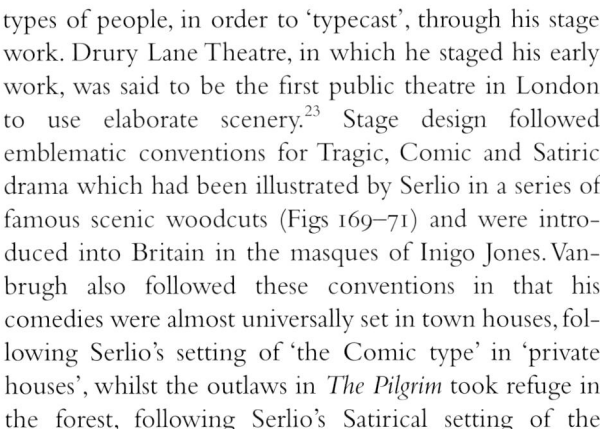

types of people, in order to 'typecast', through his stage work. Drury Lane Theatre, in which he staged his early work, was said to be the first public theatre in London to use elaborate scenery.[23] Stage design followed emblematic conventions for Tragic, Comic and Satiric drama which had been illustrated by Serlio in a series of famous scenic woodcuts (Figs 169–71) and were introduced into Britain in the masques of Inigo Jones. Vanbrugh also followed these conventions in that his comedies were almost universally set in town houses, following Serlio's setting of 'the Comic type' in 'private houses', whilst the outlaws in *The Pilgrim* took refuge in the forest, following Serlio's Satirical setting of the

'corrupt and the criminal' in 'wooded groves' (as was the legend of Robin Hood celebrated by Vanbrugh's Yorkshire Well; see Fig. 69).[24] Moreover the Prologue to Vanbrugh's *The Mistake* notes, with some irony, that in order to soften the mood, 'In Lace and Feather Tragedy's express'd,/And Heroes die unpity'd, if ill dress'd'.[25] In Restoration comedy a character's costume usually signified their status,[26] as for example with the Beau's costume in *The Relapse* examined shortly; these stage principles had much in common with those of heraldry since it was a herald's job to match the appropriate ceremonial dress to status and occasion (Figs 172, 173). Costume design had by tradition involved the recognisable – and therefore customary – characterisation of a variety of occupations, classes, virtues and vices, often based on Renaissance conventions established by catalogues of moral emblems and hieroglyphs. An edition of the most famous emblem book of all, Cesare Ripa's *Iconologia, or, Moral Emblems*, was published in England in 1709 and was used in the internal scheme of the great hall at Castle Howard.[27] Here again, through working with painters, Vanbrugh would have come into contact with emblematic conventions governing the representation of character and type similar to the rules of heraldic and architectural decorum.

172 Detail from William Hogarth's *Marriage à la Mode* (1745), in which an eighteenth-century Beau admires his reflection in the mirror, engraving, 68 × 89 cm.

(Fig. 174; see Fig. 144). It is within this development of Vitruvius's principles of decorum, emphasising a link between architectural and moral decorum, that Vanbrugh's general concern with ornamental propriety and his more specific recommendations to the Church Commissioners for 'a plain, but Just and Noble Stile', rather than 'such Gayety of Ornaments as may be proper to a Luxurious Palace', should be understood. Indeed, his call for propriety and plainness reflected the moral restraint in outward show that was widely seen by contemporaries as appropriate to Protestant buildings. Given these links between ornamental and moral decorum, it is fruitful to examine Vanbrugh's own attitude to morality and religious conformity for further insight into his approach to the appropriate display of luxury in buildings and dress.

★   ★   ★

173 The ceremonial costumes of the Garter Order, from Elias Ashmole's *The Institution, Laws and Ceremonies of the Most Noble Order of the Garter* (1672), pp. 234–5.

According to Serlio the corruption of traditional ornamental forms – the splitting of pediments and the addition of volutes – was not only best suited to particular, decorative buildings and elements, such as gates, but it also had a moral dimension in producing a style which he called 'licentious'.[28] This style was so called not only because it lacked the 'licence' of classical canonics but because it expressed the evils of the natural world – ranging from human vices to monstrous forms – which might more naturally be expressed by particular types of building, for example garden gates and festival buildings

174   Model gate design from Alexandre Francini's *Livre d'archi-tecture* (1640), pl. XXXVIII.

'THE REFORMATION HAS REDUC'D THINGS TO A TOLERABLE MEDIUM': FOPPINGTON'S POCKET AND VANBRUGH ON MORALITY AND ORNAMENT

It was noted in the Preface that the term 'Whig' generally connoted nonconformity not only in State but also in religious affairs. In thus stressing the value of individual freedom, Whigs included amongst their number nonconformists such as Quakers and Deists. Nonconformists considered the history of organised Christianity to be the story of the triumph of superstition over reason, symbolised by the Church's execution of Galileo and its opposition to early science. For example Lord Shaftesbury, a zealous Whig, was a nonconformist in religious matters, appearing to argue that there was no necessity for fixed religious doctrine since a tendency to virtue existed naturally in all men.[29] Lord Carlisle's religious sympathies were latitudinarian (that is, indifferent

to the particular creeds and government of the English Church), whilst there is strong evidence for the influence on him of Deist and Quaker beliefs.[30] True to his Whig affiliations, Vanbrugh famously lampooned the clergy both in his correspondence and his plays. Writing to the Duke of Newcastle on Christmas Day 1718, for example, concerning the repeal of the 'Occasional Conformity and Schism Act' he comments: 'I rejoyce with your Grace most heartily, on the destruction of the Earl of Nottinghams Bill. I find many of the Clergy of this Country, dispos'd to be more drunk than ordinary this Christmass, to enable them to bear this Great Affliction with such humility as becomes the Cloath'.[31] On the idea for a mausoleum at Castle Howard, he wrote to Lord Carlisle on 19 June 1722 that this form of burial was what 'has been practic'd by the most polite peoples before Priestcraft got poor Carcases into their keeping, to make a little money of'.[32] Carlisle's quintessentially Whiggish nonconformity in religious matters was seen, at least by some, to have influenced his novel choice of a pagan mausoleum, in preference to a Christian parish church, as his place of burial (Fig. 175).[33] Later, on 18 February 1724 Vanbrugh added to Carlisle that the 'true Spirit of the Clergy' was 'to meddle in everything'.[34] However, these apparent nonconformist statements do not mean that Vanbrugh was against organised religion *per se*, rather that he was in favour of an unpretentious, simple form of worship. The 'polite peoples' he refers to ranged from the Mogul rulers whose tombs he had witnessed on his travels in India (see Fig. 5), to the first, or so-called 'primitive', Christians whose liturgical and burial practices were projected by contemporary theologians as a model for those of the Church of England. Perhaps Vanbrugh had in mind the mausoleum of Constantine's daughter Costanza, built near Rome, or Theodoric's magnificent mausoleum, situated near Ravenna (Figs 176, 177).

Moreover as a writer of comedies, Vanbrugh was naturally deeply interested in questions of morality. As noted in Chapter One, his accounts record that he subscribed to the second edition of John Dennis's *Select Works* (1721), for example, including *Original Letters, Familiar, Moral and Critical* (1721),[35] and that he owned a quarto edition of Milton's *Poetical Works* (1720). The Vanbrugh family Bible and Book of Common Prayer which had belonging to his mother passed, on Vanbrugh's death, to his wife.[36] On the stage he sought to characterise immorality and vice as a warning and means of correction and, following in the footsteps of Aesop, each of Vanbrugh's plays has a moral. In echoing Aristotelian ideas as to the purpose of the stage, he comments in *A Short Vindication of The Relapse and The Provok'd Wife,*

175 Hawksmoor's Mausoleum at Castle Howard, 1728–42.

from Immorality and Profaneness (1698): 'For the Business of Comedy is to shew People what they shou'd do, by representing them upon the Stage, doing what they shou'd not'.[37] He continues that it was the business of plays 'to recommend Virtue and discountenance Vice: To shew the Uncertainty of Human Greatness; the sudden Turns of Fate, and the unhappy Conclusions of Violence and Injustice: That 'tis to expose the Singularities of Pride and Fancy'.[38] Vanbrugh must have seen the same reversals of fortune reflected in the ruins of English castles whose austere façades would readily have displayed the equivalent moral restraint, in terms of luxury, that he admired.

Nevertheless, given Vanbrugh's fondness for the 'comedy of errors' and for merriment even bordering on excess, he not surprisingly disliked the absolute models of moral behaviour cultivated by contemporary Catholics and arch-Protestants alike. In *The Relapse* (1696), for example, he observes in the Preface: 'As for the Saints (your thorough-pac'd ones I mean, with screw'd Faces and wry Mouths) I despair of them; for they are Friends to no body. They love nothing, but their Altars and Themselves: they have too much Zeal to have any Charity; they make Debauches in Piety, as Sinners do in Wine; and are as quarrelsome in their Religion, as other People are in their Drink'.[39] The (incorrect) impression that he therefore tolerated the adultery and immorality of the characters in his plays led to his being attacked by a puritanical clergyman named Jeremy Collier and in turn to the publication of his *Vindication* in 1698. In this defence Vanbrugh confirms his fundamental belief in the Christian – indeed, Protestant – moral order: 'I am fully convinc'd, as the most Pious Divine, or the most Refin'd Politician can wish me, how necessary the Practice of all Moral Virtues is to our Happiness in this World, as well as to that of another', adding:

176   The mausoleum of Costanza, built near Rome, from Sebastiano Serlio's *Terzo Libro* (1540), p. xx.

177   Theodoric's mausoleum, near Ravenna, *c.*520.

There is still in the Gown of the Church of *England* a very great Number of Men, both Learned, Wise and Good, who thoroughly understand Religion, and truly love it: From amongst these I flatter my self some Hero will start up, and with the naked Virtue of an Old Generous *Roman*, appear a Patriot for Religion indeed; with a Trumpet before him proclaim the Secrets of the Cloyster, and by discovering the Disease, guide the World to the Cure on't.[40]

In echoing the sentiments of the theologians of primitive Christianity, Vanbrugh goes on to link this call for 'naked virtue' in religion to its physical expression: 'Religion is not a Cheat, and therefore has no need of Trappings: Its Beauty is in its Nature, and wants no Dress'.[41] In *Aesop* he presents the love of 'Luxury' by contemporary noblemen as the antithesis of being what he calls 'Friends to Virtue' and in *The Confederacy* the ridiculous Clarissa is described as 'an expensive luxurious Woman, a great Admirer of Quality'.[42] Clearly this dislike of inappropriate luxury directly informs his recommendations to use a 'plain and noble' style for the London churches (in contrast to the 'gayety' of ornaments 'proper' to a 'luxurious palace') and, no doubt, his preference for the unadorned, enduring English castle whose beauty was equally 'in its Nature'. Following his attack on the clergy, Vanbrugh proposed interring the Duke of Marlborough at Blenheim 'with some plain, but magnificent & durable monument over him'.[43] Once again ostentation is to be avoided, for Vanbrugh did not see plainness and magnificence as incompatible.

The corollary of this attitude is Vanbrugh's distaste – and also that of Wren and Hawksmoor – for the opulence of foreign fashion and for the art of Roman Catholicism in particular. Echoes of this attitude are to be found in *The Relapse*, for example in Coupler's swipe at the Grand Tour when he says to Young Fashion: 'Hast thou then been a Year in *Italy*, and brought home a Fool at last? By my Conscience, the Young Fellows of this Age profit no more by their going abroad, than they do by their going to Church'.[44] Vanbrugh's stance against Rome and its Counter-Reformation baroque pomp is made explicit in his *Vindication* when in attacking 'the Grandeur of the Clergy' he clarifies that 'my Thoughts are got to *Rome*' and adds that 'The Reformation has reduc'd things to a tolerable Medium'.[45] Here again Vanbrugh avoids the extremes of piety and pomp. In this preference he echoes a fundamental precept of early Protestantism, since John Calvin had sought a 'middle way' in Protestant aesthetics which in its desire to temper extremes, whether moral or ornamental, stemmed from Aristotle's work on ethics.[46] The Protestant theologians

178   Inigo Jones's portico to St Paul's, Covent Garden, 1631–3.

of Vanbrugh's day identified a Calvinist 'middle way' in the decoration of the setting of primitive – and therefore their own – worship. This licensed ornate Gibbons carving internally but demanded a more austere exterior, in emulation of past models such as Inigo Jones's chapels and his church at Covent Garden (Fig. 178). William Cave for example observed in 1702 that 'the Christians of those [primitive] times spared no convenient cost in founding and adorning public places for the worship of God, yet they were careful to keep a decent mean between a sordid slovenliness and a too curious and over-nice superstition . . . so far as consisted with the ability and simplicity of those days'.[47] Vanbrugh would have seen firm, moralistic strictures linked to ornamental display in a much more immediate work, Campbell's introduction to the first volume of *Vitruvius Britannicus* (1715). As seen, Vanbrugh gave drawings to Campbell for his engravings, and is listed amongst the subscribers.[48] Taking his lead from Palladio, Campbell hardly surprisingly condemned the 'affected and licentious' works of Bernini and Carlo Fontana, and the 'widely Extravagant' designs of Borromini, 'who has endeavour'd to debauch Mankind with his odd and chimerical Beauties'.[49] As also seen, Vanbrugh was well aware of the work of the Italian baroque masters, in studying Bernini's fountain and adapting Michelangelo's doorcases (see Figs 56, 58).[50] Campbell also observed that 'the *Italians* can no more now relish the Antique Sim-

plicity, but are entirely employed in capricious Ornaments, which must at last end in the *Gothick*'.[51] Just as Collier had attempted to set standards of morality on the stage, so Campbell was here attempting to set them in architecture.

In fact Campbell's dislike of showy excess echoed sentiments to be found in the earliest of the English treatises on architecture. John Shute in 1563 had likened the decorative Composite Order to evil Pandora (Fig. 179); and whilst Henry Wotton in 1624 had associated the Tuscan column with the virtues of a 'sturdy well-limmed Labourer, homely clad', the Corinthian followed national Puritan tastes in being described in moralistic terms as 'laciviously decked like a Curtezane'.[52] At stake was the timeless balance between free expression, even moral 'licentiousness', in architectural decoration on the one hand, and a proper respect for the classical rules of decorum and ornamental canonics outlined by Vitruvius on the other. Under the watchful eye of the likes of Collier, Vanbrugh clearly also came across this tension in his works for the stage.

Wotton's Corinthian analogy presented the Order as if clothed in the fanciful costume of the courtesan. A further scene in Vanbrugh's *The Relapse*, concerning the clothing of the fashionable man of his day, the Beau, echoes this association between excessive decoration and foolish immorality. The Beau in question, Lord Foppington (who before ennoblement had been the

179   Composite Order as Pandora, from John Shute's *The First and Chief Groundes of Architecture* (1563).

equally aptly named Sir Novelty Fashion) addresses his tailor:

> Death and Eternal Tartures, Sir, I say the Packet's too high by a Foot.
>
> TAYLOR: My Lord, if it had been an Inch lower, it would not have held your Lordship's Pocket-Handkerchief.
>
> LORD FOPPINGTON: Rat my Pocket-Handkerchief! Have not I a Page to carry it? you may make him a Packet up to his Chin a purpose for it: But I will not have mine come so near my Face.
>
> TAYLOR: 'Tis not for me to dispute your Lordship's Fancy.[53]

Here 'fancy', or in this case the whims of fashion, triumphs over utility and common sense. Implied is the

need for a balance between utility and ornamental display which, by extension, Vanbrugh sought through his 'Castle Air'. This tale of Foppington's pocket might be unerstood to ridicule, by extension, the decorative forms of continental baroque and rococo architecture which to the Protestant mind had also promoted superfluity over utility and good taste. For it has been noted that Vanbrugh, like Hawksmoor and Wren, valued more eternal qualities such as symmetry and proportion over that of fashionable decoration. Also in Vanbrugh's case native historical forms such as the castle, which had largely escaped the dictates of fashion, as well as its once functional forms (such as crenellations and portholes) were often preferred to what he saw as 'Italian' ornament in the form of the Orders. Vanbrugh's 'Castle Air' can thus be seen to have been rooted in a morality which for the most part prioritised the plain over the superfluous and only sought to express luxury when it was appropriate (as most obviously in the case of 'luxurious palaces' such as Blenheim and Castle Howard).

It is worth noting in passing that Vanbrugh's preference for Protestant plainness and his dislike of the transient, showy tastes of the town accorded with his idealisation of the simple life and, following a well established dichotomy, the equation of this with life in the country.[54] On one of his 'Journeys of Pleasure' near the end of his life (made in 1725) Vanbrugh ate 'a Chearfull Cold Loaf at a very humble Alehouse' at Middleton Stoney in Oxfordshire, adding that it was 'the best meal I ever eat, except the first Supper in the Kitchen at Barns'.[55] (He had just been refused entry to Blenheim and evidently took comfort in the simplicity of his surroundings.) Just as Foppington personified foreign-influenced town vices, such as the love of court finery, so his would-be father-in-law, the rural squire Clumsey, represented more native virtues such as honesty and simplicity which are often associated in Vanbrugh's drama with the country and the properly maintained estate. In *Aesop* the virtue of one and the vice of the other is the obvious moral of the fable of the homely country mouse versus his fashionable town, and courtly, counterpart.[56] Town life as a basis of ruination is the moral of Vanbrugh's *A Journey to London* in which, for example, one of the servants, George, concludes 'An this be *London*, wa'd we were all weel i' th' Country again'.[57] Architecture, by implication of *The Relapse's* moral, should eschew expressing personal vanity: after all, Castle Howard celebrated a dynasty and Blenheim national glory.

In the epilogue of *The Relapse* Vanbrugh allows Foppington a degree of self-defence. For despite ridiculing 'Men of Dress', their excess was relatively harmless: 'Far, give me leave t'observe good Cloaths are Things/Have ever been of great support to Kings'. Implied is the age-old moralistic and decorous principle that display should be appropriate to rank, a principle which Vanbrugh, in common with Hawksmoor, can be understood to have attempted to apply in all his built work. One group of designs in which Vanbrugh would have been particularly sensitive as to the morality of ornament, and naturally applied his preferences concerning religious display, is that of the London churches.

'IN A PLAIN BUT JUST AND NOBLE STILE': VANBRUGH'S LONDON CHURCH PROPOSALS

Quakers, Presbyterians, Anabaptists and other dissenters from the Church of England had grown in number under the relaxed Protestant atmosphere which marked the policy of successive Whig governments under William and Mary. High Churchmen opposed any accommodation with the dissenters and, together with the Tories (their natural political allies), they held that the State religion under the pious reign of Queen Anne (from 1704) needed renewed support. When the Tories came to power in 1710 the High Church part enjoyed a complete (if short-lived) revival, of which fifty new churches were to have been a tangible expression (Fig. 180; see Figs 104, 105, 139). The new churches were to be paid for from the coal tax initially levied to fund the rebuilding of churches after the fire of 1666 and were guided by a series of Commissions, the first of which was set up by the new Tory government in 1711. This Commission was comprised of Church of England divines (mostly High Churchmen), elected officials (mostly Tories) and architects in the pay of the Crown. The last group comprised Wren as Surveyor of the Royal Works, his son and clerk (also Christopher), Thomas Archer as Groom Porter in the royal household and an amateur architect of note, and Vanbrugh as the Work's Comptroller. Vanbrugh was not reappointed to the second Commission formed in 1716[58] but as his letter of advice indicates, he played an active and influential role on the first Commission, in surveying ground, approving designs and attending meetings. On one of Hawksmoor's drawings for St George-in-the-East for example a pencil scribble records 'to Mr Vanbrugh in Duke . . .', indicating that drawings were submitted to Vanbrugh for comment and approval (Figs 181a and b).[59] Writing to Henry Joynes on 30 September 1711 concerning Blenheim, he notes: 'I thought to have come downe next week but shall be hindred by the Commission for Building the Churches'.[60] On 16 July 1712 Vanbrugh attended a meeting with the full Commission which

endorsed the idea 'that one general design, or Forme ['Modell' crossed out], be agreed upon for the fifty new intended Churches'.[61] Vanbrugh would therefore have been well aware of Hawksmoor's model plan entitled 'Basilica after the Primitive Christians' of 1711–12 (Fig. 182), produced for the Commission, and the debates in the Commission about the character of primitive Christianity which the plan reflected.[62]

Vanbrugh opened his own advice to the Commission by wishing that 'the fifty new Churches the Queen has

180 Hawksmoor's Christ Church, Spitalfields, 1714–29.

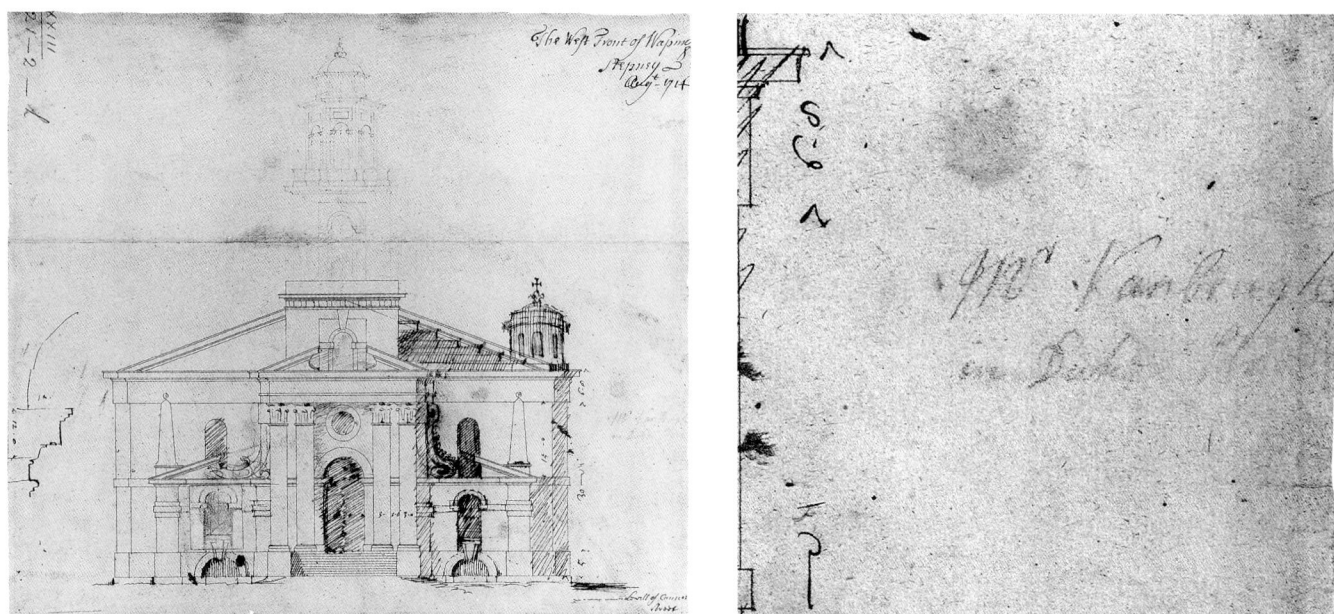

181 a and b   Hawksmoor's drawing for St George-in-the-East, August 1714, recording Vanbrugh's involvement in a faint pencil note on the right-hand side of the drawing, and detail [British Library, London].

182   Hawksmoor's plan entitled 'Basilica after the Primitive Christians', 1711–12 [Lambeth Palace Library, London].

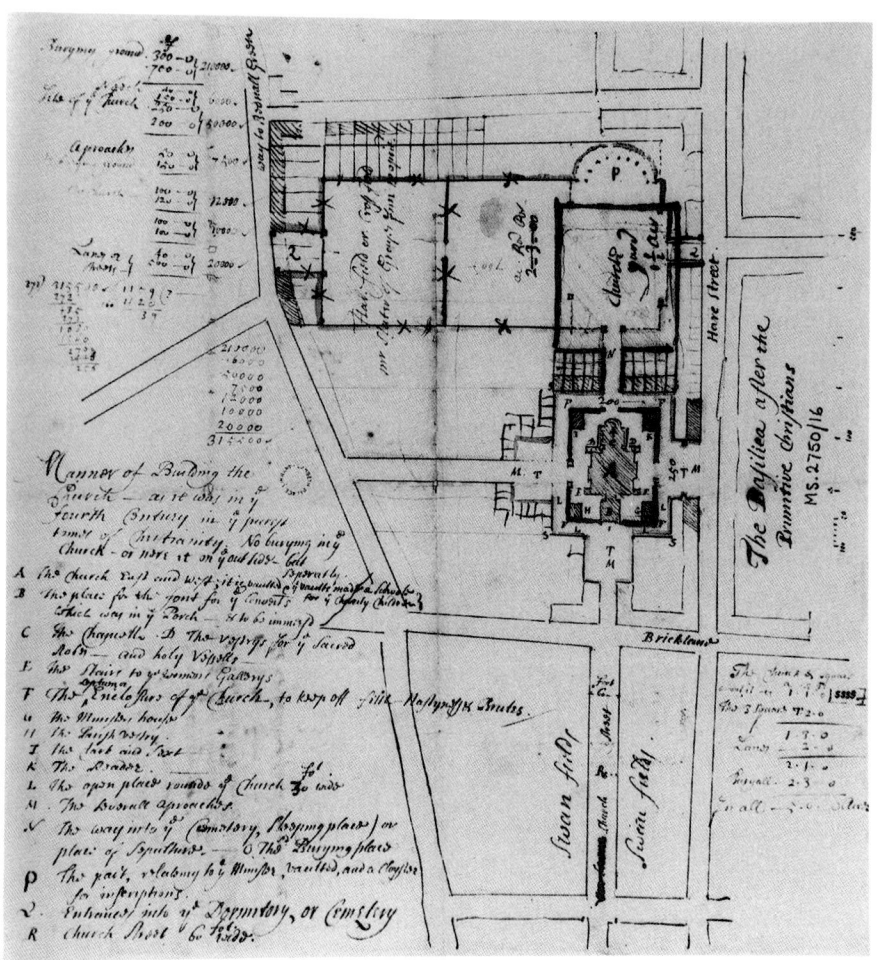

gloriously promoted the Building of' should 'remain Monuments to Posterity of Her Piety & Grandure'.[63] In his mood-orientated recommendations, it has been seen that Vanbrugh reflected contemporary ideals of primitive Christianity as well as Addison's desire for awe when observing that the

> Grace that [Church] Architecture can produce... shou'd generally be express'd in a plain, but Just and Noble Stile, without running into those many Divisions and Breaks which other buildings for Variety of uses may require; or such Gayety of Ornaments as may be proper to a Luxurious Palace. . . . That for the Lights, there may be no more than what are necessary for meer use... They ... take off very much, both from the Appearance & reality of strength in the Fabrick; giving it more the Air of a Gay Lanthorn to be set on the Top of a Temple, than the Reverend look of a Temple it self; which shou'd ever have the most Solemn and Awfull Appearance both without and within, that is possible.[64]

Just as the preacher manipulated the congregation's mood through oral images of solemnity, so Vanbrugh as a storyteller aimed to evoke these same images through form and details in stone. Here again, as previously observed, he calls for appropriate decoration matched to purpose following the principles of decorum – the 'gayety of ornaments' are seen as 'proper' to a 'luxurious palace', just as his somewhat Calvinistic desire for 'a plain but just and noble stile' is seen as best suited to a Protestant church. His expression 'meer use' suggests once

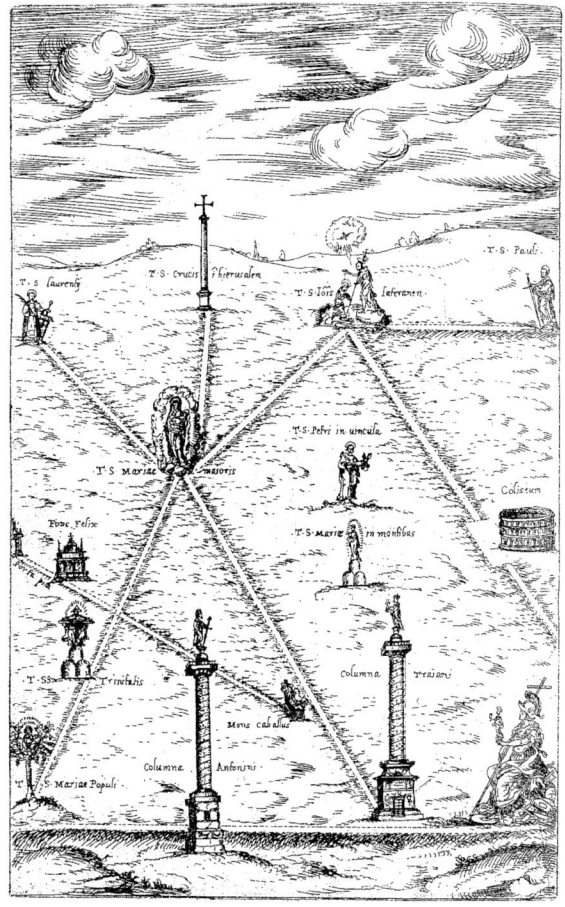

183   Diagrammatic plan of Domenico Fontana's re-ordering of Rome for Sixtus v, from Giovanni Bordino's *De Rebus Praeclare Gestis a Sixto V Pont. Max* (1588).

184   Wren's plan for London after the Great Fire of 1666 [All Souls, Oxford].

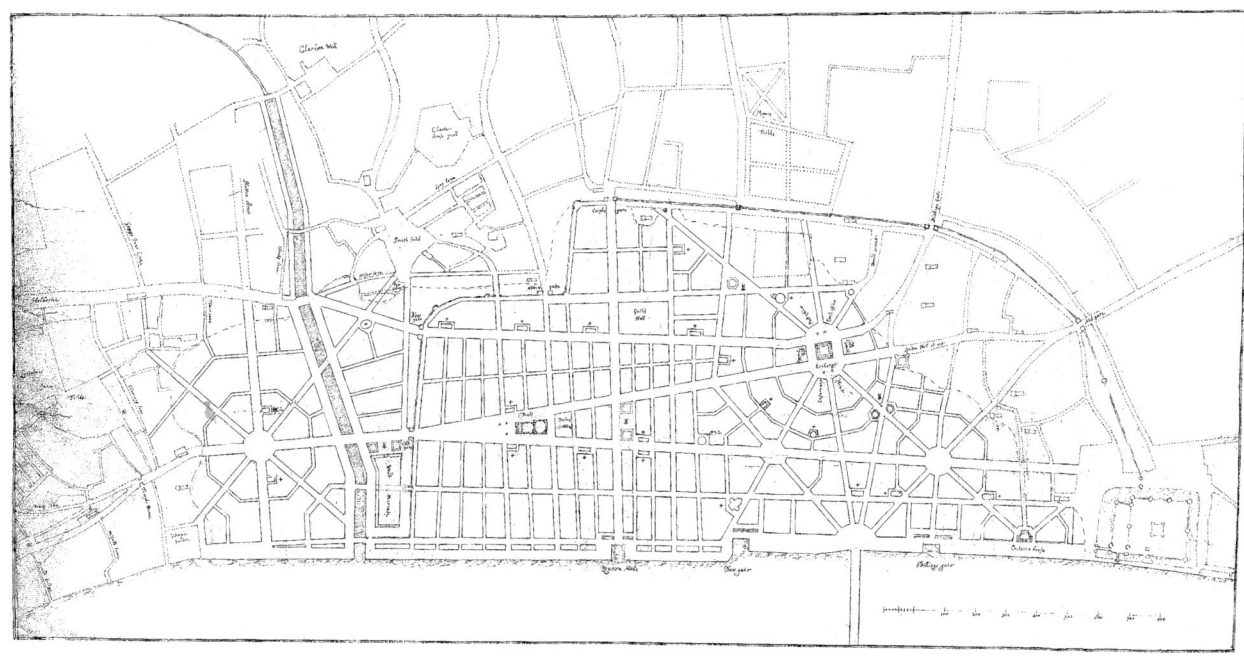

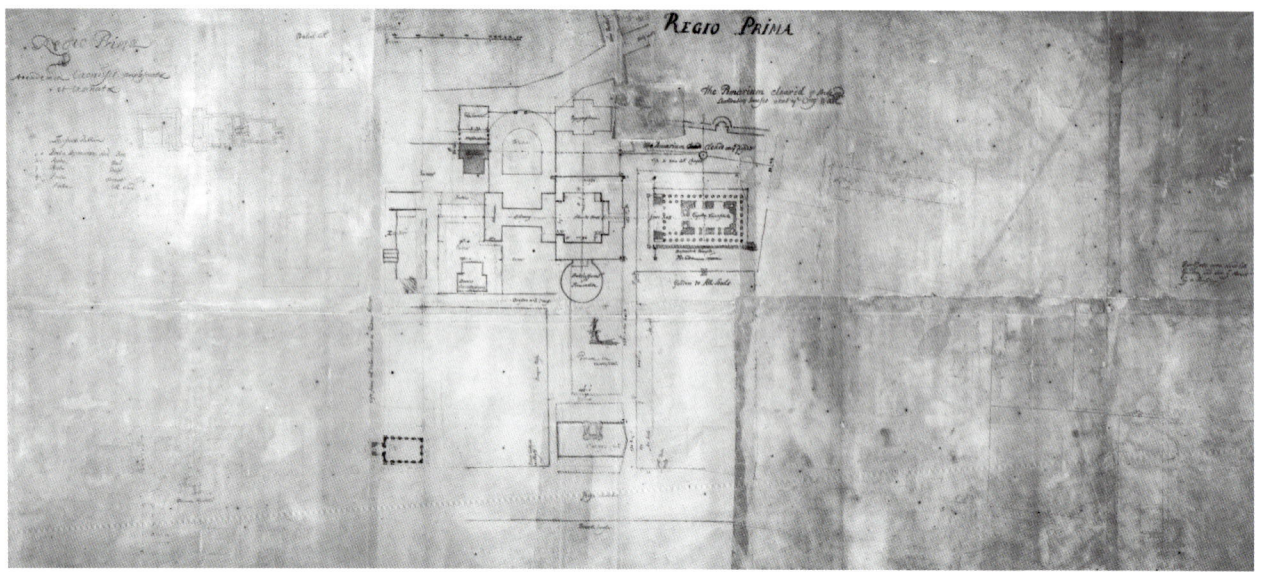

185   Hawksmoor's drawing entitled 'Regio Prima Aecademia Oxoniesis [*sic*] amplificata et exornata', *c.*1713–14 [Bodleian Library, Oxford].

186   Hawksmoor's plan for Cambridge, 1712 [British Library, London].

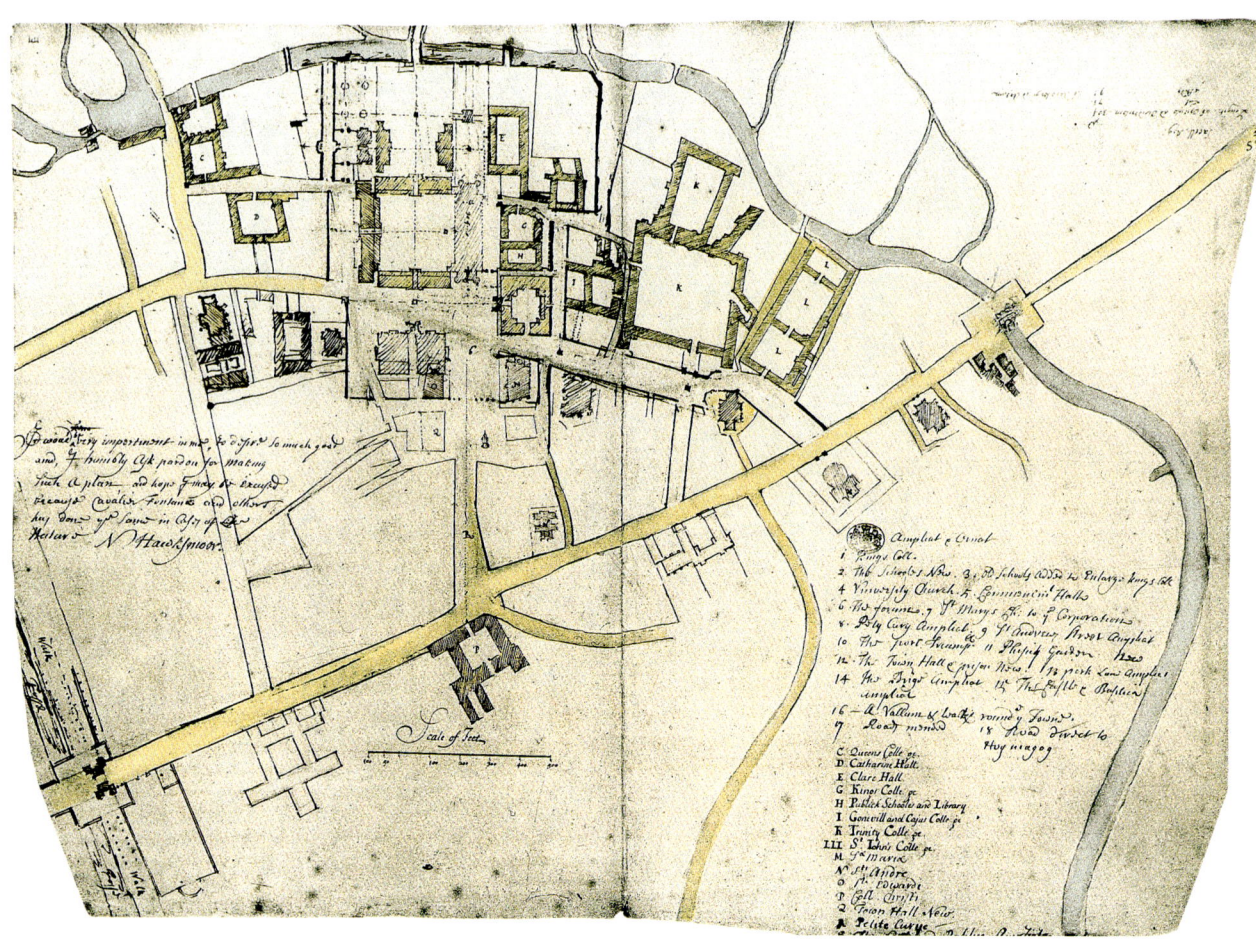

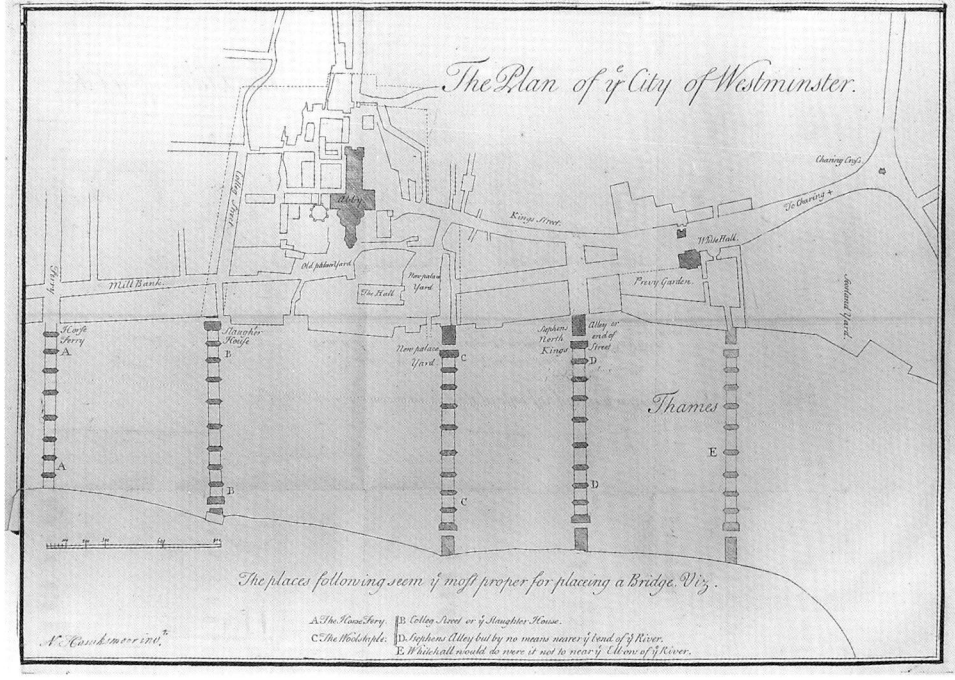

187   Hawksmoor's plan for Westminster, from his *A Short Historical Account of London Bridge* (1736).

more a preference for the symbolic and psychological purposes of architectural elements (in this case of windows and their light). This particular recommendation for plainness was influential, as Defoe records in his *Tour* of 1725 when noting that, taken together, the new London churches 'are rather convenient than fine, not adorned with pomp and pageantry as in Popish countries; but, like the true Protestant plainness, they have made very little of ornament either within them or without'.[65]

In his 'Proposals' Vanbrugh recommended freestanding churches and saw them as structuring a regular-planned city, positioned as they were 'to be fairly View'd at such proper distance, as is necessary to shew their Exterior Form to the best Advantage, as at the ends of Large and Strait Streets, or on the Sides of Squares and Other open Places'.[66] This calls to mind near-contemporary city plans with their vistas and axes by Domenico and Carlo Fontana for Rome and Wren for London (Figs 183, 184); indeed, these were the precedents which also influenced Hawksmoor in his near-contemporary plans for Oxford and Cambridge (*c.*1712–13) and his slightly later plan for Westminster (1736) (Figs 185–7).[67] Vanbrugh's preference for dignity, vistas and awe-inspiring forms echoed the recommendations of Palladio – which Vanbrugh studied carefully. For Christians should, according to Palladio in his fourth book, 'choose sites for temples in the most dignified and pres-

tigious part of the city, far away from unsavory areas and on beautiful and ornate squares where many streets end, so that every part of the temple can be seen in all its majesty and arouse devotion and awe in whoever sees and admires it'.[68] As part of this and following Vanbrugh's suggestion, the Commission had recommended burial take place in large cemeteries on the outskirts of town – albeit filled, as he advised, with 'Lofty and Noble Mausoleums' unprecedented in England.[69] As has been seen, Vanbrugh illustrated his proposals with his sketch of the obelisks, columns and pyramid mausolea at the English cemetery at Surat that he had visited when in India (reproduced in Appendix Two).[70]

Vanbrugh's involvement with the Commission led him to produce a number of actual church designs. On 2 November 1714 he submitted two designs for St Mary's in the Strand, for example, eventually built to designs by Gibbs.[71] A year later he submitted a design for St George's in Bloomsbury, which was approved, but the church was built to a different design by Hawksmoor. The surviving drawings for an unidentified church design attributed to him show a building which is indeed 'in a plain but Just and Noble Stile' (see Figs 138 and 167).[72] As was pointed out in Chapter Three, the design serves to illustrate the kind of architecture Vanbrugh had in mind as capable of evoking the mood of solemnity and awe, and clearly reflects the Calvinist aversion to rich display in favouring somewhat stark, primitive forms.

The two drawings show a tower, since he recommended that 'for the Ornament of the Towne, and to shew at a distance what regard there is in it to Religious Worship; every Church (as the Act of Parliament has provided) may have a Tower'.[73] They should be 'High and Bold Structures . . . of such Solidity and Strength, that nothing but Time, and scarce that, shou'd destroy them'. This reoccurring wish for durability was symbolised in Vanbrugh's design by the heavy quoins and keystones. In the end, none of his designs was built, possibly because of the apparent ridicule of priests in his dramas or because his dislike of the High Church faction sometimes led to indiscretions, as with his letter to a relation of 2 April 1713 with its reference to 'High-Church Blockheads'.[74] Yet in shifting the ground from design principles based on ancient Vitruvian models to those based on rhetorical ideas of visual contrast and mood, in perfect alignment with Addison's ideas, Vanbrugh's strictures obviously informed Hawksmoor's visually arresting compositions and his use of a vocabulary of keystones and quoins to form his own 'sermons in stone'.

II

'BUILDING HOUSES HERE T'OBLIGE THE PEERS': LUXURIOUS PALACES AND SHAM CASTLES

'WONDER ENOUGH IN THE STORY': CASTLE HOWARD AND BLENHEIM

Vanbrugh's best-known houses are Castle Howard and Blenheim Palace. In making explicit the emblematic, memorial role of Blenheim, I have noted that he wrote in his letter of 1709 to the Duchess of Marlborough that 'I believe it cannot be doubted, but if Travellers many Ages hence, shall be shewn the Very House in which so Great a Man Dwelt, as they will then read the Duke of Marlborough in Story'.[1] He evidently imagined that Blenheim would become a tourist attraction, on a par with the monuments of antiquity which were visited by contemporary travellers in order to understand better the legendary stories of the ancients which the history books recorded.[2] Vanbrugh goes on to make this narrative, rather than aesthetic, priority clear in somewhat modestly adding his observation that 'tho' they may not find art enough in the Builder, to make them admire the Beauty of the Fabrick they will find Wonder enough in the Story, to make 'em pleas'd with the Sight of it'.[3] As noted in Chapter One, by 'story' Vanbrugh meant nothing short of a 'legend': in his play *The Confederacy*, Clarissa recommends various extravagances to her husband by promising 'You will therefore be renown'd in Story'.[4] In these references to Blenheim are an indication, if one were needed, of Vanbrugh's intention to tell 'stories in stone' through the vocabulary of architecture. Both Castle Howard and Blenheim can thus be viewed as giant emblematic compositions narrating, rather like heraldry, the heroic character of their respective patrons and, following Marlborough's victories, the dawning of a new, particularly British Golden Age.

'PARADISE REGAINED': VANBRUGH AT CASTLE HOWARD

In 1699 Vanbrugh started to design Castle Howard in Yorkshire with Hawksmoor serving as his assistant and draughtsman.[5] This relationship continued until Van-

brugh's death in 1726, by which time he had designed the Pyramid Gate, Marlborough obelisk and the 'Temple of the Four Winds' (see Figs 153, 156, 195). Hawksmoor went on to design the Pyramid, Carrmire Gate, Temple of Venus and, most famously, the Mausoleum (Fig. 189; see Figs 136, 175, 192). The consistent element in this process was the patron, the Earl of Carlisle, and the interests which the Earl shared with his principal architect.

189   Hawksmoor's pyramid at Castle Howard, 1728.

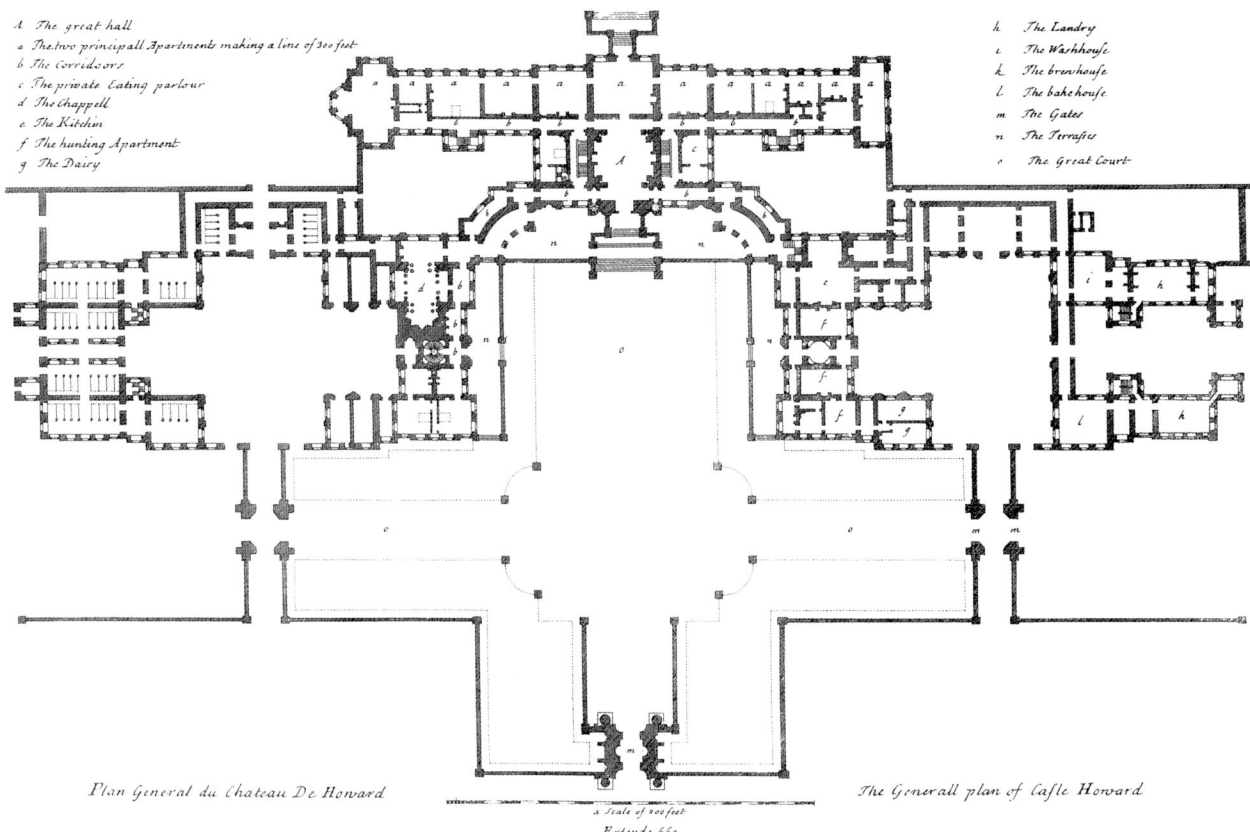

A The great hall
a The two principall Apartments making a line of 300 feet
b The Corridoors
c The private Eating parlour
d The Chappell
e The Kitchin
f The hunting Apartment
g The Dairy

h The Landry
i The Washhouse
k The brewhouse
l The bakehouse
m The Gates
n The Terrasses
o The Great Court

Plan General du Chateau De Howard   The Generall plan of Castle Howard

a Scale of 200 feet
Extends 660

190   Engraved general plan of Castle Howard, from Colen Campbell's *Vitruvius Britannicus*, vol. I (1715), pl. 63.

For Vanbrugh had much in common with Carlisle. As seen earlier, both men were leading Whigs, both Kit Cat members and both were interested in heraldry. Chapter Two discussed the fact that despite Vanbrugh's lack of previous experience, the Earl as Deputy Earl Marshal responsible for organising all aspects of Court ceremonial installed his architect in the revived office of Carlisle Herald in March 1703, as a reward for the early work at Castle Howard and as a prelude to Vanbrugh's becoming Clarenceux King of Arms. Carlisle's interest in heraldry was despite – or perhaps because of – the newness of the Carlisle line. Although the 'house' of Carlisle was an old title (of the Hay family), it had been re-established in the seventeenth century by the first Earl, Charles Howard (1628/9?–85). Carlisle was thus not naturally part of the landed class: a hostile manifesto issued on 10 December 1701 noted sarcastically 'wee the Gentlemen of Ancient Families & substantiall Freeholders of the County of Cumberland . . . First and principly we commend our dying Liberties, Properties, Priviledges, and Immunities into the hands of the Noble Peer the Lord C[arlisle] to be disposed of according to his discretion for ye supporting & Maintaining his Grandeur at

Court'.[6] In the light of the associations between Vanbrugh's roles as herald and architect, and between heraldry and architecture, the main house of Castle Howard might be seen as a vast exercise in heraldry in order to legitimise a title of relatively recent origin, clearly built as it was to celebrate the 'house' of Carlisle. After all, rather like this 'heraldic house', Castle Howard was raised on the site of the ruins of an older house, called Henderskelfe Castle. This heraldic purpose would surely have been emphasised by the use, once again, of the Doric Order, given its explicit heraldic characteristics introduced by Wotton in 1624, and by Carlisle's arms in the pediment on the rear of the house (Fig. 188; see Fig. 107).[7]

In fact an obvious distinction is made at Castle Howard between the style of the front, with its military character, and that of the rear, garden façade, with its Corinthian pilasters (Fig. 191; see Fig. 188). It is often claimed that this contrast in the ornamentation of the house produces a poor dichotomy,[8] and Hawksmoor was certainly well aware that such contrasts could be criticised. In defending Vanbrugh's design to Carlisle, he pointed out the importance of optics, since 'The South side, and the North front of your Ldships house cannot be seen together at the same Time, nor at any time upon the Diagonall (or angular view)'.[9] If the pilasters and accompanying ornament were indeed used, like heraldic emblems, to express the identity of Carlisle and his house, then the reason for this contrast may lie in the split nature of Castle Howard. For the house was conceived of as both a 'castle' imposed on the landscape, implicit in the house's name, and a domestic palace belonging to its garden.[10] Hawksmoor himself pointed out this dichotomy in a comment to Carlisle on 12 October 1734 concerning the house, that 'It is the seat of one of [the] chief nobles of Britain, it is both a Castle and Pallace conjoyn'd'.[11]

Castle Howard's identity as a military building is conveyed through a variety of means. The approach to the house is marked by ever more refined martial and heraldic elements, in the form of the crenellated walls and rustic Carrmire Gate (designed by Hawksmoor), Vanbrugh's slightly more refined Pyramid Gate followed by his inscribed obelisk celebrating Marlborough's victories (see Figs 136, 153, 156). Judging from the famous idealised view of the house published in the third volume of *Vitruvius Britannicus* (1725), triumphal arches were to have marked the entrance to the forecourt (see Fig. 151). The ornamentation on the north front of the house continues this martial theme, as a concluding backdrop to, and final refinement of, the landscape elements on the approach side. As was noted, the façade has giant pilasters of the Doric Order (which replaced Corinthian pilasters of an early scheme). I have shown that as an austere 'masculine' Order, the Doric was particularly suited to the character of soldiers according to Serlio, whose citation of St George as an example would have given the Order the special relevance to his English readers discussed in Chapter Two. The conception at Castle Howard of the Doric pilasters as a type of heraldic ensign is emphasised by accompanying martial trophy in the form of flags, breastplate and cannon (symbols absent on the earlier designs; see Fig. 93). The pilasters are set against walls with incised joints that result in a form of smooth-faced rustication particularly suitable, according to Serlio, to castles.[12] This lent a further 'masculine' character to the façade, following Hawksmoor's remarks regarding the pillars on the Temple of Venus in the grounds that 'Without the Rusticks they will be too feminin (*trop Megre*) as the French call it'.[13] Moreover the façade rests on a basement which, according to Hawksmoor, 'is plain and represents (or intended so to do) a grand entire plinth made out of one solid Rock of Stone', thereby signifying 'Strength'.[14] Here Hawksmoor refers, like Vanbrugh, to the use at Castle Howard

191   The north, front façade of Castle Howard, from 1699.

of the decorum-based concept that ornament and texture could symbolise particular human and natural qualities.

This work is in strong distinction from the delicate (feminine) ornamentation of the private, south façade, which celebrates the contrasting ideal of the house conceived as a palace set in nature tamed by art (see Fig. 188). The façade faces the garden and its parterre, lake,

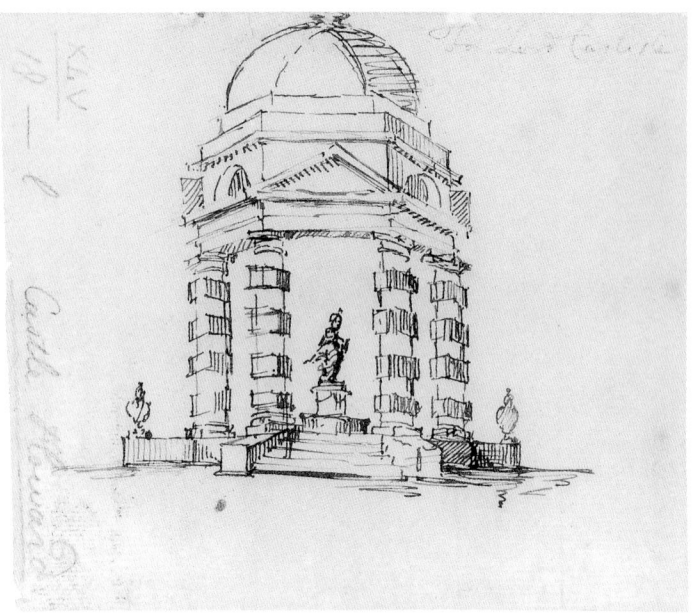

192   Hawksmoor's sketch of the octagonal Temple of Venus at Castle Howard, undated [British Library, London].

wilderness and temples to the Four Winds (Belvedere) and to Venus (Fig. 192). Giant pilasters, this time of the Corinthian Order – the feminine Order most appropriate to Venus and Flora according to Vitruvius[15] – are accompanied by leaf motifs, boys blowing conch shells at seahorses and a general ornamental flamboyance. Appropriately, the pediment serves as a plinth to statues of Pallas Athene (Minerva), Flora with a cornucopia of flowers and Ceres with a sheaf of corn (see Fig. 310). Again appropriately, a large relief of Diana on the east end of the garden wing (Fig. 193) faces Ray Wood, which is described as the goddess's 'fav'rite Grove' in a poem of around 1733 by Carlisle's daughter, Lady Anne Irwin.[16] This poem opens with a quotation from Virgil's *Georgics* in celebrating Castle Howard as a product of a new Golden Age, that is, 'happy Plenty, the Effect of Peace'. Slightly later, Thomas Gent's *Pater Patriae: Being, An Elegiac Pastoral Dialogue occasioned by the most lamented Death of the Late Rt. Honble and Illustrious Charles Howard* (1738) grieved 'Ah, me! dear Stephon! Is my Lord then dead!/That God-like Soul, with Astrael Virtues, fled'. A woodcut used to illustrate Gent's poem pictures the house and landscape at Castle Howard in this Arcadian light (Fig. 194). According to Virgil, the age of iron and war gave way to that of gold and peace under the rule of the legendary virgin Astraea. Vanbrugh was well aware of Virgil's work: as noted in Chapter One, in *The Mistake* he ridiculed the quotation of Virgil out of context.

Thus a form of integrated symbolic (or emblematic) programme can be suggested for Castle Howard, compatible with Hawksmoor's reference to the house as both a castle and a palace.[17] Clearly conceived as a 'gateway' to the garden beyond, Vanbrugh's house marks the physical boundary between two opposing 'realms'. Just as the north (public) face is masculine in character, dramatically triumphing over the forces of human conflict and mortality, the south (private) front is feminine and celebrates, through traditional Golden Age imagery, the ideals of peace and a renewed harmony with nature. Encircling the dome are the busts of antique philosophers – including Seneca, Socrates, Cicero and Plato[18] – which look down from all sides of their 'heaven' on this timeless narrative of war giving way, as it were, to peace. As already seen, the return of the age of peace and plenty (symbolised by Venus and Diana) after the Civil War (symbolised by Mars) is the theme of Dryden's masque at the close of *The Pilgrim* adapted by Vanbrugh (first performed at the dawn of a new century, in 1700). The idea of the façades as presenting ornamental 'opposites' was emphasised by Hawksmoor when noting that, whereas 'The South Front is Smooth in ye upper order, with, a continuall arcade, and The Basement Rusticated, per Contrà The North ffront is Rusticated in the order, and so is the Wing, and the Basement, Like a sollid rock quit plain'.[19] This narrative may account for the (otherwise inexplicable) change in the style of the north front, from the Corinthian of the early schemes to the Doric of the built façade. For as time went on the project came increasingly to celebrate the military glory of Whig rule which had become evident from Anne's succession in 1702 – eventually explicitly commemorated by Vanbrugh's obelisk – and the new Golden Age of peace and plenty expected in its wake. The massive crenellated walls enclosing the estate also play their part in this scheme (see Fig. 128). As a committed Protestant and reader of Milton,[20] Vanbrugh would have been well aware of the potency of the image of the biblical paradise which had, after all, been surrounded and defined by walls, and it was noted that the Castle Howard walls were primarily symbolic structures.

In keeping with the understanding of the house and landscape at Castle Howard as a paradise inspired by the study of Virgil and ancient literature, Vanbrugh's 'Temple of the Four Winds' was conceived as a garden 'temple' to reading and writing (Fig. 195). The 'temple' was intended as a place for Carlisle to read, study and enjoy wine-assisted contemplation – for annotated on Hawksmoor's drawing of an alternative design of 1723 are 'Books' and 'A Bot Wine' in the alcoves (Fig. 196) and his accompanying letter to Carlisle pointed out that his

193   The large relief of Diana on the east end of the garden wing at Castle Howard.

designs would 'make a very good Studdy'.[21] As noted earlier, Vanbrugh emphasised the status of the new building by insisting on the name of 'Temple', rather than mere 'Belvedere', when linking form and situation by observing 'this Building I fancy wou'd more naturally take the Name of Temple which the Situation likewise is very proper for'.[22] The importance to Vanbrugh of his building's temple character is underlined by the fact that he was equally clear that in this case it should be purely *all'antica* in style, continuing:

> But I still flatter my Self, nothing of this plain or Gothick Sort will be determin'd on at last . . . The first Design I sent, with the 4 Porticos will be found very near (perhaps quite) as cheap, as any Gothick Tower, that has yet been thought of. My Lord Morpeth about a month ago, View'd all the Designs I had sent, He declar'd his thoughts utterly against anything but an Italian Building in that Place, and entirely approv'd the first Design'.[23]

Carlisle rejected the alternative designs submitted by Hawksmoor, which were more rustic in character – that is, as Hawksmoor put it, 'built with rough stone'.[24] For the 'Italian Building', or 'Temple with the four Porticos'

194   Woodcut illustrating the Castle Howard landscape as an arcadia, from Thomas Gent's *Pater Patriae* (1738).

195　Vanbrugh's 'Temple of the Four Winds' (Belvedere) at Castle Howard.

as Vanbrugh also described it,[25] its architect turned once again to Palladio's domestic architecture. As Chapter One noted, the Temple is most obviously based via Palladio's famous Villa Rotonda on his reconstruction of the Temple of Fortuna Primigenia at Praeneste[26] (see Figs 60, 61), as well as alluding, perhaps, to more ethereal garden structures such as the domed Temple of Venus described in the *Hypnerotomachia Poliphili* (Fig. 197), with its eight rotating winged figures representing the winds.[27] Following the example of the porticoes of the Villa Rotonda, Vanbrugh used Ionic columns, a choice perfectly appropriate given the literary purpose of his Temple. For echoing Vitruvius, who had emphasised the Ionic's 'middle quality'[28], Serlio specified the Order's suitability to 'men of letters and of a quiet life – not robust, but also not delicate'. Vanbrugh's application of these principles of decorum to his design was indicated by Hawksmoor (who as Vanbrugh's assistant would surely have known his intentions) when reassuring Carlisle that the design was 'founded upon ye Rules of ye Ancients' (adding with a nod to the importance of the spectator

that 'we are assured of ye good effect of it').[29] The statues of the sibyls guarding the entrances, which stand in place of the sphinx initially proposed by Hawksmoor (Fig. 198; and which echoed the pyramids elsewhere in the landscape), were put there after Vanbrugh's death but they make clear the association between his *all'antica* garden 'temple' and prophetic wisdom and ancient learning, initiated by the writer–architect and executed by Hawksmoor under Carlisle's learned direction.[30] Here again, appropriately enough a boundary between two distinct realms is marked symbolically through ornament. Like Vanbrugh, Hawksmoor was, after all, also acutely aware of the importance of using ornament to convey the character of his patron and of a building's situation and function.[31] Indeed, the garden location of the temple is reflected in its flora and fauna decoration over the doors, as well as the shells over the windows which were carved in 1727, a year after Vanbrugh's death (Figs 199, 200).

Elsewhere the theme of the four winds had been represented in the form of the blowing cherubs' heads on

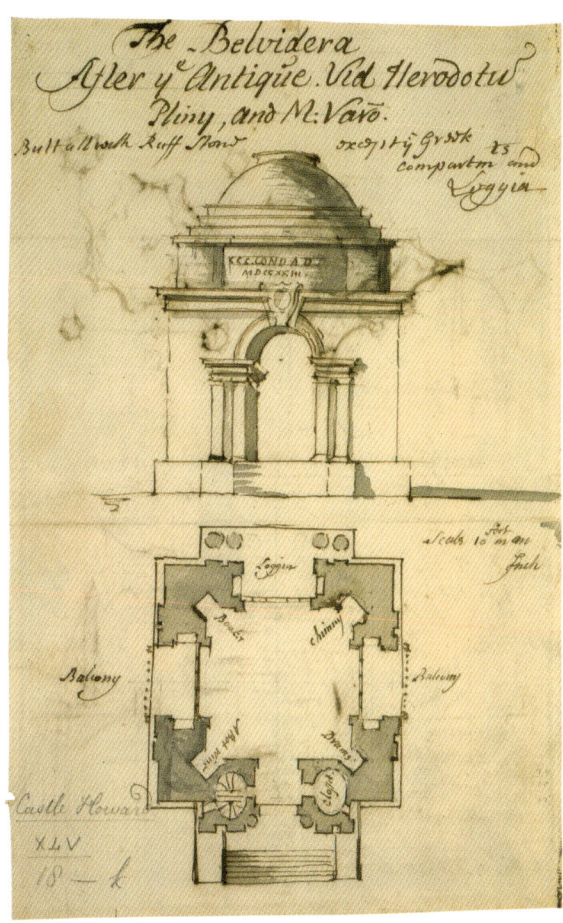

196 (*above left*) Hawksmoor's proposed square Belvedere at Castle Howard, 1723 [British Library, London].

197 (*above right*) The domed Temple of Venus from the *Hypnerotomachia Poliphili* (1499).

198 (*right*) Hawksmoor's sketch of a sphinx, for the base of Vanbrugh's 'Temple of the Four Winds' at Castle Howard, from his letter to Carlisle of 11 April 1730 [Castle Howard Collection, Yorkshire].

the west façade of the Painted Hall at Greenwich Hospital (see Fig. 37), where they patriotically emphasised Britannia's status as ruler of the waves and centre of world trade. The house and garden of Castle Howard can in turn be seen not only to reflect the character and family of Lord Carlisle but, more generally, to 'dramatise' the eternal, cyclical theme of temporal glory, mortality and the long-expected natural rejuvenation of the nation brought about by Whig rule.

★   ★   ★

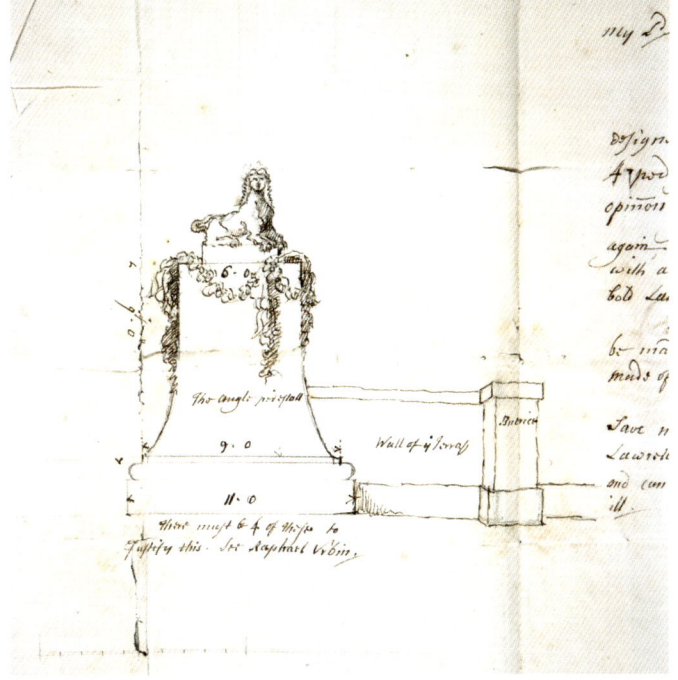

199   Flora and fauna decoration over the doors of Vanbrugh's 'Temple of the Four Winds', carved in 1727.

'READ THE DUKE OF MARLBOROUGH IN STORY': VANBRUGH AT BLENHEIM

Vanbrugh's installation as Comptroller of Works in 1702 led to his appointment as architect of Blenheim in 1705, the foundation stone of which was laid that year (Fig. 201). Hawksmoor again served as his assistant, since the work was (in principle) paid for by the government and was therefore within the scope, if not the direct responsibility, of the Office of Works.[32] As Vanbrugh explained, 'The Queen having resolv'd to build a House for the Duke of *Marlborough*, at her own Expence, and thinking fit, that the Method for defraying that Expence should be, by issuing Moneys to his Grace, for that end, without Account; The Building was not conducted by her Board of Works, but left to him, to employ such Officers and Workmen as he should see fit'.[33] Writing to the Duchess of Marlborough on 27 May 1710, Vanbrugh justified his additional remuneration for work on Blenheim by defining his responsibilities: 'I am *here Surveyor*, which

Relates to the Designing and Direction of the Building'.[34] In contrast, fifteen years later, Hawksmoor wrote to the Duchess on 2 September 1725 somewhat immodestly that 'when the Building began, all of them (the Builders) put-together, could not stir an inch without me'.[35] Vanbrugh evidently drew on his knowledge of human nature when directing the building site at Blenheim, since unlike Hawksmoor he had never served as a Clerk of Works; he urged his clerk, Boulter, for example not to 'endeavour to terrify Men from giving us Information when they think they see us wrong'd, tho' it may happen there is only the Appearance of it'.[36] Despite his success in designing one of the grandest houses in Europe, by 1716 Vanbrugh had quarrelled with the Duchess and resigned, as the Introduction outlined, and initially taken Hawksmoor with him.

At least publically, both Marlborough and his architect wisely considered the house a memorial to the deed (the Duke's defeat of the French in 1704) and not to the doer. In Kneller's oil sketch celebrating the reward of the

200 Shells over the windows of Vanbrugh's 'Temple of the Four Winds', carved in 1727.

house to the Duke (Fig. 202), the Queen presents a drawing of Blenheim not to Marlborough but to a figure representing 'Military Merit'.[37] Shaftesbury had attacked opulent palace-building by the nobility – with Blenheim and Castle Howard in mind – in moralistic terms, noting in 1712 that such building was performed 'at a vast expense' and represented 'a false and counter-feit Piece of Magnificence' which could be 'justly arraign'd for its Deformity'.[38] The Aristotelian ethical concept of 'magnificence' (*magnificentia*) had been used by architectural writers from Alberti onwards to justify expenditure on large-scale public works and, as a matter of architectural decorum, distinguish appropriate public and charitable displays of magnificence from inappropriate ones of luxury.[39] Vanbrugh reflected this concept when defining the role of Blenheim as that of a public memorial in his letter to the Duchess of 27 May 1710: 'This Building, tho' ordered to be a Dwelling house for the Duke of Marlborough, and his posterity, is at the Same time *by all the World esteemed, and looked on as a Publick Edifice,*

raised for a Monument of the Queen's Glory through his great Services. Which (I desire leave by the way to observe) is a most ample justification of the great Expence, which has been made for the beauty, Magnificence and Duration of the shell'.[40] Writing on 30 September of the same year to Lord Poulet and Robert Harley (the Chancellor of the Exchequer), Vanbrugh reiterates that he could be forgiven for seeing the building 'as an intended Monument of the Queens Glory, than a private Habitation for the Duke [of] Marlborough'.[41] He added that the house should be 'consider'd as both a Royall and a National Monument.' Nevertheless, Vanbrugh clearly also saw his role at Blenheim as helping to represent the Duke's legend in stone, an ambition finally achieved by the Duchess with Hawksmoor's assistance after Vanbrugh's resignation. This aim was much like – albeit on a far grander scale – his sponsorship of one of the plates in Tonson's publication of Clarke's *C. Julii Caesaris* (1712; see Fig. 91).[42] For as was noted in Chapter Two, with its opening portrait of, and

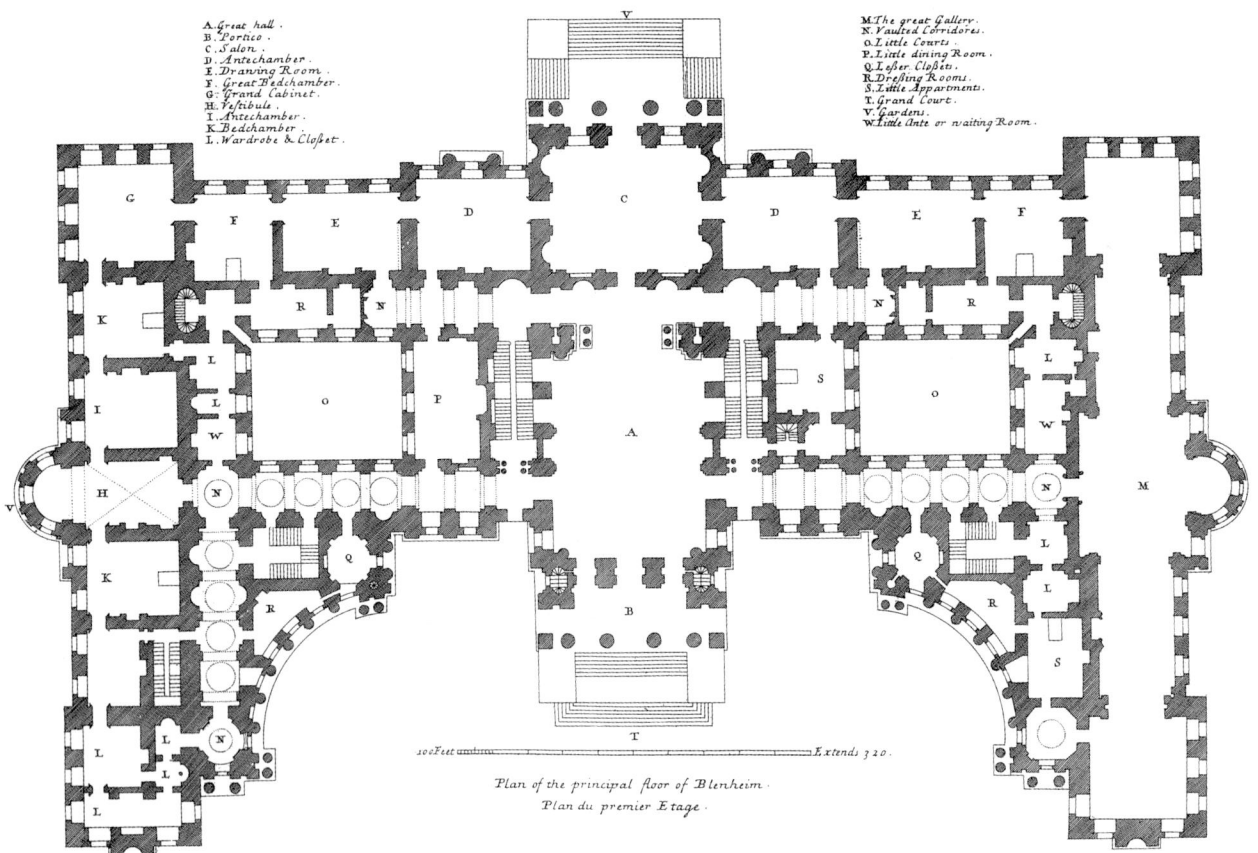

A. Great hall.
B. Portico.
C. Salon.
D. Antechamber.
E. Drawing Room.
F. Great Bedchamber.
G. Grand Cabinet.
H. Vestibule.
I. Antechamber.
K. Bedchamber.
L. Wardrobe & Closset.

M. The great Gallery.
N. Vaulted Corridores.
O. Little Courts.
P. Little dining Room.
Q. Lesser Clossets.
R. Dressing Rooms.
S. Little Appartments.
T. Grand Court.
V. Gardens.
W. Little Ante or waiting Room.

100 Feet   Extends 320.

Plan of the principal floor of Blenheim.
Plan du premier Etage.

201   Engraved plan of the principal floor of Blenheim, from Colen Campbell's *Vitruvius Britannicus*, vol. 1 (1715), pl. 56.

dedication to, the Duke and its subsequent plates of Caesar, Clarke's book was intended to emphasise the Duke's legendary status as Caesar's modern – although as a Whig convert, more politically enlightened – military equivalent. In so doing the book's intentions mirrored those at Blenheim, in serving as inspiration for Clarke's own age.

Given Vanbrugh's unambiguous reference to the narrative role of architecture, made explicit here yet fundamental to the reading of all his buildings, how exactly did he tell the 'story' of the Duke of Marlborough at Blenheim? Much as at Castle Howard, at Blenheim the ornament and forms were conceived of in heraldic terms to emphasise British military glory under the Duke's command. Once inside the great court, the visitor passes Vanbrugh's side gates to the kitchen court, with their giant pared-down Doric columns (without triglyphs) and rustic bands recalling in style Giulio Romano's 'Porta Cittadella' in Mantua and Serlio's fortified gates in his Book VII (Figs 203, 204). Heraldic beasts in the form of the British lion savaging the French cockerel surmount these gates, relating Marlborough's victory in

graphic terms and, as noted in Chapter One, a verbal pun translated into the decoration. Progressing towards the house, the square towers crowned by giant finials of upside-down French fleurs-de-lys supported by cannon balls tell the same story (Fig. 205).[43] Marlborough was, after all, Master of the Ordnance.

This mood is continued by the giant Corinthian portico to the house, either side of which are fictive arcades of Doric pilasters which sweep out as if to form the apse of a Roman forum (Fig. 209). In fact the portico was originally intended also to be of the Doric Order, as might be expected given the Order's associations with martial and masculine strength made explicit at Castle Howard and elsewhere on Vanbrugh's front façades. However, the style was changed to the Corinthian during construction (in the winter of 1706–7) – that is after the column diameters had been fixed – due to a need to increase the height of the portico and, in following the canonic proportions of the columns, thereby use a more slender Order.[44] The Duke's heraldry is blazoned in the tympanum and the pediment is surmounted by a statue of Pallas Athene (here in her

202   Queen Anne presenting a drawing of Blenheim to a figure representing 'Military Merit', by Sir Godfrey Kneller, 1708, oil on canvas, 127 × 101.5 cm [By Kind Permission of His Grace The Duke of Marlborough].

203   Vanbrugh's inner gate to the kitchen court at Blenheim.

204   A fortified gate from Sebastiano Serlio's *Settimo Libro* (1575), p. 95.

205   Towers at Blenheim crowned by giant finials of upside-down French fleurs-de-lys supported by cannon balls.

206 and 207   Vanbrugh's outer gate to the kitchen court at Blenheim.

war-like guise) together with those of chained captives on the broken pediment above (recalling the iconography of imperial Rome).[45] The overall arrangement of the front façade, with its curved wings, statues, heavy cornice and giant Corinthian portico, bears a striking similarity to that of the temple of Mars Ultor as illustrated by Palladio and discussed and illustrated in plan by Wren (Fig. 208).[46] There is no doubt that Vanbrugh used his copy of Palladio in the design of Blenheim, for he writes to his Clerk of Works, Henry Joynes, in February 1710, 'Pray ask Kitt Cash if the French book of Paladio be not in Mr Strongs Shedd; I thought we had had it in Towne but don't find it'.[47] Palladio's illustration of the ancient temple to war would have been perfectly appropriate as a model at Blenheim. Wren for one clearly understood the form of ancient temples as expressive of their dedication. He notes in his fourth 'Tract' on architecture that 'As studiously as the Aspect of the Temple of *Peace* was contrived in Allusion to Peace and its Attributes, so is this of *Mars* appropriated to War: a strong and stately

208   Temple of Mars Ultor, from the fourth book of Andrea Palladio's *I quattro libri dell'architecture* (1570), ch. vii, p. 16.

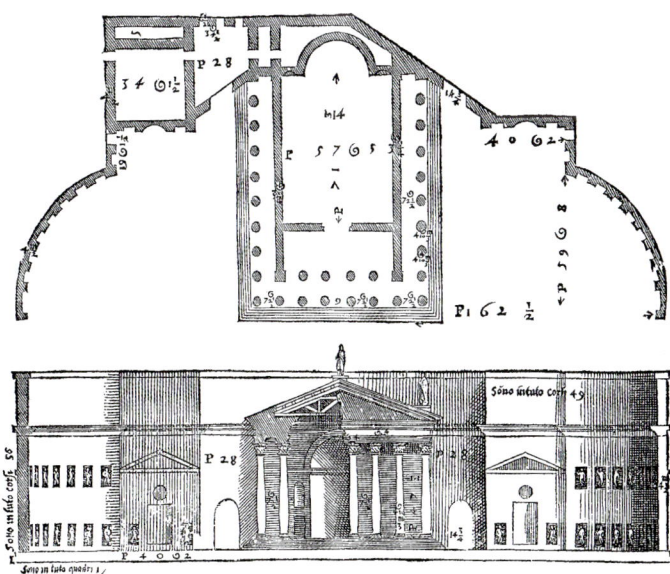

209   The north, front façade of Blenheim.

Temple shews itself forward'.[48] Indeed, much like at Blenheim, Wren records that this temple front was built 'to muster up at once a terrible Front of Trophies and Statues, which stand here in double Ranks . . . Thus stands the Temple like the *Phalanx*, whilst the Walls represent the Wings of a *Battalia*'. It is tempting to imagine the heroic British General and Master of the Ordnance viewing his Blenheim façade in a similar way, with the legion of Doric and Corinthian columns deployed like military ensigns, surmounted as these columns were by statues and trophies of war.

In line with Vanbrugh's awareness of the evocative power of names, evident in his plays and in the associational quality of the name 'Castle Howard', so at Blenheim the archetype of the medieval castle was recalled semantically through the Office of Works's reference to the palace as 'Blenheim Castle', an association reinforced through the cannon balls and other trophies of arms, the fortress-style gates and the battlements to the kitchen court.[49] Unlike at Castle Howard, though,

at Blenheim the triumphalism of the front extends to the rear. Here the Doric pilasters of the earliest known design, of 1704–5, were again modified to a more regal fluted Corinthian portico as built, above the cornice of which is an actual trophy of victory (Figs 210, 211).[50] The engraving of this garden façade in *Vitruvius Britannicus* (1715) depicts an equestrian statue of Marlborough crushing his enemies, either side of which stand the lion and eagle of the Duke's crest (see Fig. 99). On the façade as built, a captured bust of Louis XIV in the guise of a Roman general (taken by the Duke from the Porte Royale of Tournai in 1709) forms the centrepiece, in triumphalist reference to the iconography of the archetypal palace of the age, Versailles. The caryatids on the west front continue this narrative theme, given their traditional role in Greek architecture as representations of the captured women of Carya (see Figs 134, 135).

It has even been speculated that Vanbrugh's magnificent, if somewhat useless, bridge at Blenheim (see Figs 7, 8) was built to 'recall' the Duke's crossing of the Nebel

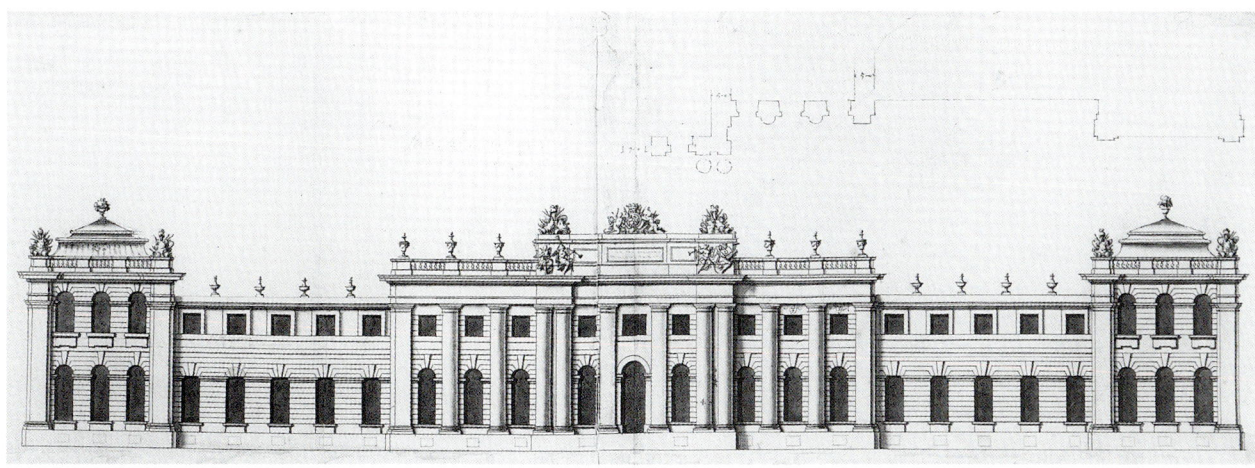

210 Hawksmoor's drawing illustrating the original Doric theme of the south façade of Blenheim, c.1704–5 [Bodleian Library, Oxford].

that had preceded victory near the Belgian village of Blenheim.[51] Certainly the huge lake which now gives purpose to the bridge was put there long after Vanbrugh's death, by Lancelot 'Capability' Brown. Vanbrugh was passionate about this bridge and commented to the Duchess on 10 July 1716 that 'I am mighty willing to defer the Greenhouse for a very natural reason which is, I dont love it. As for the Bridge I do love it; but will overcome my passion and not be troublesome about it'.[52] And again on 27 July he adds:

211 Rear, garden façade of Blenheim.

And I hope you will in almost every article of the Estimate for finishing this great design, find the expence less than is there allow'd. Even that frightful Bridge, will I believe at last be kindlier look'd upon if it be found (instead of twelve thousand pounds more) not to cost above three; and I will venture my whole prophetick skill, on this one Point, That if I liv'd to see that extravagant project compleat, I shall have the satisfaction to see your Grace fonder of it, than of any part whatsoever of the House, Gardens or Park: I don't speak of the Magnificence of it, but the agreeableness which I do assure you Madam has had the first place in my thoughts and contrivance about it: which I have said little of hitherto; because I know it wont be understood till tis seen; and then every body will say, *t'was the best money* laid out in the whole design *And if at last,* there is a house found in that *Bridge your Grace will go and live in it.*[53]

Vanbrugh obviously intended the illusion of Blenheim's size, to which this bridge contributed, to form part of the theatricality of the house and as such to evoke the desired feeling of wonder in the spectator. Moreover whilst many other houses had more outbuildings than at Blenheim, elsewhere according to Vanbrugh these 'look like a Ragged Village Wheras these being Compriz'd within One regular Handsome Wall, (And being likwise regularly dispos'd within) Form a Court, which by this means Adds to the Magnificence of the Dwelling, but not to the Quantity of it'.[54] Fully aware of the grandiosity of his architecture, and his undoubted need to form an architectonic equivalent to Dryden's revival of heroic verse, Vanbrugh constantly had to reassure Lord Carlisle and the Duchess of Marlborough regarding what he termed the 'conveniency' of his 'long Passages, High Rooms &c'.[55]

The landscape which today surrounds the main house at Blenheim is the work of later hands, and of Brown in particular. Yet clues as to the meaning, or conception, of the original gardens can be found in contemporary literature. Addison and Thomas Clayton's semi-opera *Rosamond* was first performed in Drury Lane in March 1707, with stage sets depicting Woodstock Park. The work dramatised the murder of Rosamond by the jealous queen of Henry II and was dedicated to the Duchess of Marlborough. It ran to many editions and was published in Addison's collected *Works* of 1721 to which, as noted, Vanbrugh subscribed.[56] Clearly his letter to the Duchess of 1709 concerning Woodstock Manor, with its special mention of 'Rosamond's bower', was intended to recall this eponymous drama of two years earlier and its romantic associations, especially given that the drama

had been dedicated to her, and further underlines the links between Addison and Vanbrugh discussed in Chapter Three. The Duchess must have particularly identified at this time with Rosamond's plight, awaiting her lover's return from martial conflict, and Vanbrugh no doubt considered that this gave poignancy to his appeal to save the Manor. After all, he is careful to remind her of the Manor's role concerning the king, as 'the Scene of his Affections'.[57]

In *Rosamond* the king seeks solace in the bower for, much as Marlborough rested in his garden from his victories against the French, so Henry rested from his wars, also with the Gauls,

> Not the loud *British* shouts that warns
> The Warrior's Heart, nor clashing Arms,
> Nor Fields with hostile Banners stow'd,
> Nor Life on prostrate *Gauls* bestow'd,
> Give half the Joys that fill my Breast,
> While with my Rosamond I'm blest.[58]

The opera plays with the timeless idea of the garden as the setting for love and death, reflected in the 'Et in Arcadia Ego' theme of the 'Arcadian Shepherds' by Poussin and the popular 'ruins in nature' theme of what Vanbrugh has been seen at Blenheim to refer to as contemporary 'Landskip Painters'. In idealising the garden, and the bower in particular, as a paradise, Addison's opera surely reflects the intentions behind Vanbrugh's proposals for the landscape at Blenheim as a refuge from, rather than a celebration of, martial conflict memorialised by the house. The queen introduces the scene in Act One:

> Enchanted Ground
> And soft *Elysiums* rise
> Flow'ry Mountains,
> Mossie Fountains,
> Shady Woods,
> Chrystal Floods
> With wild Variety Surprize.[59]

Vanbrugh echoed this aspect of visual surprise, or rather the need for it, when observing to the Duchess that 'That Part of the Park which is Seen from the North Front of the New Building, has Little Variety of Objects Nor dos the Country beyond it Afford any of Vallue. It therefore Stands in Need of all the helps that can be given'.[60] Later in the opera a Page enjoys a vista of the type commonly employed by Vanbrugh:

> O the soft delicious View,
> Ever Charming, ever New!
> Greens of various Shades arise,

Deck'd with Flowers of Various Dies:
Paths by meeting Paths are crost,
Alleys in winding Alleys lost;
Fountains playing through the Trees,
Give Coolness to the passing Breeze.

This might be taken for a description of the garden at Blenheim as planned and in part realised by Vanbrugh and others, with its crisscrossing paths, 'cabinets' and water features (see Fig. 133).

In the printed edition of *Rosamond* dedicated to the Duchess, the opening poem 'to the author' by Addison's friend Thomas Tickell confirms the contemporary understanding of the intention behind the gardens at Blenheim as the recreation of an ancient paradise:

Nature and Art in all their Charms
  combin'd,
And all Elysium to one View confin'd!
No further could Imagination roam,
Till Vanbrook fram'd, and Marlbo' rais'd
  the Dome.[61]

In making explicit the idea that Vanbrugh was recreating this paradisiacal setting for the enactment of British history, the opera went on to visualise his design for the house at the opening of Act Three. Here Marlborough is alluded to as one of 'Britannia's Heroes, yet unborn' and Henry stands in, as it were, for the Duke in dreaming about the house rising from the ruins of the bower. A guardian angel exclaims

To calm thy Grief, and lull thy cares,
Look up and see
What, after long revolving Years,
Thy Bow'r shall be!
When Time its Beauties shall deface,
And only with its Ruins grace
The future Prospect of the place.
Behold the glorious Pile ascending!
Columns Swelling, Arches bending,
Domes in awful Pomp arising,
Art in curious Strokes surprizing,
Foes in figur'd Fights contending,
Behold the glorious Pile ascending![62]

The scene changes from medieval Woodstock to the plan of Blenheim Castle, thus offering further evidence, if any were needed, of Addison's close partnership with Vanbrugh. A second angel then exclaims: 'He sees, he sees the great Reward/For Anna's mighty Chief prepar'd'. Once more the opera prefigures Vanbrugh's letter to the Duchess, in linking the bower's ruins to Blenheim's prospects, whilst his argument against the destruction of the Manor on the grounds of failing to consider the importance to 'Travellers many ages hence' echos the sentiments of the opera towards the recognition of 'Heroes immers'd in time's dark womb'.[63] Here again, in these images of 'swelling columns' and 'bending arches' conjured up by Addison himself is a clear indication of the staged effect of wonder which Blenheim was intended to evoke in the onlooker.

212   The north, front façade of Seaton Delaval, Northumberland.

Chapter 6

'SOMETHING OF THE CASTLE AIR': CHARACTERS IN STONE AT KIMBOLTON AND SEATON DELAVAL

In Chapter Three it was pointed out that Vanbrugh followed the conventions of Restoration drama in giving his *dramatis personae* and their buildings descriptive names evoking their intended character – Beast Hall, Headpiece Hall, Wagonrut-Lane, Smoke-dunghil Farm and so on. In *The Relapse* (1696) the country squire Sir Turnbelly Clumsey lives in a primitive castle complete, as the text makes clear, with gate, drawbridge and moat. The old house is evidently a stranger to classical principles of proportion and order. Young Fashion comments: 'the Seat of our Family looks like *Noah's* Ark, as if the chief part on't were design'd for the Fowls of the Air, and the Beasts of the Field'; to which his servant Lory replies: 'Pray, Sir, don't let your Head run upon the Orders of Building here', and adds the previously quoted line: 'Igad, Sir, this will prove some Inchanted Castle; we shall have the Gyant come out by and by with his Club, and beat our Brains out'.[1] True to convention, Clumsey's castle or fortified house matches perfectly his rough but honest 'down-to-earth' character. Unfortunately for Vanbrugh, Swift had also followed these allegorical conventions when identifying the diminutive character of 'Goose-Pie' house with, as Swift saw it, the character and achievements of its architect.

In line with the rhetorically based principles of architectural decorum outlined in Chapter Four, Vanbrugh saw his domestic architecture as akin to these stage buildings and indeed to heraldry in using ornament and forms (the castle chief among them) to express the patron's character, social position and consequent level of refinement. After all, through his role as a herald Vanbrugh was well aware of the efficacy of symbols to express a patron's nobility and character. Concerning character, Caroline Van Eck has noted that the 'concept connecting the visual arts with rhetoric and drama is that of character, the visual or outward appearance of a building by which its true nature and that of its owner is revealed, just as

the character of a dramatic personage is revealed by speech, actions and gestures'.[2] Hawksmoor had also worked references to his patron's identity into his buildings: on the façades at Easton Neston, for example, the Composite capitals have, in place of their canonic rosette, lion's heads in direct reference to the patron, Lord *Leominster* (Fig. 213), whilst at Greenwich Hospital (where Vanbrugh served on the Board of Directors and

213   Detail of a Composite capital on the pilasters at Easton Neston, Northamptonshire, 1695–1710, designed by Hawksmoor.

214   The east, front façade of Kimbolton Castle, Cambridgeshire, by Vanbrugh, the portico added by Alessandro Galilei *c.*1719.

later as Surveyor) it has been seen that the four Ionic capitals on the east front of the King William Building of 1702 have festoons with shellfish in reference to the building's maritime associations (see Fig. 38). Much as Vanbrugh sought through a vocabulary of symbols to tell what he termed the heroic 'Story' of the Duke of Marlborough at Blenheim, so at Kimbolton in his ornamental additions he aimed at 'a very Noble and Masculine Shew' appropriate to the character of the Earl of Manchester.[3]

'A VERY NOBLE AND MASCULINE SHEW': KIMBOLTON AND THE 'CASTLE AIR'

Early in the summer of 1707 Vanbrugh was called by the Countess of Manchester to Kimbolton (Fig. 214), near Huntingdon in Cambridgeshire, whilst her husband, Charles Montague (a fellow Kit Cat member and the fourth Earl) was serving as ambassador extraordinary in Venice. Kimbolton was a four-square medieval house remodelled at various times, the last involving the addi-

tion of an *all'antica* skin to the interior courtyard in the 1690s. The south façade of the house had collapsed and the proposals by the local carpenter–builder, William Coleman, were asymmetrical and judged inadequate. Vanbrugh reported to the Earl on 18 July 1707 that 'the Whole Garden Front has come downe' and that the Countess 'did me the honour (when she saw it must do so) to, ask my Advice in carrying it up Again'.[4] He took Hawksmoor along as his draughtsman to assess the situation. The problem at Kimbolton was how best to relate the centre line of the new façade (Fig. 215), by preference symmetrical, to the existing rooms and courtyard behind and to the garden and ornamental canal in front.[5] The desirability of imposing symmetry was stressed by Vanbrugh in his letters to the Earl, continuing for example in the July letter: 'we all Agreed Upon the enclos'd Design; which Differs very much from what Coleman had drawn, And particularly in that he had not brought the Door of the House into the Middle of the Front', adding on 22 March 1708: 'And the Salon beyond it, is Almost as big as the Hall, and looks mighty pleasantly Up the Middle of the Garden and Canall'.[6] Van-

215 *(facing page)*   The south façade of Kimbolton Castle.

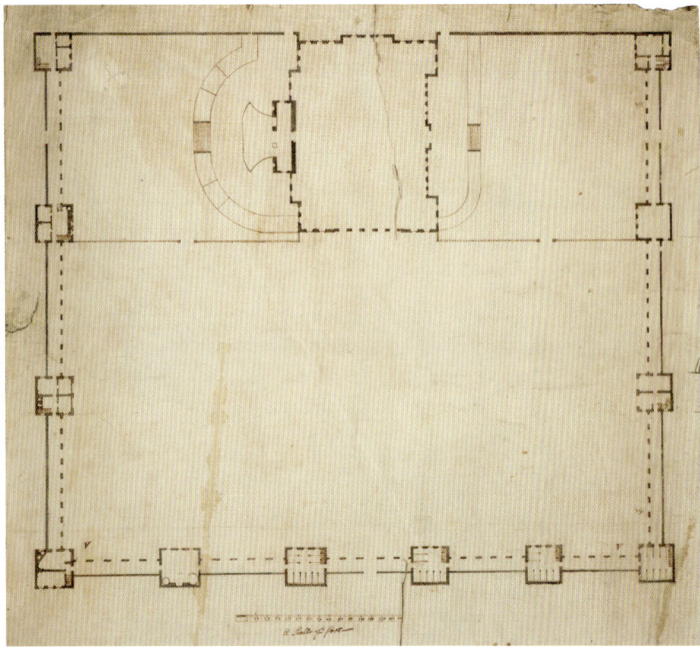

216   Vanbrugh's preliminary plan for Kimbolton Castle with a perimeter wall and towers similar to those at Vincennes château, drawing by Vanbrugh's Office [Huntingdon County Records].

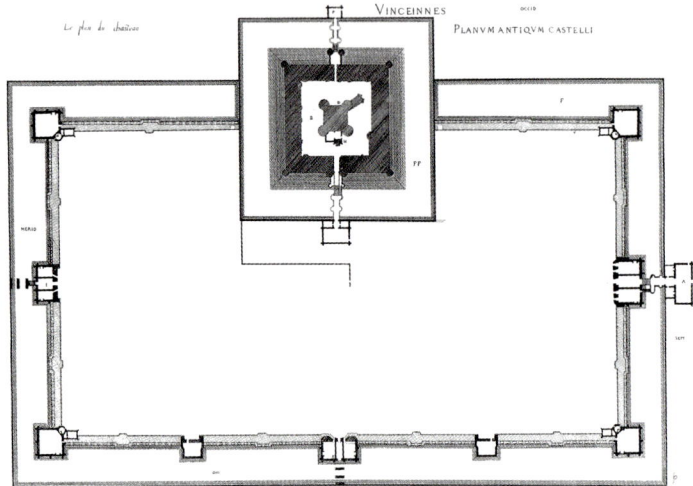

217   The plan of Vincennes, from Jacques Androuet du Cerceau's *Les plus excellents bastiments de France* (1576–9).

brugh employed his sense of the theatrical in his replanning of the house, in designing what he called a novel 'Room of Parade' which recalled the French 'salon'. This type of room had been illustrated in Serlio's seventh book and was no doubt seen by Vanbrugh when in France. He explains the novelty to the Earl on 18 July 1707:

> Your L^dship will here See something, that differs in the Cast of the Rooms, from the Common mode;

which is, to go immediately out of the Drawing Room into the Bedchamber. But the Drawing room here, falling in the beginning of the Line, had the Bed Chamber been next, there cou'd have been no regular nor propper way out of this Front into the Garden, which wou'd have been an Unpardonable want. There was therfore a necessity for some new Contrivence. And I thought, there cou'd nothing in reason be Objected to being Surpris'd with a large Noble Room of Parade between the Drawing room and Bedchamber; especially since it falls so right to the Garden, that the Door is in the Middle of the Room, and takes exactly the Middle Walk and Canall. For my part; I cannot but hope, 'twill prove in the generall Opinion An Agreable (tho' Unusuall) Accident in the Appartment . . . I wish it cou'd have been made a reall Salon, by carrying it up into the Next Story, but that wou'd have destroy'd one of the three Bedchambers Above, which My Lady thinks cannot be Spar'd. 'Twill however be eighteen foot high, which is no contemptible thing, tho' not what in Strictness One wou'd wish.[7]

Concerning this south, garden façade, Vanbrugh continues with a key passage which explains much of his general intentions and associational stylistic approach. As Chapter Two discussed, he clearly intended to evoke in the mind of the onlooker not only the image of the castle but also that of the archetypal chivalric castle – none other than Windsor, home of his beloved Garter: in his letter of 1707 he explains in the previously quoted lines that

> As to the Outside, I thought 'twas absolutely best, to give it Something of the Castle Air, tho' at the Same time to make it regular. And by this means too, all the Old Stone is Serviceable again; which to have had new wou'd have run to a very great Expence; This method was practic'd at Windsor in King Charles's time, And has been universally Approv'd, So I hope your L^dship won't be discourag'd, if any Italians you may Shew it to, shou'd find fault that 'tis not Roman, for to have built a Front with Pillasters, and what the Orders require cou'd never have been born with the Rest of the Castle: I'm sure this will make a very Noble and Masculine Shew; and is of as Warrantable a kind of building as Any.[8]

The castle theme seems to have been in Vanbrugh's mind from the start of his work at Kimbolton, since a drawing survives of a preliminary scheme which included a perimeter wall and towers similar to the arrangement at Vincennes (Figs 216–18; see Fig. 19).[9] In the event he achieves his 'Castle Air' principally through

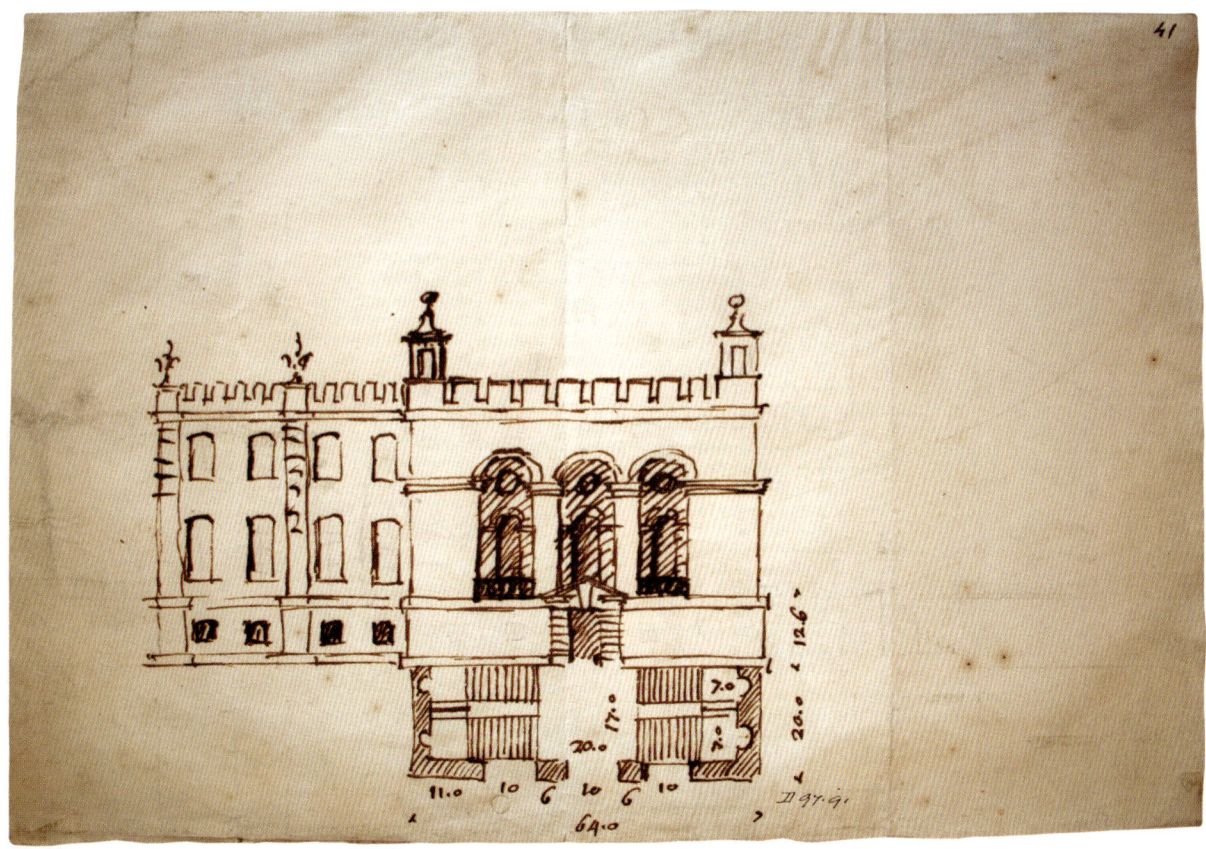

218   Vanbrugh's preliminary design for the east entrance of Kimbolton Castle, *c.*1707 [Victoria and Albert Museum, London].

219   The south façade of Kimbolton Castle, drawing by Vanbrugh's Office, 1707 [Victoria and Albert Museum, London].

220   The north façade of Kimbolton Castle.

the presence of the 'battlements' along the roofline (Fig. 219), as he describes them in a letter to the Earl on 17 August 1708.[10] In addition, the massive walls with their quoins, the unadorned central door on the western façade without porch or applied bay, the rough materials indicative of what he terms 'Manly Beauty',[11] the astylar façades with their crenellations and the suggestion of corner towers in the projecting western end blocks are all intentionally reminiscent of the medieval fortified house (Figs 220, 221). The modern, symbolic and associative roles of these elements at Kimbolton are obvious, given that any danger of actual attack had long passed. As noted in Chapter Three, since Kimbolton was the house within which Henry VIII imprisoned his wife Katherine of Aragon, it carried rich historical associations which Vanbrugh's dramatic crenellated motifs sought to evoke. Perhaps the observer was meant to reflect on the liberties of a more enlightened age.[12] Van-

brugh's reference to Windsor, closely followed by his rejection of Italian decorative forms, strongly implies that the work at Kimbolton was seen by him as explicitly British in character. Given his subsequent identification of masculinity with astylar façades, a use of the Orders as either columns or pilasters in this context seems not only to have been alien or foreign but to have carried an implicitly female character, as a form of superfluous, over-decoration, reflecting the prejudices of Wren.[13] Vanbrugh was anxious to reassure the Earl that, in the absence of the Orders, the astylar character of the façade was a suitable reflection of the nobility of both his house and (male) title.

However, in Vanbrugh's desire for 'Something of the Castle Air, tho' at the Same time to make it regular', the 'tho' implies the distinction between the noble but unruly native style (the 'Castle Air') and the classical principles of regularity and proportion. Indeed, as

221   The west, rear façade of Kimbolton Castle.

quoted earlier, on 9 September 1707 he further observed to Manchester: 'I shall be much deceiv'd if People don't See a Manly Beauty in it when tis up, that they did not conceive cou'd be produced out of such rough Materialls; But tis certainly the Figure and Proportions that make the most pleasing Fabrick, And not the delicacy of the Ornaments: A proof of wch I am in great hopes to Shew y^r L^{d}ship at Kimbolton'.[14] Vanbrugh thus repeats his association between the symmetries and proportions of a house and its owner's level of refinement – qualities which evidently transcended a house's richness of decoration, as his preference for plainness here demonstrates. The emphasis placed on the observers' perception ('See a Manly Beauty') once again resembles the manipulation of the audiences' emotions through stage scenes and dramatic effects in Vanbrugh's opera house or when watching one of his dramas. It is as if a dramatic character is being introduced, in this case the Earl, whose character of 'noble masculinity' is flattered by Vanbrugh's new castle-like façade with its combination of masculine details and proportioned symmetry.

It follows that Vanbrugh may well have seen the all-important use of these *all'antica* principles of proportion and order, and on occasions even the additional display of what Lory called 'the Orders of Building', as in some way taming uncivilised forces. These forces were reflected, for Lory at least, in the archetypal 'Inchanted Castle' to which the existing medieval house at Kimbolton inevitably alluded. After all, the virtue of taming unruly characters is one of Vanbrugh's principal dramatic themes, as for example with the disciplining of Sir John Brute in *The Provok'd Wife*. Moreover, as noted in Chapter One, in 1726 Vanbrugh almost certainly purchased for his son Charles Ovid's *Metamorphoses*, with its stories of the subjugation of a chaotic universe into harmonious order (Fig. 222).[15] Stories drawn from Ovid

222   Frontispiece of Book v (including the rape of Proserpine, centre right) from Jacob Tonson's 1717 folio edition of Ovid's *Metamorphoses*, engraved by Elisha Kirkall.

were later represented through the two statue groups on the skyline at Grimsthorpe Castle as well as the representation of Phaeton at Castle Howard (see Figs 50, 305, 306).[16] This tension between order and chaos is also to be found in the satyr gate of 1705 at Castle Howard, by Vanbrugh and Hawksmoor, which has two playful satyr masks emerging, as it were, from the regular stone quoins of the *all'antica* gate (Fig. 223). On advising on the condition of the walls of Nottingham Castle, which had been rebuilt to an *all'antica* design between 1663 and

1678, Vanbrugh observed that 'you'll think it Stairs you in the face, wth a pretty Impudent countenance'.[17] It is as if its façades resemble an unruly Vanbrugian stage character, in need of reform. In referring to Lumley Castle as 'a Noble thing' (Fig 224), and therefore an appropriate residence for his patron Lord Lumley, Vanbrugh described his 'General Design' for the medieval castle in the same 'civilising', even Vitruvian, spirit as consisting 'in altering the House both for State, Beauty and Convenience, And making the Courts Gardens and

223   The satyr gate at Castle Howard by Hawksmoor and Vanbrugh (carved by Samuel Carpenter), 1705.

224   The west façade of Lumley Castle, Durham, remodelled by Vanbrugh in 1722 with a new staircase, door and sash and bull's-eye windows.

Offices Suitable to it' (here translating the Vitruvian triad of *firmitas*, *utilitas*, *venustas*).[18] Once again the existing house went through a process of refinement in order to express his patron's nobility. Of course in describing his intentions for Kimbolton, Vanbrugh echoed the timeless schema in which virtuous but unruly native arts are civilised, or classicised, by Vitruvian principles. This schema had been advanced by, amongst others, Inigo Jones in his history of Stonehenge[19] and it reflected in particular the historical narrative of Caesar taming the ancient British race through military might and Roman wisdom outlined in Clarke's edition of the commentaries which Vanbrugh supported.[20]

Manchester was evidently pleased by Vanbrugh's south, garden façade at Kimbolton because within three years most of the exterior had been remodelled to match

it. Writing to the Earl on 22 March 1708 Vanbrugh had predicted 'And I Apprehend but One thing from the Whole, wch is, That your L^dship will two or three years hence find your self under a violent Temptation to take downe and rebuild (suitable to this New front) all the Outside Walls round the Castle'.[21] In the end, despite Vanbrugh's original recommendations, a 'violent temptation' to use the Orders proved irresistible to Manchester, for in order to celebrate his elevation to a dukedom he turned to the Florentine architect Alessandro Galilei around 1719 to add a massive Doric portico to the main, eastern façade (Fig. 225). Here again, at Kimbolton there is the heraldic link between the Orders and ennoblement made by Hawksmoor at Easton Neston and elsewhere.[22]

★   ★   ★

225 The Doric portico by Alessandro Galilei added to the main, east façade of Kimbolton, *c.*1719.

'WITH A PRETTY IMPUDENT COUNTENANCE': SEATON DELAVAL AND THE PLAY OF OPPOSITIONS

Seaton Delaval (1720–28) is a good example of Vanbrugh's wish to represent the virtues of his patron's character through the use of ornament, iconography and architectural form (Figs 227, 228).[23] Like the Duke of Marlborough and indeed Vanbrugh himself, the patron in this case, George Delaval (*c.*1660–1723), was a military man – or an admiral to be precise.[24] Although from a noble family, he was self-made, having profited through his appointment as Queen Anne's Envoy to Morocco (1707) and Portugal (1710–13) with responsibility for buying supplies for the British Army. In 1715 he had been elected as the Whig Member of Parliament for West Looe in Cornwall. Vanbrugh was well aware of Delaval's military rank and social status, referring to the new house on 20 February 1721 as 'Admll: Delavals' and reporting to another soldier, Brigadier-General William Watkins on 26 August of the same year: 'The Admiral is very Gallant in his operations, not being dispos'd to starve the Design at all. So that he is like to have, a very fine Dwelling for himself, now, and his Nephew &c hereafter'.[25] I shall now show how Vanbrugh represented in his design these traditionally male chivalrous virtues of gallantry and military prowess, together with the ancient lineage of the Delaval family in Northumberland which could be traced to William the Conqueror.

The nephew in question was Captain Francis Blake Delaval (1692–1752), also a navy man, who succeeded his uncle in June 1723 after the latter's death in a riding accident. The Delavals had further connections with the navy. George Delaval's kinsman, Sir Ralph – the grandson of the first baronet of Seaton Delaval – was also an admiral and Lord of the Admiralty; he distinguished himself against the French in the battle of Barfleur in May 1692.[26] No doubt of particular appeal to Vanbrugh as a fellow Whig was the fact that a Delaval had been amongst the Barons who had witnessed the Magna Carta (a fact which Francis Blake Delaval's heraldry celebrated).

Vanbrugh's general predilection for 'Something of the Castle Air' was achieved at Seaton Delaval not through medieval details but through the imposing military feel, or effect, of the overall design of the house and its landscape complete with mock-defensive ditches and walls (Fig. 226). As a basement course to the house Vanbrugh adapted a pulvinate frieze, found for example in Serlio's fourth book (referred to as a 'bulging frieze') and on his 'licentious' Rustic gates (Fig. 229, see Fig. 142).[27] This

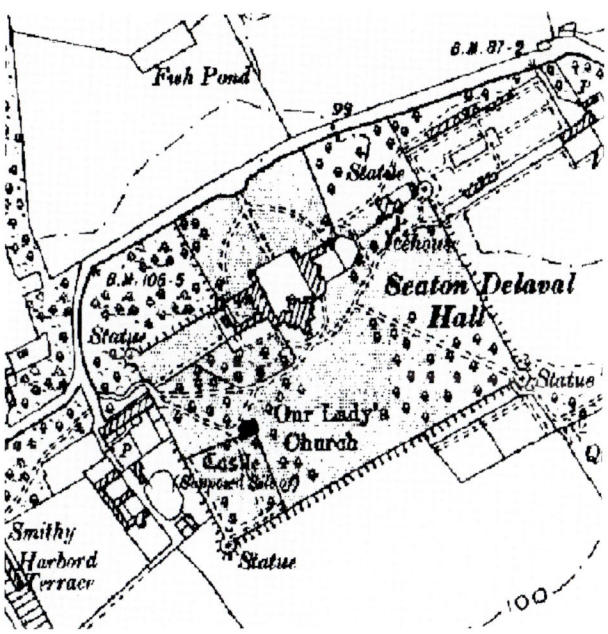

226 Vanbrugh's mock garden defences comprising ditch, platform and bastions at Seaton Delaval, from Victorian Ordnance Survey Map (1888 revised series).

novel rearrangement of classical details by Vanbrugh gives expression to the great weight of his masonry walls and literally cushions the building (and, as one might expect from the writer of comedies, is a visual

227   The north, front façade of Seaton Delaval, Northumberland.

228   Engraving of the north, front façade of Seaton Delaval from Colen Campbell's *Vitruvius Britannicus*, vol. III (1725), pl. 20.

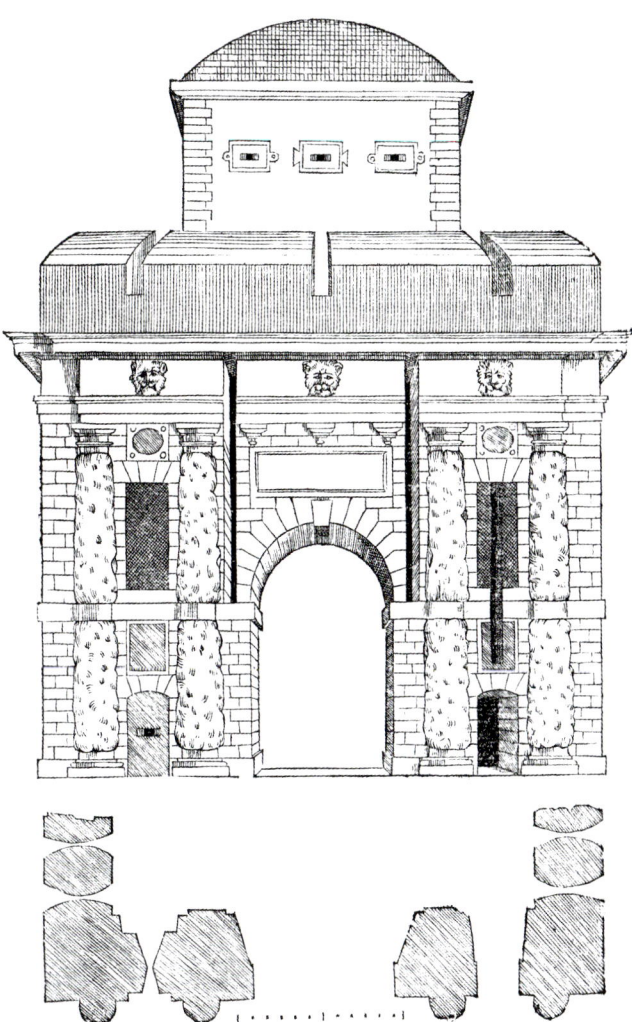

229   Detail of the basement at Seaton Delaval.

230   A fortified gate from Sebastiano Serlio's *Settimo Libro* (1575), p. 93.

pun on the Latin *pulvinus*, meaning cushion). Here, as also at Blenheim, Vanbrugh exploits the metaphorical language of architecture. His use of the Serliana form for the windows on the two towers might be a clue to the importance, as a general design source, of Serlio's books, where, as the name suggests, the form is much in evidence. In fact, the whole arrangement of this façade resembles that of one of Serlio's fortified gates in his Book VII (Fig. 230; see Fig. 204).[28] Both the house and the gates combine a giant Doric Order – including its frieze of metopes and triglyphs – with incised joints, dropped keystones and even lion heads (as described by Vitruvius; see Fig. 233b).[29]

The use at Seaton Delaval of giant Doric columns in a non-structural, decorative role has been something of a puzzle to historians[30] but, as noted earlier, Serlio regarded the Order as particularly appropriate to a military commander or 'men of arms'.[31] The military char-

acter of the north façade is enhanced by Roman military insignia – arrows, shields and eagles – which are carved into the metopes, as they had been at Castle Howard in 1706 (Fig. 231, see Fig. 93).[32] It was pointed out in Chapter Two that, as a herald and former soldier, Vanbrugh was especially interested in military insignia. This is shown by his subscription to 'Browns book of Medals' and to Haym's *Del Tesoro Britannico*, published by Tonson in London in 1719–20, that is, just before the design of Seaton Delaval.[33] Amongst the many insignia which Haym illustrates are Neptune's trident and the eagle which appear at Seaton Delaval (Fig. 232). Also featured in the metopes on the house are more explicit military and naval details – a hunter's face over the central window with his arrows (possibly a caricature of Delaval), an admiral's hat with an anchor in direct reference to Delaval's naval rank, and what appear to be sea monsters with Neptune's trident (Figs 233a and b). Nep-

231   Roman military insignia in the frieze on the north façade of Seaton Delaval.

232   Insignia on ancient medals from Nicola Haym's *Del Tesoro Britannico . . . over il Museo Nummario* (1719–20), pp. 144, 153.

tune's trident reappears in the pediment (Fig. 234). In this way, as at Greenwich Hospital for seamen, Vanbrugh's attempt to give expression to the English boast as to their supremacy of the seas forms part of his general ambition to formulate a national architectural style (Vanbrugh was proud of what he termed 'our Fleet'[34]). More specifically the pediment celebrates, and by implication narrates, the Delavals' achievements. Trade such as that undertaken by George Delaval depended on this naval supremacy, in order to achieve which the sea monsters have, by necessity, been tamed with the help of Neptune, both on the house and on the seas. For this reason sea monsters together with Neptune's trident had appeared on the west façade of the Painted Hall at Greenwich Hospital (see Fig. 37). At Seaton Delaval the taming of unruly natural forces might also be seen dramatised through the giant non-structural Doric columns applied to, yet contrasting with, the rustication on the north façade, given that such forces are made explicit through the bestial forms – a heraldic griffin and sea monsters – which are carved above the rustication in the frieze; here too a lion roars at a timid sheep (a battering ram; Figs 235a and b).

This ornament also fitted perfectly the house's location a short distance from the Northumberland coast visible from the upper rooms of the house. Given Vanbrugh's admiration for medieval ruins, he must have been particularly charmed by the sight of the ruin of Tynemouth Priory to the south. The Saxon chapel of 1102 in the grounds, with its primitive, round-headed openings (Fig. 236), together with the site of the old fortified house of the Delavals, gave Vanbrugh's new house a more immediate local context. Location was certainly a factor in the house's design: with its rustication it is clearly suited to the rugged character of the north of England, in contrast to what he referred to as the 'tame' south. Vanbrugh reports from York to Brigadier Watkins that 'I return'd but last night from the North (for here you must know we are in the South,) where I have been near three weeks finding a vast deal to do, both at Delavals and Lumley Castle . . . If I had had good weather in this Expedition, I shou'd have been well enough diverted in it; there being many more Valluable and Agreeable things and Places to be Seen, than in the Tame Sneaking South of England'.[35]

233a and b A hunter's face, an admiral's hat with an anchor, and Neptune's trident with sea monsters in the frieze on the north façade of Seaton Delaval.

234 Delaval family heraldry, together with Neptune's trident, in the pediment on the north façade of Seaton Delaval.

235a and b   Lions, griffins and sea monsters carved in the frieze on the north façade of Seaton Delaval.

236   Round-headed openings in the Saxon chapel of 1102 in the grounds of Seaton Delaval.

Passing through the front façade of Seaton Delaval, the visitor enters the great central hall (finished after Vanbrugh's death) with its statues of the Liberal Arts (here redefined for the modern era as music, painting, sculpture, architecture, geography and astronomy; Fig. 237).[36] The hall's symbolic role as a pantheon of the arts is extended on the south, garden front by a portico of the Ionic Order (Fig. 239) – the Order suitable, according to Serlio, for 'men of letters' (such as Vanbrugh himself) whose life was 'not robust, but also not delicate'. In this sense the house is a celebration not just of the patron and his status but also of the Liberal Arts enjoyed by its architect. On the north façade the Doric Order has in fact been softened by the addition of delicate carving, in the form of flowers and egg and dart mouldings – although here the egg has been replaced by forms which resemble sea shells (a further specific reflection, perhaps, of location and – like in heraldry – of the family's naval traditions; see Fig. 235b). According to Serlio, this kind of fine detail reflected a patron with a 'delicate side to him' and as such the work should be 'carved with some delicacy'.[37] I have quoted Vanbrugh referring to Delaval's 'gallantry' towards, and appreciation of, the house's design as an expression of his wealth, and his judicious role as an envoy to Queen Anne has been noted. This more delicate aspect of the design would thus naturally have expressed the sophistication of the Whig Member of Parliament, familiar as he probably was with

237 (facing page)   The great central hall at Seaton Delaval (finished after Vanbrugh's death) with its statues of the Liberal Arts [Country Life Picture Library].

238   The winding staircase in the west tower at Seaton Delaval, *c*.1724.

the architecture of Europe.[38] His heir, Francis Blake Delaval, was married to Rhoda Apreece, a rich heiress from Huntingdonshire and, by eighteenth-century standards, the family lived in wealthy gentility.

Indeed, the tension of opposites can be detected throughout the ornamentation of the house's façades, in thus expressing the contrasting aspects of his patron's character and achievements. For example Vanbrugh uses rough and smooth surfaces, and forms whose origins were either medieval (as with the fortified outworks) or *all'antica* (as with the Serliana windows, the Ionic portico and the Palladian arrangement of the side wings; Fig. 240).[39] As Vanbrugh's comparison between 'rustics' and 'fluting' at Castle Howard indicates, he certainly chose contrasting decorative effects in his buildings with care.[40] Contemporaries including Alexander Pope had advocated the interplay of such contrasts and oppositions, based on poetic conventions, in the case of garden design.[41] Furthermore, the interplay of oppositions – virtue and vice, love and hate, innocence and guilt – is a major dramatic device in Vanbrugh's comedies, in which characters are most often simply either 'good' or 'bad'.

In *The False Friend*, for example, the villainous Don John observes 'Leonora's Charms, turn Vice to Virtue, Treason into Truth'.[42] Aesthetic oppositions are one of the main themes in *Aesop*, where the beautiful Euphronia has nightmares involving 'Monsters and Hobgoblins' due to her father's wish that she wed the ugly Aesop: the nurse Doris concludes, 'He loves my mistress, because she's handsome; and she hates him, because he's ugly'.[43]

Seaton Delaval also expresses gender-related contrasts, in that the public (robust and male) Doric columns and incised-jointed stone face defends, as it were, the private (delicate and female) fluted Ionic loggia and smooth-jointed stone face to the garden. With its broken pediment over the central door (which the engraving of the elevation in *Vitruvius Britannicus* of 1725 indicates was to hold a delicately carved bust; Figs 241, 242), the garden façade is clearly more playful. As Serlio had observed, contrasting human characteristics of strength and delicacy, associated with gender differences, were easily transferable to inform architectural character in thereby expressing an Aristotelian truth concerning Nature and her opposites.[44] Vanbrugh was well aware of the contrasting gender associations between different surfaces and ornamental types, an awareness underlined by the fact that his 'Castle Air' was intended as particularly male, following his comments regarding the 'noble and masculine show' and 'manly beauty' of astylar façades and rough materials. Hawksmoor too was fully aware of the traditional links between gender and ornamental type. On rejecting the Ionic Order for his Mausoleum colonnade at Castle Howard (see Fig. 175), for example, he wrote to Lord Carlisle on 19 April 1729 that the Doric 'will make ye fabrick more firm and masculine', recalling later that 'I esteem'd the Dorick most suitable to the Masculin strength we wanted'.[45] Discussing the octagonal Temple of Venus at Castle Howard (see Fig. 192) he observed on 4 January 1732 'that the 8 pillars may be Rusticated as I have hinted to you, in ye drawing, for the more firm and masculin they appear, the better they will suit our Rurall, Sylvan, Situation. Without the Rusticks they will be too feminin (*trop Megre*) as the French call it'.[46] The smooth-jointed south façade of Seaton Delaval should surely also be seen as 'delicate' (as Vanbrugh described the same effect on the 'Temple of the Four Winds') and therefore 'feminine', in contrast to the undoubted 'masculine beauty' of the incised-jointed, or rusticated, north façade.

As Vanbrugh's role as Garter Herald indicates and his letter concerning Woodstock Manor and the legend of Rosamond's Bower confirms, he had a deep affinity to the medieval romantic tradition; this tradition emphasised such gender associations, in which a bower was

239   The south, garden façade of Seaton Delaval.

necessarily female and a manor house or castle necessarily male. Vanbrugh's plays exploit these differences in gender and much mishap arises through sexual inequality. The theme of gender difference, illustrated through the device of a woman disguised as a man, is most fully played out in *The Mistake*.[47] True to traditional stereotypes, his leading men are frequently brutish, as epitomised by Sir John Brute, whereas his women are for the most part more delicate, playful (even wilful) and, sometimes despite appearances, vulnerable (even weak). In *The Mistake*, for example, Sancho observes that 'a Woman in all Times has been observ'd to be an Animal hard to understand, and much inclin'd to Mischief', whilst Leonora justifies herself by noting 'Women have their

Frailties'.[48] Don Carlos comments that 'I am a Man, by Nature meant for Power; the Scepter's given us to wield, and we betray our Trust, whene'er we meanly lay it at a Woman's Feet'.[49] On the character of Amanda in *The Relapse*, Vanbrugh explains the weakness of her defences: 'Here's a Woman whose Virtue is rais'd upon the utmost Strength of Foundation: Religion, Modesty, and Love, defend it. It looks so Sacred, one wou'd think no Mortal durst approach it: and seems so fix'd one wou'd believe no Engine cou'd shake it: Yet loosen one Stone, the Weather works in, and the Structure molders apace to decay'.[50] Vanbrugh's use of an architectural metaphor here – and a fortification one at that – surely confirms the examination of his buildings for expressions of such

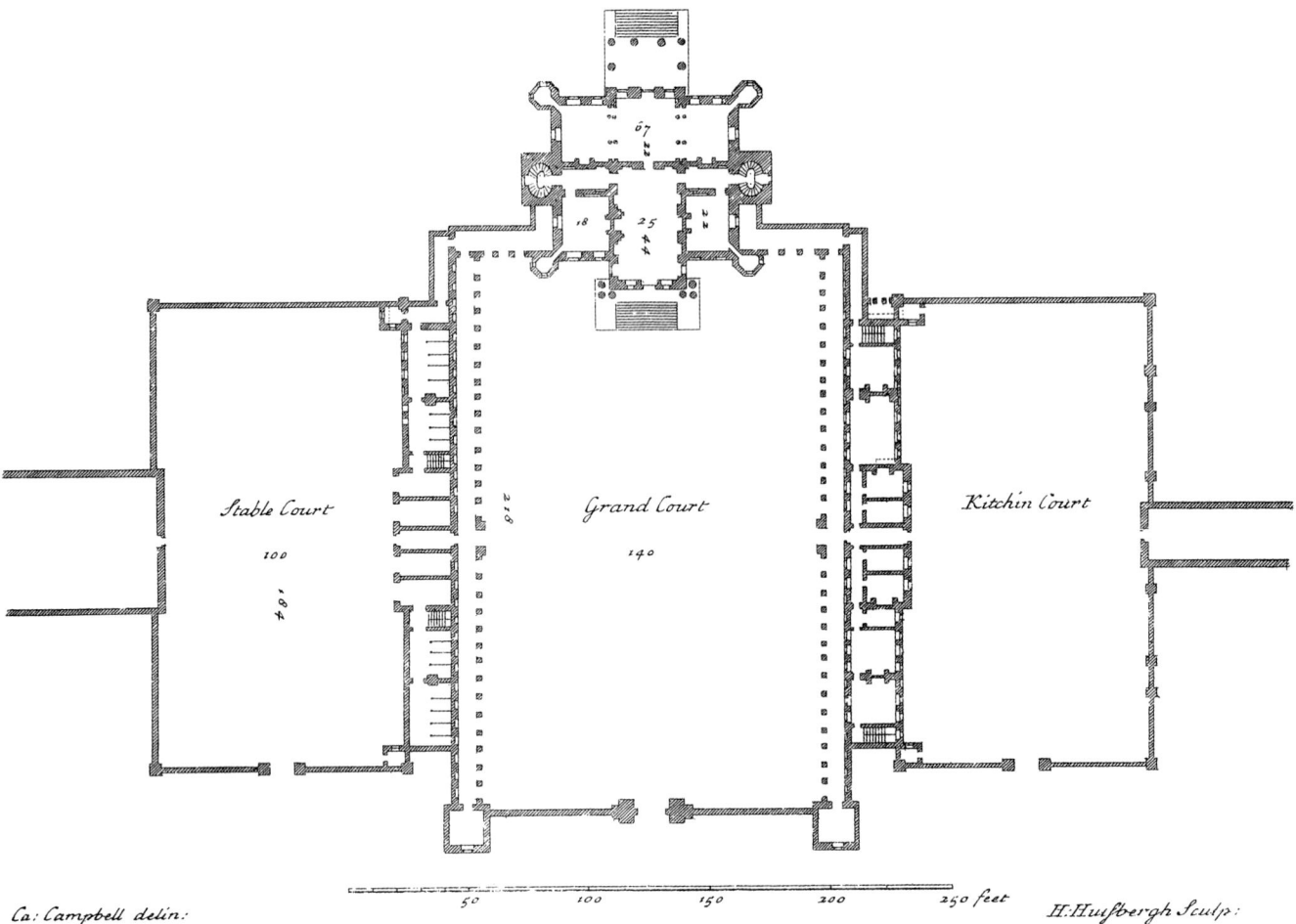

Stable Court
100

Grand Court
140

Kitchin Court

Ca: Campbell delin:

50   100   150   200   250 feet

H. Hulfbergh Sculp:

240   Engraving illustrating the Palladian arrangement of the 'Grand Court' at Seaton Delaval, from Colen Campbell's *Vitruvius Britannicus*, vol. III (1725), pl. 20.

gender-based virtues of strength and frailty, as part of the general reflection by these works of what their architect evidently saw as the natural order.[51]

In his plays Vanbrugh uses actual fortifications to bar ever-present town vices (as dramatised, for instance, in Foppington's visit to Clumsey's fortified country seat in *The Relapse*, a play sub-titled 'virtue in danger'[52]) and he uses metaphorical barricades as symbolic defences of, or supports for, virtue and as signs of moral resolve. In *The Provok'd Wife*, for example, Bellinda exclaims: ''Tis well *Constant* don't know the weakness of the Fortifications; for o'my Conscience he'd soon come on to the Assault'.[53] In both instances – 'fortified' character and building – a worthy or refined interior (and, in the case of building, its patron) is protected by an 'exterior countenance' which is necessarily sometimes threatening (as with Nottingham Castle or Sir Turnbelly) and sometimes restrained (as with Kimbolton or Bellinda). Understood in this context, the masculine castle-like towers

either side of the 'Nunnery' at Greenwich might be seen to protect the female virtue of its inhabitants (see Fig. 332). It has equally been seen at Seaton Delaval and elsewhere in Vanbrugh's work how an essentially masculine front façade defends and protects, as it were, a feminine private one.[54] Thus the decorative (that is, non-functional and skin-deep) fortifications such as towers and crenellations on his buildings might reasonably be understood as performing the same symbolic roles as those referred to in his plays. They outwardly both protect and, like heraldry, proclaim the strength of, his patrons' masculine character and moral rectitude, as well as the nobility of their dynastic line. These were, after all, the eternal qualities symbolised for Vanbrugh by the medieval ruins at Woodstock and elsewhere, as opposed to the ephemeral ones pursued by contemporary followers of fashion ridiculed in his plays – namely by the 'beau' and those female characters subject to this vice. Yet as in Vanbrugh's plays, appearances can be deceptive:

clearly such applied fortifications are similarly only 'façades' and cannot offer any active protection against the vices of the world or even the follies that may lie 'within'.

It was noted in Chapter Two that Wren had warned of the dangers of fashionable taste in matters of architectural design, associating this influence with women at Versailles. The answer to the contemporary quest for a national style in architecture was thus to be founded by Wren and Vanbrugh on what they saw as the certainties of the male character, and not the vagaries of the female (which are associated by Wren with England's great rival, France). However, if for Jones and Wren this style had been necessarily classical, it has been seen that for Vanbrugh – as his desire for the 'Castle Air' implies – the character could be refined from a variety of sources, most notably from native medieval buildings. Vanbrugh's cel-

241 (*right*) Broken pediment on the south, garden façade of Seaton Delaval.

242 (*below*) Engraving of the south, garden façade of Seaton Delaval, from Colen Campbell's *Vitruvius Britannicus*, vol. III (1725), pl. 21.

The South front of Seaton Delaval in the County of Northumberland the Seat of Francis Delaval Esq. design'd by S.' *Iohn Vanbrugh K.'* 1721.

Ca: Campbell delin: H: Hulsbergh Sc.

243   The south, garden façade of Seaton Delaval.

244   The west, gaden façade of Seaton Delaval.

245 Obelisk in the landscape at Seaton Delaval, erected c.1737.

ebration of the strength of masculine character and nobility, and its corollary, the frailties of the feminine, at Seaton Delaval and elsewhere, followed in the tradition of the 'masculine and unaffected' façade famously advocated by Jones and which had triggered in the onlooker associated ideas of the medieval lord's military and economic strength.[55] Just as Vanbrugh's front façades at Blenheim, Castle Howard and Seaton Delaval can thus be understood to have worn the costume, or 'livery' as Wren put it, of male nobility, so his garden façades generally took on a more feminine character (Figs 243, 244).[56] Women and their genteel occupations were traditionally seen as unsuitable for public life, as Wren's letter emphasises and Vanbrugh's lines echo, and were identified rather with interiors and with the garden.[57] Giving onto the garden at Seaton Delaval was the Saloon, with its maidenly Corinthian columns and elegant plaster ceiling by Francesco Vassalli.[58]

Much like the picture art of heraldry, Vanbrugh's ornamentation of Seaton Delaval thus expresses the self-identity and character of the Delaval family, and in par-

ticular their naval traditions and ancient roots in the Northumberland area. As if to emphasise this ambiguity between Delaval's new, physical house and his ancient, heraldic one, the ancient heraldry of the Delavals' (ermine with two bars) and the more modern alternative of Frances Blake Delaval (a chevron between three garbs – that is, wheat sheaves) appears in the house's pediment alongside the trident and trophies of arms (a pickaxe; see Fig. 234). More traditional memorials to George Delaval were erected in the grounds of Seaton Delaval by his nephew, in the form of three obelisks – one supposedly marking the spot where the Admiral was unseated from his horse and another the place to which he was dragged and died (Fig. 245). These are thought to have been included in Vanbrugh's original scheme for the grounds, although they were not finally erected until about 1737.[59] In commemorating his patron through these obelisks, much in the way that memorial forms were used elsewhere in his work, Vanbrugh told the last act in his patron's 'story'.

'PLEAS'D TO STORM MY CASTLE': ENGLISHMEN'S HOMES AND CASTLES AT KINGS WESTON, EASTBURY, GRIMSTHORPE AND STOWE

Vanbrugh's predilection towards the medieval country house was sometimes expressed literally in his work, through clearly identifiable elements – such as the crenellations at Kimbolton that gave, in his own words, 'Something of the Castle Air' – and at other times in more allusive ways, for example through the upper room and corner towers at Seaton Delaval (see Fig. 227). The tension between the use of *all'antica* elements on the one hand and medieval ones on the other is critical in many of Vanbrugh's domestic designs and reflected nuances of site and patron. With this mix of forms he sought to merge the rugged character of the English castle with the more refined aspect of the Palladian country house, to create a unique architecture at once expressive of national traditions but tempered and enhanced by the universal virtues of classicism.

In his country houses at Kings Weston, Eastbury and Grimsthorpe, Vanbrugh can be seen to have represented the particular virtues of his patrons and their ancestors through his novel adaptation of traditional domestic forms – chimneys and porticoes, towers and crenellations – and through his choice of *all'antica* ornamentation – heraldry and columns, carving and statuary. Elements of the medieval fortified house featured in all three designs, as more universal signs of strength and protection – virtues that were of fundamental importance to Vanbrugh in his conception of the English country house (and, given such virtues were also fundamental to the more noble of his male stage characters, to his desire for 'Manly Beauty'). Writing to the Duke of Newcastle in 1719 from Greenwich he noted: 'I hear your Grace was pleas'd to Storm my Castle yesterday: I hope next time you'll be so Gallant to let me know of your Design, which if I do, I'll endeavour to give you a Warmer Reception'.[1] Vanbrugh here makes explicit the meta-phorical nature of his defensive forms such as 'battlements' and 'fosses'. For his houses were built to celebrate the age-old adage that 'an Englishman's home is his castle'.[2]

'YOUR CHATEAU': KINGS WESTON FOR EDWARD SOUTHWELL

Kings Weston in Gloucestershire was built between 1710 and 1714 (Figs 247, 249, 250). The date '1711' is inscribed on one of the beams of the house, alongside the letter 'T' (Fig. 251) – probably the mark of the mason, George Townesend, who also worked at Blenheim.[3] Although the interior was not finished until the 1760s (by Robert Mylne), Vanbrugh was responsible for the house's plan, its façades and the central newel staircase of about 1719–20 (Figs 252, 253). The grisaille paintings of urns and niches in the staircase hall are also thought to have been carried out to Vanbrugh's designs and lend the hall the quality of a stage set (Fig. 248). The centralised atrium with fictive niches and statues reflects the known influence on Vanbrugh of Palladio's houses. Vanbrugh was evidently happy with the design of the house, for it became something of a model: writing to the Duchess of Marlborough on 19 August 1716 he observes: 'I am very glad your Grace is pleased with Mr Southwell's house; it being the sort of Building I endeavour to bring people to, who are disposed to ask my advice or assistance: 'tis certain his work has been done cheap and a great deal of it tolerably well'.[4] The Right Honourable Edward Southwell (1671–1730) was a Member of Parliament from 1702 to about 1714, accounted *doctissimus juvenis* and, following his father, served as Secretary of State for Ireland from 1702. He was made clerk to the

247 (*above*)   The south, front façade of Kings Weston, Gloucestershire, 1710–14.

248 (*right*)   Grisaille (*trompe l'oeil*) painting of an urn in a niche in the staircase hall at Kings Weston, probably carried out to Vanbrugh's designs [Regional Building Record, Bath University].

Privy Council of Great Britain on 10 May 1708.[5] Southwell had been well educated, at first under the supervision of his father, Sir Robert (who was President of the Royal Society from 1690), and then at Merton College in Oxford, after which he spent time travelling in Europe.

Having never served as a military commander, Southwell was thus unlike Vanbrugh's other patrons such as Delaval, Doddington and Marlborough. The gentler, civilian nature of his profession and that of his father may well account for the unusually feminine character of Vanbrugh's front façade at Kings Weston, with its pilasters of the Corinthian Order (see Fig. 247). In this regard the house is atypical given the fact that Vanbrugh commonly used the masculine Doric Order on his front façades,

249 (*facing page*)   The west façade of Kings Weston.

250 (*above*)   The east façade of Kings Weston.

251 (*left*)   The date '1711' and a 'T' inscribed on a beam in Kings Weston [Regional Building Record, Bath University].

252 (*facing page top*)   The inner hall at Kings Weston, with its apparently unsupported, 'hanging' staircase (*c*.1719–20) [Regional Building Record, Bath University].

253 (*facing page bottom*)   Ground-floor and first-floor plans of Kings Weston, from Colen Campbell's *Vitruvius Britannicus*, vol. I (1715), pl. 47.

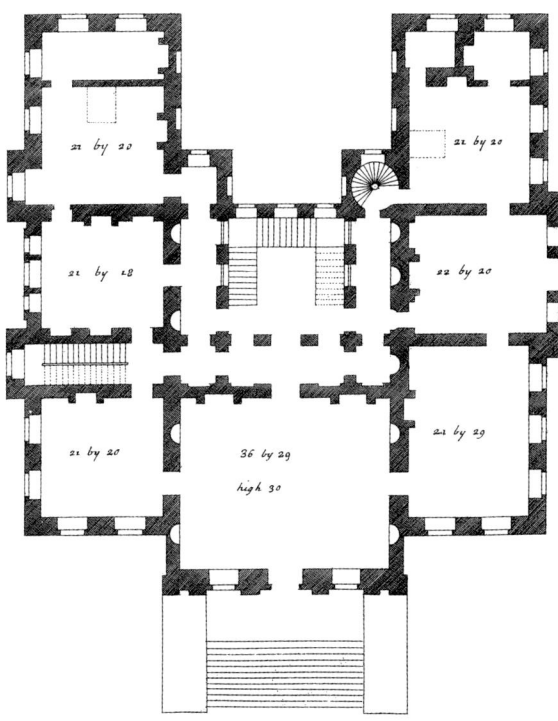

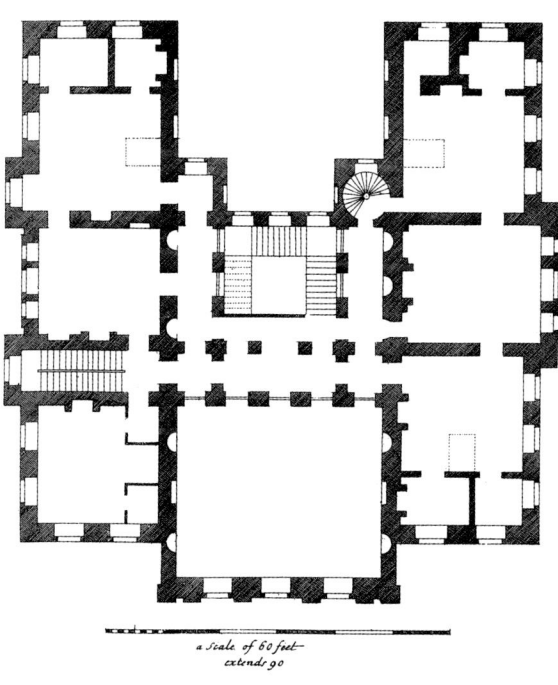

a Scale of 60 feet
extends 90

The Plan of ye Principal floor of Kings Weston

Plan du Premier Estage de Kings Weston

The Plan of ye Chamber floor of Kings Weston

Plan du Second Estage de Kings Weston

254 The main door on the south façade of Kings Weston.

255 Doorway on the east façade of Kings Weston.

256 Drawing for the east façade of Kings Weston, Vanbrugh's Office [Victoria and Albert Museum, London].

257 The Banqueting House Loggia facing the east façade of Kings Weston, attributed to Vanbrugh.

258 Grotesque masks on urns surmounting the Banqueting House Loggia, Kings Weston.

259 A design for a garden gate attributed to Vanbrugh, anonymous drawing dated March 1722, from 'The Kings Weston Book of Drawings' [Bristol Civic Trust].

260 (*right*)
Projected stables at
Kings Weston
(eventually built to
a design by Robert
Mylne), anonymous
drawing dated 1720
attributing the design
to 'Mr Price' (thought
to be the mason
who succeeded
Townesend)
influenced by
Vanbrugh, from
'The Kings Weston
Book of Drawings'
[Bristol Civic Trust].

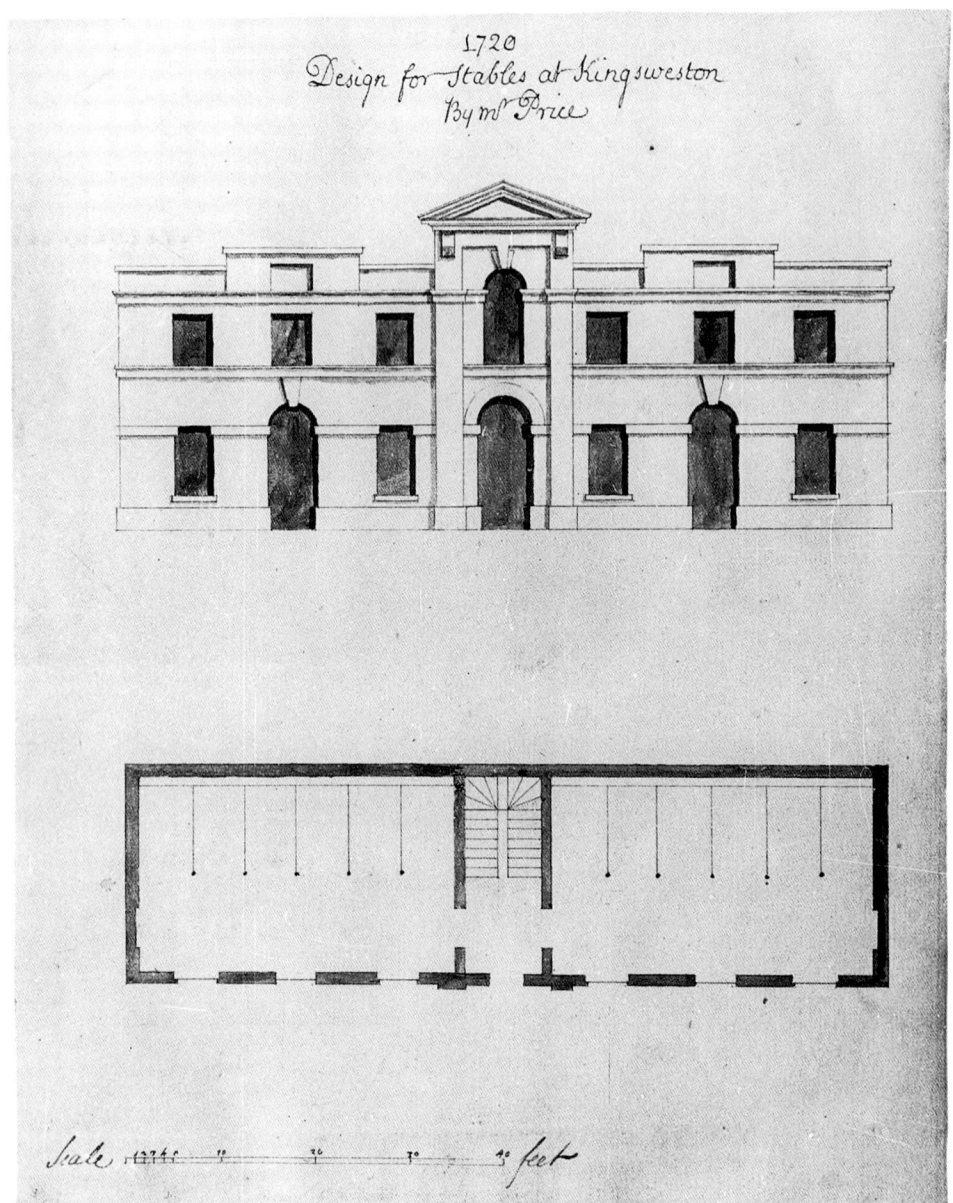

261 (*below*)
Projected brew-house
at Kings Weston,
anonymous drawing,
*c.*1718, influenced by
Vanbrugh, from
'The Kings Weston
Book of Drawings'
[Bristol Civic Trust].

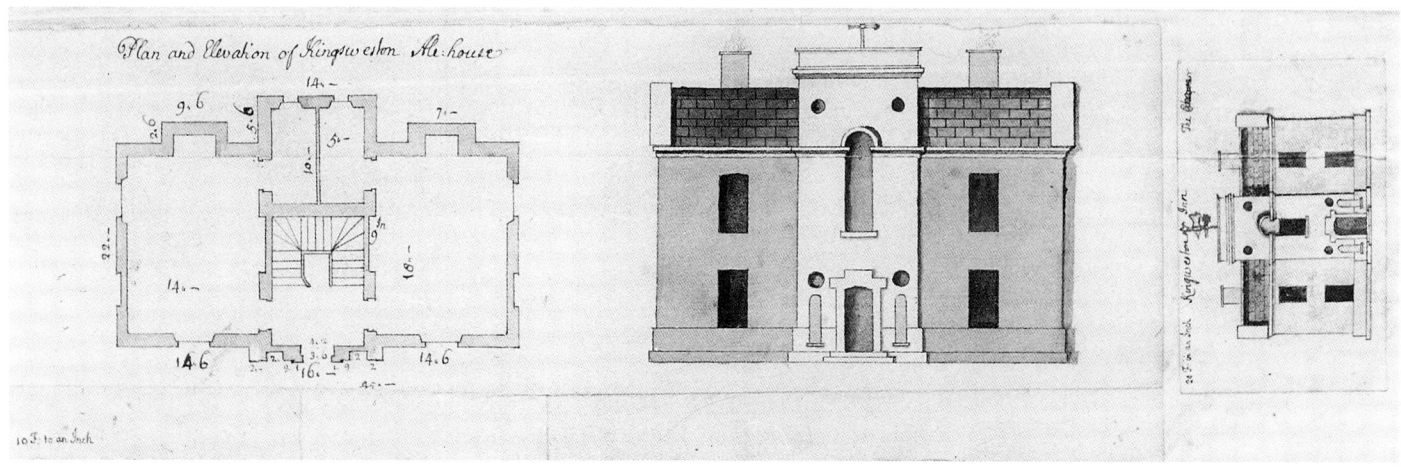

which on this occasion is relegated to the main door in a somewhat simplified form and to the doorway on the eastern side (Figs 254–6).[6] Here the Order is perfectly matched to its location facing the garden, however, through its embellishment with frostwork reflecting that used on the Banqueting House Loggia, which the doorway faces, and on a garden gate design (Figs 257, 259), both works attributed to Vanbrugh.[7] The presence of grotesque faces on the urns which crown this loggia further emphasise its rustic, untamed character suited to its location (Fig. 258). That Vanbrugh respected the hierarchical character of the *all'antica* ornamental language at Kings Weston is indicated by the fact that the Corinthian Order is restricted to this entrance façade, whilst the other façades are left astylar (excepting this Doric garden entrance on the east) and that designs for outbuildings which were clearly influenced by Vanbrugh – the brew-house and stables – are also astylar (Figs 260, 261).[8] Instead of using the Orders, these designs have a characteristic Vanbrugian eclectic mix of *all'antica* and medieval details – Venetian windows and bulky towers, broken pediments and portholes. Despite the Corinthian front to Kings Weston, Colen Campbell was moved to remark that 'the Architecture is great, and Masculine'.[9] Moreover a hint of Vanbrugh's familiar military theme is to be found in the proof produced for the engraving of the front façade published in Campbell's *Vitruvius Britannicus* (1715), where a warrior is sketched in an anonymous hand surmounting the pediment; this figure is dispensed with in the actual engraving and on the house itself (Fig. 263; see Fig. 164).[10] In this engraving

The Elevation of KINGSWESTON in the County of GLOCESTER the Seat of the Rt Honble EDWARD SOUTHWELL, Esqr Principal Secretary of State for the KINGDOM of IRELAND Designed by Sr Io: Vanbrugh Kt
Co: Campbell Delin: Elevation de la Maison De KINGSWESTON dans la Comte de GLOCESTER.

262 (*above*) Vanbrugh's neo-Palladian design for the Penpole Gate at Kings Weston (a garden structure built in 1723 largely to a design by Colen Campbell, now destroyed), drawing by Vanbrugh's Office, bound in the Elton Hall volume [Victoria and Albert Museum, London].

263 (*left*) Engraving of the front façade of Kings Weston, from Colen Campbell's *Vitruvius Britannicus*, vol. 1 (1715), pl. 48.

264 (*above*) The three-sided rooftop colonnade linking the chimneys on the skyline at Kings Weston [Regional Building Record, Bath University].

265 (*left*) The 'Edifice des Tuteles', from Claude Perrault's *Vitruvius* (1684 edition), p. 219.

Campbell's inscription at the base links the façade design to Southwell's civilian status and administrative role, as indeed I have suggested the ornamentation should be understood, by including the fact that he was Principal Secretary of State for Ireland. Campbell must have known Kings Weston well, for along with Vanbrugh he produced designs for the Penpole Gate there (Fig. 262) and, in reference to Giacomo Angarano – an early patron of Palladio – he underlines artistic taste as a key aspect of Southwell's character by describing him as 'the *Angaranno* of our Age, to whom my Obligations are so deep, that to repeat the least Part of them, would offend the Modesty of my Benefactor'.[11]

What is one to make of the strange three-sided rooftop colonnade linking the chimneys on the skyline at Kings Weston (Fig. 264; see Fig. 137)? Vanbrugh later proposed using a similar form at Eastbury, around 1716, but subsequently much adapted it in execution (see Fig. 284).[12] The form with its ornamental keystones is entirely non-functional and, as a colonnade, obviously out of place – although sitting as it does above urns and a giant-order Corinthian portico it recalls the upper colonnade in the 'Edifice des Tuteles' illustrated in Perrault's French edition of *Vitruvius* of 1673 (Fig. 265), a work which was fully available to Vanbrugh through his time in Paris and was known to Hawksmoor.[13] As a purely decorative feature, its principal purpose must surely be to create a dramatic effect when seen from a distance – a smoking form whose brooding silhouette set against the sky produced, as Addison might reasonably have concluded, a sense of foreboding in the onlooker. This intention is reflected in the drawing of the façade, attributed to Vanbrugh, in which the rooftop 'arcade' is shaded and smoke is seen to issue from the chimneys, as in his early Eastbury drawing, lending a distinctly melancholic air to the element (see Figs 145, 146, 163).[14] The urns at the base of the 'arcade' certainly reinforce this feeling (and echoed the equally inventive use of morbid sarcophagus forms as chimneys on the gatehouse at Anet illustrated in de l'Orme's *Le Premier tome de l'architecture* of 1567, which, as Chapter Three noted, Vanbrugh must have seen given his interest in French architecture). After all, the appearance of architectural forms when viewed from a distance was one of Vanbrugh's fundamental concerns. The appearance of these chimneys at Kings Weston, especially with regard to their height, was no exception. He writes to Southwell on 28 September 1713 that 'I am in so much care about this one point of the Chimneys answering what I expect from them that I cou'd be glad to make some tryalls with boards about height &c, before they are carried up', re-emphasising on 23 October that, 'In my last I told you I wished you would not go up with the chimneys till I was with you on the spot, to make tryall of the heights etc, with boards . . . for I would fain have that part rightly hit off'.[15]

Clearly in transforming the chimneys into fictive crenellations Vanbrugh gave them 'Something of the Castle Air', an allusion that might reasonably be confirmed by his subsequent passing reference to Southwell's house as 'your Chateau' in this letter concerning the chimneys.[16] Indeed, the chimney was a prominent feature of the French castle, as Vanbrugh was well aware through his travels – the Château de Boulogne (called 'Madrid') has arched openings in various chimneys, for example, and Serlio provides *all'antica* models for such French chimneys in his seventh book (Figs 267, 268).[17] Probably the most famous French château of them all, Chambord, has decorative chimneys and a rooftop arcade over the central staircase (Fig. 269). Closer to home, Wollaton in Nottinghamshire, Burghley House in Lincolnshire and Hampton Court Palace all have flues which form a row of pillars (Figs 270, 271; see Fig. 76).[18] The rooftop colonnade at Kings Weston also makes an allusion to the freestanding arcades of English medieval ruins, an association which assists in evoking a sombre mood in the onlooker when this form is seen from afar.

The freestanding colonnade has the added virtue of representing what Vanbrugh saw as a basic element of architecture – which he defined to the Earl of Carlisle as comprising 'Pillars, & Arches and Round Windows & Square Windows'[19] – and the spirit of which was further articulated on the façades of Kings Weston by the plain, unembellished window openings (the traditional object of decorative embellishment with richly moulded architraves, tabernacles and pediments; Fig. 266). The same paired-down, plain style was executed by Vanbrugh at

266 The plain, unembellished window openings at Kings Weston.

267   The Château de Boulogne (called 'Madrid') with arched openings in the central chimneys, from Jacques Androuet du Cerceau's *Les plus excellents bastiments de France* (1576–9).

268   Sebastiano Serlio's *all'antica* models for French chimneys in his *Settimo Libro* (1575), pp. 70–71.

269   The rooftop arcade over the central staircase at the Château de Chambord, Loire-et-Cher, France.

270 Flues forming a row of pillars at Burghley House, by Robert Smythson.

271 Chimney columns at Hampton Court, with crenellations.

272 The East Wing lantern at Blenheim.

Chargate, whilst arched forms, open to the elements and without apparent function, were used by him at Blenheim as part of the East Wing lantern (Fig. 272),[20] and at Morpeth on the Town Hall (built to Vanbrugh's design in 1714 but rebuilt as a replica in 1869–70[21]; Fig. 273). These haunting details exemplify Vanbrugh's pref-

erence, outlined at Kimbolton, for the form and proportions of architectural elements over the 'delicacy' of their ornament.

Given Vanbrugh's sensitivity to the historical associations of a particular site, as powerfully outlined by him at Woodstock, his crenellated chimney form would have carried particular potency as an allusion to the history of the estate at Kings Weston. No less than the 'Bravest and most Warlike of the English Kings', as Vanbrugh described Henry II, had granted Kings Weston to Robert Fitz-Harding as part of the Lordship of Berkley and as a reward for his services to Henry I. Berkley was a royal demesne and the name 'Kings Weston' is probably derived from this. These associations cannot have escaped Vanbrugh's attention and the old Tudor manor house with its crenellations (as illustrated by Kip around 1700; Fig. 274) would have formed a powerful 'memory' to which he surely would have wished to allude in his new house. With the appearance of a medieval, crenellated 'core' surrounded by classical façades, a (false) sense of a history of architectural addition and embellishment is

273   The Town Hall at Morpeth, built to Vanbrugh's design in 1714 (rebuilt as a replica in 1869–70).

conveyed at Kings Weston, as with the signification of a heraldic lineage from past to present or, to use a dramatic analogy, Lord Foppington's inappropriate ennoblement and dress. Just as the medieval ruins of Woodstock gave Blenheim a tangible sense of history, stretching back to the heroic medieval kings and queens, so 'fictive' medieval elements in Vanbrugh's work – the crenellations and towers of his 'Castle Air' – gave his houses and their patrons a 'false' or invented link with the nation's past. This embellishment is in keeping with Vanbrugh's conception of medieval architecture made virtuous through the application of Vitruvian principles,

producing a higher form of architecture than a purely classical design. In its altered state, Lumley Castle (see Fig. 224) for example combined the tripartite Vitruvian virtues of 'State, Beauty and Convenience', as Vanbrugh put it.[22] This was similar to the process of heraldic design, where traditional medieval forms – castles and gates amongst them – were combined using essentially Vitruvian principles, as discussed in Chapter Two.

The castle theme at Kings Weston was perhaps most obvious in the outworks. For some time between 1717 and 1718 Vanbrugh planned a forecourt surrounded by a wall, fosse and giant archway surmounted by a pyramid (some forty feet high) – resembling the Pyramid Gate at Castle Howard and corner towers at Eastbury (Fig. 275; see Figs 156, 286). Anonymous annotations to drawings of this project attribute it to Vanbrugh, although the drawings are also not in his hand.[23] The pyramid is a direct allusion to archetypal tomb architecture, examples of which had made a strong impression on him at Surat. As monumental, and elemental, forms of masonry, these memorials were compatible with the castle structures which so enthralled Vanbrugh. The fosse was a fortification device, akin to the walls at Castle Howard, which at Kings Weston served to extend the fortification allusions made by the chimney 'crenellations' at rooftop level. Vanbrugh would have been made fully aware of fortification theory through his time imprisoned at Calais, for example, since the citadel had been reinforced by the leading French engineer Errard (see Fig. 17). His

sponsorship of plate 62 in Clarke's 1712 edition of Caesar's 'Commentaries' indicates his knowledge of the book's other plates, with their illustration of Caesar's encampments (see Fig. 91).[24] It is as if Vanbrugh's fosse and mock crenellations guard against unwanted visitors. After all, this was the unwelcome fate that perpetually befell the country house in Vanbrugh's play of that name and he clearly saw his actual buildings as in need of such symbolic protection.[25]

★   ★   ★

274   The old Tudor manor house at Kings Weston viewed from the south-west, engraved by Leonard Knyff from Johannes Kip's *Britannia Illustrata* (1740 edition), pl. 32.

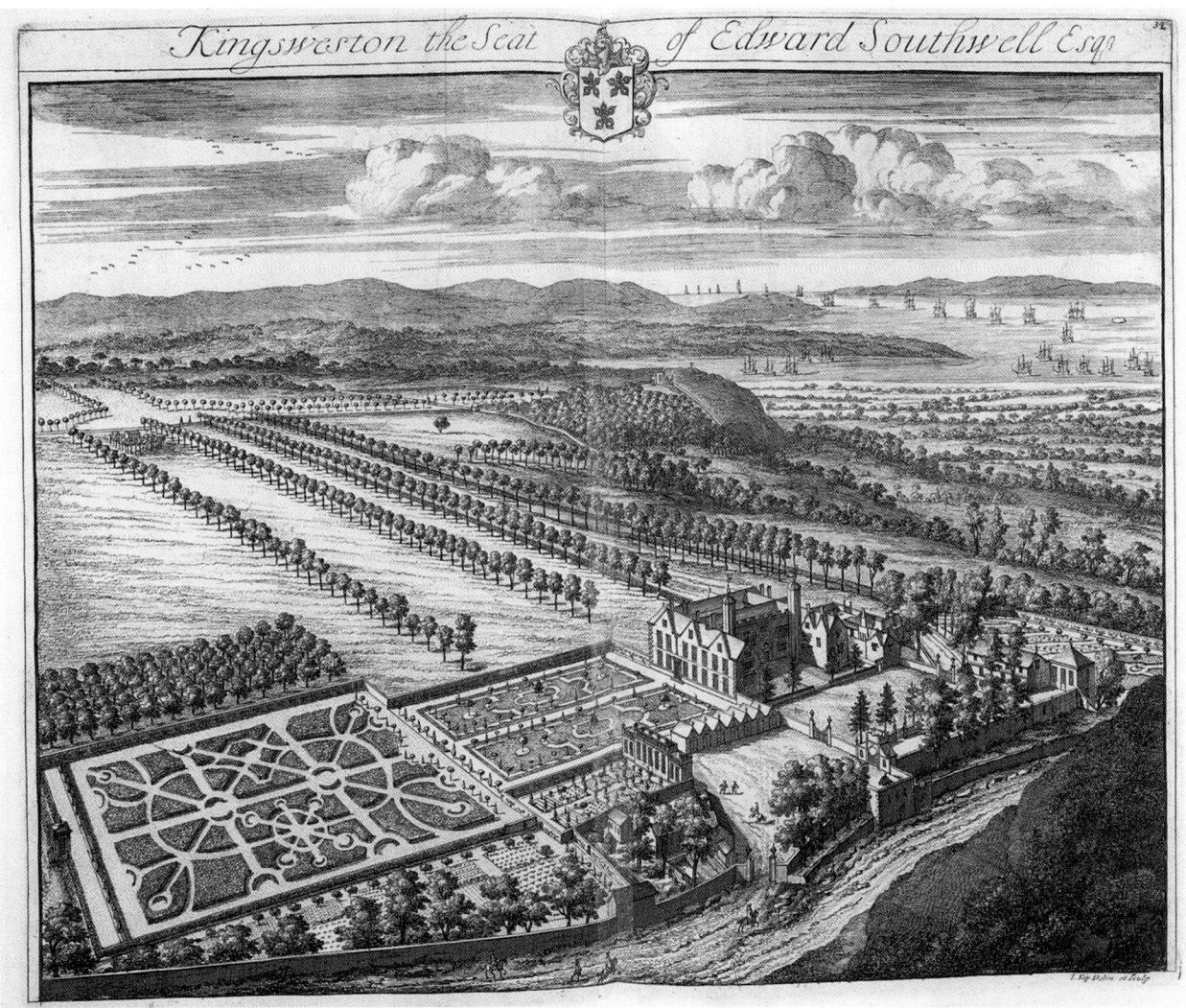

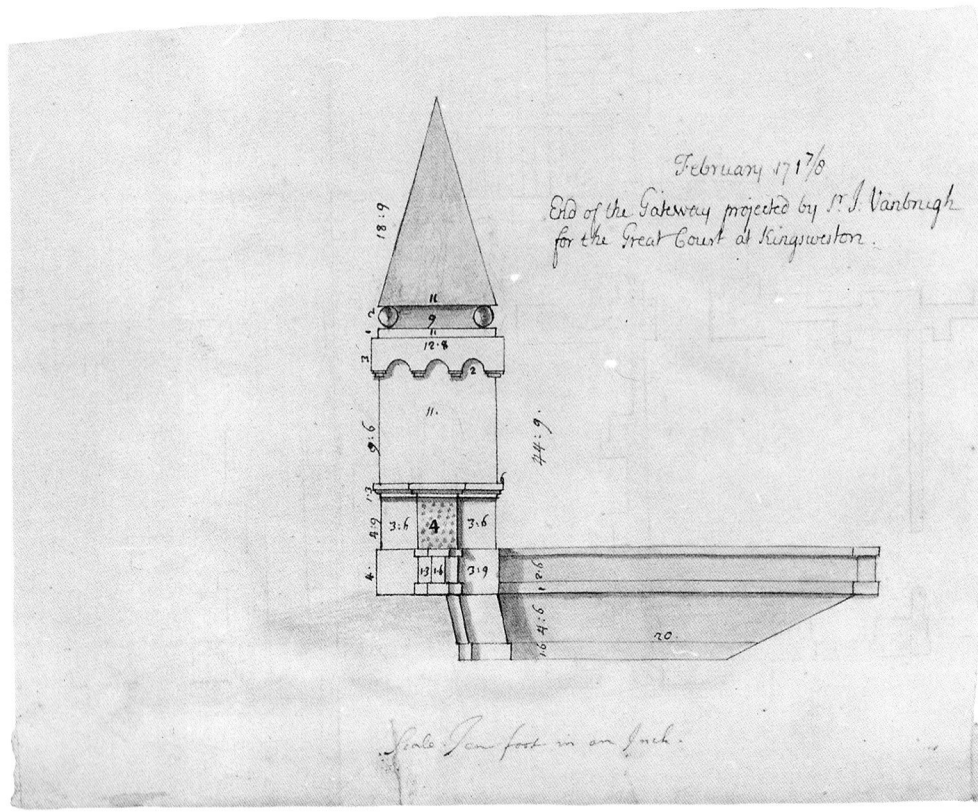

275   Vanbrugh's planned giant archway surmounted by a pyramid at Kings Weston, in an anonymous drawing, February 1718, from 'The Kings Weston Book of Drawings' [Bristol Civic Trust].

'A NEW DESIGN FOR A PERSON OF QUALITY IN DORSETSHIRE': EASTBURY HOUSE FOR GEORGE DODDINGTON

Eastbury House in Dorset was originally designed by Vanbrugh for George Doddington, a Lord of the Admiralty under George I. When he died in 1720 his nephew, George Bubb Doddington, Baron Melcombe, completed the house. Writing to Lord Carlisle on 19 July 1722 Vanbrugh reported that 'I am now going into Dorsetshire, Mr Dodingtons Trustees having met here in Towne, and adjusted all things for executing the Trust, in regard to the Building, which from this time is to go on without any Stop as fast as the Revenue the South-sea has left will allow of, which will be about £1800 a year'.[26] Once again, medieval houses influenced Vanbrugh's design, since Eastbury was closely modelled on Wollaton Hall (through its corner towers and planned sentry-boxes on the parapet), whilst the first design paid homage to Hardwick Hall (see Figs 77, 79).[27] Appropriately enough given George Doddington's Admiralty role, the masculine and 'martial' Doric Order was finally settled on for the front portico at Eastbury, after a number of Corinthian designs, whilst as a quintessential castle form, the corbel-table appears on the surviving great gateway to the north court and, together with portholes, on towers in the first design for the garden front (Figs 276, 279).[28]

Eastbury House was completed after Vanbrugh's death by the arch-Palladian Roger Morris (who added a conventional pediment to the Doric portico, in place of the planned unconventional chimney arcade) and it was demolished in 1775. Today only the gateway and part of the north wing survive (Fig. 278) but it is fortunate that a number of scheme drawings and engravings which record Vanbrugh's development of the design and its themes have been preserved. The design by Vanbrugh for the entrance front of about 1713 has, together with the smoking chimneys, two giant altar-like forms decorated with what look like Terms which cap paired columns (see Figs 145, 146).[29] These are *all'antica* versions of the medieval corner turrets found, for example, at Wollaton and which were later echoed in cylindrical towers at Vanbrugh Castle and House (see Figs 323, 334). In thus adapting traditional medieval domestic elements into

276   Vanbrugh's first design for the garden façade of Eastbury House, Dorset, c.1714–15 [Victoria and Albert Museum, London].

277   Alternative scheme for the garden façade of Eastbury House, c.1716 [Victoria and Albert Museum, London].

Garden Front.

278 Surviving north wing at Eastbury House.

what appear to be ancient forms Vanbrugh provides a graphic example of his quest for a British architectural style based on the dual virtues of the classical and medieval. In the centre of the house, set back from the front (judging from the shading on the drawing) are arched openings formed from chimneys, a variation on the open colonnade used at Kings Weston. Here Vanbrugh's intention for a dramatic effect and brooding presence on the skyline is emphasised by this shading of these haunting forms and the smoke issuing from their tops. The sheer scale of these twenty-five-foot high arches, rather than suggesting an element of 'self-parody' as some have claimed,[30] surely indicates their importance in Vanbrugh's scheme to evoke an effect of wonder or awe in the onlooker. A further elevation, for the garden front of about 1716 (Fig. 277), has a row of flaming urns similar to those at Kings Weston, traditionally symbolising death and resurrection.[31]

From the outset of its design, the roofscape of Eastbury was therefore conceived in terms of evoking a

mood of awe and melancholy in the onlooker, the thematic development of which is recorded in the unusually complete collection of Vanbrugh's subsequent scheme drawings which have survived. In an engraving of a revised design for the front (as of 1716) by Vanbrugh published in the second volume of Campbell's *Vitruvius Britannicus* of 1717 (Fig. 280), aptly entitled 'a New Design for a person of Quality in Dorsetshire', flaming urns have replaced the 'altars', a pediment befitting the patron's high social status has been attached, whilst the chimney arches remain.[32] Open mini-turreted forms resembling sentry-boxes have been added to the skyline, which in association with the flaming urns might be taken for memorial forms with the same brooding purpose. The accompanying side elevation has feminine cartouches over the windows at either end, whilst the rear façade has, appropriately enough for an elevation facing the garden, a bowed bay with giant Corinthian pilasters and female statues, possibly representing the Muses, on the parapet (Figs. 281, 282).[33] An

279 Surviving gateway at Eastbury House.

40 Feet ⊏⊐⊏⊐⊏⊐⊏⊐⊏⊐⊏⊐ *Extends 140*

The Elevation of a New Design for a person of Quality in Dorsetshire as Designed by Sr Iohn VanbrughKt.
Elevation D'un Nouveau Dessein.

Ca: Campbell Delin: *H. Hulsbergh Sc:*

280 (*above*)   Engraving of the front façade of Eastbury House in a design of 1716, from Colen Campbell's *Vitruvius Britannicus*, vol. II (1717), pl. 53.

40 Feet ⊏⊐⊏⊐⊏⊐⊏⊐⊏⊐⊏⊐ *Extends 100*

The Elevation of One End of a New Design for a person of Quality in Dorsetshire, as Designed by Sr Iohn Vanbrugh Kt.

Ca: Campbell Delin: *H. Hulsbergh Sc:*

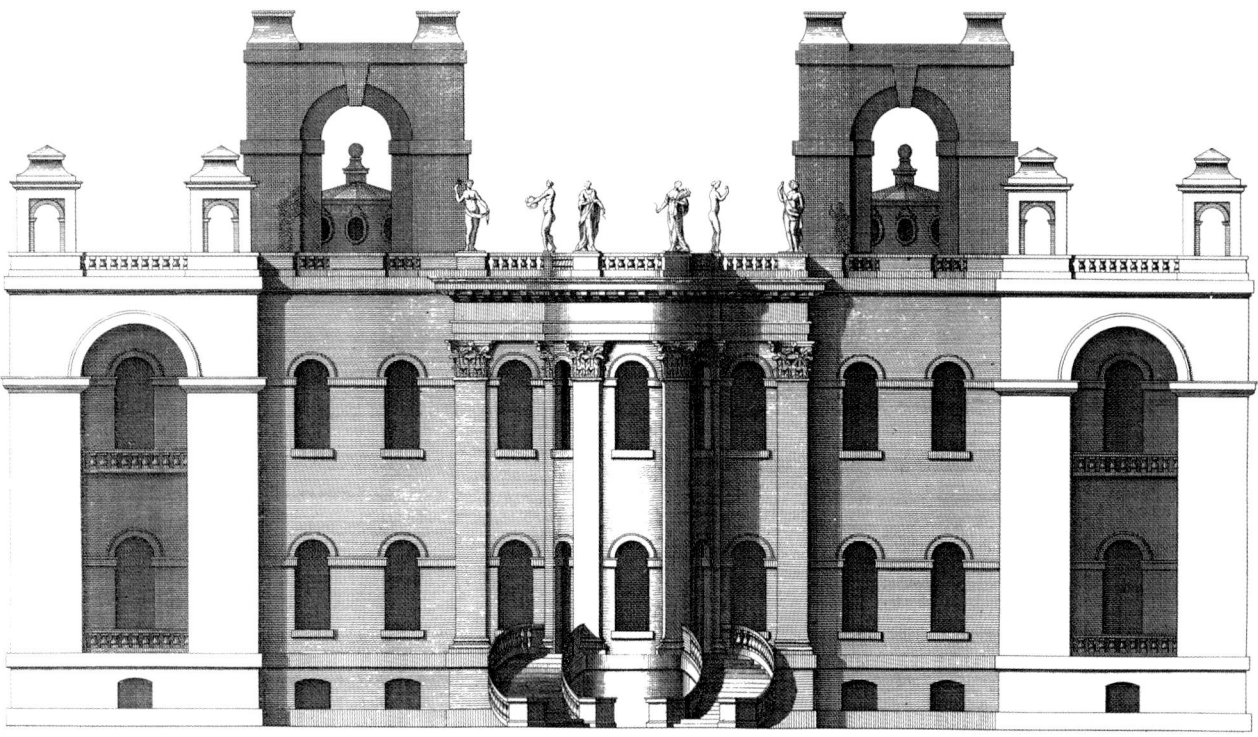

The Garden Front of a New Design for a person of Quality in Dorset-shire, as Designed by Sr. John Vanbrugh Kt.
Elevation D'un Nouveau Dessein du Coté des Jardins

Ca: Campbell Delin: H: Hulsbergh Sc:

282   Engraving of the rear, garden façade of Eastbury House, from Colen Campbell's *Vitruvius Britannicus*, vol. II (1717), pl. 54.

283 (*left*)   An alternative intermediary scheme for the front façade and plan of Eastbury House [Worcester College, Oxford].

281 (*facing page bottom*)   Engraving of a side façade of Eastbury House, from Colen Campbell's *Vitruvius Britannicus*, vol. II (1717), pl. 55.

alternative entrance scheme survives of uncertain date, which has a row of urns capping the Corinthian portico and smoking chimneys in the form of Roman altars over each side tower (Fig. 283); the centre is flanked by what seem to be obelisks, once again emphasising a melancholic memorial theme.[34]

In a subsequent drawing of the entrance front (Fig. 284), the fine ornament of previous schemes has gone.[35] The Order has been changed from Corinthian to Doric, perhaps because this was felt to be more in keeping with the military role of the first patron of the house and, of course, with Vanbrugh's own preferences. The front elevation has become more masculine and castle-like, with a fully crenellated rooftop arcade uniting the chimneys as at Kings Weston, portholes in the base of the portico,

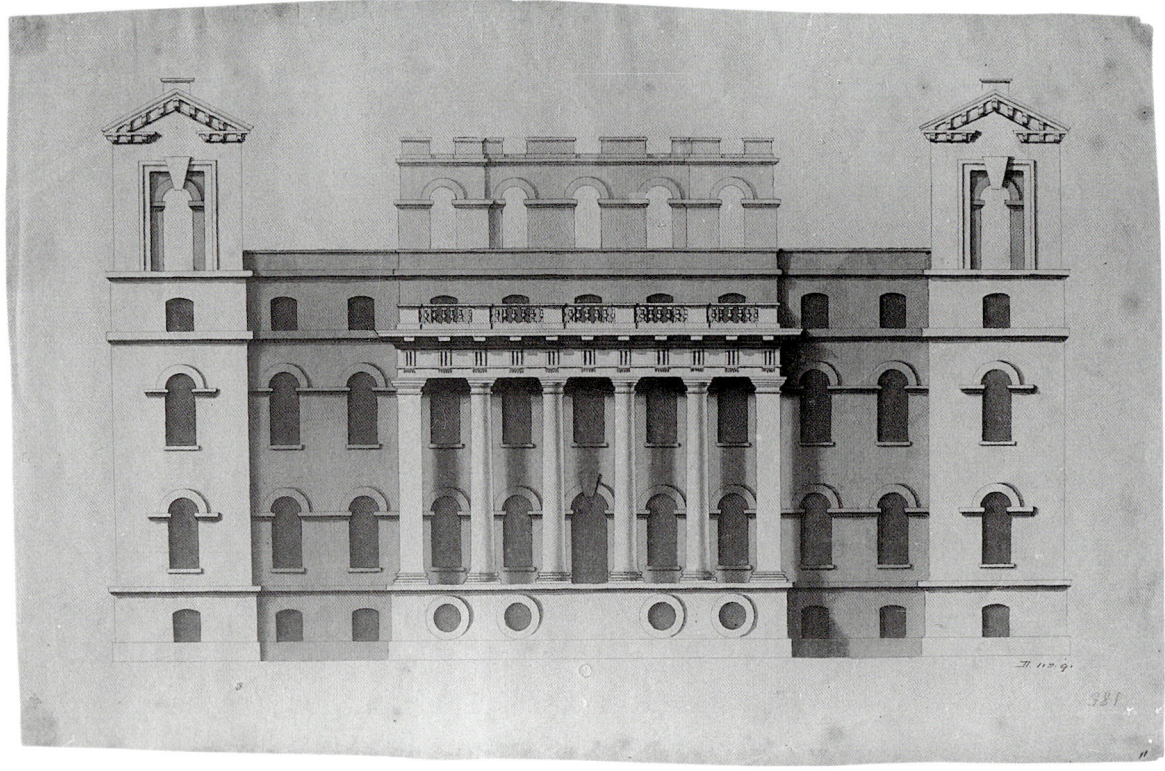

284 A further (Doric) intermediary scheme for the front façade of Eastbury House [Victoria and Albert Museum, London].

285 Final design for the front façade of Eastbury House, c.1716, drawing by Vanbrugh's Office, bound in the Elton Hall volume [Victoria and Albert Museum, London].

286 Computer model of Vanbrugh's final design for Eastbury House (the chimney arcade was not built) [author].

Elevation of Eastbury in Dorsetshire the Seat of the Right Hon.ble George Dodington Esq.r
Design'd by S.r John Vanbrugh K.t

Ca: Campbell delin: H. Hulsbergh Sculp:

287 and 288   Engravings of the front façade and the plan of the final design for Eastbury House, *c.*1721, from Colen Campbell's *Vitruvius Britannicus*, vol. III (1725), pls. 16 and 17.

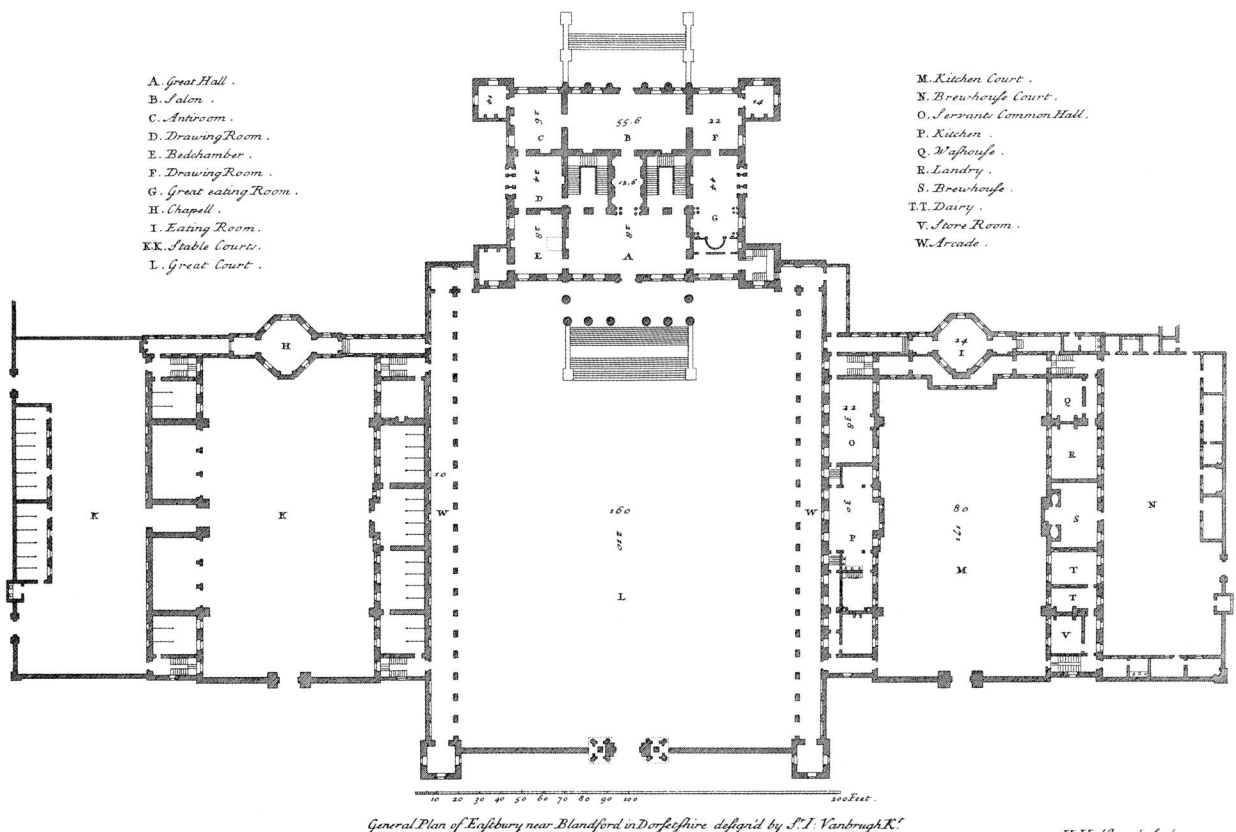

A. Great Hall .
B. Salon .
C. Antiroom .
D. Drawing Room .
E. Bedchamber .
F. Drawing Room .
G. Great eating Room .
H. Chapell .
I. Eating Room .
KK. Stable Courts .
L. Great Court .

M. Kitchen Court .
N. Brew-house Court .
O. Servants Common Hall .
P. Kitchen .
Q. Washouse .
R. Landry .
S. Brewhouse .
T.T. Dairy .
V. Store Room .
W. Arcade .

General Plan of Eastbury near Blandford in Dorsetshire design'd by S.r I. Vanbrugh K.t

Ca: Campbell delin: H. Hulsbergh Sculp:

simplified string-courses and corner towers (in the tradition of the medieval fortified house) capped by the
sentry-box forms and with heavy ornamental keystones
scaled to be seen from a distance. Thus the whole front
façade, not just the roofline, is more brooding in character. The final design of 1721, published by Campbell
this time in the third volume of *Vitruvius Britannicus* of
1725 (Figs 285, 287, 288) was clearly developed from this
scheme.[36] This design can be visualised in three dimensions using the computer (Fig. 286). Here the transformation from feminine to masculine is completed by the
addition of rusticated surrounds to the windows,
banding to the Doric columns and the re-appearance of
the row of urns. Eastbury has developed into a 'classical'
house – having a symmetrical front and Doric portico –
with medieval overtones – having corner towers and
rooftop arcade. The brooding, melancholic feel of the
original rooftop altars and urns has been retained and
pervades the whole façade, perhaps once again with the
intention of serving, much like the obelisks at Seaton
Delaval, as a memorial to the original patron.

'THE SEAT OF . . . THE HEREDITARY LORD GREAT CHAMBERLAIN OF ENGLAND': GRIMSTHORPE CASTLE FOR THE FIRST DUKE OF ANCASTER

Grimsthorpe Castle in Lincolnshire was Vanbrugh's last
major house, planned to be constructed on the foundations of an existing thirteenth-century manor which had
been enlarged in the reign of Henry VIII and remodelled
during the 1660s with a new north front (Fig. 289).[37]
Given that in this case the existing front façade was not
Tudor but classical (that is, symmetrical with Corinthian
pilasters), Vanbrugh's refacing with Doric columns was
obviously driven by his patron's iconographic requirements rather than a mere change in stylistic preferences.
Vanbrugh was a friend and distant relative of Grimsthorpe's owner, Robert Bertie (1660–1723), who was
the sixteenth Baron Willoughby de Eresby and from 1715
the first Duke of Ancaster and Kestevan. He was a fellow
Whig and a member of the party which travelled to The
Hague. Vanbrugh was also on close terms with the

289 Grimsthorpe Castle, Lincolnshire, before refacing by Vanbrugh, engraved by Leonard Knyff from Johannes Kip's
Britannia Illustrata (1707), pl. 20.

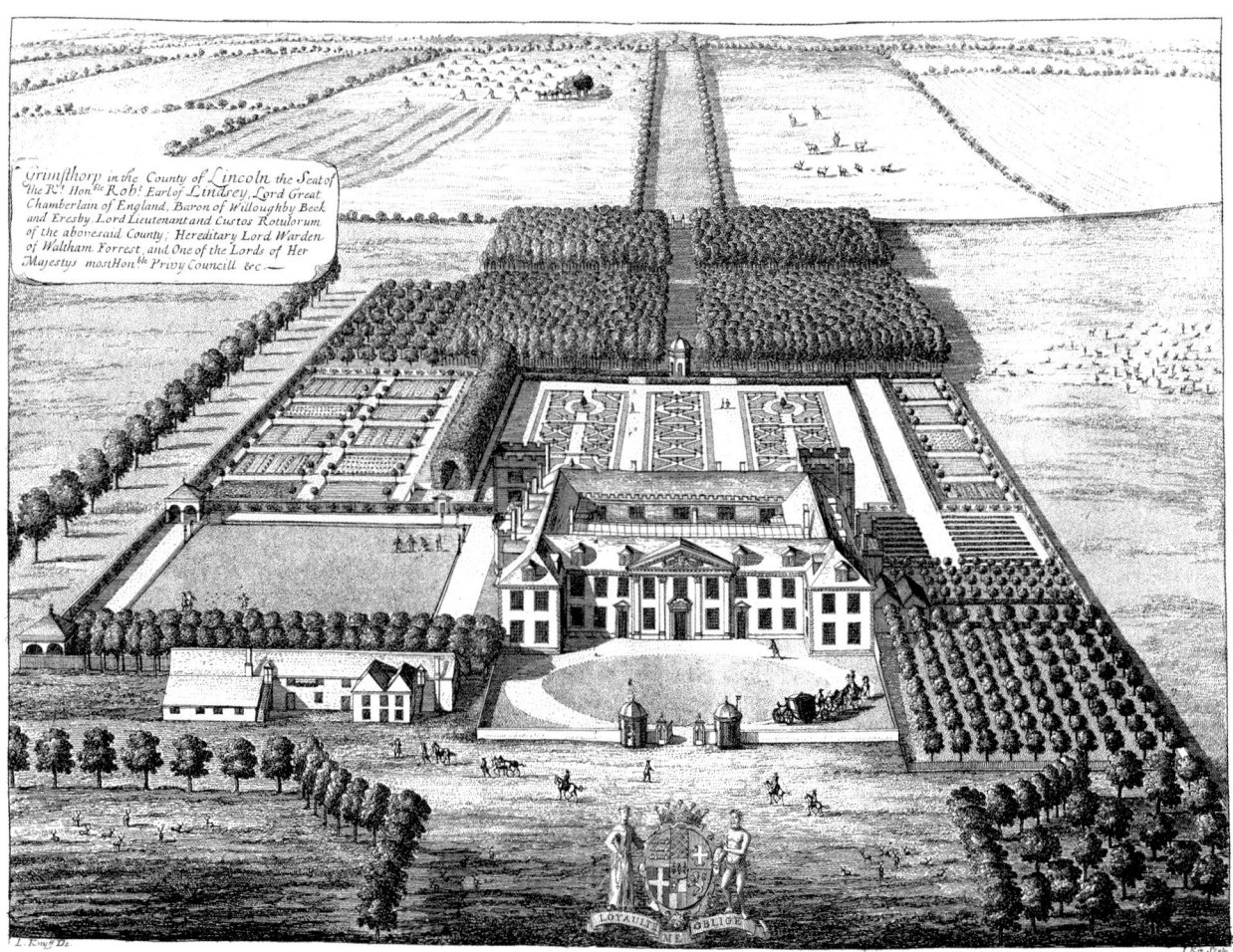

290   The north, front façade of Grimsthorpe Castle, with forecourt.

Duke's brother, Peregrine Bertie.[38] Writing to the Duke of Newcastle on 20 August 1723 Vanbrugh reports that in returning to London from Scarborough his plan was to 'wait upon his new Grace of Ancaster in my way, having the honour of an Invitation from him, to consult about his Building; by which I believe he is inclin'd to go on upon the General Design I made for his Father last Winter and which was approv'd of by himself'.[39] In the event only Vanbrugh's forecourt, the north front and Great Hall behind it, and the corner towers on the east and west elevations and a small summer house in the estate (at Swinstead and attributed to Vanbrugh) were built by the time work was halted in 1730, four years after his death (Figs 290–3). The low walls and pavilions which define the forecourt were probably designed by

the mason Edward Nutt, possibly under the direction of Hawksmoor, and are based on the towers on the north front.[40] The gardens were laid out by Stephen Switzer from 1711, with a concentric series of bastions extending the castle theme across the parkland (Fig. 294). In addition to the castle, Vanbrugh is credited with other work for the first Duke in the form of a large house at Swinstead a few miles from Grimsthorpe, which was also on the Ancaster estate and is now demolished (see Fig. 362). Drawings equally survive possibly of a hunting lodge (Figs 295, 296), designed in the typical Vanbrugian astylar, crenellated manner.[41] At the castle Vanbrugh proposed to follow his by then standard formula of a masculine, that is Doric, front façade and a feminine, that is Corinthian, rear-garden one. Corner towers were

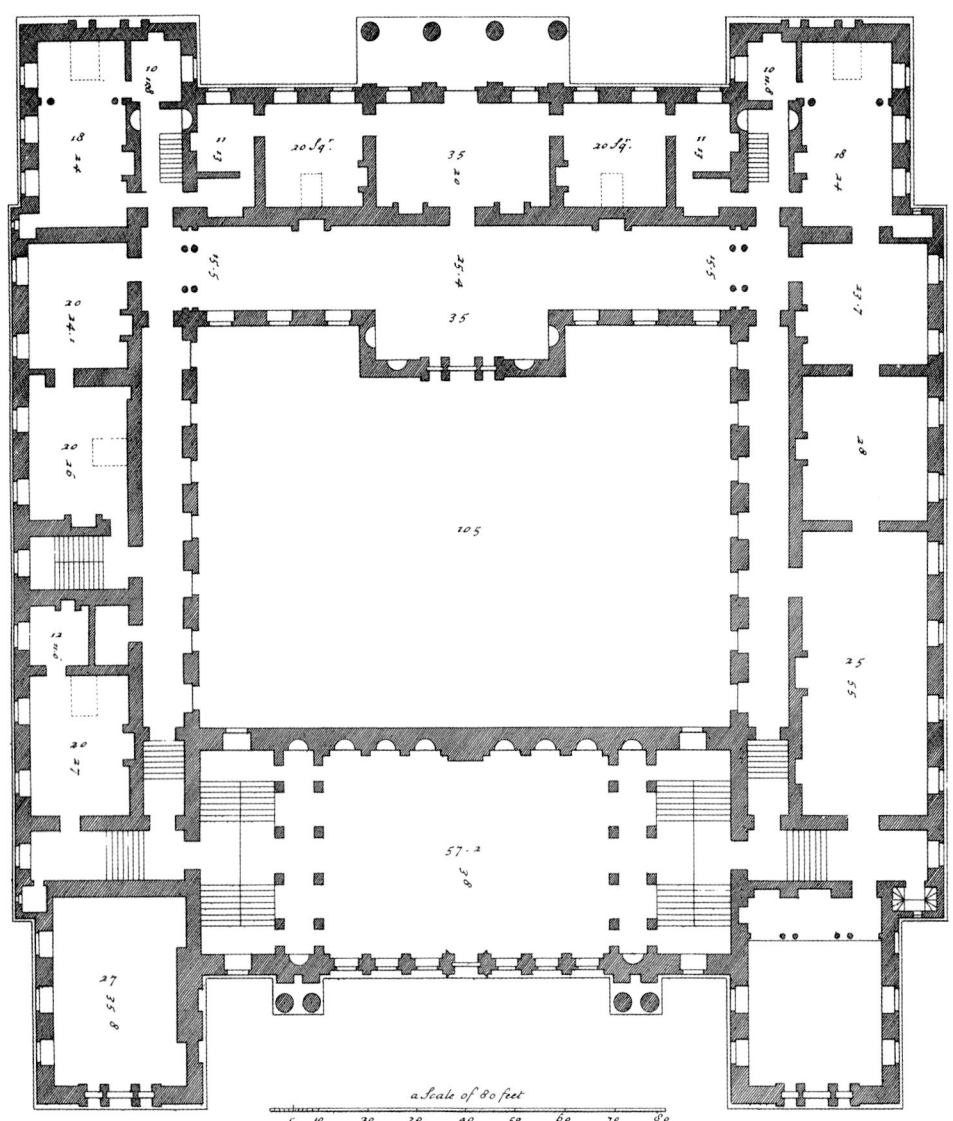

Plan of the Principall Floor of Grimsthorp in the County of Lincoln the Seat of his Grace the Duke of Ancaster and Kesteven Hereditary
Lord great Chamberlain of England. Defign'd by Sʳ Iohn Vanbrugh Kᵗ 1723.

Ca: Campbell delin: H. Hulfbergh Sculp:

291   Engraving of the plan of Grimsthorpe Castle, from Colen Campbell's *Vitruvius Britannicus*, vol. III
(1725), pl. II.

planned to frame each façade in order to suggest, once
more, the air of a medieval fortified house. After all, he
had worked on Lumley Castle just the previous year (in
1722; see Fig. 224). Here again urns and Roman altars
(serving as chimneys; see Fig. 165) appear on the skyline
at Grimsthorpe – the urns coming to memorialise,
perhaps, Vanbrugh's first patron Robert Bertie who had
died before building work commenced. The garden

façade was unbuilt but it is recorded in the third volume
of *Vitruvius Britannicus* published in 1725 (Fig. 297).
    The Willoughby de Eresbys held ancient hereditary
office as the Lord Great Chamberlain of England,
serving as Master of the Household at the Palace of
Westminster. Vanbrugh observed to Newcastle on 30 July
1723, 'I have just now a Message from Grimsthorpe, That
my Old Friend & Ally the Great Chamberlain is at last,

292   The east, corner façade of Grimsthorpe Castle.

293   The old summer house on the Grimsthorpe Estate at Swinstead, Lincolnshire, *c.*1720.

294   The Duchess's Bastion in the garden woods at Grimsthorpe Castle, laid out by Stephen Switzer from 1711, as drawn by William Stukeley in 1736 [Bodleian Library, Oxford].

The Duchesses Bastion in Grimsthorp gardens. Aug. 10.1736.

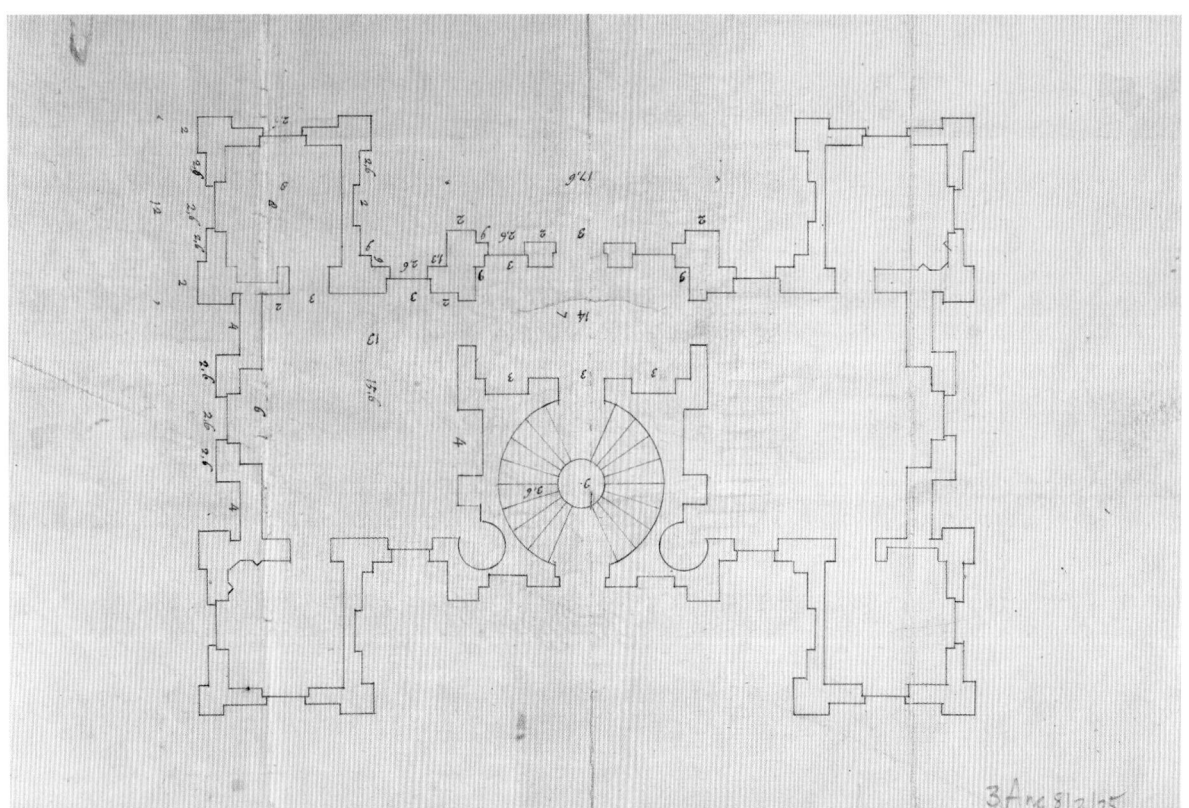

295 and 296   Elevation and plan of a house or hunting lodge near Grimsthorpe, design attributed to Vanbrugh, *c*.1710 [Lincolnshire Archives Office].

297   Engraving of the unbuilt south, garden façade of Grimsthorpe Castle, from Colen Campbell's *Vitruvius Britannicus*, vol. III (1725), pl. 13.

298   Engraving of the north, front façade of Grimsthorpe Castle, from Colen Campbell's *Vitruvius Britannicus*, vol. III (1725), pl. 12.

299 Vanbrugh's or Hawksmoor's fireplace and Thornhill's paintings of English kings in the Great Hall at Grimsthorpe Castle.

gone. I have no particulars how matters are left, But I think the Son he has left, will prove the best Soveraign that has Sate upon that Throne, and I hope all reasonable means will be us'd to Cultivate him, for I don't take him to be of an Ungratefull Soyle'.[42] Vanbrugh's metaphor links, in time-honoured fashion, the ancient family to the agricultural virtues of its estate (which are celebrated by a statue with a sheaf of corn, probably Ceres, in Campbell's 1725 engraving of Grimsthorpe's north façade in the third volume of *Vitruvius Britannicus*; Fig. 298). In both its ornamentation and form, Grimsthorpe can be seen as a celebration of the 'antiquity' of the Ancaster family, a link emphasised by Campbell in the base inscription to these engravings (quoted in the heading above). Vanbrugh's Hall at Grimsthorpe consciously recalled the medieval tradition of the Great

Hall[43] and this link is further authenticated by the fact that the Hall was constructed round an existing medieval house. The appearance of a medieval core surrounded by *all'antica* façades conveyed at Kings Weston was achieved at Grimsthorpe through the actuality of refacing a thirteenth-century manor. This was an arrangement that once again (and with greater veracity) emphasised a quasi-heraldic lineage from past to present. The fusion of, and continuity between, medieval and modern is given thematic emphasis in the Great Hall by Thornhill's paintings of English kings whom, by tradition, the Lord Chamberlain served and who had granted lands and titles to the Bertie clan – namely George I, William III, Henry VIII, Henry VII, William I, Edward III and Henry V (Figs 299, 300). Not only did this sequence connect the present to the medieval past, it also celebrated the

300 *(facing page)*   The Great Hall at Grimsthorpe Castle.

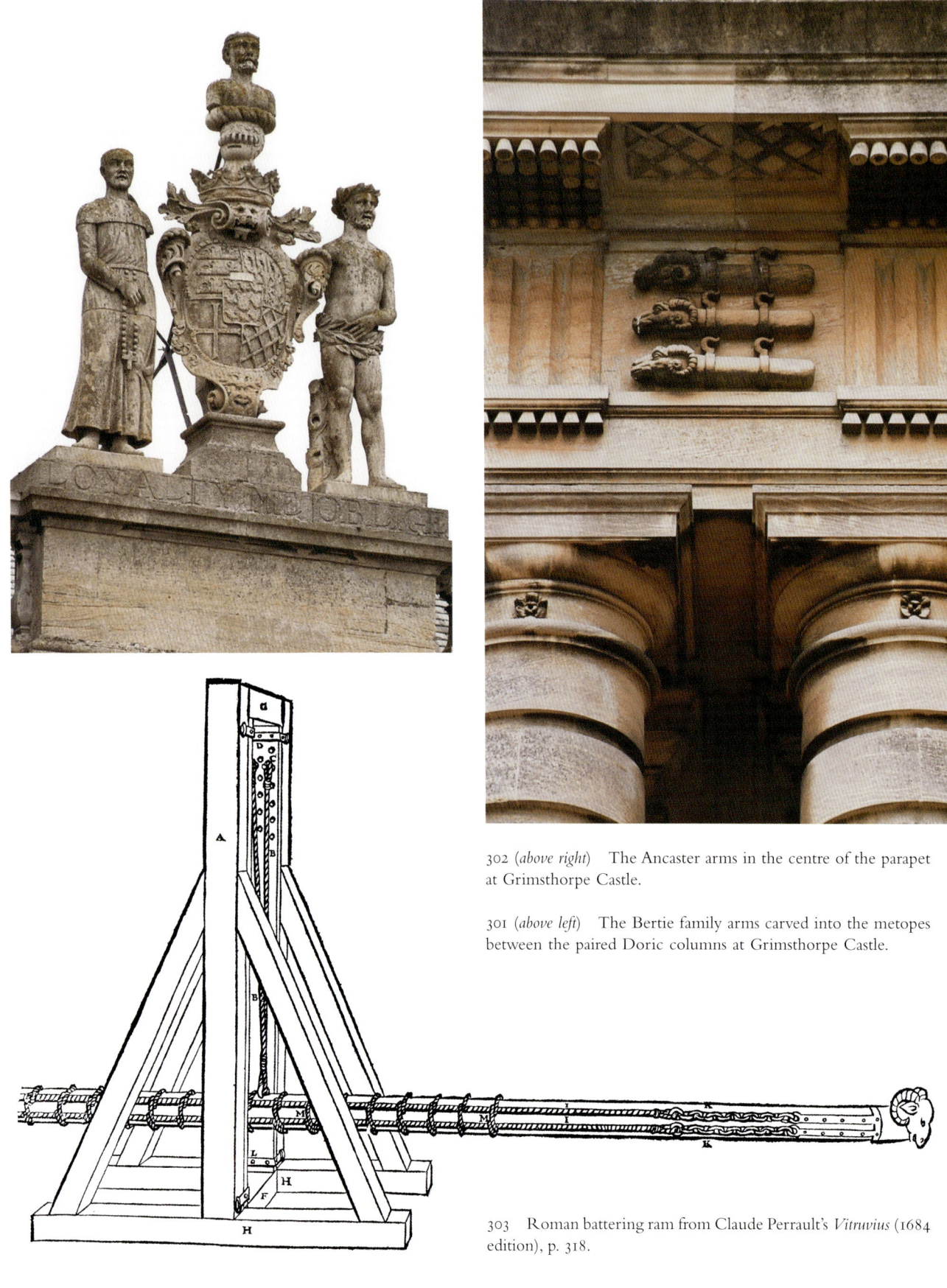

302 (*above right*)   The Ancaster arms in the centre of the parapet at Grimsthorpe Castle.

301 (*above left*)   The Bertie family arms carved into the metopes between the paired Doric columns at Grimsthorpe Castle.

303   Roman battering ram from Claude Perrault's *Vitruvius* (1684 edition), p. 318.

304   Vanbrugh's first project for the north façade of Grimsthorpe Castle, *c*.1715, drawing by Vanbrugh's Office, bound in the Elton Hall volume [Victoria and Albert Museum, London].

particular history of the house and its patron in the manner Vanbrugh's architecture generally aimed to do. His new north front had been first commissioned in 1715, during the reign of George I, whilst the old house came into the possession of the family in 1516 when it was granted by Henry VIII to the tenth Baron Willough-by de Eresby on the occasion of his marriage to Maria de Salinas, kinswoman and lady-in-waiting to Queen Katherine of Aragon. Indeed, Henry VIII had visited the house in 1541.[44] The paintings constitute a medieval revival and celebration, of which Vanbrugh's physical fabric should be seen as forming a part.

Vanbrugh's ornamentation on the north front closely follows a heraldic purpose and theme, since its commissioning in 1715 had been to mark Bertie's ennoblement as the first Duke of Ancaster and Kestevan. The façade celebrates this fact both directly, through the presence of the Ancaster arms in the centre of the parapet (Fig. 302), and indirectly, through the traditional identification of its Doric Order with heraldry, masculine nobility and, via Serlio, the legends of Hercules and St George.[45] A

drawing of Vanbrugh's first project for the north front (*c*.1715) indicates the presence of the Doric theme from the earliest days (Fig. 304). The heraldic character of the built scheme is made even more explicit through the presence of the Bertie family arms, comprising a stack of three Roman battering rams, which are carved into the metopes between the paired Doric columns (Fig. 301). This type of ram is described by Vitruvius in his tenth book[46] and illustrated in Perrault's edition of 1673 (which, as noted earlier, Vanbrugh may well have owned; Fig. 303). Vanbrugh's placing of the device in this prominent position clearly adds to the military character of these columns and of the façade as a whole. It represents yet another expression of his understanding of the essentially heraldic nature of the Doric Order, together with his fascination with Roman military history, and one is reminded of the metopes at Seaton Deleval taken from Roman coins and medals (see Figs 231, 232). A statue of a Roman soldier or warrior is depicted above the left-hand pair of Doric columns in the engraved north front published in *Vitruvius Britannicus* (1725; see Fig. 298). The

305   Pluto's rape of Proserpine, the statue group on the left-hand pedestal above the cornice at Grimsthorpe Castle.

306   Neptune's rape of Medusa, the statue group on the right-hand pedestal above the cornice at Grimsthorpe Castle.

warrior personifies the masculine character and intended martial aspect of the façade and the onlooker would have been eloquently prompted to recall the nation's warrior traditions. Here again, this particular 'Englishman's home' is most definitely his 'castle'.

In the event the paired Doric columns support statues representing scenes drawn from Roman mythology, which were in place by 1753 and perhaps as early as 1745. It is thought that they formed part of Vanbrugh's 'General Design' mentioned in 1723, carved possibly with Hawksmoor's help (given that Vanbrugh died in 1726 and work was probably continued by his assistant).[47] The pair on the left (when facing the building) represent the rape of Proserpine by Pluto, based in composition on the famous sculpture by Bernini although here accompanied by the guardian dog of the underworld, Cerberus (Figs 305, 308). Vanbrugh's admiration for Bernini's sculptures has been noted and he may have known of the version of this particular work by François Girardon at Versailles. The story of Pluto and Proserpine

is described by Ovid in Book Five of the *Metamorphoses* (see Fig. 222). Pluto, the god of the underworld, arose from the earth to capture Proserpine, whom he fell in love with because of an arrow shot by Cupid. Proserpine was the daughter of Jupiter and Ceres. Ceres searched the land for Proserpine and could not find her. Being the goddess of the earth, she refused to let things grow. Thus Jupiter arranged for Proserpine to return to her mother. However, because of Pluto's trickery, Proserpine could stay with her mother for only half the year, spending the other half with Pluto. When Proserpine is united with her mother it is said that spring comes, but when she is with Pluto winter arrives. The statue group on the right (Figs 306, 309) has been variously identified as Hercules holding aloft Antaeus or Neptune with Amphitrite accompanied by Neptune's traditional servant, the dolphin.[48] Given that the female figure clasps a snake-like form emerging from her hair, the more likely depiction is that of Neptune's rape of Medusa which is also described by Ovid in the *Metamorphoses*,

307   Bosses of flower-heads carved in the underside of the entablature above each metope at Grimsthorpe Castle.

this time in Book Four. Neptune had raped Medusa in the temple of Minerva, fathering Pegasus and Chrysaor, and in retribution for this violation of her temple Minerva changed Medusa's beautiful hair into snakes.[49]

The pairing of the two rapes, Neptune's of Medusa and Pluto's of Proserpine, reflects the wider theme of masculine strength – or 'Masculine Shew' – tempered by feminine virtue and beauty which is represented in the overall treatment of the Doric ornamentation on the façade. Vitruvius recommended that, on account of Proserpine's 'gentleness', works suitable to her should be adorned with flowers and foliage and this characteristic is reflected in the bosses of flower-heads carved in the underside of the entablature above each metope and in the frieze of the Doric capitals, thereby providing the ornamentation with what Serlio calls 'greater delicacy' (Fig. 307; see Fig. 302).[50] The same softening of – and duality in – the ornamentation at Seaton Delaval has been observed. Here at Grimsthorpe the dual aspect of male and female can also be seen reflected in the pairing

of the statue of a Roman soldier with that of the female figure carrying her sheaf of corn (which as noted most probably represented Proserpine's mother Ceres who was the goddess of the harvest and corn), in the engraving of the north façade published in *Vitruvius Britannicus* in 1725, a year before Vanbrugh's death (a scheme of 1723; see Fig. 298). Ceres was a common enough figure in Vanbrugh's work, having been represented above the pediment at Castle Howard (Fig. 310). The presence of Ceres and the bosses of flower-heads indicate the season of spring at Grimsthorpe, in keeping with Vanbrugh's use of Golden Age imagery elsewhere in his work.

It was noted in Chapter Six that the representation of unruly characters and forces, and their eventual subjugation, was one of Vanbrugh's principal dramatic themes. Here at Grimsthorpe this theme is powerfully translated into statuary. Indeed, the attempted rape of Leonora by Don John in *The False Friend*, which leads to Don John's death at the end of the play, carries with it a moral which might be seen to be particularly appropriate in under-

308 and 309 *(following pages)*   Left- and right-hand column groups and statues at Grimsthorpe Castle.

310   Ceres above the pediment at Castle Howard.

hereditary role as Lord Great Chamberlain of England and owners of a productive estate. The urns and altars also on the skyline echo the themes of sacrifice, death and resurrection implicit in the stories related by the two statues and unite to make a powerful and dramatic impression on the spectator consistent with Addison's theories. Here again Vanbrugh is literally a 'storyteller in stone'.

'MUCH ENTERTAIN'D WITH (BESIDES HIS WIFE) THE IMPROVEMENTS OF HIS HOUSE AND GARDENS': STOWE FOR THE FIRST VISCOUNT COBHAM

On 12 August 1725 Vanbrugh wrote to Tonson that 'we Stay'd at Stowe a Fortnight, a Place now, so Agreeable, that I had much ado to leave it at all'.[52] Whilst Bridgeman laid out the gardens at Stowe (Fig. 311) to a grand formal design inspired by the tastes of the leading Whig Richard Temple, First Viscount Cobham, in 1719–20, Vanbrugh's landscape works included the Temple of Sleep, Pyramid, Doric Arch, Nelson's Seat, Rotunda and The Cold Bath (Figs 312, 313; see Figs 130, 148, 149, 246).[53] These buildings, and the general reordering of the house and garden at Stowe of which they formed a part, can be understood as conceived round, amongst other themes, the celebration of love between Cobham and his wife. To build in order to celebrate the love of a husband for his wife was, after all, a timeless theme, as perhaps most famously of all with Shah Jahan's building of the Taj Mahal for Queen Mumtaz Mahal (which Vanbrugh may even have seen whilst in northern India, given his interest in Mogul mausolea; see Fig. 152). Just as Vanbrugh contrasted the building of the old manor at Woodstock by 'One of the Bravest and most Warlike of the English Kings' with Rosamond's Bower, which was 'tenderly regarded as the Scene of his Affections', so the theme of love was a common one in the gardens he influenced. Lady Irwin's poem celebrating the Castle Howard landscape notes that 'Perpetual Verdure all the Trees disclose,/Which like true Love no Change of Seasons knows' and that 'Not greater Beauty boasts th' *Idalian* Grove,/Tho' that is sacred to the Queen of Love'.[54]

As the Preface pointed out, gardens were frequently the setting of love and secret assignations in Vanbrugh's plays (much as the town was for villainous comedy, the forest was for outlaws and the country was for wholesomeness).[55] In *The Provok'd Wife*, for example, the amorous conspiracies of Lady Fancyfull are set in Spring Garden, a name used for several London pleasure gardens

standing how these statues were intended to be viewed. As Chapter One noted, Vanbrugh's liking for the morality of Ovid is indicated by the fact that in 1726 he almost certainly purchased an edition of the Roman writer for his son Charles, probably Tonson's 1717 illustrated folio edition of the *Metamorphoses*, with these very stories of the subjugation of a chaotic universe into harmonious order (see Fig. 222).[51] Such statuary inevitably reminds the onlooker of the timeless battles between the forces of order and disorder and, in standing either side of the Ancaster arms, more specifically of the heroic virtues of the house's patron and his ancestors as bringers of harmony and order to the country at large through their

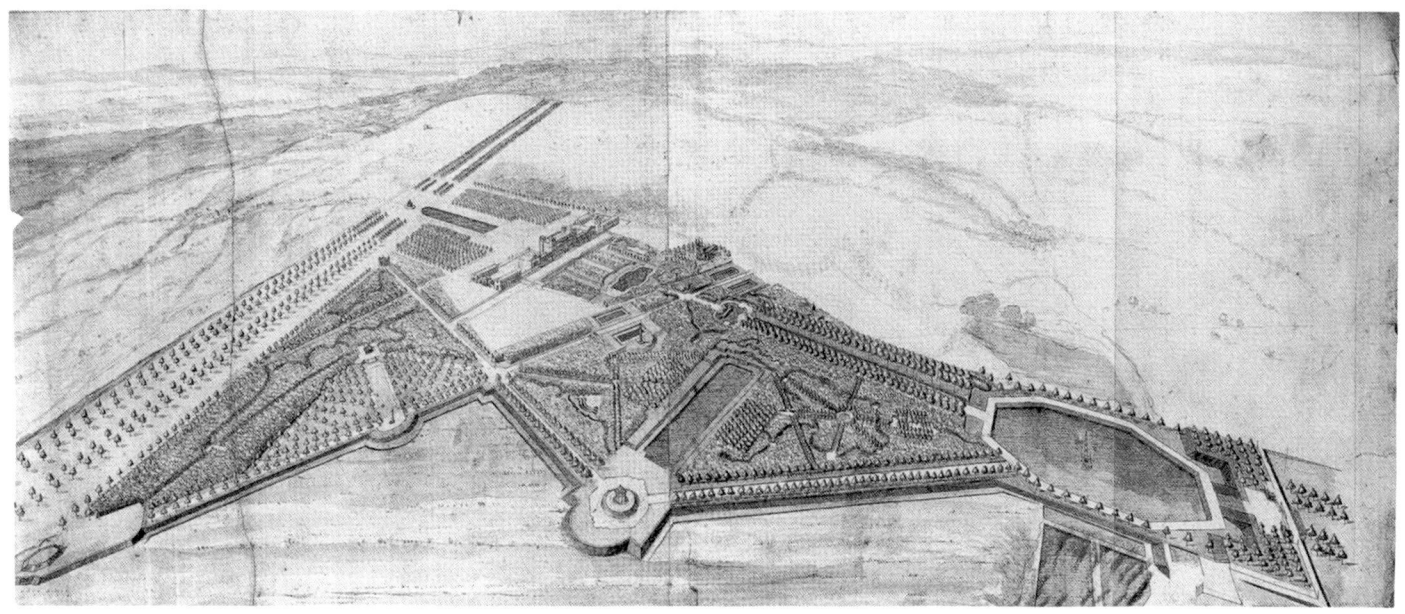

311 Bird's-eye view attributed to Charles Bridgeman of the Stowe landscape in 1719–20, with Vanbrugh's Rotunda as the focus of the garden (rather than the main house) [Bodleian Library, Oxford].

312 Vanbrugh's Rotunda at Stowe, 1720–21, which housed a gilt statue of Venus under a dome supported by Ionic columns, engraving by Jacques Rigaud (c.1733–4) [The Metropolitan Museum of Art, New York].

View of the Queen's Theatre *from the* Rotunda.   Veüe du Theatre de la Reine *prise a coté de la* Rotonde.

313   The Doric Arch at Stowe, adapted and re-positioned in 1767 using parts from Vanbrugh's original arch.

noted as places of assignation and intrigue.[56] In *The Mistake* Jacinta comments to Don Carlos: 'my Lady'll give you a Meeting in the Close Walk by the back Door of the Garden; she thinks she has something to propose to you, will certainly get her Father's Consent to marry you'.[57] In *The Relapse* Loveless's soliloquy on the subject of love opening the second scene of the third act is set in a garden. In *The False Friend* Don John remarks: 'The Wall [Don Guzman] past, to attempt your Wife, let us get over to prevent his doing so any more. 'Twill let us into a private Apartment by his Garden, where every Evening in his Amorous Solitudes, he spends some time alone'.[58] The theme of Cobham's love for his wife found particular expression in the Stowe landscape through

Dido's Cave, possibly designed by Vanbrugh around 1720, with its later painting (added by 1738) depicting Dido and Aeneas attended by a pair of cupids with torches to signify marriage. The theme was also celebrated through Vanbrugh's Rotunda of 1720–21 which originally housed a gilt statue of Venus, goddess of love, under a dome supported by Ionic capitals (see Figs 246, 312) – appropriately given the Order's established association with matrons and, according to Vitruvius, with 'womanly gracefulness'.[59] The specific requirement to celebrate Venus clearly limited Vanbrugh in his design to a canonic interpretation of an appropriate *all'antica* model, and the building is probably intended as a re-creation of the (destroyed) circular Temple of Aphrodite Knidos, or Venus, which housed Praxiteles's famous statue of Aphrodite/Venus. Perhaps this 'feminine' temple was also intended as a contrast to the 'male' Doric Arch designed by him which was taken down in 1767 and remodelled into the existing arch at Stowe (see Fig. 312).

The Ionic portico on the northern, front façade at Stowe, which is traditionally attributed to Vanbrugh (*c.*1720; Fig. 314), seems to have been added to honour the ennoblement of Sir Richard Temple as the first Viscount Cobham in 1718 and therefore represents a further expression of the conception of the architectural Orders as heraldic. With its origins in the ancient temple front, the pedimented portico would have been particularly appropriate as a celebration of a patron whose name was 'Temple'. However, the use of the Ionic Order here strongly contrasts with the masculine character of the majority of Vanbrugh's front façades. Perhaps the dimensions of the existing house, to which the portico was added, played a part in dictating the use of the Ionic's more slender proportions, as they had at Blenheim. Alternatively Giles Worsley has explained this apparent anomaly as a product of the fact that Stowe was a 'classical house' remodelled, unusually in Vanbrugh's designs, as the dominant feature in a self-consciously 'classical garden' and true to the principles of decorum, 'this purer Classical manner would have seemed more appropriate' than the more common one of 'masculine licentiousness' expressed in houses such as Seaton Delaval not set in this kind of garden.[60] As such the portico conforms to a further general distinction in architectural style observable throughout Vanbrugh's designs, whereby garden buildings such as the 'Temple of the Four Winds' at Castle Howard are far more canonically *all'antica* than are their main houses.[61] Although this explanation does not account for the specific use of the Ionic Order, it certainly echoes the association between feminine Orders and gardens found in Vanbrugh's work.

314 The Ionic portico on the north, front façade at Stowe, traditionally attributed to Vanbrugh (c.1720).

Moreover it has been seen that Vanbrugh associated the 'matronly' Ionic Order with Venus, the goddess of love, elsewhere in the Stowe landscape in celebration of the love between Temple and his wife. A carving of Venus and Adonis by Peter Scheemakers formerly graced the south portico at Stowe, put there around 1726, thereby further implying the link between porticoes and love. The fortune of Temple's wife, the heiress of a rich London brewer, had greatly assisted the work at Stowe, so the north Ionic portico may well have been conceived as a celebration of her contribution to the work, as well as the love between the pair and their recent ennoblement. House and wife were, after all, united as the two great loves of Temple's life. On 1 July 1719 Vanbrugh wrote to Tonson that 'I lately went to make my Ld Cobham a Visit at Stowe. Where he is very well, and in very good humour: and much entertain'd with (besides his Wife) the Improvements of his House and Gardens, in which he Spends all he has to Spare'.[62]

Chapter 8

'A SORT OF CHILD OF MY OWNE' AUTOBIOGRAPHY IN STONE AT 'GOOSE-PIE' HOUSE, GREENWICH AND CHARGATE

Vanbrugh designed a number of houses for himself and his family. These were a house at Esher in Surrey called Chargate, his 'Goose-Pie' townhouse at Whitehall and a group of family houses at Greenwich comprising Vanbrugh Castle, Mince-Pie House, the 'Nunnery' and two White Towers.[1] Freed from the normal constraints of patronage and immediate context (except, that is, at Whitehall), whilst tailored to Vanbrugh's resources and social status, these houses might be expected to represent the clearest architectural expression of his own character and stylistic preferences. Certainly this was how one contemporary, Jonathan Swift, famously portrayed 'Goose-Pie' House. If at Blenheim it was Vanbrugh's intention for the viewer to read 'the Duke of Marlborough in Story' – where he added that 'I cannot help looking on this Building wth. y^e. tenderness of a sort of Child of my Owne'[2] – it follows that in these houses built for himself and his family one might read something of his own 'story' and, as the most personal of his architectural 'offsprings', see reflected his self-image most clearly of all.

'PRETTY FOR A CHILD': JONATHAN SWIFT AND 'GOOSE-PIE' HOUSE IN WHITEHALL

A fire in January 1698 had destroyed a large part of the palace at Whitehall and it was at first planned that Wren should design a sumptuous building as its replacement. However, the intention was never realised and instead Vanbrugh – having only just turned his attention to architecture – was given permission to build a 'private' court lodging, suited to his future role as Comptroller

of the Works, on part of the site. Built by 1701, this was his first completed house (Fig. 316). The house was eventually demolished in 1895 but it is recorded in its enlarged state in a coloured wash made for Sir John Soane around 1803 and in an ink drawing (Fig. 317; see Fig. 29).[3] Vanbrugh attempted to give the new dwelling a 'guard-house' character, with four sentinel towers at its corners, consistent with his use of military typology elsewhere.[4] Although symmetrical, the façade was again astylar and emphasised notions of strength and impregnability, rather than classical order, through the quoins at the corners of the towers. With its curious crenellations implied by the panels in the parapet and banded rustication of the stucco in the central bays, the house appears to have been designed to give the impression of being larger than it was. For as Downes points out, Vanbrugh 'achieved a kind of grandeur on a small scale' by treating the middle three arched bays of the symmetrical elevation as a unit.[5] Houses of this size were usually part of a terrace; only grand houses in the centre of towns would have freestanding side elevations. Through this attempt at giving the effect of grandeur Vanbrugh no doubt sought to express his impending official role as Comptroller, given that this was the reason for the house's existence on this particular site. Ever conscious of the visual effect of forms, Vanbrugh here assembled parts and details which were drawn from a much larger composition (the quoins in particular) in order to give the impression to the onlooker of scale and importance, an effect which in the event seems to have been unsuccessful judging from the variety of records as to how the house was actually viewed by contemporaries.[6]

In 1701 an anonymous pamphlet appeared entitled 'A True Character of the Prince of Wales's Poet, with a Dis-

315 *(facing page)*   Vanbrugh Castle, Greenwich, north, rear garden façade.

316   Computer reconstruction of Vanbrugh's 'Goose-Pie' House as enlarged with side wings in 1719 [author].

cription of the newly erected Folly at White-hall'. The fact that the house failed to conform visually to any canonic domestic model was used as a sign of moral corruption on the part of its architect. The house was described as 'of mixt Preposterous kind', since Vanbrugh 'knows no *Sense, nor Place, nor Unity*'.[7] More damagingly for Vanbrugh, however, was the fact that Swift took up the attack and, as the Introduction noted, wrote three poems directly satirising both the new house, nicknamed by him 'Goose-Pie', and its architect. These poems were called 'Vanbrug's House' (manuscript version, *c.*1703), 'Vanbrug's House, built from the Ruins of Whitehall that was burnt' (1709) and 'The History of Vanbrug's House' (1710).[8] Given the understanding of Vanbrugh as a 'storyteller in stone' examined here, curiously enough in the 1709 version Swift read the fabric of the house, albeit sarcastically, as if it were a five-act play with its author-architect as the chief character:

> The building, as the poet writ,
> Rose in proportion to his wit:
> And first the Prologue built a wall
> So wide as to encompass all.
> The scene, a wood, produced no more
> Than a few scrubby trees before.
> The plot as yet lay deep, and so

> A cellar next was dug below:
> But this a work so hard was found,
> Two Acts it cost him underground.
> Two other Acts we may presume
> Were spent in building each a room;
> Thus far advanc't, he made a shift
> To raise a roof with Act the fift.
> The Epilogue behind, did frame
> A place not decent here to name.

Vanbrugh was unique amongst the architects of his day in receiving such direct criticism from Swift, attacks that continued throughout his career. Superficially both men were similar, both popular writers and almost the same age – Swift was born three years after Vanbrugh, in 1667. However, Swift was a Tory and Vanbrugh a Whig. Vanbrugh's evident popularity with the great and the good and his lack of respect for the Cloth added to Swift's disapproval. If on the political seesaw Swift's fortunes had declined with the death of Queen Anne in 1714, Vanbrugh's were rising – as has been seen, he was dismissed from the Comptrollership under Tory pressure in 1713 only to be re-instated two years later under the new Whig administration. In the context of the eighteenth-century battle between the so-called 'Ancients' and

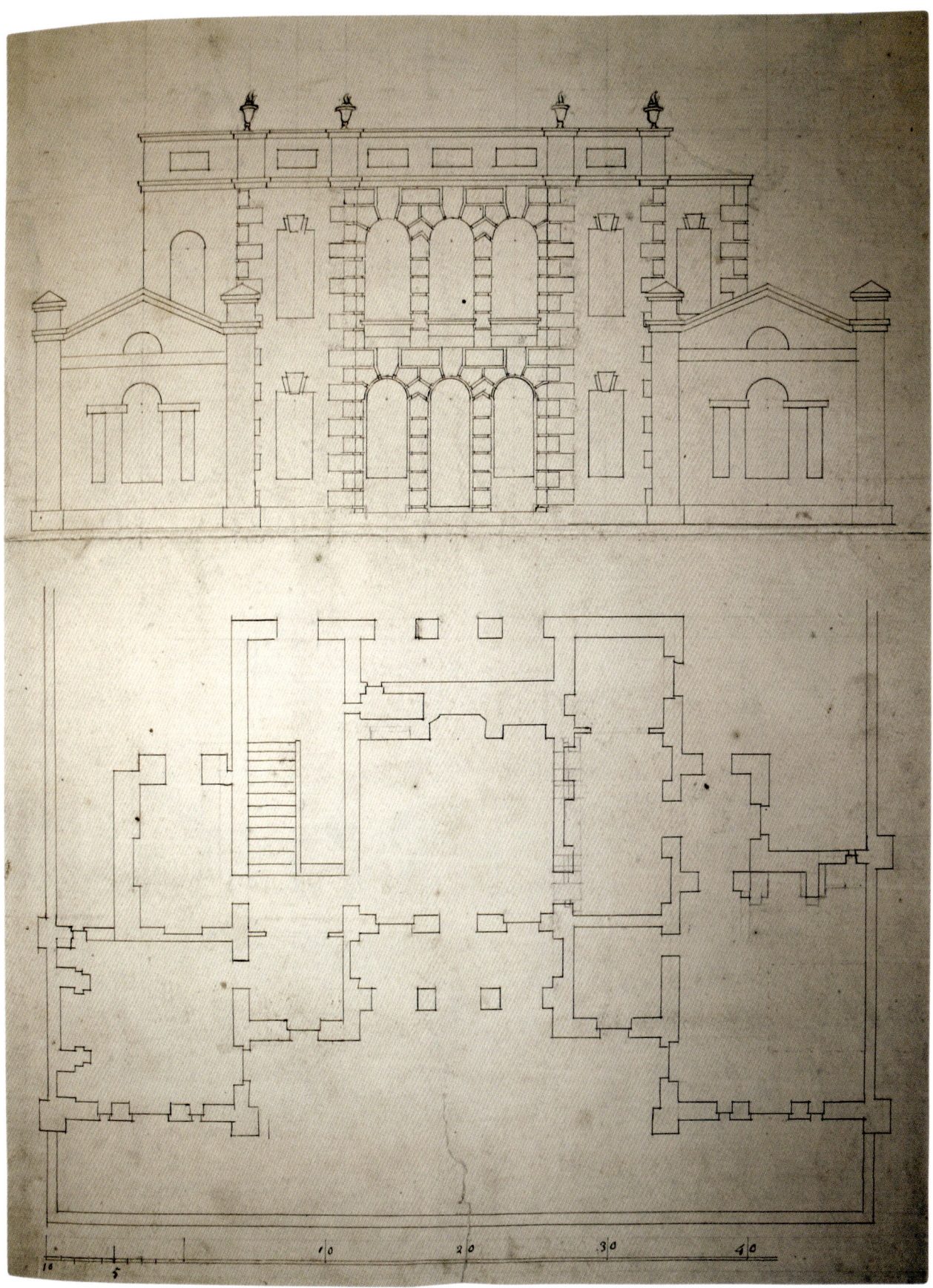

317   Elevation and plan of Vanbrugh's 'Goose-Pie' House, unknown draughtsman, bound in the Elton Hall volume [Victoria and Albert Museum, London].

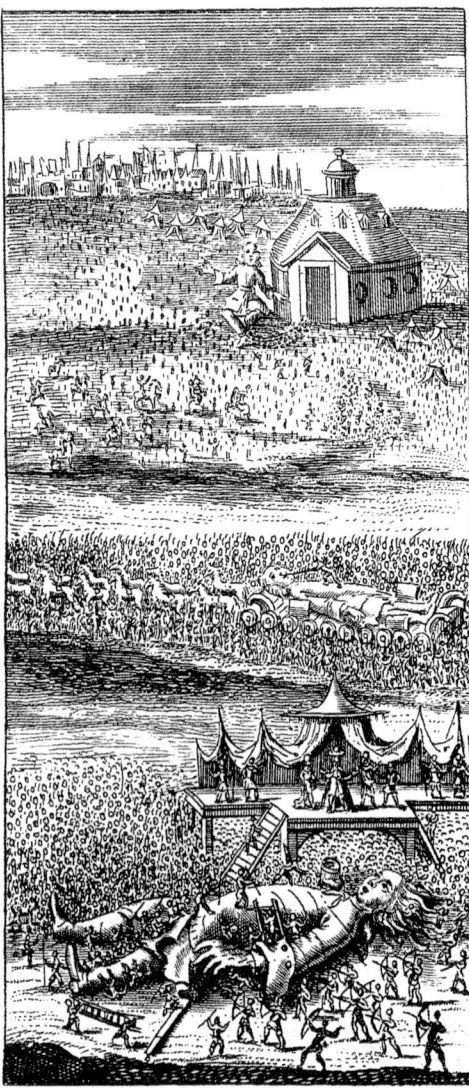

318 Illustration of the house for a 'big' man from Jonathan Swift's *Gulliver's Travels* (1727 edition).

One Storey high, one postern Door,
And one small Chamber on a Floor . . .

He saw the edifice, and smiled,
Vowed it was pretty for a child . . .

Thrice happy poet, who may trail
Thy house about thee, like a snail;
Or harnessed to a nag, at ease,
Take journeys in it like a chaise;
Or in a boat, whene'er thou wilt
Canst make it serve thee for a tilt.

Compare these lines with Swift's fictional history for Gulliver's 'little' house in Book II of the *Travels* of 1726:

. . . a wooden chamber of sixteen foot square, and twelve high, with sash windows, a door, and two closets, like a London bed-chamber.

. . . not much bigger than what I have seen in a London toy-shop, for the furniture of a baby-house.

In journeys . . . a servant on horseback would buckle my box, and place it on a cushion before him . . . My box . . . floated about five foot deep in water . . . they had seen a swimming house . . . he laughed at their folly (II, III–VIII).

Swift's fictional history of Vanbrugh's 'Goose-Pie' house told first in public by him in 1709 becomes that of Gulliver's doll's house in 1726. To both fall the same ridiculous consequences of being seen by Swift as toy buildings. As an integral part of Swift's satire in *Gulliver's Travels*, the book's domestic architecture would surely have been readily identifiable with Vanbrugh's buildings to the contemporary reader, since they had been a frequent target of Swift's poetic satire. For example one 'Signor Carolini' (acknowledged only as a 'noble Venetian now residing in London') in his *Key, or Gulliver Decypher'd* (1727) saw in Book III, 'A New method (perfectly Vanbrughian) for building Houses, by beginning at the Roof, and working downwards to the foundations'.[10]

In Swift's attacks on 'Goose-Pie' he identifies both house and architect as attempting to signify the effect of grandeur without merit, just as diminutive Gulliver was seen to do. As if in direct reference to Vanbrugh and his house, Guilliver reflects:

how vain an attempt it is for a man to endeavour doing himself honour among those who are out of all degree of equality or comparison with him. And yet I have seen the moral of my own behaviour very frequently in England since my return, where a little contemptible valet, without the least title to birth, person, wit, or common sense, shall presume to look

'Moderns', Swift was indisputably on the side of the former, whilst Vanbrugh and his new Whitehall house came to symbolise for Swift all the modern delusions of 'Reason' and Whig values of progress that much of his work, including his most famous book, *Gulliver's Travels*, ridiculed.

Indeed, Blenheim is the clear object of ridicule behind the large, state-financed house provided for the giant Gulliver in Book I of the *Travels* (Fig. 318), published in the year of Vanbrugh's death, 1726, just as the description of Guilliver's little house in the second book clearly parallels that of Vanbrugh's 'Goose-Pie'.[9] A simple comparison shows this, taking firstly Swift's fictional history for Vanbrugh's 'Goose-Pie' house from the poems of 1703, 1709 and 1710:

with importance, and put himself upon a foot with the greatest persons of the kingdom (II, v).

Here again is an echo of Swift's earlier attacks in 'The History of Vanbrug's House', where he had observed that 'Van's genius, without thought or lecture,/Is hugely turned to architecture'. On the architect being installed in the revived office of Carlisle Herald in March 1703, it was seen that Swift commented: 'Now Van will be able to build houses'. Swift is alluding to the idea that Vanbrugh was dependant on the rules of other crafts when designing his buildings, in this case heraldry, and he goes on to include the influence of stagecraft when observing of 'Goose-Pie' in 1709 that 'The building, as the poet writ,/Rose in proportion to his wit' and that the house represented 'A type of modern wit and style,/The rubbish of an ancient pile'.

Judging from Vanbrugh's reaction to Swift's mockery, discussed in the Introduction, the poet seems to have hit a nerve. The house was enlarged with the side wings in 1719, following Vanbrugh's need for extra space after his marriage in that year but perhaps also as a response to Swift's criticisms, since the result was to give the house greater actual presence. Swift plainly disliked the false crenellations and overblown scale of Vanbrugh's architecture, factors which he clearly identified less with function than with the need for visual effect. Somewhat ironically given Vanbrugh's general ambition to use architecture to tell his patron's 'story', Swift saw 'Goose-Pie' and its attempt to signify the effect of grandeur to passers-by as a perfect expression of its architect's own character and artistic pretensions. In so doing he provides a valuable clue as to how the other houses Vanbrugh designed for his own use should be seen.

'A TOWER OF WHITE BRICKS . . . UNDER THE CANNON OF THIS CASTLE': VANBRUGH AT GREENWICH

Following Vanbrugh's appointment as Surveyor of Greenwich Hospital in 1716, his association with the town became more intimate still. Whilst staying in Greenwich he rented a house which he somewhat mockingly referred to in Christmas 1717 as his 'Country morsell',[11] but his impending marriage evidently led to new requirements. For in an entry for 3 March 1718 his account book records that he 'took a Lease from Sr Michll. Biddulph at Greenwich, of a Field & Other Grounds, at the Rent of Sixteen Pounds a year for 99 Years' and that he had 'pd Mr Fuller for drawing the Lease'.[12] This was in reference to a plot on Maze Hill

and a twelve-acre triangular field to the south. Vanbrugh built a 'castle' and gated forecourt for himself and his new wife on this plot between 1718 and 1719, whilst in the field (which became known as Vanbrugh Field) he built a gateway, which comprised two habitable towers joined by an arch, and four houses for members of his family (Figs 319, 320). Vanbrugh House, or what later became known as 'Mince-Pie House' (1721–2), was built for his brother Charles (Figs 321, 322). Befitting the building's military style and location, Charles was a captain in the navy, as the inscription on an elevation drawing of about 1721 emphasised – 'Capt Charles Vanbrough's house at Greenwich' (Fig. 323).[13] The house was little more than fifty-odd feet across with two stairtowers either side and three ground-floor rooms. The so-called Nunnery (1719–20; Figs 324–8) was probably intended for his maiden sisters but was let after Christmas 1720 to his widowed brother Captain Philip Vanbrugh (another naval man who may well have been nursed by the sisters). This building consisted of a symmetrical central block joined by small courtyards to two detached single rooms on either side, both of which had large hearths in the almshouse tradition. The form thereby expressed the building's intended charitable purpose, to house two elderly women, further signified by its associative name and the cross over the central tower.[14] To one side of this, on the north, stood the New White Tower (1722–3), built by Vanbrugh for his son Charles, whilst on the other side stood the South White Tower (1723–4), built for his youngest son John – both towers were originally identical but were altered over time (Figs 329–33). Vanbrugh Castle was also much altered, not least by Vanbrugh himself with a large eastern extension, but it can be shown in its original form using the computer (Fig. 334). In Greenwich, as in Whitehall, Vanbrugh's houses grew in proportion to his family. Of these buildings, the only survivor is Vanbrugh Castle (Figs 335–8) and its track (the street now called Vanbrugh Fields) but the original complex is recorded in a variety of sketches and once again can be visualised using the computer (Fig. 341). William Stukeley documented the Greenwich compound for the Society of Antiquaries in a series of sketches in June 1721, and then in August 1722 when he drew Vanbrugh House (Fig. 339; see Fig. 322).[15] It was Stukeley who recorded the name of 'The Nunnery' on one of his sketches, although in the light of the humorous and, here again, the associational qualities of the name, it is quite likely that it was Vanbrugh's own for the building. Given Stukeley's antiquarian interests, these sketches are a clear indication of the contemporary observer's association of Vanbrugh's Greenwich buildings with English medieval architecture.

319   Computer reconstruction of Vanbrugh's Greenwich compound [author].

320   Gateway to Vanbrugh Fields [Martin Collection, Greenwich Heritage Centre].

321   Computer reconstruction of Vanbrugh House (1721–2) [author].

322   Vanbrugh House drawn by William Stukeley in 1722 [Bodleian Library, Oxford].

Castellulum Vanbrugiense apud Gronovicum
18 Aug. 1722.

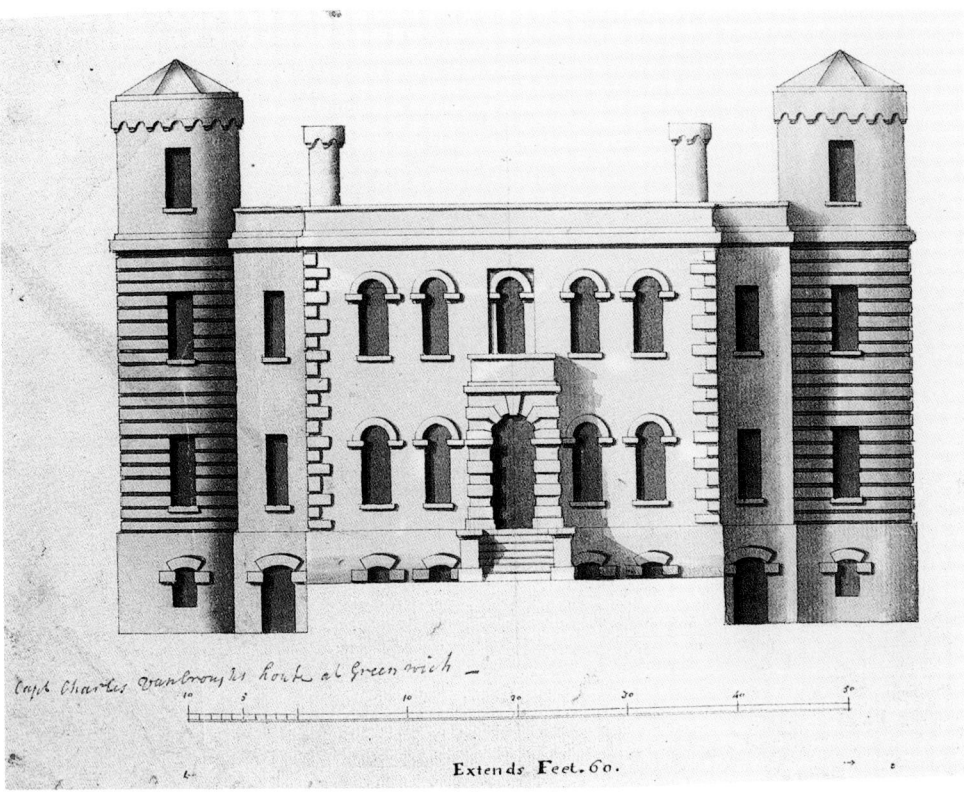

323 Preliminary design for the front façade of Vanbrugh House, *c*.1721, or what became known as 'Mince-Pie House' (destroyed), Vanbrugh's Office, bound in the Elton Hall volume [Victoria and Albert Museum, London].

With their corbel-tables and mock crenellations, astylar façades and heavy quoins, together with their portholes and gates, Vanbrugh's Greenwich buildings were obviously intended, somewhat self-consciously, to recall in the observer's imagination traditional fortification structures. Vanbrugh Castle for example owes much to the Little Castle at Bolsover, whilst Vanbrugh House may well have been inspired by Worksop Manor (see Fig. 78).[16] At Vanbrugh House, outworks were again added which in this case – judging from the surviving preliminary drawing of 1721 and Stukeley's sketch of the actual building (see Figs 322, 323) – took the form of a stepped gateway, raised entrance platform and two corner mini-towers resembling sentry-boxes. The cylindrical towers which are attached to either side of the building, as well as the one in the centre of the south elevation of Vanbrugh Castle, are reminiscent of much smaller forms on the main façade of Wollaton Hall (see Fig. 79).[17] These details once more reflected Vanbrugh's lifelong concern for military structures and are here realised in their purest form. At about the same time as designing these Greenwich buildings, around 1720, he even produced a scheme at Inveraray for a full-blown castellated house set on an earth mound, complete with corner towers capped with pyramidal roofs, arrow slits and crenellations (Fig. 340) but this (albeit symmetrical) medieval fantasy remained unbuilt.[18] Vanbrugh's probable influence over the design of actual military structures realised in the same astylar manner – which has become known as the 'Ordnance Vanbrugh' style (see Figs 112–17) – no doubt lent an air of authenticity to such fantasies, as well as to the castellated houses built at Greenwich.[19] Vanbrugh certainly saw his own fortified houses in traditional, defensive terms. For, as noted in the previous chapter, when writing to the Duke of Newcastle concerning the Duke's surprise visit to Vanbrugh Castle he had observed: 'I hear your Grace was pleas'd to Storm my Castle yesterday: I hope next time you'll be so Gallant to let me know of your Design, which if I do, I'll endeavour to give you a Warmer Reception'.[20]

Whilst Vanbrugh Castle was undoubtedly designed to evoke the image of the archetypal medieval castle in the mind's eye of contemporary observers, it was also a deeply personal statement of its architect's identity and character informed by such roles as that of Garter Herald. It was pointed out that Vanbrugh was fully aware

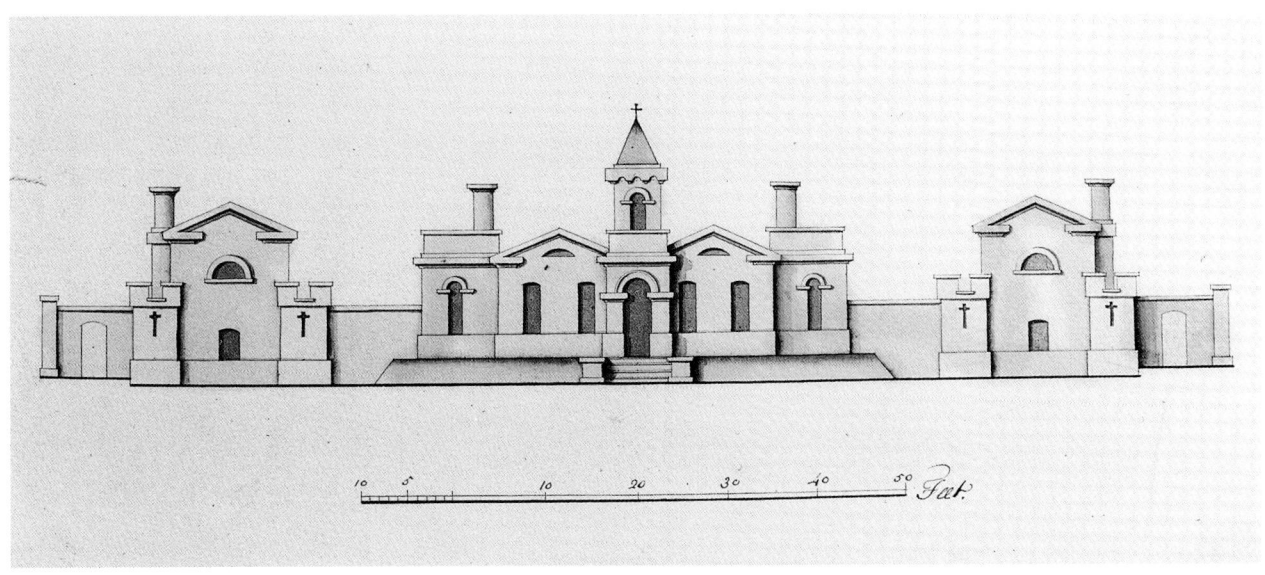

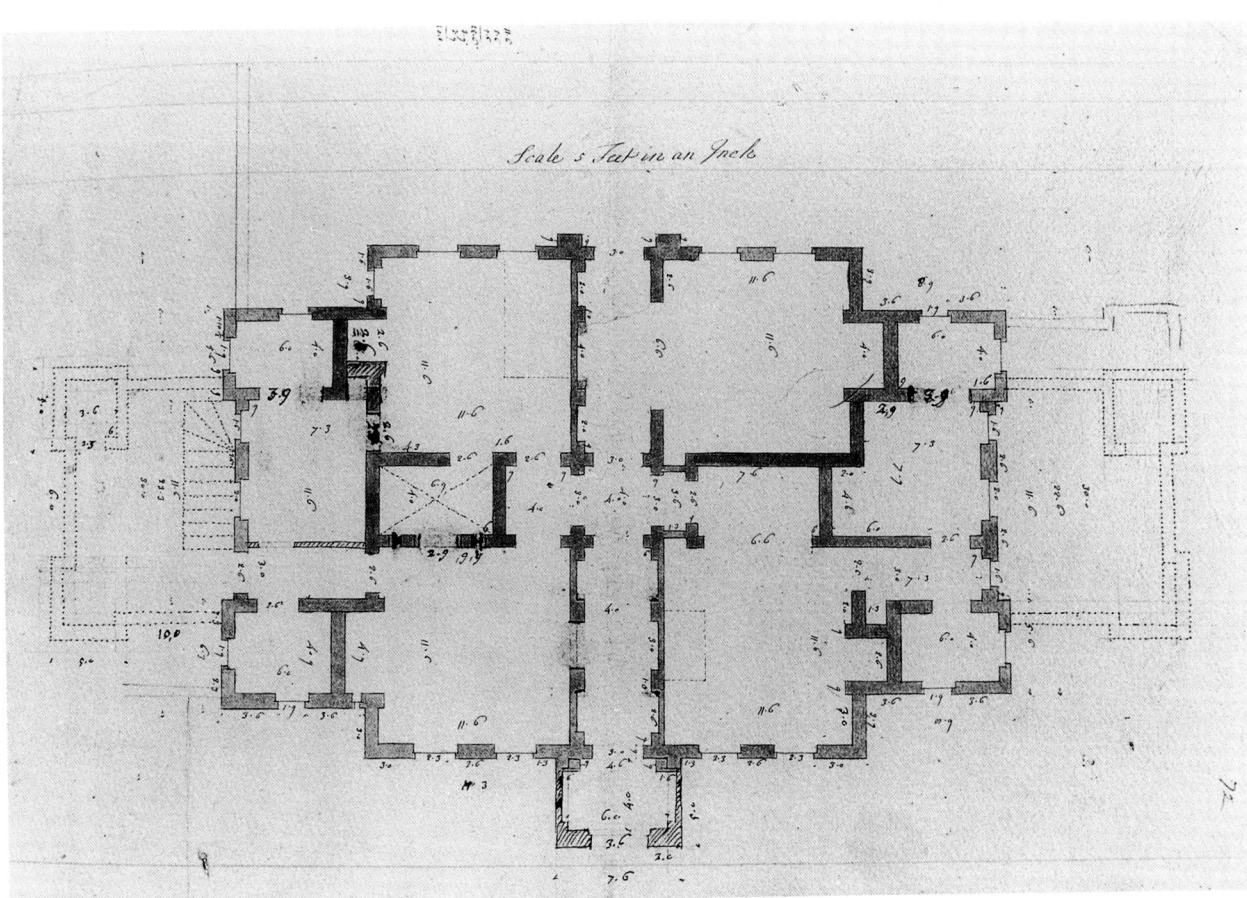

324 and 325   The so-called Nunnery (1719–20; destroyed), front façade and plan, Vanbrugh's Office, bound in the Elton Hall volume [Victoria and Albert Museum, London].

326, 327 and 328   The 'Nunnery', exterior view and details [Martin Collection, Greenwich Heritage Centre].

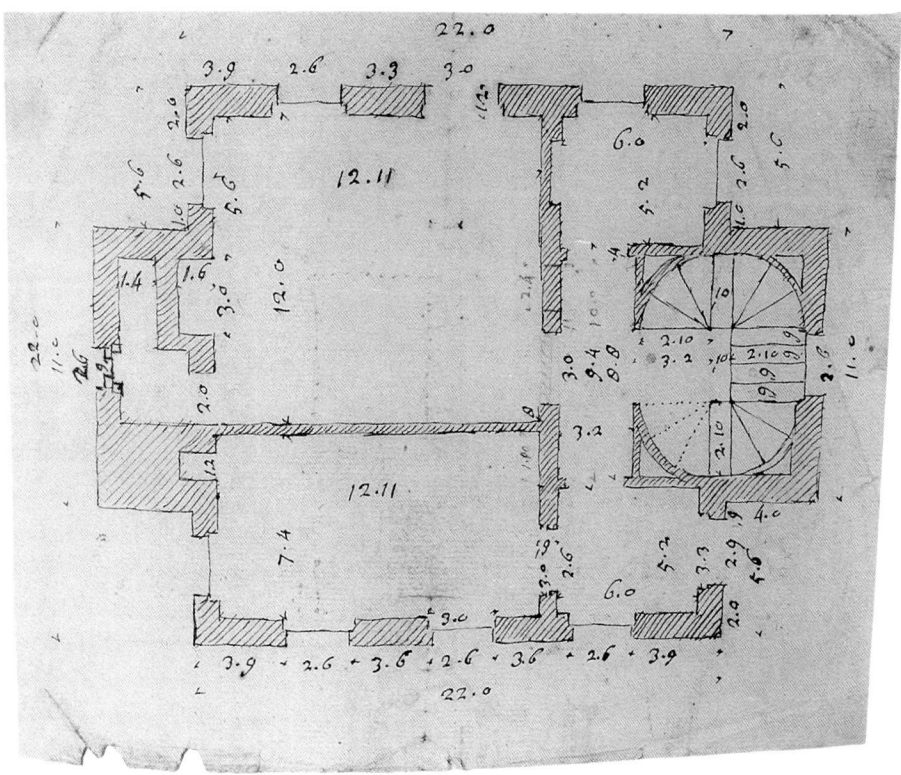

329 and 330 The New White Tower (1722–3; destroyed), elevation and plan, Vanbrugh's Office, bound in the Elton Hall volume [Victoria and Albert Museum, London].

331 and 333 (*above and facing page*) Two views of the South White Tower (1723–4; destroyed), *c*.1910 [Martin Collection, Greenwich Heritage Centre].

332 Computer reconstruction of the two White Towers and the 'Nunnery' [author].

of the archetypal image of the castle in the medieval myths and legends which the Garter cultivated. Well versed in the use of metaphor and the theory of association, he was also fully aware of the romantic potency of his architectural forms. In his copy of Ovid's *Metamorphoses* the young Charles, no doubt helped by his father, could have read about the romance of fortifications, with tales of a beleaguered city's ramparts and the citizens' panic when enemy soldiers were undermining the walls from the outside, as well as the building of Troy's walls and the defence of the gateway to Rome.[21] Vanbrugh's adaptation of the playful architecture of towers, castles and fortifications may well have been inspired by his, and his sons', childhood passions. Swift certainly thought so, reflected in the lines on the doll's house 'Goose-Pie' in 'The History of Vanbrug's House' which ran: 'He saw the edifice, and smiled, / Vowed it was pretty for a child' and when noting that Vanbrugh,

> . . . found the boys at play,
> And saw them dabbling in the clay;
> He stood behind a stall to lurk,
> And mark the progress of their work:
> With true delight observed 'em all
> Raking up mud to build a wall;
> The plan he much admired, and took

> The model in his table-book;
> Thought himself now exactly skilled,
> And so resolved a house to build.[22]

Vanbrugh most obviously drew inspiration from Charles when building the tower for him at Greenwich. It was noted in the Introduction that he wrote to Carlisle on 19 July 1722: 'I fancy your Lordships Godson will be a Professor that way, for he knows Pillars, & Arches and Round Windows & Square Windows already, whether he finds them in a Book or in the Streets, and is much pleas'd with a House I am building him in the Field at Greenh: it being a Tower of White Bricks, only one Room and a Closet on a floor'.[23] The tower as built, with its square- and round-headed windows, was clearly intended to reflect this elemental definition of architecture understood by Charles. Given the associative quality of names in Vanbrugh's plays, his emphasis on 'white bricks' evokes the image of a child's tower, built from blocks.

Ironically enough, Vanbrugh's description of his tower to Carlisle echoes that by Swift of 'Goose-Pie' as 'One Storey high, one postern Door, / And one small Chamber on a Floor'. Carlisle would have known of Swift's verse, as it was circulated widely, and the theft of a goose pie in *A Journey to London* shows that Vanbrugh could exploit this particular joke at his own expense elsewhere in his

334a–d   Computer reconstruction of the original form of Vanbrugh Castle, before the eastern extension [author].

work.[24] Swift's 'Vanbrug's House' had included the lines 'Leaving the wits the spacious air,/With licence to build castles there'. Here, as if in answer to Swift's jibes, Vanbrugh's New White Tower is designed to be self-consciously permanent with its heavy brickwork and castellated forms. Free from the normal constraints of function and built as it was for a child, the White Tower can be seen as Vanbrugh's idea of a fantasy building or ideal structure, an archetypal nursery 'model' from which all his work might well have stemmed. Echoing his earlier reference to the Duke of Newcastle as having 'stormed his castle', Vanbrugh concludes his letter to

335 *(facing page)*   Vanbrugh Castle, Greenwich, south, front forecourt façade, 1718–19.

336　Vanbrugh Castle, east, side façade.

337　One of the portholes on the south, front forecourt façade of Vanbrugh Castle.

Carlisle by fantasising that if the Earl's own child, Lady Irwin, 'ever has a House under the Cannon of this Castle' he would be glad to see Charles provide 'some amusement to her'.

The use of medieval architectural forms and details at Greenwich – the manner that Hawksmoor called the 'monastic style' – not only evoked the nation's glorious history with which the style was associated by Stevens and Dugdale but it also liberated Vanbrugh from the obligation to follow the formal rules dictating symmetry and order as prescribed by classical canons when it

came to the overall landscape composition of the buildings. Indeed, his arrangement of these buildings, including his own mock-monastery in the form of the 'Nunnery' complete with its tower and cross, coincided with his subscription to Stevens's study of the monasteries of England, with its 'picturesque' plates of medieval ruins in harmony with their landscape (see Figs 73–5). On Maze Hill Vanbrugh had the opportunity to adjust the silhouette of a group of buildings, and of Vanbrugh Castle in particular, to suit a moving spectator and various vantage points in the landscape – an opportunity

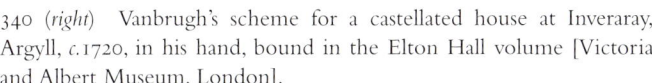

338 (*top*) Computer reconstruction of Vanbrugh Castle, as extended by Vanbrugh [author].

339 (*above*) Vanbrugh Castle drawn by William Stukeley for the Society of Antiquaries in 1721 [Society of Antiquaries, London].

340 (*right*) Vanbrugh's scheme for a castellated house at Inveraray, Argyll, *c*.1720, in his hand, bound in the Elton Hall volume [Victoria and Albert Museum, London].

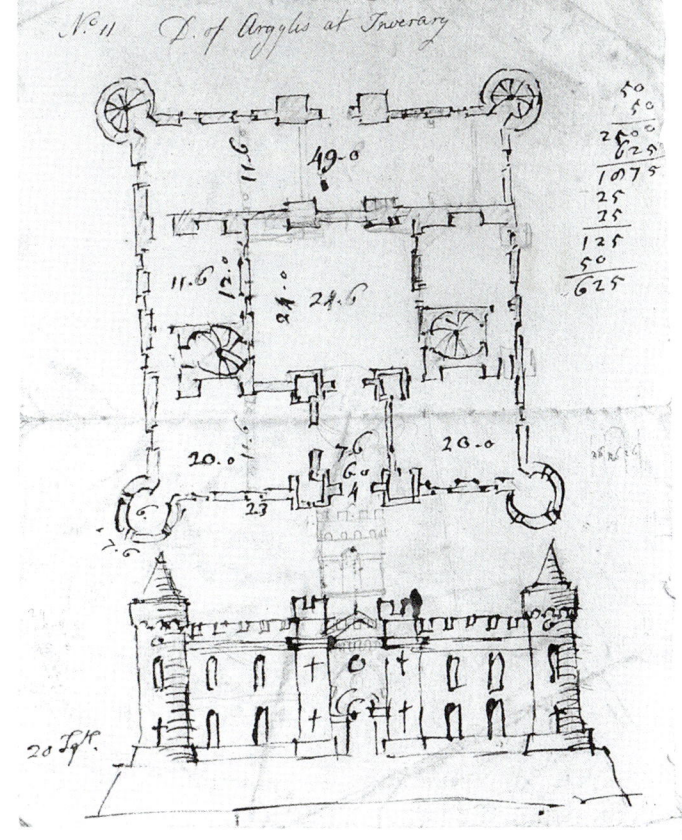

341   Computer model of Vanbrugh's lost buildings at Greenwich, looking north [author].

denied him at Woodstock a decade before. These picturesque qualities are, of course, fully understood and
expressed in Stukeley's sketches and can be visualised
once again using the computer (see Figs 131, 341). Initially built with a symmetrical plan, Vanbrugh Castle was
enlarged on the birth of the architect's sons – Charles in
1720 and John in 1722 – and became asymmetrical.[25]
The south front, for example, is subtly asymmetrical (see
Fig. 335). This work also coincided with Vanbrugh's subscription to Addison's collected works (in 1721), and,
given that a sense of impregnability was one of his
express aims at Vanbrugh Castle with its imaginary
cannons, the intended emotions in the onlooker must
surely have been a certain apprehension and respect balanced by a pleasure in the natural beauty of the arrangement. For at Woodstock too the composition was clearly
arranged to comprise a picturesque whole, such that it
'might Appear' as 'One of the Most Agreable Objects

that the Best of Landskip Painters can invent'. In the
symmetrical arrangement of the individual parts yet the
asymmetry of the ensemble at Greenwich, Vanbrugh
found the perfect expression for the classical virtues of
harmony and balance combined with the emerging picturesque sensibility of irregularity that became identified
with the gardens of the Whig aristocracy.[26] In stylistic
terms too Vanbrugh explored a non-dogmatic balance at
Greenwich, in using certain adapted yet recognisable
antique (astylar) forms – most obviously the broken
pediment – within an overall medieval style (see Fig.
326). By recalling British history whilst hinting at classical virtue, this eclectic mix might easily be associated
in an observer's mind with the prevailing Whig values
commonly understood to be held dear by its author, of
national glory founded on classical ideals of liberty, in
strong contrast with the absolutist monarchies and richly
ornamental rococo palaces of France and Spain.

The vision of a walled and gated compound enclosing fortified buildings has inevitable utopian connotations, with its ancient antecedent in the Roman military camp or *castra* of the type illustrated by the plate sponsored by Vanbrugh in Clarke's *C. Julii Caesaris* (1712; see Fig. 91). Through his involvement with this work, if from no other source, Vanbrugh would have been well aware of this Roman pedigree for the military compound (and its relationship to the antique city). However, with Addison's ideas concerning the association between architectural forms and mental images fresh in Vanbrugh's thoughts, his crenellated walls must also have recalled more immediate precedents such as his own childhood experience of Chester and possibly his later one of the Bastille, here again lending an autobiographical aspect to the buildings. The stair-towers to the sides of Vanbrugh House have caps of the type he identified at Chester and later recommended to Carlisle ('a Cap is all that those sort of Towers shou'd have, and I have seen one upon a round Tower on the Walls of Chester, that I thought did extreamly well'[27]). These defensive forms, when used by Vanbrugh on his own houses and understood, as Swift suggests, as a type of heraldry or 'expression of character', would also have represented to the public at large his life-long interest in fortifications and his own military past.[28]

Looking out over his castle walls, Vanbrugh could easily have imagined himself in the role once more of the military commander, a role reinforced by the proximity of the naval hospital and the site of his knighthood at the Queen's House. Indeed, the reference by him to imaginary cannons suggests that he indulged in just such a fantasy. For clearly the Greenwich compound was self-consciously constructed to suite Vanbrugh's mood and frame of mind, serving as it did as a peaceful retreat from his current disputes with the outside world, in particular his lawsuit with the Duchess of Marlborough.[29] He had been forced to come to terms with the loss of Blenheim, finally reduced a year before he died to peering over the wall to see what progress had been made. The Introduction quoted Vanbrugh's telling comments to Carlisle on 8 June 1721 that he had

every day of my Life Since twenty years old, grown more and more of opinion, that the less one has to do, with what is call'd the World, the more Quiet of mind; and the more Quiet of mind, the more Happyness. All other delights, are but like debauches in Wine; which give three days pain, for three hours pleasure. It has however been my chance, to lead a Life quite against my Sentiments hitherto; But I have made a Virtue of Necessity, from Some rebuffs I have met with in this Reign, and lessen'd my concern in things I was tempted before to be busy about which has eas'd me a good deal, and I hope will Still do more.[30]

Greenwich should be seen as an expression of these embattled sentiments, in brick and stone.

Much as in a military camp or even a heraldic composition, Vanbrugh also used the hierarchy of the family of buildings at Greenwich to express that of his own family, ranging from a large castle for himself, redolent of the 'Masculine Shew' achieved at Kimbolton, through a fortified house for his brother and two single-room towers for his boys, to two adjoining single-storey almshouses for his maiden sisters. Moreover Vanbrugh used the physical arrangement of these buildings on the site to express the relationship of family members – with his own castle on the summit and the other buildings marshalled symmetrically in a line, as if on parade (see Fig. 332). As a further aspect of this link between these particular works and their author's identity, Vanbrugh's Greenwich buildings can be viewed as an attempt by him to establish a form of patriarchal utopian settlement, in line with his preferences for heroic, patriarchal military commanders. For as a former soldier, Vanbrugh naturally approved of patriarchs and of strong, necessarily male, military leaders – most obvious in his admiration for Marlborough and in his celebration of Delaval and his military past. Yet he was also fully aware of the legendary heroic deeds of Alexander the Great, who as has been seen could symbolise William III, of Caesar, who prefigured the achievements of both Edward III and Marlborough, of Henry II as 'the Bravest and most Warlike of the English Kings' and of St George – patron saint of the Garter as symbolised by the Doric Order and the chapel at Windsor. In the case of Louis XIV, Vanbrugh took Colbert's 'brave designs' and, consistent with Whig ideology, freely adapted them for less absolutist, British royal projects such as Greenwich Hospital. The mock-fortified style of many of the front façades of Vanbrugh's houses, with their giant Doric columns, can be understood as an explicit celebration of the male patriarch, just as it was the business of heraldry to celebrate the male bloodline. This conception of society lies at the heart of Vanbrugh's group of buildings at Greenwich, the hierarchical arrangement of which emphasised his own role as the head of the Vanbrugh clan. In this way here again his buildings tell their story.

★ ★ ★

342   Chargate, Surrey, sketch plan and elevation, undated, unknown draughtsman, bound in the
Elton Hall volume [Victoria and Albert Museum, London].

'A FEW SHILLINGS WORTH OF DISTINCTION': CHARGATE INTO CLAREMONT

Vanbrugh built Chargate at Esher in Surrey around 1709 in the parish next to his mother's, although she died shortly after, in 1711. Commentators have noted the close connection between Chargate's original form, of which sketch plans and elevations survive (Figs 342–4),

and the traditional Tudor manor-house 'H' plan.[31] Here too the kitchen garden was to be given a military feel, with massive brick walls and doorways (Figs 345; see Figs 347, 354).[32] The drawings of Chargate's front elevation show a crenellated, astylar façade with small split pediments and windows without surrounds. A dramatic presence was achieved by using components which were in themselves small – the rooms in the wings were tiny and the overall façade was little more than ninety-odd feet

343   Chargate, Surrey, elevation by Vanbrugh, *c.*1703 [Victoria and Albert Museum, London].

344   Computer model of Chargate, Surrey [author].

345   Chargate, Surrey, a plan of Vanbrugh's garden, c.1709–15, with the Belvedere (centre) and walks cut through Chargate Wood [Bodleian Library, Oxford].

in length. Consistent with the reading of the style of Vanbrugh's own domestic buildings as an expression of their architect's character and story, when the owner of Chargate changed, so too did its identity. For Vanbrugh's subsequent alteration of this house into one suitable to the young Earl of Clare (Thomas Pelham-Holles, later the Duke of Newcastle), on the Earl's purchase of the house from him in October 1714 directly following his ennoblement, was not just a matter of extension and renaming (appropriately enough to Claremont) but also involved the stylistic transformation of the house from

medieval to *all'antica* and the addition of huge side wings. The house was demolished in the 1760s but it is shown in a landscape sketch possibly from Vanbrugh's office, an engraving by John Rocque of 1738 and an anonymous painting of about 1750 (Figs 348, 349, 350).[33] In 1715 Vanbrugh also designed the brick Belvedere, which survives (Fig. 346, see Fig. 70). The medieval character of this Belvedere served to emphasise its role as a garden building, distinct from the emerging 'classical' character of the altered house. With its crenellated corner towers and stark astylar walls, its hilltop location

346   Vanbrugh's Belvedere tower at Claremont, 1715.

347   Vanbrugh's massive walls surrounding the kitchen garden at what became Claremont.

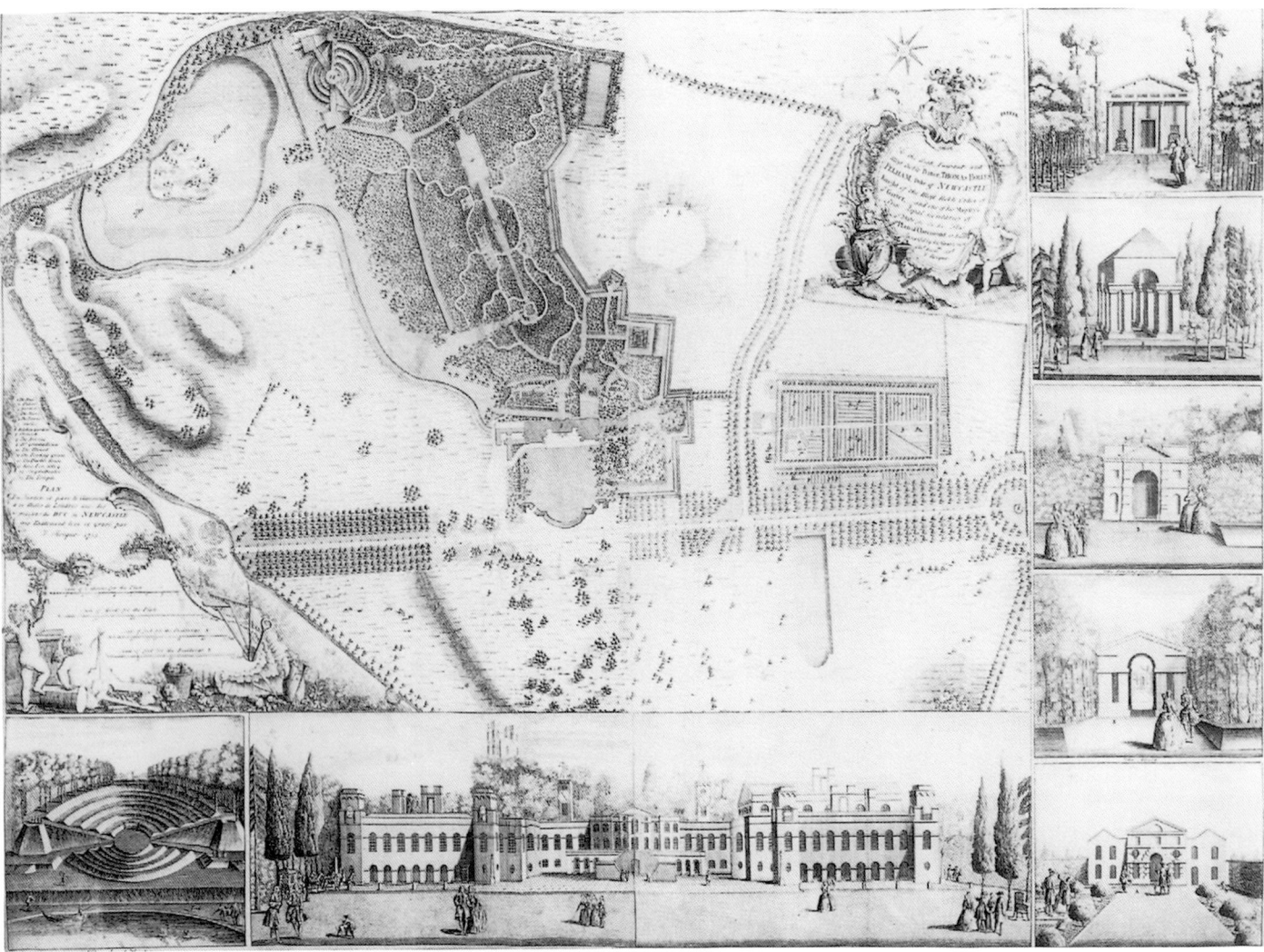

348   Claremont, 1715–20, engraving by John Rocque of 1738 showing Vanbrugh's pyramidal temple (second vignette from top) [British Library, London].

and symmetrical façades, the building had no practical function other than as a small summer retreat and therefore represented a golden opportunity for Vanbrugh to indulge his medieval stylistic preferences.

Evidently this indulgence was not forthcoming elsewhere at Claremont. For in a letter to the Duke of Newcastle, undated but probably written in 1718, Vanbrugh writes concerning a detail of, or most likely all, the conversion work of the house:

> I am very proud of my Lady Dutchesses Approbation, And shall ever have a great deal of pleasure in doing any thing that can give her the least Satisfaction. And I do assure both her and your Grace, That the dislike I had, to this piece of work in general, has been so far from making me move Idly or Sowerly about it, That I took a Resolution (from the time I found you wou'd

not quit it) To try if 'twere not possible to fetch good out of Evill, by the Manner of doing, what I wish'd might never be done.[34]

Clearly Vanbrugh was troubled by some aspect of the conversion – perhaps the toning down of the medieval character or the addition of such large wings, or a mixture of both. Yet it is fair to say that the removal of the battlements – in favour of a full pediment – illustrates their 'add-on' or stage-set character and that iconography appropriate for one scale of building and patron, in this case Vanbrugh himself, was not necessarily considered appropriate for another.

Vanbrugh seems to have had a problem convincing his patrons that the medieval style was one suitable to express their nobility, judging from this work and his reassurances at Kimbolton. Newcastle identified himself

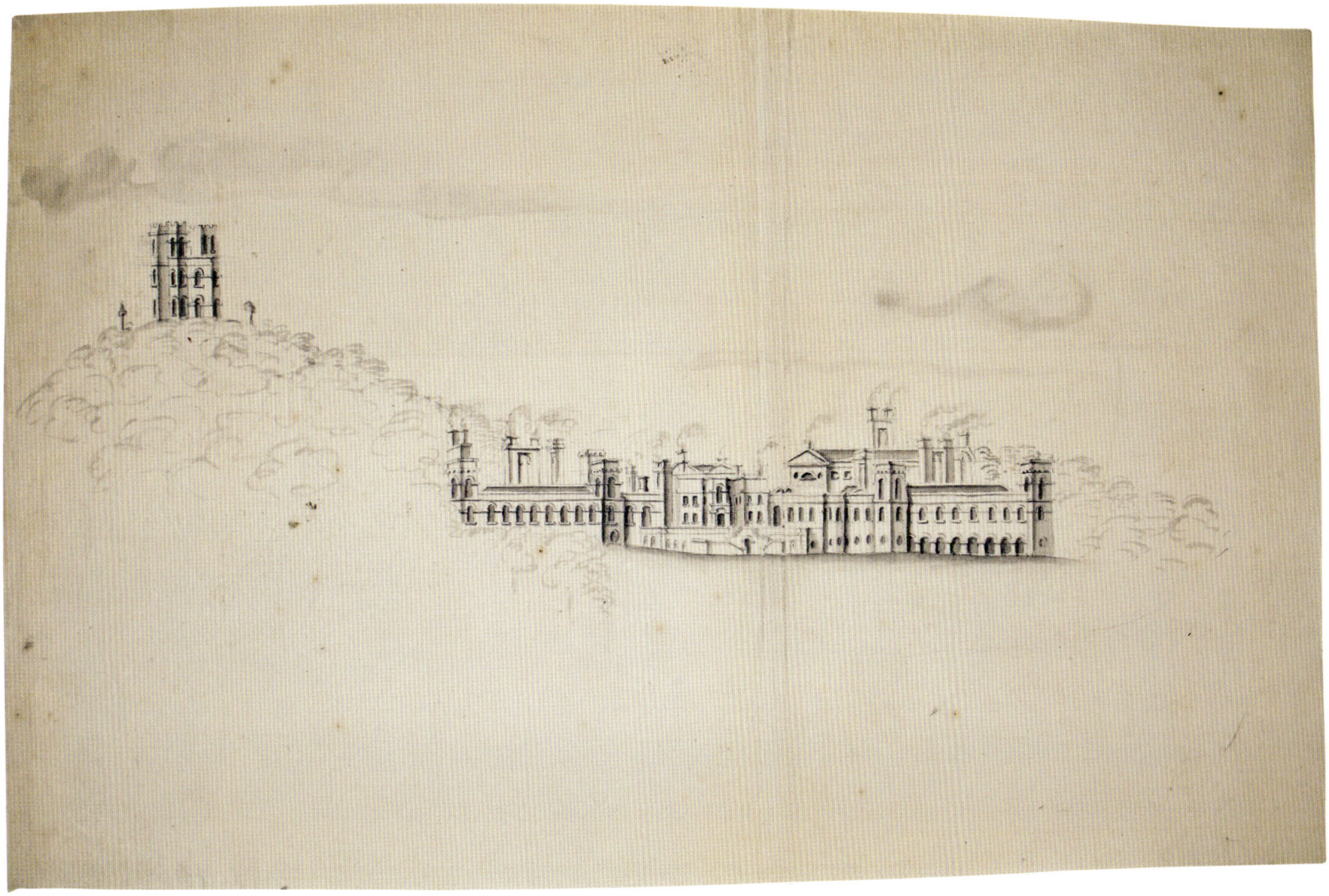

349 Sketch illustrating the compositional effect of Claremont and the Belvedere in the landscape, possibly from Vanbrugh's Office, undated, bound in the Elton Hall volume [Victoria and Albert Museum, London].

350 Anonymous painting of Claremont, *c.*1750, oil on canvas [private collection].

351 (*above*) Vanbrugh's 'Newcastle Pew', Esher Old Church (St George's), Surrey, built 1723–5.

352 (*right*) Vanbrugh's entrance to the 'Newcastle Pew', Esher Old Church.

most emphatically with the pure *all'antica* style elsewhere, for Vanbrugh employed a Corinthian temple front – complete with its pediment – when designing the 'Newcastle Pew' of 1723–5 nearby the house, in Esher Old Church (Figs 351, 352). Concerning porticoes, he recommended to the Church Commissioners that no element was 'so solemnly Magnificent'. As seen at Stowe, Vanbrugh is thought to have added the north, pedimented portico (*c*.1720; see Fig. 314) as a sign of the nobility of his patron, the first Viscount Cobham, and, perhaps significantly, in the houses he built for himself he avoided the use both of *all'antica* columns and of a central 'noble' pediment; appropriately enough the presence of a pediment is merely implied, in a much paired-down and broken form, on Chargate or either side of the front door in the 'Nunnery' for example. At Blenheim it is the minor buildings which have broken pediments (such as the kitchen court), whilst the main front has a full one. The most obvious contextual opportunity for Vanbrugh to have placed a full pedimented front on one of his own houses would have been at 'Goose-Pie', given the proximity of Jones's Banqueting

House which the house overlooked, but here again the style of the original building is rusticated astylar (the later side wings have Serliana, perfectly in keeping with the Banqueting House; see Figs 29, 316, 317). Perhaps the absence of this element in the buildings Vanbrugh designed for himself is not surprising, for in the *Quattro Libri* Palladio had implied the importance of the pediment as the signifier of social status, considering it the rightful place for the display of nobility through heraldry.[35] Almost every pediment of the houses which he illustrates is adorned with a coat of arms, a fact that must have given the architectural element a special significance to Vanbrugh as a keen herald. A scheme by Vanbrugh possibly representing an early proposal for Claremont clearly demonstrates this (Fig. 353).[36] Elsewhere, in Vanbrugh's designs for ordinary citizens such as 'The Vine' for Colonel Lambert of about 1718 he equally avoided the overt use of *all'antica* decoration in favour of heavy string courses, portholes and corner towers (judged suitable, no doubt, to the colonel's occupation; Fig. 355).[37] Certainly Kings Weston has a pediment but Southwell's artistic status as the 'new Angarano'

353   Scheme by Vanbrugh possibly representing an early proposal for Claremont, with a shield in the pediment, *c*.1715 [Victoria and Albert Museum, London].

355   The front façade of 'The Vine', Sevenoaks, Kent, designed by Vanbrugh for Colonel Lambert, *c*.1718, drawing by Vanbrugh's Office [Victoria and Albert Museum, London].

gave him especial significance, as did the house's historical and etymological connection with royalty. Vanbrugh's eye for the appropriateness of the use of ornament at Claremont is confirmed by a note to Newcastle in 1719 concerning instructions to a mason in which the architect observes: 'he will See, that the Tablet is design'd only to give the Middle break, a few Shillings worth of distinction. The Other Windows have all the respect paid them that's due to their Quality, I Speak in a Stile, I reckon he'll like'.[38] Here Vanbrugh makes clear that elements of his buildings were decorated according to their importance, much as a herald expressed the hierarchy of the court and following classical notions of decorum in which ornament was seen to express the relative importance of the various parts of a building and of different patrons.

As has been shown, Vanbrugh adapted and applied the *all'antica* rules governing appropriate decorative styles to incorporate medieval forms and elements, and as a consequence his work ranged from projects where the classical language is merely implied (at the 'Nunnery', for example), through those where the *all'antica* rules are strictly applied and the language is purely expressed (at the 'Temple of the Four Winds'), to those where it is

'abused' in the baroque manner (as at Castle Howard and Blenheim). This approach to architecture as a language capable of expressing variations in mood and effect is not surprising given Vanbrugh's friendship with Addison and his experience with scenography. In Vanbrugh's private work, as elsewhere, a house's particular context evidently also influenced this choice of architectural style – using a mixture of *all'antica* and medieval forms in city contexts such as at Whitehall – with Inigo Jones's Banqueting House nearby – and a more pure medieval style in the country at Greenwich and at Chargate – with no neighbouring buildings to relate to or patrons to please. Indeed, all Vanbrugh's private residences, from his adaptation of Woodstock Manor with its new enclosing wall,[39] to the newly built houses at Whitehall, Greenwich and Chargate, eschewed the use of columns in favour of traditional elements drawn from the fortified house, with battlements and corner towers being the most prominent.[40] These buildings should thus be seen as a pure expression of Vanbrugh's own architectural tastes and medieval fantasies – fantasies which, in the imaginative spirit of association, he played out at Vanbrugh Castle when defending the phantom storming of its walls with his make-believe cannon.

354 *(facing page)*   A doorway forming part of Vanbrugh's walls surrounding the kitchen garden at what became Claremont.

Conclusion

'STARV'D LONDON ROGUES'
COUNTRY ESTATES AND NATIONAL DECAY

'THE ENEMY APPROACHES, WE MUST SET OUT OUR FALSE COLOURS': MASKS AND FAÇADES

Vanbrugh's description of the walls of Nottingham Castle as bearing an expression, or 'countenance', suggests not only that he saw the character of his buildings as akin to that of his *dramatis personae*, but also the possibility that he considered his façades as analogous to human faces, or perhaps somewhat like theatrical face-masks. The oculus – as used at Claremont, at Vanbrugh Castle and on the west façade of Lumley castle (see Figs 224, 337) – had traditionally been seen, following Serlio and other Renaissance commentators, as an eye. Indeed, Serlio's famous rustic gates were described by the Italian as 'Doric but disguised and masked' through a rustic appearance similar to that of Seaton Delaval (Fig. 357).[1] Vanbrugh would also have been well aware of the dual meaning of the word 'façade', both as an architectural element and as a false veneer or face-mask, just as he would have been familiar with the idea of the stage as a mask or illusion, expressed by the face-masks bearing comic and tragic expressions which symbolised the duality of the classical theatre. Moreover much as the proscenium arch and its curtain veils or masks the drama, so a façade conceals, as it were, the life of the inhabitants. Vanbrugh's façades proclaimed the public virtues of his patrons whilst concealing their private vices, and it follows that he might well have viewed his façades as just such a curtain or mask hiding the 'drama' played out by the occupants – similar to the fans and the black velvet masks used by contemporary ladies in the playhouse to disguise their enjoyment of rude jokes (Fig. 358).[2] After all, the point of both the mask and the fortified wall (according to Vanbrugh's architectural stage metaphors concerning the protection of chastity) was to conceal and protect female virtue from the threat of external vices. Rhetorical theory, with which Vanbrugh may well

have been familiar, emphasised the importance of concealment and surprise in the act of eloquent speech and, by implication, design.

There are clues to this reading of Vanbrugh's façades in the buildings themselves. The notion of the façade as a mask is obviously literally true in the case of his re-

357 Sebastiano Serlio's Rustic gate VI, described as 'disguised and masked', from the *Libro Extraordinario* (1551), fol. 5v.

356 *(facing page)*   The estate walls at Casle Howard, Yorkshire.

358   William Hogarth's *The Laughing Audience*, 1733, etching, 18.8 × 17.1 cm [Fitzwilliam Museum, Cambridge].

359   Face strongly resembling a mask in the entablature at Castle Howard.

resembles a mask, as do the satyrs on the Satyr Gate of 1705 by Vanbrugh and Hawksmoor, whilst the stone 'drapery' in the south pediment was described as such in the 'Bill' by Samuel Carpenter (Fig. 359; see Fig. 223).[4] The paired giant order columns used to frame the

360   Arcades used as a screen to veil the medieval chapel, Vincennes, Paris.

facing of Lumley Castle and Kimbolton, as it had been in Hugh May's much admired work at Windsor. At Kings Weston and in the early Doric design for Eastbury (see Figs 247, 284), the castellated form was effectively hidden (that is, set back) behind, and even disguised or veiled by, the classical façade. The double-height arcade at 'Goose-Pie' (see Figs 29, 316, 317), with its false stucco stonework, similarly veiled the face behind, just as the stone screen at the south end of the Great Hall at Audley End (tentatively attributed to Vanbrugh)[3] and the largely functionless double-arcaded screens at Grimsthorpe both playfully half-conceal the staircases beyond (Fig. 361; see Fig. 100). Perhaps most tantalising of all, the elevation of Vanbrugh's Queen's Theatre facing the Haymarket (see Fig. 52) – where one might reasonably expect this allusion to the façade as a mask – had oval oculi at the upper level and an arcade at ground level affording glimpses of the hidden world behind. Vanbrugh would have seen such arcades used as a screen to veil, from the vantage point of the courtyard, the medieval chapel at Vincennes (Fig. 360). On a less literal, more metaphorical level, at Castle Howard a face with its exaggerated expression carved in the entablature strongly

361 (*facing page*)   The double-arcaded screen in the Great Hall at Grimsthorpe, half-concealing the staircase.

entrance elevations at Grimsthorpe, Seaton Delaval and in an early scheme for Eastbury, and the use of a giant arch on schemes for Swinstead and Eastbury (Fig. 362; see Fig. 281), resemble a giant proscenium and assist the dramatic effect of the framed central section of the façade conceived as a curtain or screen.[5]

At Grimsthorpe the double-height arcaded form used in the hall screen mirrors that on this external front face (see Figs 290, 300, 361), further suggesting its role as a screen and lending an air of ambiguity between inside and out. Screen walls, with arcades, were also used by Vanbrugh to enclose the front court at Seaton Delaval and Eastbury (Fig. 363; see Fig. 286) and these 'false' façades have the effect of making the houses seem larger than in actuality. Here again, Vanbrugh plays with a sense of ambiguity, or 'complexity and contradiction' as Robert Venturi observed, in which nothing is ever quite

what it seems.[6] He was well versed in the manipulation of optical effect through his probable use of *trompe l'oeil* paintings (those which literally 'mislead the eye') on the walls and ceilings at the Haymarket and through Giananbrugh's interest in this art of illusion is further attested by his endorsement of Pozzo's *Perspectiva* (1707).[8] The inner hall at Kings Weston is a triumph in the art of illusion, with its *trompe l'oeil* urns and apparently unsupported 'hanging' stair of about 1719 (Fig. 364; see Fig. 252). Vanbrugh's design for his own coat of arms (finally officially registered by him in 1714; see Fig. 91) can be seen to have expressed this liking for architectural ambiguity, in incorporating a bridge which was upside down (a somewhat ironic image given his problems with the bridge at Blenheim).[9] This sense of ambiguity and abuse of archi-

362   A giant arch resembling a proscenium on a scheme for a house at Swinstead, near Grimsthorpe, attributed to Vanbrugh, *c*.1710 [Lincolnshire Archives Office].

363 Screen walls, with arcades, Seaton Delaval, used by Vanbrugh to enclose the forecourt.

364 The hanging staircase at Kings Weston [Regional Building Record, Bath University].

tectural form is present also in his ornamentation, in which ponderous keystones are enlarged beyond structural necessity and string-courses double as paired down pediments that seemingly hint at a language of architecture suppressed and barely visible.

Indeed it is easy to find evidence for a concealed or secretive side to Vanbrugh's life and character – in his possible envoy mission to The Hague, his supposed spying activities in France, his membership of secretive clubs and in his matchmaking for, and general dealings with, the Duchess of Marlborough.[10] Disguise and pretence, and eventual revelation, are central themes in Restoration comedy and its source in the French tradition of the Comédiens Italiens, in which once again nothing is ever quite what it seems (Fig. 365). This is true with William Congreve's only novel, entitled *Incognita* and centred on the mistaken identities and fanciful deceits of the Florentine masqued ball (as Defoe observed, Vanbrugh was himself involved with these

form of 'masquerades' at the Haymarket[11]). It is also true with Vanbrugh's plays, and in particular with *The Pilgrim* and *The Mistake* or with *The False Friend* where falsehood is a central theme. In *The Mistake* Isabella says of Camillo's concealing costume, 'this Disguise hides other Mysteries, besides a Woman; a large and fair Estate was cover'd by't'.[12] In this case architecture, or at least a country estate, is clearly the subject of the disguise. Here the dramatic comedy of errors centres on misunderstandings arising from the fact that not only fine ladies but also whores wore their velvet masks in the park or at the play.[13] Vanbrugh's heroes frequently mistake the heroines when in disguise, as in *The Provok'd Wife* where the two heroines, Lady Brute and Bellinda, enter 'mask'd and poorly dress'd' and the errant gentlemen of the play remark to each other, 'How now, who are these? Not our Game I hope'.[14] As a former soldier Vanbrugh would have been equally well aware of the role of disguise in military conflict. In George Farquhar's *Love and a Bottle*

365   French almanac for the year 1689 entitled *La Troupe royale des Comédiens-Italiens*, engraving [Louvre, Paris].

of 1698 the lady and her maid put on their masks saying, 'the enemy approaches, we must set out our false colours', and the heroine continues, 'I dread these blustering men-of-war who . . . are for boarding all masks they meet as lawful prize'.[15] In this sense the false defensive crenellations and portholes on Vanbrugh's façades and fortified outworks 'mask' the domestic character of his buildings and also aim to deceive. They are rhetorical and pretentious forms designed for visual effect.

'A GOOD ESTATE, BUT IT'S A LITTLE AUT AT ELBOWS': ENGLISH HOMES AND CASTLES

At Blenheim park Vanbrugh designed probably the greatest building of his age. Today his achievement is seen in terms of the house and garden but this overlooks one

further important ambition on Vanbrugh's part, namely to establish an estate. For the outworks here and at Castle Howard, Seaton Delaval and Eastbury were as much a part of his original conception of the houses they served as were his grand entrances and porticoes (see Fig. 356). Concerning the estate garden at Sacombe Park in Hertfordshire which Vanbrugh designed for Edward Rolt (d. 1722), Sir Matthew Decker recorded in his diary: 'The Kitchin Garden is by itself, 3 acres and within walls, with 4 Towers one on each corner so strongly built by Van Brock, as if they were to defend a Citty'.[16] As has been seen, these mock walls and towers, together with those around the estate at Castle Howard and the ditches at Seaton Delaval, were rhetorical works, functionless in purely utilitarian terms. Rather, they were intended to perform a symbolic role in signifying qualities of massiveness and permanence to the onlooker and thereby offer the protection which Vanbrugh considered the country estate required given what he saw as its vulnerability to threats from both within and without.

A number of Vanbrugh's plays focus on the virtues of efficient estate management and on the neglect of agricultural estates by the foolish landowners of his day. Such neglect is the principal theme in his adaptation of Florent Carton de Dancourt's *The Country House*, for example, whose serious purpose has often been overlooked.[17] The play's eponymous dwelling is vulnerable to intrusion by all types of scroungers, a condition emphasised by its comic conversion to an inn under the protective sign of a rusty sword. The drama offers a clue as to the symbolic purpose of its author's mock outworks in protecting the estate from the threat posed by unarmed yet uninvited visitors encountered both on stage and, on one memorable occasion, by Vanbrugh himself at Greenwich. The house's ineffectual squire, Mr Bernard, observes 'What will become of me? Since I bought this damn'd Country House, I spend more in a Summer than wou'd maintain me seven Years'. His brother advises him that 'If you don't order your Affairs better, you'll have your Fowl taken out of your very Yard, and carried away before your Face'.[18] The theme of inefficient and neglectful estate management is echoed in *Aesop*, where the aptly named Squire Polidorus Hogstye, when asked 'How do you use your Tenants?', replies: 'Why I Skrew up their Rents' till they break and run away, and if I catch 'em again; I let 'em Rot in a Gaol'.[19] Forced to reduce his gluttony because of taxation, Hogstye considers felling his forests, 'which he wou'd willingly preserve, against an ill run at Dice'. Vanbrugh presents the neglect of estates such as these as a symbol of national decay – in much the same vain as, ironically enough given their mutual animosity, Swift would do in the form of Lord Munodi's estate in *Gulliver's Travels*.[20]

After all, the English nation was characterised by such houses, whose efficient management was a model for that of the country at large.[21] As such the country house was the quintessential building type of Vanbrugh's era, the ornamentation of which commonly expressed both individual and national identity. The Golden Age imagery used on the façades and in the landscapes of Vanbrugh's houses testifies to their ideal status as Arcadian models, firmly rooted in English soil, just as the contrasting martial aspect of these houses celebrated England's national glory in the best traditions of heraldry. It was noted in Chapter Seven that the agricultural virtues of the estate at Grimsthorpe were celebrated through the representation of a statue with a sheaf of corn, most probably Ceres, in Campbell's 1725 engraving of the north façade published in the third volume of *Vitruvius Britannicus*, and that Ceres also featured above the pediment at Castle Howard (see Figs 298, 310). At a practical level Lord Carlisle saw it as his moral duty to develop the agriculture and forestry on the estate, much as Addison had emphasised the economic advantages of productive park land over formal parterre.[22]

Behind Vanbrugh's concern for the nation's country estates, and indeed his stylistic preference for the patriotic 'Castle Air' and celebration of the male bloodline, lay a form of social idealism on his part. For uniting his work as a dramatist, herald and country-house architect was his wish to remind his audience of a lost medieval world of the patrician landowner, who cared for his workforce as a matter of national wellbeing. The fact that Blenheim, Seaton Delaval and his own family houses at Greenwich were built for military commanders not only added authenticity to their own particular 'Castle Air' but also to the feudal aspects of their hierarchical organization, expressed through a central house surrounded by the often extensive outbuildings, estate offices and mock-fortified walls. According to this feudal tradition the owners of country houses supported the poor on their estates – a hospitality symbolised by the Great Hall which Vanbrugh included in all his country house designs[23] – just as his beloved heraldic Orders of chivalry had a charitable mission. One of the consistent themes of Vanbrugh's plays was the mistreatment of the underclass – tradespeople and labourers – by the privileged. In *A Journey to London* the extravagant Lady Arabella remarks in exaggerated self-justification for not paying for her goods, 'Tradesmen are strange unreasonable Creatures, refuse to sell People any more Things, and then quarrel with 'em because they don't pay for those they have had already'.[24] Lady Arabella had simply gambled her money away.

Vanbrugh was evidently compassionate towards his workforce and was keenly aware of their economic and social circumstances, frequently unaided as these workers were by national institutions of Church and State. He championed the labourers at Blenheim, for example, writing to Lord Poulet on 30 September 1710 that 'finding things here on the point of falling into a Distraction not to be Express'd, from the Great Arrears due to a vast Number of poor familys, and not hearing any thing certain of mony being imediately Order'd in some measure to releive them I thought it might not be Amis to Acquaint your Lordship in particular with something relating to this Worke'.[25] Then, on 3 October to the Duke of Marlborough regarding the sudden stop to the work at Blenheim ordered by the Duchess, he notes:

> the Labourers, Carters, and other Country People, who us'd to be regularly paid, but were now in arrear, . . . finding themselves distress'd by what they ow'd to the People where they lodg'd &c. And numbers of them having their Familys and Homes at great distances in other Countys, twas very much to be fear'd such a general Meeting might happen, that the Building might feel the Effects of it . . . Your Grace won't blame me, if asham'd to continue there any Longer on such a foot.

Concerning the 'Poor Labourers', he adds on 10 October, 'Mr Travers arrived at Blenheim just upon the execution of my Lady Duchess's Order and immediately got 500£ upon his own Credit to satisfy the poorer and most distressed labourers'.[26]

Clearly like his near contemporary William Hogarth, Vanbrugh was far from blind to the inequalities of contemporary society and took his chance on the stage to poke fun at the national institutions of Church, Parliament and, on occasions, even the Court (Fig. 366). The corruption and vanity of courts is dwelt upon in *Aesop*, for example, whilst the new Member of Parliament in *A Journey to London*, the appropriately named Sir Francis Headpiece, naïvely boasts:

> But then when we consider that what we undergo, is in being busy for the Good of our Country, – O, the Good of our Country is, above all Things; what a Noble and Glorious Thing it is . . . that *England* can boast of five hundred zealous Gentlemen, all in one Room, all of one Mind, upon a fair Occasion, to go all together by the Ears for the Good of their Country . . . at the end of the Sessions, you will find your self so ador'd, that your Country will come and dine with you every Day in the Week.[27]

In this play Vanbrugh's patriotically motivated apparition of institutional corruption is presented as synonymous with the physical and moral decay of London and more-

366 William Hogarth's *Some of the Principal Inhabitants of Ye Moon: Royalty, Episcopacy and Law*, 1724, etching and engraving, 18.8 × 24.6 cm in which a guinea (bribery), a Jew's harp (sanctimonious sermonising) and a mallet (coercion) take the place of the faces of king, bishop and judge respectively [British Museum, London].

over of the nation at large. This decay is made clear when, on arrival in the capitol, Sir Francis's party are robbed of their pie by beggars. In a scene reminiscent of one from the work of Hogarth (Fig. 367), the cook explains 'up comes two of these thin starv'd *London* Rogues, one gives me a great Kick o' the – here; [*Laying her Hand upon her Backside*] Whilst t'other hungry Varlet twitcht the dear Pye out of my Hands'. Lady Headpiece asks if 'they make a Practice of these things often here?' to which the landlady, Mrs Motherly, replies 'Madam, they'll twitch a Rump of Beef out of a boiling Copper; and for a Silver Tankard, they make no more Conscience of that, than if it were a *Tunbridge* Sugar-box'.[28] No sooner has this misfortune befallen the group than their coach is deliberately broken up for scrap: a servant, George, concludes, 'Sir, I have no good Opinion of this Tawne, it's made up of Mischief, I think . . . An this be *London*, wa'd we were all well i' th' Country again'.[29] Sir Francis, Vanbrugh implies, is to blame since he has aban-

doned his country estate – described as 'a good Estate, but it's a little aut at Elbows'[30] – for an ineffectual Parliament and the pleasures and vices of the town.

Vanbrugh had had first-hand experience of Parliament's shortcomings. In 1723 he had supported an ultimately unsuccessful Parliamentary scheme for new street paving and drainage in the cities of London and Westminster; on 26 March 1724 he lamented to Carlisle that 'My Lord Morpeth is often low Spirited about this Paving Bill; and often much Inclin'd to give it up, till another Sessions, thinking the Great Men don't appear in it, as he expected they wou'd. But for my part, I see no rubs or delays, more than what I reckoned upon, from the natural Course of everything moving in Parliamt: thats worth having'.[31] Vanbrugh had also proposed the paving of the market-place in Oxford, in the ill-fated letter which led to his dismissal as Comptroller.[32] These paving schemes, together with his proposal for a new front for the town hall in Oxford of 1713 and his new town hall built in Morpeth in Northumberland a year later (see Fig. 273), are a further sign of his civic sensibility towards what he refers to as 'Publick Work' and his support for rural market towns which served their neighbouring estates, as Oxford did Blenheim and Morpeth did Seaton Delaval.[33]

In his recommendations for the new London churches Vanbrugh had attempted to correct national ills: he concluded by reminding the Commissioners of their duty to posterity and of the timeless link between architectural and civic virtue in urging that future generations should identify 'the Politeness of the Age, by finding the Edifices Suitable to what produc'd them'.[34] Given that his actual church designs were rejected, however, his preferred vehicles for moral and social reform of the town became limited to the opera and the theatre, both artforms which most united his talents as architect and dramatist. As has been seen, he makes perfectly clear in his *A Short Vindication* that 'the Business of Comedy is to shew People what they shou'd do, by representing them upon the Stage, doing what they shou'd not'.[35] Meanwhile Vanbrugh fortified his family against town vices through the embattled style of his domestic residences in and about London.[36] His comment at Greenwich that visitors without invitation needed to 'storm his castle', with its imaginary cannons, speaks volumes as to his desire for protection from what he saw as outside intrusion. Contemporary London, after all, was the setting for such Hogarthian sites as 'Drab-Alley at Wapping', as featured in *The Relapse*, or the New Exchange with its 'well-shap'd Ladies' in *The Provok'd Wife*.[37] In contrast, the country was frequently projected by Vanbrugh as the setting for unpretentious virtues,

367 William Hogarth's *A Rake's Progress*, 1733–4, II, 'The Levée', oil on canvas, 62.2 × 75 cm: Tom entering London Society through recklessly spending his father's wealth, much like Sir Francis Headpiece in Vanbrugh's *A Journey to London* [Sir John Soane's Museum, London].

symbolised by the honest 'home-bred Village-Mouse' in *Aesop*.[38] As Chapter Four noted, Vanbrugh's letters record his personal enjoyment of many simple and unpretentious country pleasures, such as his 'eating a Chearful Cold Loaf at a very humble Alehouse' at Middleton Stoney, on one of his 'Journeys of Pleasure' through the country near the end of his life – in this case from Blenheim to Stowe in August 1725.[39] Throughout his career as an architect, Vanbrugh had been most successful, in terms of judgements of scale and detail, in the country, a fact famously underlined by the failure of 'Goose-Pie' to suit its Whitehall site and of his church designs to find favour.[40] Whilst Blenheim was considered by some too grand a country house, to his mind its size was wholly appropriate as an expression of patriotism.

Vanbrugh's *A Journey to London* was composed within the fortified world of his castle at Greenwich and turned out to be his last play, left incomplete at the time of his death. In thus speaking of the inability of national institutions to deal with emerging urban-based social ills – the begging and stealing of the lower classes, the idleness and licentiousness of the upper ones – the play's themes are indicative of Vanbrugh's growing distaste for the city and the role of its institutions as agents of social welfare and reform. In ever sharper contrast, as he grew older, stood the ancient feudal form of land-based charity, symbolised by the heraldic nobility of his Whig patrons and of the Garter, and architecturally by his beloved medieval castles, fortified houses and country estates. Vanbrugh's most personal architectural expression of this feudal vision made near the end of his life was, of course, at Vanbrugh Castle itself, in which its architect could play the part of the medieval lord fending off besieging visitors.

This sensibility was perfectly compatible with support for the Whig ideal of a constitutional monarchy, and Vanbrugh's consequent definition of the King's charitable role as 'the fountain of Justice and the Guardian of the Rights of the subjects' and his hope at Blenheim that the King 'will relieve the Distress of the Numerous Familys of poor Workmen employed in the Building'.[41] Moreover it was this Whig vision of English feudal society and its ancient rights over royalty, established by Magna Carta, which might also be seen as expressed through Vanbrugh's eclectic architectural style in blending medieval and *all'antica* forms. For he seems to have considered that the warlike aspects of English medieval architecture and indeed monarchy – as jointly identified by him in Woodstock Manor – could be harmonised or tamed by *all'antica* principles and architectural forms, or 'The Orders of Building' as Lory put it; this process would have been further enhanced by the general identification amongst Whigs of *all'antica* forms with Republican Rome. These applied porticoes and pediments were

no doubt in turn equally enhanced and authenticated in Vanbrugh's mind through association with the chivalrous spirit of national history which medieval architecture represented. In using this mix, albeit to different degrees depending on location and circumstance, Vanbrugh attempted to formulate an heroic architecture which reflected national traditions traced back to the archetypal British feudal castle, the 'restored' Windsor.

In his lectures to students delivered between 1809 and 1815, Sir John Soane captured something of this patriotic understanding of Vanbrugh when describing him as 'the Shakespeare of architects'.[42] Here too is a hint of the architect's role as a 'storyteller in stone'. Of all the houses designed by this most literary of architects, Seaton Delaval is one of the clearest, if one of the final, affirmations of its author's land-based, feudal vision. The house tells the story of its patron's chivalrous virtues through its very own 'Impudent Countenance' far removed from the urban vanities and fashions which Vanbrugh's drama forcefully ridiculed. In this way, through giving literal expression to the common-law adage that 'an Englishman's home is his castle', Vanbrugh sought to help correct national decay and thereby bring about a new and glorious Golden Age under Whig rule.

Appendix I

TRANSCRIPTION OF VANBRUGH'S 'REASONS OFFER'D FOR PRESERVING SOME PART OF THE OLD MANOUR' OF 11 JUNE 1709, SENT TO THE DUCHESS OF MARLBOROUGH[1]

There is perhaps no One thing, which the most Polite part of Mankind have more universally agreed in; than the Vallue they have ever set upon the Remains of distant Times. Nor amongst the Severall kinds of those Antiquitys, are there any so much regarded, as those of Buildings; Some for their Magnificence, or Curious Workmanship; And others; as they move more lively and pleasing Reflections (than History without their aid can do) on the Persons who have Inhabited them; On the Remarkable things which have been transacted in them, Or the extraordinary Occasions of Erecting them. *As I believe it cannot be doubted, but if Travellers many Ages hence, shall be shewn the Very House in which so Great a Man Dwelt, as they will then read the Duke of Marlborough in Story; And that they Shall be told, it was not only his Favourite Habitation, but was Erected for him by the Bounty of the Queen and with the Approbation of the People, as a Monument of the Greatest Services and Honours, that any Subject had ever done his Country: I believe, tho' they may not find art enough in the* Builder, to make them *admire the Beauty of the Fabrick* they will find Wonder enough in the Story, to make 'em pleas'd with the Sight of it.

I hope I may be forgiven, if I make some faint application of what I say of Blenheim, to the Small Remains of ancient Woodstock Manour.

It can't indeed be said, it was Erected on so Noble, nor on So justifiable an Occasion; But it was rais'd by One of the Bravest and most Warlike of the English Kings; And tho' it has not been Fam'd, as a Monument of his arms, *it has been tenderly regarded* as the Scene of his Affections. *Nor amongst the Multitude of People, who come daily to View what is raising to the Memory of the Great Battle of Blenheim; are there any that do not run eagerly to See* what Ancient Remains are to be found of Rosamonds Bower. *It may perhaps be worth some Little Reflection Upon what may be said, if the Very footsteps of it are no more to be found.*

But if the Historicall Argument Stands in need of Assistance; there is Still much to be said on Other Considerations.

That Part of the Park which is Seen from the North Front of the New Building, has Little Variety of Objects Nor dos the Country beyond it Afford any of Vallue. It therefore Stands in Need of all the helps that can be given, which are only Two; Buildings, And Plantations[.] These rightly dispos'd will indeed Supply all the wants of Nature in that Place. And the Most Agreable Disposition is to Mix them: which this Old Manour *gives so happy an Occasion* for, That were the inclosure fill'd with Trees (principally Fine Yews and Hollys) Promiscuously set to grow up in a Wild Thicket. So that all the Building left, (which is only the Habitable Part and the Chappel) might Appear in two Risings amongst 'em; it wou'd make One of the Most Agreable Objects that the Best of Landskip Painters can invent. And if on the Contrary this Building is taken away; there then remains nothing but an Irregular, Ragged Ungovernable Hill, the deformitys of which are not to be cured *but by a Vast Expence. And that at last will only Remove an Ill Object* but not produce a good One. Whereas to finish the present Wall for the Inclosures, to forme the Sloops and make the Plantation (which is all that is now wanting to Compleat the Whole Designe) wou'd not Cost Two Hundred pounds.

I take the Liberty to offer this Paper, with a Picture to Explain what I endeavour to describe, That if the Present Direction for destroying the Building, shou'd happen hereafter to be Repented of, I may not be blam'd for Neglecting to Set in the truest Light I cou'd, a Thing that Seem'd at least to me so very Matteriall.

J Vanbrugh
June the 11th 1709

---

1   British Library, Additional MS 61353, nos 62–63; (other copies nos 64–65, 66–67). This letter has been transcribed (inaccurately) on a number of occasions: in Dobrée, B., and G. Webb (eds), *The Complete Works of Sir John Vanbrugh*, vol. 4 [Letters], (1928), pp. 29–30; Dixon Hunt, J., and P. Willis (eds), *The Genius of the Place: The English Landscape Garden 1620–1820* (1975), pp. 119–21; Ridgway, C. and R. Williams (eds), *Sir John Vanbrugh and Landscape Architecture in Baroque England 1690–1730* (2000), p. 191; Van Eck, C. (ed.), *British Architectural Theory 1540–1750* (2003), p. 165; Mallgrave, H. F. (ed.), *Architectural Theory: Volume 1: An Anthology from Vitruvius to 1870* (2006), p. 230.

Appendix II

TRANSCRIPTION OF
'MR VAN-BRUGG'S PROPOSALS ABOUT
BUILDING YE NEW CHURCHES', ADDRESSED TO THE
CHURCH COMMISSIONERS AROUND 1711.[1]

Since it will perhaps be thought reasonable, that the fifty new Churches the Queen has gloriously promoted the Building of, in London and Westminster; shou'd not only serve for the Accommodation of the Inhabitants, in the Performance of their Publick Religious Dutys; but at the same time, remain Monuments to Posterity of Her Piety & Grandure And by consequence become Ornaments to the Towne, and a Credit to the Nation; the following Considerations are humbly offer'd, to the Commissioners who are Instructed with the direction of them.

That amongst the several kinds of Buildings by which Great Citys are Adorn'd; Churches, have in all Ages, and with all Religions been placed in the first Rank. No Expence has ever been thought too much for them; Their Magnificence has been esteem'd a pious expression of the Peoples great and profound Veneration towards their Deitys, And the contemplation of that Magnificence has at the same time augmented that Veneration.

If therefore on one hand it be reasonable to design Churches in such Manner, that the People may both hear what is utter'd by the Minister, and at the same time be so accommodated, as not to be disturb'd in their devotions by one an Other, or by the Inconveniencys of too much heat or cold; So on the other, these necessary dispositions in the usefull part of the Fabrick, shou'd be made consistent with the utmost Grace that Architecture can produce, for the Beauty of it: which Grace shou'd generally be express'd in a plain, but Just and Noble Stile, without running into those many Divisions and Breaks which other buildings for Variety of use may require; or such Gayety of Ornaments as may be proper to a Luxurious Palace.

To form the Churches now to be built, to these two general Propositions, it will be necessary to observe these following Rules.

First. That their Situation may be ever Insulate. This do's not only give them that Respectfull Distinction & Dignity which Churches Always ought to have; but it makes the Access to them easy, and is a great Security from Fire.

2dly. That they may be so plac'd, to be fairly View'd at such proper distance, as is necessary to shew their Exterior Form to the best Advantage, as at the ends of Large and Strait Streets, or on the Sides of Squares and Other open Places.

3dly. That they may be all Accommodated and Adorn'd with Portico's; no part in Publick Edifices being of greater use, nor no production in Architecture so solemnly Magnificent.

4ly. That they may be form'd for the utmost duration both in respect of the material, the Solidity of their Walls, and the Manner of their Construction: The extraordinary Expence of which is so small, That in a Church of Ten thousand pounds cost, it turns upon five hundred, whether it shall be crippled in a hundred Years, or stand like a Rock a Thousand.

5ly. That for the Ornament of the Towne, and to shew at a distance what regard there is in it to Religious Worship; every Church (as the Act of Parliament has provided) may have a Tower, but to Answer those ends, they shou'd be all of Stone or Brick; High and Bold Structures; and so form'd as not to be subject to Ruin by fire, but of such Solidity and Strength, that nothing but Time, and scarce that, shou'd destroy them.

6ly. That as to the Insides, both for the Accommodation of the Ordinary People, and the Beauty of the Place, they may not be too much crowded with Pews: but that a considerable Space may be left in the Middle Line with decent Forms regularly plac'd for People to repose themselves by Turns.

1 Bodleian MS Rawlinson B. 376, fols 351–52; see also a contemporary copy from which this title is taken, Bodleian MS Eng. Hist. b. 2. fol. 47 [transcribed in Whistler, L., *The Imagination of Vanbrugh and his Fellow Artists* (1954), Appendix 2; Downes, K., *Vanbrugh* (1977), Appendix E, pp. 257–8].

7ly. That for the Lights, there may be no more than what are necessary for meer use; many Windows making a Church cold in Winter, hot in Summer, and being very disagreeable and hurtfull to the sight. They likewise take off very much, both from the Appearance & reality of strength in the Fabrick; giving it more the Air of a Gay Lanthorn to be set on the Top of a Temple, than the Reverend look of a Temple it self; which shou'd ever have the most Solemn and Awfull Appearance both without and within, that is possible.

8ly. That they may be free'd from that Inhumane custome of being made Burial Places for the Dead. a Custome in which there is something so very barbarous in itself besides the many ill consequences that attend it; that one cannot enough wonder how it ever has prevail'd amongst the civiliz'd part of mankind. But there is now a sort of happy necessity on this Occasion of breaking through it: Since there can be no thought of purchasing ground for Church Yards, where the Churches will probably be plac'd. And since there must therefore be Cæmitarys provided in the Skirts of the Towne, if they are ordered with that decency they ought to be, there can be no doubt but the Rich as well as the Poor, will be content to ly there.

If these Cæmitarys be consecrated, Handsomely and regularly wall'd in, and planted with Trees in such form as to make a Solemn Distinction between one Part and another; there is no doubt, but the Richer sort of People, will think their Friends and Relations more decently inter'd in those distinguish'd Places, than they commonly are in the Ailes and under Pews in Churches; And will think them more honourably remember'd by Lofty and Noble Mausoleums, erected over them in Freestone (which no doubt will soon come into practice,) than by little Tawdry Monuments of Marble, stuck up against Walls and Pillars.

Noble a Generosity, that 'twere pitty Posterity shou'd not have an equal opinion of the Politeness of the Age, by finding the Edifices Suitable to what produc'd them.

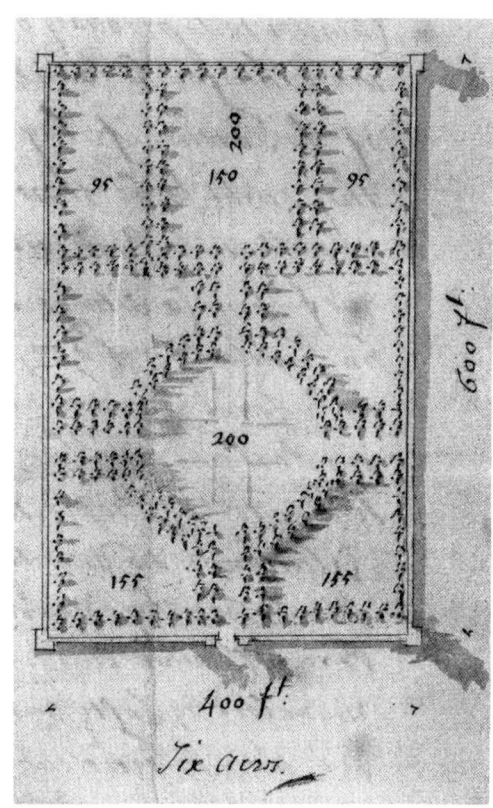

Manner of planting the Cæmitarys.

This manner of Interment has been practic'd by the English at Suratt and is come at last to have this kind of effect.

Upon the whole, it may be worth considering, That since Christianity began, there is but one Instance, where the Inhabitants of a City have had so Glorious an Occasion as this, to Adorn both their Religion and their Towne at once. A Resolution taken, and money provided to raise fifty New Churches in so short a time shews so glowing a Zeal, and so

Notes

PREFACE AND INTRODUCTION

1 Transcribed in Dobrée, B., and G. Webb (eds), *The Complete Works of Sir John Vanbrugh*, vol. IV, 'Letters' (1928), p. 59.

2 See Norberg-Schulz, C., *Late Baroque and Rococo Architecture* (1985 ed.), p. 196.

3 On the Whigs see Downes, K., *Vanbrugh* (1977), pp. 18–19.

4 See Hart, V., *Nicholas Hawksmoor: Rebuilding Ancient Wonders* (2002).

5 Downes, K., *Sir John Vanbrugh* (1987).

6 See Mowl, T., and B. Earnshaw, *An Insular Rococo* (1999), p. 20. See also Downes, K., *English Baroque Architecture* (1966), p. 86. Dobrée and Webb (1928), vol. IV, p. xxxiv. For comparisons between Vanbrugh's work and that of Palladio, see Lang, S., 'Vanbrugh's Theory and Hawksmoor's Buildings', *Journal of the Society of Architectural Historians*, vol. XXIV (1965), pp. 138–9.

7 Campbell, C., *Vitruvius Britannicus, or the British Architect*, vol. I (1715), p. 5.

8 V&A, E2124.1–254–1992. See Colvin, H., and M. Craig (eds), *Architectural Drawings in the Library of Elton Hall by Sir John Vanbrugh and Sir Edward Lovett Pearce* (1964). Vanbrugh's drawings for: Welbeck, Nottingham (*c.*1703), are held at Welbeck; houses for Robert Bertie in Lincolnshire (*c.*1710) are held in the Lincolnshire Archives Office; a plan for the layout of Kimbolton courtyard is held in the Huntingdon County Records Office, DDMIA/3/22; a design for an altar wall, All Souls College, Oxford, by 'Mr V. B. & H' (1713), is held in the Ashmolean Museum, Oxford, supplement to Gibbs Collection; plans for St James's Palace (*c.*1712–14) are held in the Royal Library, Windsor; a plan of Kensington Palace (*c.*1714) is held at Windsor and All Souls College; plans for house and gardens at Sacombe, Herts (*c.*1720), are held at the Victoria and Albert Museum, London (Elton Drawings, no. 56), and the Bodleian, Oxford, Gough Drawings a.3.64; sketches for Inveraray Castle, Argyll (*c.*1720), are held at the Victoria and Albert Museum, Elton Drawings, no. 79; a plan endorsed 'Earl of Islay' is held at the National Library of Scotland, Edinburgh, Milton of Saltoun Papers; a design for a pavilion at Claremont in Surrey (*c.*1724) is held in the British Library, Add. MS 33064, fol. 276. Additionally, an album of drawings of Kings Weston, not in Vanbrugh's hand, was bought in 1973 by the Bristol Civic Trust: see Downes, K., 'The Kings Weston Book of Drawings', *Architectural History*, vol. X, (1967), pp. 7–88. Undated drawings for Kings Weston, catalogued as by Vanbrugh, which illustrate the built scheme are held at the Yale Center for British Art, New Haven, basement and ground-floor plan, garden and side elevation, B1977.14.1235–36, 38–39, front elevation, B1977.14.1237. These drawings are similar, but not identical, to those in the so-called 'Kings Weston book'. The Canadian Centre for Architecture, Montreal, has two drawings (elevation with measurements and plan with compass holes indicating tracing) of a study of a castle attributed to Vanbrugh via a separate backing sheet with the inscribed title 'L'elevation d'un chateau fait en Espagne par le Chevallier/vanbrugh/en son stile propre', DR 1986: 0708X:001–004. A book plate indicates this study once belonged to 'The Hon'ble Edward Monckton/Sumerford Hall County of Stafford'. These drawings certainly appear to be by Vanbrugh given the smoking chimneys, the Doric doorcase, the round-headed windows and absence of 'unnecessary' mouldings, the urns and the blind arcade to the chimney/attic storey, a favorite Vanbrugian feature deployed at Kings Weston. The plan too has much in common with that of Kings Weston and may be a preliminary astylar scheme for the house.

9 A complete list of Vanbrugh's letters appears in Downes (1987), Appendix B, pp. 517–25. The unsigned letter of 16 August 1722 at Seaton Delaval reproduced and transcribed in Bingham, M., *Masks and Façades: Sir John Vanbrugh The Man in his Setting* (1974), pp. 345, 363, is not by Vanbrugh: see Downes (1987), p. 525.

10 'Journal of all Receipts, Payments and other Transactions, 1715–26', transcribed in Downes (1977), pp. 180–233.

11 See McCormick, F., *Sir John Vanbrugh: The Playwright as Architect* (1991), pp. 107–31.

12 Congreve was Vanbrugh's partner at the Queen's Theatre in the Haymarket. Congreve is mentioned in letters, Dobrée and Webb (1928), vol. IV, pp. 4 ('if Congreve's Play don't help 'em they are undone. 'tis a Comedy and will be play'd about Six weeks hence. Nobody has seen it yet'), 8 ('I was sitting downe to dinner with my Lord Hallifax and Congreve'), 146 ('Congreve says he'll poke out a letter to you'). In 1704 Vanbrugh collaborated with Congreve and Walsh in translating Molière's *Monsieur de*

Pourceaugnac as *Squire Trelooby*, each author taking one act. The Prologue, Epilogue, Dialogue and Masque to Vanbrugh's *The Pilgrim* (adapted from Fletcher's original) are by his friend John Dryden: see Dobrée and Webb (1928), vol. ii, p. 89.

13 This continuity of practice has been examined by McCormick (1991).

14 Dobrée and Webb (1928), vol. i, p. 206.

15 Dixon Hunt, J., *Gardens and the Picturesque: Studies in the History of Landscape Architecture* (1992), pp. 68–9.

16 On the 'entertaining wildernesses' of Castle Howard, see Mowl and Earnshaw (1999), p. 54.

17 Dobrée and Webb (1928), vol. ii, pp. 113, 135.

18 See Appendix One.

19 Vanbrugh's complete design for the bridge represented in the engraving by H. Terasson is held at the Bodleian Library, Oxford, Gough Maps 26, fol. 51.

20 On Aesop and Alberti see Marsh, D., 'Aesop and the Humanist Apologue', *Renaissance Studies*, vol. xvii no. 1 (2003), pp. 9–26.

21 Dobrée and Webb (1928), vol. ii, p. 15.

22 On the churches and the stimulation of awe, see Chs 3 and 4 below. See also Hart (2002), pp. 157–8.

23 Dobrée and Webb (1928), vol. iv, p. 163.

24 Ibid., pp. 9, 236. Tonson was Secretary of the Kit Cat club: see Downes (1977), p. 18. On Tonson see Geduld, H. M., *Prince of Publishers: A Study of the Work and Career of Jacob Tonson* (1969).

25 Tavernier, J.-B., *Travels in India by Jean-Baptiste Tavernier*, trans. V. Ball (1925), Book 1, ch. 1, pp. 5–7.

26 See also Downes (1977), pp. 257–8; Williams, R., 'A factor in his success. The missing years: did Vanbrugh learn from Mughal mausolea?', *Times Literary Supplement* (3 September 1999), pp. 13–14. Williams, R., 'Vanbrugh's India and his Mausolea for England', in Ridgway, C., and R. Williams (eds), *Sir John Vanbrugh and Landscape Architecture in Baroque England 1690–1730* (2000), pp. 114–30.

27 On this army service, see Bingham (1974), pp. 28–30.

28 In the Epilogue to *The False Friend*, addressed to the men in the audience, he observes on courtship, 'You won't attack the Town, which you besiege': see Dobrée and Webb (1928), vol. ii, p. 204. On Kimbolton see Ch. 6 below.

29 For the letter see Downes (1977), p. 250; on this event see Downes (1987), p. 61.

30 The Old Town Hall is one of the earliest Renaissance buildings of any size in the northern provinces. Concerning the royal palaces, that called 'Noordeinde' was built for the Orange family in 1533 and altered by Jacob van Campen and Pieter Post in 1639, whilst the 'Huis ten Bosch' (house in the forest) was built in the 1640s by Pieter Post and belonged to William iii. For a survey plan similar to this house, contemporary with Vanbrugh, see Bolton, A. T., and H. P. Hendry (eds.), *Wren Society Volumes* (1924–43), vol. xii, pl. xviii. On the influence of these buildings in Stuart England see Worsley, G., *Inigo Jones and the European Classicist Tradition* (2007), pp. 49–69.

31 Downes (1977), p. 247.

32 See McCormick (1991).

33 Dobrée and Webb (1928), vol. iv, p. 71.

34 See Luttrell, N., *A Brief Historical Relation of State Affairs from September 1678 to April 1714*, 6 vols (1969 ed.); see Downes (1977), p. 248.

35 Dobrée and Webb (1928), vol. ii, p. 10.

36 See Osborne, P., *A Journal of the Brest-expedition* (1694), p. 38.

37 Whilst Thomas Archer probably experienced Rome and its baroque masterpieces at first hand on his travels in Italy, neither Vanbrugh nor Wren visited Rome. On Wren's possible trip to the German territories, including The Hague and Heidelberg, in the train of the newly restored Elector Palatine Karl Ludwig, see Jardine, L., *On a Grander Scale: The Outstanding Career of Sir Christopher Wren* (2003), pp. 79–84.

38 Dobrée and Webb (1928), vol. iv, p. 207.

39 Swift's *Journal to Stella*, 7 November 1710, i, 83–4 [in Rogers, P. (ed.), *Jonathan Swift: The Complete Poems* (1983), p. 626].

40 Dobrée and Webb (1928), vol. iv, p. 116.

41 Ibid., p. 135.

42 Ibid., vol. iii, p. 11.

43 Ibid., vol. iv, p. 122.

44 On the marriage see Downes (1977), p. 98; Downes (1987), p. 378.

45 Dobrée and Webb (1928), vol. iv, p. 111.

46 Ibid., p. 146.

47 Ibid., p. 149.

48 On Hawksmoor and Freemasonry, see Hart (2002), esp. pp. 91–101.

49 Dobrée and Webb (1928), vol. iv, p. 12.

50 Hart (2002), p. 100.

51 Ibid., p. 127.

52 Ibid., pp. 59, 100. See Ward, E., *The Secret History of Clubs, particularly the Kit-Cat, Beef-Stake, Vertuosos, Quacks, Knights of the Golden-Fleece, Florists, Beaus, &c. with their original* (1709). Bingham (1974), pp. 88–103. Downes (1987), pp. 81–3.

53 Dobrée and Webb (1928), vol. iv, p. 59.

54 Ibid., p. 100.

55 Ibid., p. 167.

56 Ibid., p. 77. See Rogal, S. J., 'John Vanbrugh and the Blenheim Palace Controversy', *Journal of the Society of Architectural Historians*, vol. xxxii (1974), pp. 293–303.

57 Dobrée and Webb (1928), vol. iv, p. 77.

58 Ibid., p. 79.

59 Ibid.

60 See ibid., p. 215. On the bridge and its domestic interiors see Colvin, H., and A. Rowan, 'The Grand Bridge in Blenheim Park', in J. Bold and E. Chaney (eds), *English Architecture, Public and Private* (1993), pp. 159–75 [republished as 'The Grand Bridge in Blenheim Park', in Colvin, *Essays in English Architectural History* (1999), pp. 245–61.]

61 Dobrée and Webb (1928), vol. iv, p. 233.

62 In 'Sir *John Vanbrugh's* Justification of what he depos'd in the Duke of *Marlborough's* late tryal', transcribed in ibid., p. 185.

63 Ibid., p. 77.

64 Ibid., p. 85.

65 Ibid., pp. 86–7.

66 Ibid., pp. 132, 133.

67 Ibid., p. 145.

68 On this incident see Green, D., *Blenheim Palace* (1951); Downes (1987), p. 487.

69 Dobrée and Webb (1928), vol. IV, p. 167.

70 Ibid., pp. 170–71.

71 Ibid., p. 125.

72 See Bingham (1974), pp. 328–9; Downes (1987), p. 437.

73 Downes (1977), p. 203 (4 June 1720, 'pd upon Two Sub-scriptions in the South Sea').

74 Dobrée and Webb (1928), vol. IV, p. 131.

75 Vanbrugh owned and redeveloped a house and build-ings in Old Palace Yard at Westminster Abbey, e.g., enter-ing into a dispute concerning the amount charged by the workmen and the quality of the work carried out: see National Archive, Kew, C5/314/25; McKellar, E., *The Birth of Modern London: The Development and Design of the City 1660–1720* (1999), p. 84.

76 Dobrée and Webb (1928), vol. II, p. 76.

77 See esp. Colvin, H., *The History of the King's Works (1660–1782)*, vol. V (1976), pp. 36–40.

78 See ibid., p. 52; Dobrée and Webb (1928), vol. IV, pp. 117–19, 138, 169.

79 Dobrée and Webb (1928), vol. IV, p. 93. For attribution of this letter see Whistler, L., *The Imagination of Vanbrugh and his Fellow Artists* (1954), p. 246.

80 Dobrée and Webb (1928), vol. IV, p. 76.

81 Ibid., p. 11. In fact, no such undertaking had been made in the 1663 instructions concerning the Board's legal authority: see Downes (1987), p. 250.

82 Ibid., p. 247.

83 See Colvin (1976), p. 52.

84 Dobrée and Webb (1928), vol. IV, p. 117.

85 Ibid., p. 123.

86 Colvin (1976), pp. 36–7.

87 See ibid., pp. 59–60; Dobrée and Webb (1928), vol. IV, p. 98.

88 Dobrée and Webb (1928), vol. IV, p. 109.

89 Colvin (1976), pp. 62–5.

90 Dobrée and Webb (1928), vol. IV, p. 105.

91 Ibid., p. 124.

92 See Bold, J., *Greenwich: An Architectural History of the Royal Hospital for Seamen and the Queen's House* (2000), pp. 98, 135, 142–5. Bolton and Hendry (1924–43), vol. IV, pp. 30, 44–79.

93 Downes, K., *Hawksmoor* (1959), p. 249, no. 85.

94 Bold (2000), p. 144.

95 Dobrée and Webb (1928), vol. IV, p. 55. See Bingham (1974), pp. 240–64.

96 Dobrée and Webb (1928), vol. IV, p. 54.

97 Ibid., p. 73.

98 Wren, C., 'Tract I', *Parentalia* (1750), p. 351 [transcribed in Soo, L., *Wren's 'Tracts' on Architecture and other Writings* (1998), p. 153].

99 Dobrée and Webb (1928), vol. IV, p. 138.

100 See McEwen, I. K., 'On Claude Perrault: Modernising Vitruvius', in V. Hart and P. Hicks (eds), *Paper Palaces: The Rise of the Renaissance Architectural Treatise* (1998), pp. 321–7. In his copies of Blondel's *Cours*, Hawksmoor would also have seen that an *ordonnance* might be termed a *columnaison*, a coinage of Blondel's own invention that specifically concerns the column because it is 'the column that gives the rule and measure to everything else', Blondel, F. N., *Cours d'architecture* (1675–83), vol. I, p. 4; see Watkin, D. (ed.), *Sale Catalogue of Libraries of Eminent Persons* (1975), vol. IV (Architects), pp. 45–105, lots 90, 124 and 146.

101 Harris, E., and N. Savage, *British Architectural Books and Writers 1556–1785* (1990), p. 370. See also Ch. 1 below.

102 On Hampton Court see Colvin (1976), p. 178 fig. 6 C (pl. 14 illustrates the drawing by Thomas Fort of this scene). See also Thurley, S., *Hampton Court: A Social and Architectural History* (2003), pp. 258–60. Plan at the National Archive, Kew, Work 34/32. On Vanbrugh's pro-jects for the palaces of St James's and Kensington (Royal Library, Windsor, Portfolio 58, unsigned but inscribed by Vanbrugh; another version of the Kensington plan at All Souls College, I, 4), see Downes (1977), pp. 88–9.

103 For Vanbrugh's work at Hampton Court see Colvin (1976), p. 178; see also Dobrée and Webb (1928), vol. IV, pp. 73, 77, 154.

104 Dobrée and Webb (1928), vol. II, p. 196.

105 Colvin (1976), p. 169; Wind, E., 'Julian the Apostate at Hampton Court', *Journal of the Warburg and Courtauld Institutes*, vol. III (1939), pp. 127–37. See also 'Shaftesbury as a Patron of Art', ibid., vol. II (1938), pp. 182–5.

106 Discussed by Bennett, J. A., *The Mathematical Science of Christopher Wren* (1982), p. 117. See also Soo (1998), p. 212. Mowl, T., 'Antiquaries, Theatre and Early Medieval-ism', in Ridgway and Williams (2000), p. 86.

107 See Everett, N., *The Tory View of Landscape* (1994), p. 7; p. 38: 'Daniel Defoe, writing in the 1720s, saw the pro-liferation of country villas with informal parks and gardens as the best indication of a trading and improv-ing country, the most flourishing and opulent in the world, and luxuriant in culture and commerce'. See also Anne, *The Blessings of Peace: Queen Anne's Speech to Par-liament* (1713).

108 Vanbrugh alluded to the Golden Age topos in writing to the Earl of Manchester on 18 July 1707: 'We are here in Vast Expectations about the Thoulon expedition Sure if it Succeeds, it must bring things to a Speedy Issue. I wish it may; And that we may See your L^dship quickly here Again in peace and Plenty'; Dobrée and Webb (1928), vol. IV, p. 14.

109 Ibid., vol. III, p. 128.

110 Ibid., vol. II, pp. 144–5.

111 Transcribed in Downes (1959), p. 263.

112 At the time of Castle Howard's conception, Carlisle was on the threshold of a political career. He served as a min-ister under William III and, briefly from December 1701, as First Lord of the Treasury (the most important polit-ical office in the realm). His political ambitions proved short-lived, however, following the death of William on 8 March 1702 and the accession of Anne. At least at the start of her reign, Anne favoured the Tories as the 'Church party' over the Whigs whom she saw as polit-

ical republicans. Carlisle was dismissed in May 1702 but he remained a committed Whig and was even briefly re-instated as First Lord of the Treasury in 1715. See Saumarez Smith, C., *The Building of Castle Howard* (1997), esp. pp. 16–17: 'The trajectory of the third Earl's brilliant, but brief, political career as a minister of William III indicates that the plans for Castle Howard were made at exactly the moment when he was looking for promotion at Court. Building a great house was a means of drawing attention to his capabilities, of demonstrating his potential usefulness as an ally of the King'.

113   See ibid., pp. 6, 12–17, 38. On the Kit Cat Club, see Downes (1977), pp. 18–19.

114   See Saumarez Smith (1997), pp. 39, 43.

115   See Downes (1977), p. 33. Although he is sceptical of this interpretation, Saumarez Smith (1997), p. 105, notes: 'When Verrio chose as subject for the Queen's staircase at Windsor the scene of Apollo giving Phaeton permission to drive the chariot of the sun, he must have known that it would have been identified in the minds of contemporaries with autocratic monarchy (following Versailles) and the Divine Right of Kings. When, thirty years later, Pellegrini was invited to paint the Fall of Phaeton on the dome, it could be concluded that contemporaries would have seen it as an image of the collapse of such ambitions, of the detestation of the English for French forms of government and a celebration of the individual liberty established by the Glorious Revolution'. But see also p. 106, where the Great Hall is interpreted as a palace of the sun (although the political overtones are still inescapable and by no means incompatible).

116   Downes (1977), Appendix J, pp. 263–6.

117   William Kent, in the Temple of British Worthies at Stowe (*c.*1735), included busts of those who had opposed 'slavish systems' of artistic, political and religious prejudice, fought for the glory of Britannia or expanded the horizons of exploration and trade (Queen Elizabeth, King Alfred and William III). The gothic temple was originally dedicated to Liberty. The Greeks Lycurgus, Socrates, Homer and Epaminondas, all honoured in Kent's Temple of Ancient Virtue, were promoters of Virtue, Justice, Liberty and the Welfare of Mankind: see Everett (1994), p. 48. Kent's work makes explicit the emblematic nature of informal gardens of the period, and their meaning as the embodiment of the values of the Glorious Revolution and the subsequent ideal of Whig rule as the most 'natural' form of government known to humanity. Everett, p. 44, notes: 'writing in 1760, the poetess Anna Seward depicted the improvements at Shugborough as an image of national liberty, since only in "Freedom's Land" could forms reminiscent of the "Mandarins' despotic power" be happily combined with "Grecian domes" and be taken as images of pure delight rather than oppression'.

118   Chatsworth was rebuilt during the 1680s for William Cavendish who became the first Duke of Devonshire and a political associate of Carlisle. Lowther Castle in Westmorland was built by John Lowther, Viscount Lonsdale, Carlisle's political ally and rival in the north. For Saumarez Smith (1997), pp. 19, 22–3, these houses were 'striking monuments to the consequences of the Revolution Settlement'.

119   Everett (1994), p. 21, notes that Tory landowners had 'eschewed many fashionable activities, including forms of architecture and gardening which seemed devoted to private opulence, luxury and narrow ideas of possession'. See also Estienne, C., and J. Liebault, *Maison rustique, or, The countrey farme* (1616), p. 13, which notes: 'For as great cages make the birds never a whit the better, even so it is not safe and sure a course to have a large and costly building upon the ground'.

120   See Hart and Hicks (1998), pp. 287–318. See also Ch. 4 below.

121   North, R., 'Notes of Building' (1698) [transcribed in H. Colvin and J. Newman, *Of Building: Roger North's Writings on Architecture* (1981)], p. 3. Charles Davenant, *The True Picture of a Modern Whig, Set Forth in a Dialogue between Mr. Whiglove and Mr. Double. Two Under-Spur-Leathers to the Late Ministry* (1701), p. 31, noted: 'Now I am at my Ease, I have my Country-House where I keep my Whore as fine as an Empress'.

122   See Hart, V., 'Vanbrugh's Travels', *History Today*, vol. XLII (July 1992), pp. 26–32; Hart (2002), pp. 252–4.

123   See Everett (1994), p. 7; p. 38: 'Various attempts have been made in this century, as in the eighteenth, to argue that the style of informal landscape design that seemed to pervade England in the early eighteenth century was a "national style" based on ideas of constitutional liberty expressed in the Glorious Revolution of 1688. This style of improvement is often contrasted with the formality of less fortunate nations, in which nature was suppressed by a "presumptuous art", and topiary, avenues, and parterres could be seen as manifestations of some despotic tendency. In this view, liberty in Britain, together with security of property, created the condition for a rapid increase in national wealth and the general improvement of the landscape'. See Colley, L., *In Defiance of Oligarchy: The Tory Party 1714–60* (1982), pp. 9–10, 85, 99–100, 162–3, 195, 217, 274. See also Downes (1977), pp. 109–10: 'The seventeenth-century formal garden was based on the Cartesian concept of Nature as orderly and regular – Nature as exemplified in the heavenly bodies and the truth of mathematics, so that Wren could identify natural with geometrical beauty. There was a parallel in the minds of men like Shaftesbury or Addison, in the opening years of the eighteenth century, between the Whig liberation of the People from the toils of Absolutism and the liberation of natural forms from the topiarist's shears and the gardener's straight-edge. Vanbrugh was well aware of such parallels.'

124   See Bergdoll, B., *European Architecture, 1750–1890* (2000), p. 75.

125   Bond, D. F. (ed.), *The Spectator: by Joseph Addison, Sir Richard Steele et al.* (1965), vol. III, no. 412, 23 June 1712, p. 541.

126   See Dobrée and Webb (1928), vol. IV, pp. 63, 83, 87, 88, 93, 127, 128, 129, 132, 142, 143, 150, 151, 152, 156, 160, 165, 169, 170.

127 See Everett (1994), p. 47.

128 Dobrée and Webb (1928), vol. IV, pp. 150–51. See also 'Journal of all Receipts', transcribed in Downes (1977), pp. 180–233, which records in October 1716 that Vanbrugh made a journey of eleven days to 'Mr Walpoles'.

CHAPTER 1

1 Transcribed in Dobrée, B., and G. Webb (eds), *The Complete Works of Sir John Vanbrugh*, vol. IV, 'Letters' (1928), p. 15.

2 Rogers, P. (ed.), *Jonathan Swift: The Complete Poems* (1983), p. 91.

3 Dobrée and Webb (1928), vol. IV, p. 168.

4 Ibid., pp. 9, 236. See also Ch. 4 below.

5 'Journal of all Receipts, Payments and other Transactions, 1715–26', transcribed in Downes, K., *Vanbrugh* (1977), pp. 180–233.

6 On the possible influence of Alberti on Vanbrugh see Lang, S., 'Vanbrugh's Theory and Hawksmoor's Buildings', *Journal of the Society of Architectural Historians*, vol. XXIV (1965), pp. 129–31.

7 Preamble in John James's translation of Pozzo's *Perspectiva* (1707).

8 See Saxl, F., and R. Wittkower, *British Art and the Mediterranean* (1948), p. 48; Bold, J., *Greenwich: An Architectural History of the Royal Hospital for Seamen and the Queen's House* (2000), p. 143.

9 Harris, E., and N. Savage, *British Architectural Books and Writers 1556–1785* (1990), p. 115.

10 Dobrée and Webb (1928), vol. IV, p. 40.

11 See Hart, V., *Nicholas Hawksmoor: Rebuilding Ancient Wonders* (2002), p. 123.

12 Specchi published in Rossi, D., *Studio d'architettura civile*, vol. I (1702), pl. 5; See Saxl and Wittkower (1948), p. 66.

13 Dobrée and Webb (1928), vol. IV, pp. 29, 31. See Appendix One.

14 See Appendix One.

15 See Worsley, G., '"After ye Antique": Vanbrugh, Hawksmoor and Kent', in Ridgway, C., and R. Williams (eds), *Sir John Vanbrugh and Landscape Architecture in Baroque England 1690–1730* (2000), pp. 147–9.

16 See Downes (1977), p. 213, n. 278.

17 Fischer von Erlach, J. B., *Entwurff einer historischen Architectur* (1721); see Hart (2002), p. 33.

18 Bond, D. F. (ed.), *The Spectator: by Joseph Addison, Sir Richard Steele et al.* (1965), vol. I, no. 29, 3 April 1711, p. 123. For Vanbrugh and Addison, see Ch. 3 below.

19 Ibid., vol. V, no. 592, 10 September 1714, pp. 27–8.

20 Dobrée and Webb (1928), vol. IV, p. 112.

21 See Appendix Two. See also Williams, R., 'A factor in his success. The missing years: did Vanbrugh learn from Mughal mausolea?', *Times Literary Supplement* (3 September 1999), pp. 13–14; ibid., 'Vanbrugh's India and his Mausolea for England', in Ridgway and Williams (2000), pp. 114–30.

22 Dobrée and Webb (1928), vol. IV, p. 143.

23 As the Preface noted (n. 8), the Canadian Centre for Architecture, Montreal, has two drawings of a study of a castle attributed to Vanbrugh via a separate backing sheet with the inscribed title 'L'elevation d'un chateau fait en Espagne par le Chevallier/vanbrugh/en son stile propre'. This may be a misattribution, however, of an abortive scheme by Vanbrugh or of the early scheme for Kings Weston, with which it has much in common.

24 Blaeu, J., *Atlas Major*, 11 vols, Latin, 1662; 12 vols, French, 1663; 9 vols, Dutch, 1664; see Downes (1977), p. 193.

25 Ibid., pp. 193 (Eachard), 204, 216 (Stevens).

26 Ibid., p. 182.

27 Dobrée and Webb (1928), vol. IV, p. 107.

28 Ibid., p. 220.

29 See Appendix One.

30 Downes (1977), p. 199. These famous prints were mentioned by Steele in *The Spectator*, Monday, 19 November 1711 (see Bond (1965), vol. II, no. 226, p. 379).

31 Dobrée and Webb (1928), vol. I, pp. 198, 202.

32 Downes (1977), p. 228.

33 See Vanbrugh, J., *The Relapse, or Virtue in Danger*, ed. B. Harris, (1971), p. 46 note to line 473 (Act II, Sc. 1).

34 Downes (1977), p. 192.

35 Ibid., pp. 200, 214.

36 Ibid., p. 214.

37 Desaguliers published c.1720 a syllabus for his *Course of Experimental Philosophy* (1734–); see ibid., p. 215 n. 293.

38 Downes (1977), p. 231, n. 398. The Rev'd C. B. Norcliffe recorded that the volumes of the classics owned by Charles included Juvenal and Persius, *Genealogist*, vol. II (1878), p. 238. These were possibly Dryden, J., *The satires of Decimus Junius Juvenalis. Translated into English verse. By Mr Dryden, and several other eminent hands. Together with the satires of Aulus Persius Flaccus . . . To which is prefix'd a discourse concerning the original and progress of satire* (1693).

39 Transcribed in Downes (1977), Appendix J, pp. 263–6.

40 Dobrée and Webb (1928), vol. IV, p. 124.

41 See the Introduction above.

42 Downes (1977), pp. 181 (Gildon), 192, 199 (Prior), 203 (Milton), 220 (Settle).

43 Ibid., p. 197.

44 Ibid., p. 185, a work which seems never to have appeared; possibly Joseph Browne, whose collection was catalogued as *A Catalogue of a . . . Collection of Greek, Roman, Irish and English Coins and Medals [chiefly belonging to Joseph Browne] . . . which will be sold by auction* (1762).

45 Ibid., p. 197 (on 8 April 1719), p. 202 (25 February 1720). See Ch. 6 below.

46 Dobrée and Webb (1928), vol. IV, pp. 132, 144.

47 Rogers (1983), p. 97.

48 Dobrée and Webb (1928), vol. III, pp. 84–5.

49 See Palme, P., '"Ut architectura poesis"', in N. G. Sandblad (ed.), *Idea and Form: Studies in the History of Art* (1959), pp. 95–107; Johnson, A. W., *Ben Jonson: Poetry and Architecture* (1994).

50 See *The Annual Miscellany, for the year 1694* (R. E. for J. Tonson, 1694). Hammond, P., and D. Hopkins (eds), *The Poems of John Dryden*, 5 vols (1991–2005). See also Erskine-Hill, H., 'Heirs of Vitruvius: Pope and the Idea of Architecture', in H. Erskine-Hill and A. Smith (eds), *The Art of Alexander Pope* (1979), pp. 144–56.

51 See Johnson (1994); Erskine-Hill (1979).

52 Transcribed in Soo, L., *Wren's 'Tracts' on Architecture and other Writings* (1998), p. 154.

53 North, R., 'Of Unity and Variety' (*c.*1695–6), transcribed in Van Eck, C. (ed.), *British Architectural Theory 1540–1750* (2003), p. 39.

54 Bond (1965), vol. III, no. 417, 28 June 1712, pp. 564, 566.

55 Downes notes that in Vanbrugh's plays 'the major and minor plots are easily and skilfully interwoven, with a symmetry that is certainly deliberate and indeed architectural', in 'John Vanbrugh', *The Oxford Dictionary of National Biography* (2004), p. 73.

56 Bond (1965), vol. I, no. 59, 8 May 1711, p. 251.

57 As Downes notes, 'on the whole he used existing formulas, be they the classical orders, the obelisks, or the house plans of Palladio', in 'Nicholas Hawksmoor', *The Oxford Dictionary of National Biography* (2004), p. 953.

58 See Harris, B., 'Introduction' in Vanbrugh (1971), pp. xxii–xxiii, xvi. See also Downes, K., *Sir John Vanbrugh* (1987), pp. 125–7.

59 Dobrée and Webb (1928), vol. II, p. 19.

60 Ibid., vol. III, p. 100.

61 Ibid., pp. 100–01.

62 Bond (1965), vol. I, no. 62, 11 May 1711, p. 135.

63 See Harris, 'Introduction' in Vanbrugh (1971), pp. xxii–xxiii. See also Downes (1987), pp. 130, 134.

64 Dobrée and Webb (1928), vol. IV, p. 159.

65 Ibid., pp. 130, 131.

66 Downes (1987), p. 130 points to Vanbrugh's 'considerable reading in the Classics'.

67 Vanbrugh may have been educated in the rules of rhetoric, either by a private tutor or possibly at the King's School in Chester although there are no records of his attendance: see Downes (1977), p. 15 n. 12, Downes (1987), p. 41. On the links between rhetoric and the Orders, see Onians, J., *Bearers of Meaning: The Classical Orders in Antiquity, the Middle Ages, and the Renaissance* (1988), pp. 153–5, 269–71; Van Eck, C., '"The splendid effects of architecture, and its power to affect the mind": The Workings of Picturesque Association', in J. Birksted (ed.), *Landscapes of Memory and Experience* (2000), p. 255.

68 Vitruvius Pollio, M., *I dieci libri dell'architettura*, trans D. Barbaro, (1567), Book III ch. I, p. 115.

69 Browne, I., *On Design and Beauty: An Epistle* (1734), p. 1.

70 Listed in work carried out between 21 June 1705 and 15 December 1709; see Saumarez Smith, C., *The Building of Castle Howard* (1997), p. 65.

71 Dobrée and Webb (1928), vol. III, p. 107.

72 See ibid., vol. I, pp. xxiii, xxxi: 'Vanbrugh's work stands in the same relation to Orthodox classical architecture as the Heroic drama of Dryden stands to Classical tragedy. Indeed, Heroic architecture is as good a description of his style as could be found' . . . 'that theatrical quality in Vanbrugh's architecture which seems to ally it with the Heroic drama of Dryden and Congreve; the façade of Seaton, admirably set off by the splendid yet comparatively sober fronts of the wing blocks, even

more than Blenheim, is the final expression of what we may call "Heroic" architecture in England'. On Dryden's translation see Sowerby, R., *The Augustan Art of Poetry: Augustan Translation of the Classics* (2006).

73 Dryden (1693), 'Discourse on Epic Poetry'.

74 Dobrée and Webb (1928), vol. IV, p. 29. See Ch. 5 below and Appendix One.

75 Soo (1998), p. 63.

76 Downes (1977), pp. 200 (see n. 181), 203, 230.

77 See Smith, R., *Handel's Oratorios and Eighteenth-Century Thought* (1995).

78 See Olleson, P., 'Vanbrugh and Opera at the Queen's Theatre, Haymarket', *Theatre Notebook*, vol. XXVI (1971–2), pp. 94–101; Milhous, J., 'New Light on Vanbrugh's Haymarket Theatre Project', *Theatre Survey*, vol. XVII (1976), pp. 143–61; Sheppard, F. H. W. (ed.), 'The Haymarket Opera House', *Survey of London*, vols XXIX and XXX (1960).

79 Downes (1977), p. 42, comments that 'From what we know or suspect of Vanbrugh's eye for a setting, his fondness for the large, the dramatic and the extravagant, and his involvement with the London stage, we might imagine all sorts of fruitful connections between architect and man of the theatre. But most of the evidence is to the contrary . . . It is also extremely difficult to make valid comparisons between the different media of the time'. This present book seeks to establish just these connections, however.

80 Defoe, D., *A Tour Through the Whole Island of Great Britain* (1725), p. 162.

81 Dobrée and Webb (1928), vol. IV, p. 8.

82 Leslie, C., *The Rehearsal of Observator*, 5–12 May 1705. See also Downes (1977), p. 40; Downes (1987), p. 255.

83 Wilkinson, R., *Londina Illustrata* (1825), vol. II, p. 163, n. 163.

84 Fitzgerald, P., *A New History of the English Stage* (1882), vol. I, p. 238, n.

85 Dobrée and Webb (1928), vol. IV, p. 9.

86 See ibid., p. xxi; quoted in Whistler, L., *Sir John Vanbrugh, Architect and Dramatist, 1664–1726* (1938), p. 110.

87 Capron Watercolour, British Museum, Dept. of Prints and Drawings, Crace Collection Views, portfolio XI, sheet 51, no. 112.

88 Cibber, C., *An Apology for the Life of Colley Cibber, etc.*, vol. I (1740), pp. 321–2.

89 BM, Dept. of Prints and Drawings, Burney Collection of Theatrical Portraits, vol. IX, p. 65, no. 101.

90 Dobrée and Webb (1928), vol. IV, p. 16.

91 Ibid., p. 24.

92 Ibid., pp. 57–8.

93 Ibid., p. 123.

94 Advertisement for 22 March 1707 performance of *The British Enchanters*, in *The London Stage* (1707), part II, 2, p. 143; see Downes (1977), p. 44.

95 Dobrée and Webb (1928), vol. IV, p. 17.

CHAPTER 2

1   See Appendix One.

2   See Dixon Hunt, J., *William Kent Landscape Garden Designer: An Assessment and Catalogue of his Designs* (1987), p. 57.

3   See ibid. See also Baridon, M., 'Ruins as a Mental Construct', *Journal of Garden History*, vol. v (1985), pp. 84–96; Mowl, T., 'Antiquaries, Theatre and Early Medievalism', in Ridgway, C., and R. Williams (eds), *Sir John Vanbrugh and Landscape Architecture in Baroque England 1690–1730* (2000), pp. 91–2; Mowl, T., *Gentlemen and Players: Gardeners of the English Landscape* (2000), p. 63.

4   Dixon Hunt (1987), p. 57.

5   Giles Worsley comments that 'it is in the context of Venice's republican status that Palladio's handful of individual Serlianas on his villas can be understood', in *Inigo Jones and the European Classicist Tradition* (2007), p. 146.

6   See Clarke, G. B., 'Grecian Taste and Gothic Virtue: Lord Cobham's Gardening Programme and its Iconography', *Apollo*, vol. xcvii (1973), pp. 566–71.

7   See Ridgway, C., 'Rethinking the Picturesque', in Ridgway and Williams (2000), p. 187.

8   See Evans, J., *A History of the Society of Antiquaries* (1956). On 15 July 1718 Vanbrugh was paid the knighthood fees from Sir Thomas Jones, Secretary of the Society of Ancient Britain: see 'Journal of all Receipts, Payments and other Transactions, 1715–26', transcribed in Downes, K., *Vanbrugh* (1977), p. 194.

9   Skipwith appears to have lent Vanbrugh some money: see Bingham, M., *Masks and Façades: Sir John Vanbrugh The Man in his Setting* (1974), p. 39; Downes, K., *Sir John Vanbrugh* (1987), pp. 57–8. See also Cibber, C., *An Apology for the Life of Colley Cibber, comedian, and late patentee of the Theatre-Royal*, vol. I (1740; republished 1968).

10   Downes, K., *Hawksmoor* (1959), p. 278 no. 217; p. 256 no. 147.

11   Wren to John Fell, 26 May 1681, in A. T. Bolton and H. P. Hendry (eds), *Wren Society Volumes* (1924–43), vol. v, p. 17 [transcribed in Soo, L., *Wren's 'Tracts' on Architecture and other Writings* (1998), pp. 218–19].

12   Downes (1977), 'Accounts', p. 204. Vanbrugh's name appears amongst the subscribers in Stevens's book.

13   Stevens, J., *The History of the Ancient Abbeys, Monasteries, Hospitals, Cathedrals and Collegiate Churches* (1722–23), vol. II, pp. 55, 134.

14   Ibid., vol. I, pp. 419, 446.

15   Dobrée and Webb (1928), vol. IV, p. 4.

16   See Beard, G., *The Work of John Vanbrugh* (1986), p. 147 no. 98. Worsley, G., 'Sir John Vanbrugh and the Search for a National Style', in M. Hall (ed), *Gothic Architecture and its Meanings 1550–1830* (2002), p. 110, and 'Blenheim: Architecture of Albion', *Country Life*, vol. xcvii (9 October 2003), pp. 90–94. Vanbrugh's interest in Elizabethan architecture is noted here, following Pevsner, N., 'Good King James's Gothic', *Architectural Review*, vol. cvii (1950), pp. 117–22, and Whistler, L., *Sir John Vanbrugh, Architect and Dramatist, 1664–1726* (1938), and *The Imagination of Vanbrugh and his Fellow Artists* (1954).

17   Worsley (2002), pp. 102–5. See also Summerson, J., *Architecture in Britain 1530–1830* (1955 ed.), p. 159 (on the close connection between Chargate and Tudor manor-house 'H' plans); Downes (1959), pp. 79–80.

18   Hawksmoor [transcribed in Webb, G. (ed.), 'The Letters and Drawings of Nicholas Hawksmoor Relating to the Building of the Mausoleum at Castle Howard, 1726–1742', *Walpole Society*, vol. xix, (1930–31), pp. 111–63: 4 October 1731].

19   See Girouard, M., 'Attitudes to Elizabethan Architecture 1600–1900', in J. Summerson (ed.), *Concerning Architecture: Essays on Architectural Writers and Writing Presented to Nikolaus Pevsner* (1968), pp. 14–15. On Vanbrugh's kinsmen see Downes (1987), p. 25.

20   Dobrée and Webb (1928), vol. IV, p. 114.

21   Drawing by John Aubrey, Bodleian Library, Oxford, MS Wood 276b fol. 43*v*.

22   See Appendix One.

23   On 27 July 1716: Dobrée and Webb (1928), vol. IV, p. 74.

24   See Wagner, A., *Heralds of England: A History of the Office and College of Arms* (1967), and *A Herald's World* (1988).

25   The Dukes of Norfolk, who served as Earls Marshal, could not as Roman Catholics exercise the office of Earl Marshal but were allowed to appoint a Deputy from their Protestant cousins to act for them.

26   Dobrée and Webb (1928), vol. IV, p. 8.

27   Ibid., p. 170.

28   Rogers, P. (ed.), *Jonathan Swift: The Complete Poems* (1983), p. 97. See Hart, V., 'Vanbrugh's Travels', *History Today*, vol. xlii (July 1992), p. 30; see also Ch. 8 below.

29   Dobrée and Webb (1928), vol. IV, p. 9.

30   See Downes, K., 'John Vanbrugh' in *The Oxford Dictionary of National Biography* (2004).

31   Transcribed in Downes (1977), 'Accounts', p. 181; see also, e.g., p. 184.

32   See Bingham (1974), p. 296.

33   See Beltz, G. F., *Memorials of the most noble Order of the Garter* (1841), p. cxxiv. Vanbrugh was a frequent participant in court ritual at Windsor. To the Earl of Manchester on 9 September 1707, he wrote, 'I was at Windsor Yesterday, where the Duke of Devonshire was sworn into his Fathers Place of Steward, And a Great Dinner Was prepar'd for him at the Greencloath': Dobrée and Webb (1928), vol. IV, p. 15.

34   Ashmole, E., *The Institution, Laws & Ceremonies of the Most Noble Order of the Garter* (1672), p. 345.

35   Ibid., p. 592.

36   Downes (1977), pp. 185, 194.

37   See Rykwert, J., *The First Moderns* (1980), p. 131.

38   Dobrée and Webb (1928), vol. IV, p. 103.

39   Hart, V., *Art and Magic in the Court of the Stuarts* (1994), p. 37.

40   Drayton, M., *Poly-Olbion* (1613–22), xv, p. 244.

41   Thomas Carew's masque for the Stuart court, 'Coeleum Britannicum' (1634), closed with a view of Windsor Castle again drawn by Jones which the text made clear was 'the famous seat of the most honourable Order of the Garter'.

42   Dryden, J., *The Works of John Dryden*, ed. W. Scott, vol. vii (1821).

43 Ashmole (1672), pp. 95, 96.

44 Ibid., p. 136. On Hugh May's alterations, see Colvin, H., *The History of the King's Works, 1660–1782*, vol. v, (1976), pp. 316–17.

45 Eachard, L., *The History of England, from the first Entrance of Julius Caesar and the Romans* (1707–18), vol. I, pp. 41, 42, 365.

46 Dobrée and Webb (1928), vol. II, p. 33.

47 Ibid., vol. I, p. 188.

48 Published with a preface by George Powell (who was the first to act the part of Worthy in *The Relapse* in the same year, 1696) and adapted from a play by John Fletcher (1613?); see ibid., vol. I, p. 236.

49 Hart (1994), p. 55.

50 See Mowl, T., and B. Earnshaw, *John Wood: Architect of Obsession* (1988), pp. 186–7; Piggott, S., *The Druids* (1968).

51 Clarke, S., *C. Julii Caesaris, Quae Extant . . .* (1712). pl. 62, illustrating two square encampments (*castra*) and a circular city with a central circular temple, has the legend: 'Johanni Vanbrugh Armigero Clarenceux Regi Armorum nec non omnium Ædificiorum Regalium Serenissimæ Dnã Reginæ Annæ Inspectori Generali'. See Dobrée and Webb (1928), vol. IV, pp. 7–8, 9, 10–11.

52 See Smith, R., *Handel's Oratorios and Eighteenth-Century Thought* (1995).

53 Vanbrugh's letter to Tonson of 15 June 1703 alludes to the political overtones of the project: 'do you know that the Torys (even the wisest of 'em) have been very grave upon your going to Holland; – they often say (with a nod) that Caezar's CommTs might have been carry'd through without a voyage to Holland; there were meanings in that subscription, and that list of names may serve for farther engagements than paying three guineas apiece for a book; in short I could win a hundred pounds, if I were sure you had not made a trip to Hanover, which you may possibly hear sworn when you come home again; so I'd advise you to bring a very exact Journal, well attested': Dobrée and Webb (1928), vol. IV, pp. 7–8.

54 Downes sees these urns as reflecting 'the passage of history', (1977), p. 37. On Whitehall see Hart, V., '"A peece rather of good Heraldry, than of Architecture": Heraldry and the Orders of Architecture as Joint Emblems of Chivalry', *Res*, vol. XXIII, (1993), pp. 59–60.

55 Colvin (1976), p. 318; see also Worsley (2002), p. 119.

56 Defoe, D., *A Tour Through the Whole Island of Great Britain* (1725), Letter IV [p. 281].

57 See Colvin (1976), p. 327. In the King's Chapel the divine nature of the English monarchy was underlined by Varrio between 1680 and 1682 through his depictions of the miracles of Christ, ibid., p. 326.

58 British Library, London, Add. MS 6321 fol. 70.

59 Downes (1959), p. 208 (cat. no. 447).

60 Transcribed in full in Whistler (1954), p. 86; see Downes (1987), p. 272.

61 Dobrée and Webb (1928), vol. IV, p. 106.

62 Ibid., p. 98.

63 See, e.g., the entry for the Montagu(e) family in the *Encyclopedia Britannica* (1910–11 ed.), vol. XVIII, p. 746.

64 See the family tree in Downes (1977), pp. 6–7.

65 See Pevsner (1950), p. 117; this attribution is doubted by Paul Drury in '"No other place in the Kingdom will compare with it": the Evolution of Audley End', *Architectural History*, vol. XXIII, (1980), pp. 27–9, but later modified in Drury's *Audley End, Essex: HMSO Guides* (1984), p. 10, where the lower part of the screen 'may well be Vanbrugh's design'; see Downes (1987), pp. 332–3. See also Beard (1986), p. 134.

66 See Carter, P., 'Charles Howard', in *The Oxford Dictionary of National Biography* (2004).

67 Jardine, L., *On a Grander Scale: The Outstanding Career of Sir Christopher Wren* (2002), pp. 7, 30–42, 44–5, 48–50, 207–12.

68 Ibid., pp. 146–9, 165.

69 See Colvin (1976), p. 315.

70 Sir John Soane's Museum, London. See Jardine (2002), illustrations between pp. 446 and 447.

71 British Library, London, Stowe 246, fol. 64.

72 Dobrée and Webb (1928), vol. IV, p. 60.

73 Ibid., p. 95.

74 Ibid.

75 Ibid., pp. 96–7 (undated).

76 Ibid., p. 98.

77 Ibid., p. 104.

78 Ibid., p. 130.

79 Ibid., p. 102.

80 British Library, London, Add. MS 6321 fols 59r–61r.

81 Downes (1977), p. 33.

82 British Library, London, Add. MS 6321 fols 59r–61r. Vanbrugh arrived in Hanover on the evening of 6 June, bringing the Habit and Ensigns of the Order. The 11 June was appointed the first day of the investiture. The English party was conveyed by two coaches, each with six horses, from their lodging to the palace. Stebbing reports that following an address by Lord Halifax, 'Mr Vanbrugh addresst himself to his Hs in a few words, and presented him with the Book of Statutes. Then He withdrew into the Antechamber, and there putting on his Mantle of the Order took with him the Blew Ribbon Garter and George, and Repaired again to His Hs. And the Prince then declaring to the Commrs that He would accept the Order upon the Conditions mentioned in the statutes, His Hs redelivered the said Book to Mr Vanbrugh, who thereupon presenting the Blew Ribbon Garter to my Ld Halifax, and the Prince reposing his left leg on a Footstool the Commrs together tyed it on, Mr Vanbrugh reading the proper Admonition. Then Mr Vanbrugh delivered to my Lord Halifax the Diamond George, who holding it in his hand, while the Admonition was read, they both put it about His Hs neck.' Halifax and Vanbrugh then left the Prince and were conducted to the antechamber where they saluted members of the court.

83 British Library, London, Add. MS 61638 fol. 77; for other reports signed by Vanbrugh as Clarenceux King of Arms see Add. MS 61540 fol. 35 (29 November 1708); Add. MS 61649 fol. 124 (3 May 1717).

84 See Downes (1987), p. 526; Beard (1986), pp. 11–12.

85 See Saumarez Smith, C., *The Building of Castle Howard* (1997), pp. 9, 11–12.

86 Dobrée and Webb (1928), vol. III, p. 11. See the Introduction above.

87 Downes (1977), 'Accounts', p. 197.

88 Guillim, J., *A Display of Heraldrie* (1632 ed.), sig. A2r.

89 Ibid., in 'To the Courteous Reader'. See Hart (1994), pp. 73–4.

90 Guillim (1632), p. 307.

91 See Dobrée and Webb (1928), vol. IV, p. 100 (quoted in the Introduction above). In reference to the twin mountains that form the straights of Gibraltar, which were created by Hercules and signified the border of the known world, the mountains became represented by twin pillars in the heraldry of European royalty.

92 See Hart (1993), pp. 52–66.

93 Wotton, H., *The Elements of Architecture* (1624), pp. 35–6.

94 See Ch. 1, n. 45.

95 Book IV fol. 139r. Serlio notes in Book 'VIII' that 'Doric work is the most austere of all and truly appropriate for a soldier. The entire work is therefore to be Doric but delicate, because of the great Emperor who was such an admirer of architectural beauty', fol. 18r. Serlio, S., *Sebastiano Serlio on Architecture*, vol. II [Books VI–'VIII' of *Tutte l'opere d'architettura et prospetiva*; and the *Libro Extraordinario*, trans. V. Hart and P. Hicks], (2001), p. 454.

96 On Vanbrugh and this so-called 'national style' see Worsley (2002), p. 113.

97 Dobrée and Webb (1928), vol. I, p. 57.

98 Ibid., vol. IV, p. 14.

99 Ibid., p. 15.

100 A sketch survives (of *c*.1712) at the Victoria and Albert Museum, London, which Downes identifies with Castle Howard: see Downes (1977), p. 259.

101 Andrews Jelfe, a master-mason and His Majesty's Clerk of Works at Newmarket since 1715, was appointed Architect and Clerk of Works to the Board in January 1719, by when most of the Vanbrugian buildings had been designed. However, connections between Vanbrugh and subsequent work can be traced through Jelfe since he was in partnership with Christopher Cass, master-mason to the Ordnance and the mason Vanbrugh recommended to complete Blenheim; see Whistler (1954), pp. 212–26. Berwick gate drawing, British Library, London, Kings Topographical, XXXII.47–i. Davenport, W. O., 78/1564.

102 At Kimbolton the portico is again Doric but was added by Alessandro Galilei no doubt to assist the 'Masculine Shew'.

103 For these Welbeck designs see Bolton and Hendry (1924–43), vol. XII pl. XL (Talman), vol. XVII, pl. XIV (Vanbrugh). See Downes (1987), pp. 274–5.

104 See Ch. 5 below.

105 See Ch. 6 below.

106 Albeit used without triglyphs in the freeze. Here at Greenwich, as already shown, the Ionic Order was adapted to the building's character. On the simple ornamentation chosen for the soldier's church in the Hôtel des Invalides, a model for the layout at Greenwich, as a reflection of its purpose following the principles of decorum, see Berger, R. W., *A Royal Passion: Louis XIV as Patron of Architecture* (1994), p. 8.

107 Apparently removed in 1757 because the stucco weathered poorly; see engravings in Bolton and Hendry (1924–43), vol. XIX, pl. XL.

108 Wren, C., 'Letter to a Friend from Paris' (1665) [transcribed in Soo (1998), p. 104].

109 Dobrée and Webb (1928), vol. IV, p. 106.

110 See Appendix Two.

111 Dobrée and Webb (1928), vol. I, p. 100.

112 See Dixon Hunt (1987), pp. 64–5.

113 Colvin (1976), p. 224.

CHAPTER 3

1 On the importance of architectural 'effect' to Vanbrugh and Hawksmoor, see Cast, D., 'Seeing Vanbrugh and Hawksmoor', *Journal of the Society of Architectural Historians*, vol. XLIII (1984), pp. 314–6.

2 Transcribed in Dobrée, B., and G. Webb (eds), *The Complete Works of Sir John Vanbrugh*, vol. IV, 'Letters', (1928), p. 28.

3 Engraving, British Library, London, Map Room, K. XXXV, 28.d.

4 See Appendix One.

5 See Dixon Hunt, J., and P. Willis (eds), *The Genius of the Place: The English Landscape Garden 1620–1820* (1975), pp. 119–121; Watkin, D., *The English Vision: The Picturesque in Architecture, Landscape and Garden Design* (1982); Ballantyne, A., *Architecture, Landscape and Liberty: Richard Payne Knight and the Picturesque* (1997), pp. 144–5.

6 Dobrée and Webb (1928), vol. IV, p. 15.

7 Sir Polidorus Hogstye lives at Beast-Hall in *Aesop*: Dobrée and Webb (1928), vol. II, p. 47. Wagonrut-Lane features in *A Journey to London* and the children of the gluttonous Sir Francis Headpiece lodge at Smokedunghil Farm in the same play, ibid., vol. III, pp. 136, 137.

8 See Worsley, G., 'Sir John Vanbrugh and the Search for a National Style', in M. Hall (ed.), *Gothic Architecture and its Meanings 1550–1830* (2002), p. 125.

9 See Dixon Hunt, J., *Gardens and the Picturesque: Studies in the History of Landscape Architecture* (1992), p. 22. Worsley, G., '"After ye Antique": Vanbrugh, Hawksmoor and Kent', in Ridgway, C., and R. Williams (eds), *Sir John Vanbrugh and Landscape Architecture in Baroque England 1690–1730* (2000), pp. 147–9; on medieval sources see Mowl, T., 'Antiquaries, Theatre and Early Medievalism', in ibid., pp. 91–2.

10 On some (implausible) suggestions as to practical justifications for these walls, see Williams, R., 'Fortified Gardens', in ibid., pp. 49–70.

11 See Cottingham, J., *The Cambridge Companion to Descartes* (1992), pp. 350–8.

12 On Addison and garden design see Woodbridge, K., *The Stourhead Landscape* [National Trust Guides] (2002), pp. 6–7; Mowl, T., 'Addison, Switzer and "that inexpressible somewhat"', *Gentlemen and Players: Gardeners of the English Landscape* (2000), pp. 79–92.

13 See Smithers, P., *The Life of Joseph Addison* (1968). Van-

brugh and Addison shared an interest in ancient medals, e.g., Addison publishing *Dialogues upon the Usefulness of Ancient Medals* in 1726. And Addison's interest in architecture is attested by his subscription to *Vitruvius Britannicus*.

14 Downes, K., *Vanbrugh* (1977), p. 187.

15 See Downes, K., *Sir John Vanbrugh* (1987), p. 317.

16 Addison, J., and R. Steele *et al.*, *The Spectator* (1712–15), vol. III (opening list of subscribers). Subscriptions listed in Vanbrugh's accounts on 8 December 1719 and 31 May 1721: Downes (1977), pp. 200, 214.

17 Addison (1712–15) and *The Works of the Right Honorable Joseph Addison*, ed. Thomas Tickell, 4 vols (1721); see also Bond, D. F. (ed.), *The Spectator: by Joseph Addison, Sir Richard Steele et al.* (1965), vol. I, p. lxxxviii.

18 Addison (1712), vol. VI, p. 83; Addison (1721), vol. III, p. 502 no. 416; Bond (1965), vol. III, pp. 486–519.

19 On the influence of ideas of association in picturesque theory from the 1740s see Clark, H. F., 'Eighteenth-Century Elysiums: The Role of "Association" in the Landscape Movement', *The Journal of the Warburg and Courtauld Institutes*, vol. VI (1943), pp. 165–89; Brewer, J., *The Pleasures of the Imagination: English Culture in the Eighteenth Century* (1997); Van Eck, C., '"The splendid effects of architecture, and its power to affect the mind": The Workings of Picturesque Association', in J. Birksted (ed.), *Landscapes of Memory and Experience* (2000), pp. 245–59; and Van Eck (ed.), *British Architectural Theory 1540–1750* (2003), pp. 144, 165–6.

20 Bond (1965), vol. I, no. 110, 6 July 1711, p. 454.

21 Ibid., vol. III, no. 413, 24 June 1712, p. 547.

22 Ibid., vol. III, no. 411, 21 June 1712, p. 537.

23 Ibid., vol. III, no. 413, 24 June 1712, pp. 546–47.

24 Ibid., vol. III, no. 417, 28 June 1712, p. 562.

25 Ibid., vol. III, no. 416, 27 June 1712, pp. 558–9.

26 Dobrée and Webb (1928), vol. IV, p. 15.

27 Bond (1965), vol. III, no. 415, 26 June 1712, pp. 553–5.

28 See Ch. 8 below.

29 Bond (1965), vol. III, nos 411, 412, 21 June 1712, 23 June 1712, pp. 538, 544.

30 Dobrée and Webb (1928), vol. IV, p. 15.

31 See Evans, R., *The Projective Cast: Architecture and its Three Geometries* (1995); Pérez-Gómez, A., and L. Pelletier, *Architectural Representation and the Perspective Hinge* (1997).

32 See Bond (1965), vol. III, no. 415, 26 June 1712, p. 556.

33 Ibid., p. 557.

34 See Brownell, M. R., *Alexander Pope and the Arts of Georgian England* (1978). Mowl (2000), pp. 93–104.

35 See Clark (1943), pp. 165–89. See also in passing Beard, G., *The Work of John Vanbrugh* (1986), p. 61.

36 Bond (1965), vol. III, no. 412, 23 June 1712, p. 541.

37 See Van Eck (2000), p. 255.

38 See Davenport-Hines, R., *Gothic: 400 Years of Excess, Horror, Evil and Ruin* (1998); Hart, V., *Nicholas Hawksmoor: Rebuilding Ancient Wonders* (2002), p. 29.

39 Bond (1965), vol. III, no. 414, 25 June 1712, p. 549. On Addison and the concept of open landscape expressing political liberty see the Introduction above.

40 Ibid., p. 550. On Vanbrugh and Bridgeman see Mowl

(2000), pp. 62–78. The original lake, far smaller than that imposed on Blenheim by Brown, was formed by the River Glyme.

41 Dobrée and Webb (1928), vol. IV, p. 79.

42 On the various designers possibly involved in the landscape at Castle Howard, including William Talman, George London and Stephen Switzer, see Downes (1977), p. 109, Dixon Hunt (1992), p. 33, Mowl (2000), pp. 64, 71 (who argues for Carlisle as the inspiration at Castle Howard on the basis that Vanbrugh and Bridgeman reverted to a formal garden design at Eastbury House) and Ridgway and Williams (2000). See also Levine, N., 'Castle Howard and the Emergence of the Modern Architectural Subject', *Journal of the Society of Architectural Historians*, vol. XLII, (2003), pp. 326–51. On Vanbrugh's work on the landscape at Blenheim, see Ch. 4 below.

43 See Mowl (2000), pp. 72–6.

44 Dobrée and Webb (1928), vol. IV, p. 129.

45 See Ch. 4 below.

46 Wren, C., 'Tract II', *Parentalia* (1750), p. 355 [transcribed in Soo, L., *Wren's 'Tracts' on Architecture and Other Writings* (1998), p. 158].

47 'Mr. Van-Brugg's Proposals about Building ye New Churches'; see Appendix Two.

48 Bond (1965), vol. III, no. 415, 26 June 1712, p. 555.

49 Ibid., vol. II, no. 244, 10 December 1711, p. 447.

50 Dobrée and Webb (1928), vol. IV, p. 35. The Duchess of Marlborough endorsed the letter: 'The second green house, or a detached gallery I thank God I prevented being built; nothing, I think can be more mad than the proposal, nor a falser description of the prospect'.

51 Vanbrugh to Newcastle, 20 August 1723 and to Carlisle, 8 March 1726; see ibid., pp. 152, 173.

52 Ibid., pp. 171, 164 (Vanbrugh here recommending what Lord Cobham had seen 'done, to a Great Palace in Germany').

53 Ibid., p. 25.

54 Ibid., p. 5.

55 British Library, London, Add. MS 19607, fol. 44. See Hart (2002), p. 144.

56 Dobrée and Webb (1928), vol. IV, p. 164.

57 See Appendix Two.

58 Drawings of churches, Victoria and Albert Museum, London, D.104 and 110/1891, [Downes (1977), p. 83, fig. 70]; see also D.96.1891. See Lang, S., 'Vanbrugh's Theory and Hawksmoor's Buildings', *Journal of the Society of Architectural Historians*, vol. XXIV (1965), p. 128.

59 Bond (1965), vol. III, no. 418, 30 June 1712, p. 568.

60 Elevation, Victoria and Albert Museum, London, D.113–91; plan, D.129.B–91.

61 See, e.g., Wells, J., *Sciographia, or the art of shadowes* (1635); Dubreuil, J., *Perspective practical . . . also a treatise of shadows natural by the sun, torch, candle, and lamp: very useful and necessary for all painters, engravers, architects, embroiderers, carvers, goldsmiths, tapestry-workers and all others that work by design* (1698). On occasion Hawksmoor sketched shadows appropriate to the intended light source on designs for tapestries: see Whistler, L., *The Imagination of*

Vanbrugh and his Fellow Artists (1954), p. 57. On Hawksmoor's use of shadow see Geraghty, A., 'Nicholas Hawksmoor and the Wren City Church Steeples', *The Georgian Group Journal*, vol. x (2000), p. 5.

62 Transcribed in Yolton, J. W., *Perception Acquaintance from Descartes to Reid* (1984), p. 91.

63 Evelyn, J., 'An Account of Architects and Architecture', appended to *A Parallel of the Antient Architecture with the Modern* (1707), p. 9.

64 Breval, J., *Remarks on several Parts of Europe* (1726), vol. II, pp. 269–70.

65 Dobrée and Webb (1928), vol. II, p. 116.

66 Bond (1965), vol. III, no. 411, 21 June 1712, p. 539.

67 This first appeared in the 1628 edition. On the deliberate creation of settings conducive to the melancholic mood, see Strong, R., *The Renaissance Garden in England* (1979), pp. 215–9.

68 Burton, R., *The Anatomy of Melancholy* (1676 ed.), p. 170.

69 Downes, K., *Hawksmoor* (1959), p. 253, no. 114.

70 Dobrée and Webb (1928), vol. IV, p. 131. Saumarez Smith, C., *The Building of Castle Howard* (1997 ed.), p. 151.

71 Burton (1676), p. 170.

72 The Temple of Sleep, or Sleeping Parlour, was demolished in 1760 and the four urns with their grotesque masks, probably designed by Vanbrugh, were transferred to the Oxford Bridge which was built that year.

73 See Ch. 1 above.

74 '*Don John*, with his last breath, confesst himself the Offender', in Dobrée and Webb (1928), vol. II, p. 203.

75 See Beard (1986), pp. 84–5, nos. 8–9.

76 On the Kings Weston pyramids, see Ch. 7 below. On the 'temple' design, see Beard (1986), p. 143, no. 92.

77 Victoria and Albert Museum, London, D.106–1891. See ibid., pp. 144–5, no. 96.

78 Serlio, S., Book III, p. LXII; see *Sebastiano Serlio on Architecture*, vol. I [Books I–V of *Tutte l'opere d'architettura et prospetiva*, trans. V. Hart and P. Hicks], (1996), p. 152.

79 Drawing of the front elevation for Kings Weston, catalogued as by Vanbrugh, held at the Yale Center for British Art, New Haven, B1977.14.1237. On this drawing see the Preface, n. 8. Campbell is at pains to thank Vanbrugh for 'most generously assisting me with his Original Drawings, and most carefully correcting all the Plates as they advanced', in *Vitruvius Britannicus* (1715), vol. I, p. 5. These urns are also illustrated, in a different form and with flames, drawn on the surviving proof for the Campbell engraving preserved in an album of drawings of Kings Weston, not in Vanbrugh's hand, bought in 1973 by the Bristol Civic Trust, no. 1: Downes, K., 'The Kings Weston Book of Drawings', *Architectural History*, vol. x (1967), cat. 1, p. 39; on the surviving contract drawing for two Kings Weston urns, in an anonymous hand and with a ball finial in place of the flames, see ibid., cat. 19.

80 See Downes, K., *Hawksmoor* (1970; rep. 1994), p. 121; Hart (2002), p. 154.

81 These altars are illustrated in the plates of Seaton Delaval in *Vitruvius Britannicus*, vol. III (1725), pls 20, 21; and in a drawing for the garden elevation of Kings Weston, catalogued as by Vanbrugh, held at the Yale Center for British Art, New Haven, B1977.14.1238.

82 Wren, C., 'Tract IV', *Parentalia* (1750), p. 363 [transcribed in Soo (1998), pp. 178–9].

83 Bulls' sculls carved into the Doric entablatures of ancient temples had expressed the theme of death and sacrifice, as Serlio noted in his fourth book: 'when the ancients sacrificed bulls a plate was used, and it was their custom to set things like this in these places around sacred temples as decoration': Serlio, S., Book IV, p. XVIIIv; see Hart and Hicks (1996), p. 283.

84 Langley, B., *Grub Street Journal*, 11 July 1734; see Hart (2002), p. 154.

85 See Hart (2002), p. 145.

86 See Ch. 4 below; see also Hart (2002), pp. 131–65.

87 Dobrée and Webb (1928), vol. IV, p. 148.

88 See Appendix One.

89 Downes (1987), p. 337, notes, e.g., that, 'Hawksmoor can write as a theorist or as the learned architect he was recognized to be; Vanbrugh's opinions show a manager's confidence rather than a scholar's'. Colvin observes that in the early 1700s 'as an architect Vanbrugh was still a brilliant novice who needed the technical assistance of Hawksmoor to realize those heroic visions which were his particular contribution to English architecture', *The History of the King's Works, 1660–1782*, vol. v (1976), p. 36.

90 Palladio, A., *Andrea Palladio: The Four Books on Architecture*, trans. and ed. R. Tavernor and R. Schofield (1997), p. 217.

91 This was in line with Hawksmoor's description of gothic as the 'Monastic style' – coined to convey the style's associative, rather than its formal, qualities; see Hart (2002), pp. 57–64, 79–80.

92 Scruton, R., *The Aesthetics of Architecture* (1979), p. 138.

93 See Watkin, D., *Sir John Soane: Enlightenment Thought and the Royal Academy Lectures* (1996), Lecture IX, p. 618; Lecture XI, p. 646.

94 Ballantyne (1997), p. 144.

CHAPTER 4

1 Vanbrugh, J., 'Mr Van-Brugg's Proposals about Building ye New Churches'; see Appendix Two. On Vanbrugh's possible sources for his ideas see Lang, S., 'Vanbrugh's Theory and Hawksmoor's Buildings', *Journal of the Society of Architectural Historians*, vol. XXIV (1965), pp. 127–51.

2 Vitruvius is unspecific about the matching Order, Vitr. I.i.5 [in Vitruvius, *De Architectura*, Books I–X, trans. I. D. Rowland (1999)]. The Erechtheum is Ionic but the caryatids do not have canonic capitals (they are a form of Doric). See Colvin, H., 'Hermes, Terms and Caryatids in English Architecture', in *Essays in English Architectural History* (1999), pp. 94–135.

3 Transcribed in Dobrée, B., and G. Webb (eds), *The Complete Works of Sir John Vanbrugh* (1928), vol. II, p. 162.

4 Serlio, S., *Sebastiano Serlio on Architecture*, vol. I (Books I–V of *Tutte L'opere d'architettura et prospetiva*, trans. V. Hart and P. Hicks (1996)).

5 Serlio, S., Book VII, p. 232 [see Serlio, S., *Sebastiano Serlio on Architecture*, vol. II (Books VI–'VIII' of *Tutte l'opere d'ar-*

chitettura et prospetiva; and the *Libro Extraordinario*, trans. V. Hart and P. Hicks (2001), p. 376), here paraphrasing Alberti, Book nine, ch. two [see Alberti, L. B., *On the Art of Building in Ten Books*, trans. J. Rykwert, N. Leach and R. Tavernor (1988), p. 294]. On this aspect see esp. Onians J., *Bearers of Meaning: The Classical Orders in Antiquity, the Middle Ages, and the Renaissance* (1988), pp. 310–4. Serlio notes in his letter to the Readers in the 'Extraordinary Book of Doors': 'you, O architects grounded in the doctrine of Vitruvius (whom I praise to the highest and from whom I do not intend to stray far), please excuse all these ornaments, all these tablets, all these scrolls, volutes and all these superfluities, and bear in mind the country where I am living, you yourselves filling in where I have been lacking' (fol. 2r). Here again, context – in this case France – played its part in determining the degree of fidelity to Vitruvian forms, linked to prevailing moral norms and acceptable licences.

6 See Hart, V., and R. Tucker, 'Ornament and the Work of Inigo Jones', *Architectura*, vol. XXXII, (2002), pp. 36–52.

7 Defoe, D., *A Tour Through the Whole Island of Great Britain* (1725), Letter V, p. 333.

8 Evelyn, J., 'An Account of Architects and Architecture', appended to *A Parallel of the Antient Architecture with the Modern* (1664), p. 122; (1707), p. 15.

9 Ibid.

10 Norberg-Schulz, C., *Late Baroque and Rococo Architecture* (1985 ed.), p. 196. On Vanbrugh's preference for simplicity in the London churches, and the possible influence of René Rapin's note that the 'true Eloquence of the Pulpit should endeavour to support itself only by the Greatness of its Subjects, by its Simplicity and Good Sense', see Lang (1965), p. 141.

11 Onians (1988), p. 38, has pointed out that Cicero's three types of oratory provided 'a close model for Vitruvius's classification of Doric and Corinthian as extremes of "severity" and "softness", with Ionic embodying *mediocritas* in between'. On the links between rhetoric and architecture, see Van Eck, C., '"The splendid effects of architecture, and its power to affect the mind": The Workings of Picturesque Association', in J. Birksted (ed.), *Landscapes of Memory and Experience* (2000), pp. 245–59.

12 Dobrée and Webb (1928), vol. IV, p. 74.

13 Ibid., pp. 32–3.

14 Ibid., pp. 14, 15.

15 Ibid., p. 129.

16 Ibid., p. 131.

17 Ibid., p. 157.

18 Ibid., p. 164.

19 Ibid., p. 160.

20 Vanbrugh used his Palladio in the design of, e.g., Blenheim, see Ch. 5 below; see also Downes, K., *Vanbrugh* (1977), p. 84; Worsley, G., *Classical Architecture in Britain: The Heroic Age* (1995), p. 91.

21 Dobrée and Webb (1928), vol. IV, p. 9.

22 Palladio, A., *Andrea Palladio: The Four Books on Architecture*, trans. and ed. R. Tavernor and R. Schofield (1997), p. 216.

23 Wright, J., *Historia Histrionica: An Historical Account of the English Stage* (1699), pp. 10–11. There is no evidence that Vanbrugh designed scenery, however: see Downes (1977), p. 42. Frank McCormick has examined the influence of set design, particularly of perspective scenes and martial vocabulary, on Vanbrugh's architecture, in *Sir John Vanbrugh: The Playwright as Architect* (1991), pp. 88–94, 107–31; see also Mowl, T., 'Antiquaries, Theatre and Early Medievalism', in Ridgway, C., and R. Williams, (eds), *Sir John Vanbrugh and Landscape Architecture in Baroque England 1690–1730* (2000), p. 85.

24 Serlio, S., Book II, fols 45v and 46r; see Serlio (1996), p. 86. On 'Robin Hood's Well', designed by Vanbrugh c.1720, see Ch. 2 above.

25 Written by Richard Steel, Dobrée and Webb (1928), vol. III, p. 84.

26 E.g., the actor Tom Doggett, who played Moneytrap in *The Confederacy*, adopted a grim humour for the part, wearing an old threadbare black coat on which he had put new cuffs, pockets and buttons to make it appear even more rusty. The neck of the coat was stuffed to make him appear round-shouldered from crouching over his accounts; see Bingham, M., *Masks and Façades: Sir John Vanbrugh The Man in his Setting* (1974), pp. 116–17.

27 See Saumarez Smith, C., *The Building of Castle Howard* (1997), p. 99.

28 See Serlio (2001), pp. XXXIV–XXXVII.

29 See Shaftesbury's *Inquiry concerning Virtue or Merit*, first published in 1699 and then in *Characteristicks of Men, Manners, Opinions, Times* (1711).

30 See Story, T., *A Journal of the Life of Thomas Story* (1747). See also Saumarez Smith (1997), p. 10.

31 Dobrée and Webb (1928), vol. IV, p. 107.

32 Ibid., p. 147. See Colvin, H., *Architecture and the After-Life* (1991), p. 317 and p. 160.

33 See Hart, V., *Nicholas Hawksmoor: Rebuilding Ancient Wonders* (2002), p. 234.

34 Dobrée and Webb (1928), vol. IV, p. 158.

35 Downes (1977), p. 214.

36 Beard, G., *The Work of John Vanbrugh* (1986), p. 80 no. 2.

37 Transcribed in Dobrée and Webb (1928), vol. I, p. 206.

38 Ibid.

39 Ibid., p. 11.

40 Ibid., pp. 202, 204.

41 Ibid., p. 205.

42 Ibid., vol. II, p. 34, vol. III, p. 12.

43 Ibid., vol. IV, p. 147.

44 Ibid., vol. I, p. 29.

45 Ibid., p. 205.

46 See Carpo, M., 'The Architectural Principles of Temperate Classicism: Merchant Dwellings in Sebastiano Serlio's Sixth Book', *Res*, vol. XXII (1992), pp. 135–51; Randall, C., *Building Codes: The Aesthetics of Calvinism in Early Modern Europe* (1999); Hart, V., and R. Tucker, '"Immaginacy set free": Aristotelian Ethics and Inigo Jones's Banqueting House at Whitehall', *Res*, vol. XXXIX (2001), pp. 151–67. Drawing on Aristotle, Daniele Barbaro in his 1567 commentary *M. Vitruvii Polionis de Architectura libri decem* explained that mixing contrasting forms using reason 'can result in a beautiful median

form', Book III ch. 1, p. 115: 'però dico io, che mescolando con ragione nelle fabriche le proportioni d'una maniera, o componendole, o levandole, nè puo risultare una bella forma di mezo'. Wren had stressed a middle path when emphasising that it was the 'Variety of Uniformities' which 'makes the Mean', Tract I, *Parentalia* (1750), p. 352 [transcribed in Soo, L., *Wren's 'Tracts' on Architecture and Other Writings* (1998), p. 154].

47 Cave, W., *Primitive Christianity, or The Religion of the Ancient Christians in the First Ages of the Gospel* (6th ed., 1702), pp. 91–2. On Wren's possible use of this, see Loach, J., 'Gallicanism in Paris, Anglicanism in London, Primitivism in Both', in N. Jackson (ed.), *Plus ça change . . . Architectural Interchange between France and Britain: Papers from the Annual Symposium of the Society of Architectural Historians of Great Britain* (1999), p. 13.

48 Campbell, C., *Vitruvius Britannicus, or the British Architect* (1715), vol. I, p. 5. See Harris, E., and N. Savage, *British Architectural Books and Writers 1556–1785* (1990), p. 144 n. 1; see also the Preface and Ch. 1 above.

49 Campbell (1715), 'Introduction'.

50 See Ch. 1 above.

51 Campbell (1715), 'Introduction'.

52 Wotton, H., *The Elements of Architecture* (1624), p. 37. See Onians (1988), p. 155; Hart, V., 'From Virgin to Courtesan in Early English Vitruvian Books', in V. Hart and P. Hicks (eds), *Paper Palaces: The Rise of the Renaissance Architectural Treatise* (1998), pp. 297–318.

53 Dobrée and Webb (1928), vol. I, p. 26.

54 See, e.g., Breton, N., *The Court and the Country* (1618); Williams, R., *The Country and the City* (1985), esp. pp. 52–4. See also the Conclusion below.

55 Dobrée and Webb (1928), vol. IV, p. 167. In *c.*1715 Vanbrugh had carried out alterations at Middleton Park in Middleton Stoney for Henry Boyle, Lord Carleton (destroyed in 1755).

56 Ibid., vol. II, pp. 29–31.

57 Ibid., vol. III, p. 143; 'bringing his Wife to *London* to play off a hundred Pounds at Dice with Ladies of Quality, before breakfast', 'I am extremely sorry to see you, in the worst Place I know in the World for a good Woman to grow better in', pp. 136, 139.

58 Downes (1977), p. 83, notes the High Church and Tory motivations behind these new churches and comments, surely incorrectly, that 'as an exercise in piety, providing places of worship for the established religion of England in the new suburbs of London and Westminster, the scheme cannot have greatly interested Vanbrugh'.

59 British Library, London, Kings Topographical, XXIII–21–2–h.

60 Dobrée and Webb (1928), vol. IV, p. 240.

61 'Papers of the Commission for Building Fifty New Churches', Lambeth Palace Library, London, MS 2690, fols 42–4.

62 Lambeth Palace Library, London, MS 2750, nos 16 and 17. See Du Prey, P. R., *Hawksmoor's London Churches: Architecture and Theology* (2000); Hart (2002), pp. 140–2.

63 See Appendix Two.

64 See ibid. Vanbrugh was perfectly capable of formulating

these ideas, without the assistance of Hawksmoor (on whose possible involvement see Downes (1977), p. 84: 'on the evidence of their correspondence it is Hawksmoor who appears as the theoretician, and the more likely to have drawn up the memorandum on the churches').

65 Defoe (1725), p. 331.

66 See Appendix Two; see also Du Prey (2000), p. 56.

67 See Hart (2002), pp. 187–231.

68 See Palladio (1997), p. 215.

69 See Appendix Two.

70 See Williams, R., 'A factor in his success. The Missing Years: Did Vanbrugh learn from Mughal Mausolea?', *Times Literary Supplement* (3 September 1999), pp. 13–14; 'Vanbrugh's India and his Mausolea for England', in Ridgway and Williams (2000), pp. 114–30.

71 'Papers of the Commission for Building Fifty New Churches', Lambeth Palace Library, London, MS 2693, fol. 76.

72 Drawings of churches, Victoria and Albert Museum, London, D.104 and 110/1891, [Downes (1977), p. 83, fig. 70]; see also Victoria and Albert Museum, D.96.1891. See Smith, P., 'St Lawrence, West Woodhay: A Church by Vanbrugh?', in J. Bold and E. Chaney (eds), *English Architecture, Public and Private: Essays for Kerry Downes* (1993), p. 186.

73 See Appendix Two. On Vanbrugh's debt to Alberti see Lang (1965), p. 130.

74 Dobrée and Webb (1928), vol. IV, p. 55. See the Introduction above.

CHAPTER 5

1 See Appendix One.

2 See Stoye, J., *English Travellers Abroad 1604–1667* (1989 ed.).

3 Dobrée, B., and G. Webb (eds), *The Complete Works of Sir John Vanbrugh* (1928), vol. IV 'Letters', p. 29. See Ch. 1 above and Appendix One.

4 Ibid., vol. III, p. 57.

5 Saumarez Smith, C., *The Building of Castle Howard* (1997), pp. 51–3, notes that where 'Vanbrugh took responsibility for everything that happened at Castle Howard, Hawksmoor occupied himself with practicalities, regulating the quality of workmanship, surveying the foundations, drawing up future instructions for the workmen . . . Vanbrugh was entirely and exclusively responsible for the first ideas for the house . . . He took the project through to the stages of preparing the model in wood. At this point he realized that he would need the professional assistance of someone with more experience of the everyday practicalities of building. So he decided to employ Nicholas Hawksmoor in this capacity . . . If one single person is to be attributed with the quality of the building of Castle Howard, then it must be Vanbrugh, working within a matrix which was essentially collaborative'. Downes, K., *Sir John Vanbrugh* (1987), p. 200, notes: 'it is clear from surviving drawings and

documents that Hawksmoor performed three functions of which Vanbrugh was as yet incapable; he made most of the drawings, he designed the detailing, and he negotiated rates with the artificers and craftsmen who were to build the house'. On the development of the design and the role of both architects see Downes, K., 'Vanbrugh over Fifty Years', in Ridgway, C., and R. Williams (eds), *Sir John Vanbrugh and Landscape Architecture in Baroque England 1690–1730* (2000), pp. 1–11. See also Dixon Hunt, J., *Gardens and the Picturesque: Studies in the History of Landscape Architecture* (1992), pp. 18–46; Levine, N., 'Castle Howard and the Emergence of the Modern Architectural Subject', *Journal of the Society of Architectural Historians*, vol. LXII (2003), pp. 326–51.

6 Cumbria County Record Office, Carlisle: D/LONS/ L13.

7 See Ch. 2 above.

8 See Saumarez Smith (1997), p. 58.

9 Downes, K., *Hawksmoor* (1959), p. 254 no. 136.

10 See Dixon Hunt (1992), p. 22.

11 See Webb, G. (ed.), 'The Letters and Drawings of Nicholas Hawksmoor Relating to the Building of the Mausoleum at Castle Howard, 1726–1742', *Walpole Society*, vol. XIX (1930–31), pp. 111–63.

12 Serlio, S., Book IV, fol. 126v; see Serlio, S., *Sebastiano Serlio on Architecture*, vol. I [Books I–V of *Tutte l'opere d'architettura et prospectiva*, trans. V. Hart and P. Hicks (1996)], p. 254. In 'Book VIII' Serlio again makes clear that rustication 'is very suitable' as a symbol of protection and strength, fol. 17v, [Books VI–'VIII' of *Tutte l'opere d'architettura et prospetiva*; and the *Libro Extraordinario*, trans. V. Hart and P. Hicks (2001)], p. 452.

13 Webb (1930–31), 4 January 1732.

14 Downes (1959), p. 254 no. 136.

15 Vitruvius, I.ii.5 [in Vitruvius, *De Architectura*, Books I–X, trans. I. D. Rowland (1999)].

16 Transcribed in Downes, K., *Vanbrugh* (1977), 'Appendix J', pp. 263–6; see Saumarez Smith (1997), pp. 69, 156.

17 Downes notes 'that Castle Howard has an integrated symbolic programme is yet to be proved', in Ridgway and Williams (2000), p. 10.

18 Listed in work carried out between 21 June 1705 and 15 December 1709; see Saumarez Smith (1997), p. 65. See Ch. 1 above.

19 Downes (1959), p. 254 no. 136. Balanced opposites can also be found in the internal iconography of the house, with its vision of Apollo (sun) in the Great Hall contrasted with Diana (moon) in the Grand Cabinet at the west end of the garden front.

20 Vanbrugh owned Milton's *Poetical Works* in quarto (1720): Downes (1977), p. 203. See Ch. 1 above. On the influence of Milton's description of Paradise on garden design see Mowl, T., *Gentlemen and Players: Gardeners of the English Landscape* (2000), pp. 79–80, 81, 88.

21 Downes (1959), p. 243 no. 67.

22 Dobrée and Webb (1928), vol. IV, p. 160; see Ch. 4 above.

23 Ibid., p. 156.

24 Downes (1959), pp. 243, 244 no. 67.

25 Dobrée and Webb (1928), vol. IV, pp. 156, 157.

26 See Worsley, G., '"After ye Antique": Vanbrugh, Hawksmoor and Kent', in Ridgway and Williams (2000), pp. 147–9. The Temple also resembles the Aurora casino in the gardens of the Villa Ludovisi; see Dixon Hunt (1992), p. 27.

27 See Colonna, F., *Hypnerotomachia Poliphili*, trans. and ed. J. Godwin (1999), p. 209.

28 Vitruvius, I.ii.5, in Vitruvius (1991).

29 Downes (1959), p. 244 no. 67.

30 Hawksmoor sketched a sphinx in a letter to Carlisle of 11 April 1730: see Hart, V., *Nicholas Hawksmoor: Rebuilding Ancient Wonders* (2002), pp. 67–8. Combined with the pyramids, these proposed sphinxes show the Egyptian influence on the Castle Howard landscape consistent with Vanbrugh's Indian influences. See Grant, E., 'The Sphinx in the North: Egyptian Influence on Landscape, Architecture and Interior Design in Eighteenth- and Nineteenth-Century Scotland', in D. Cosgrove and S. Daniels (eds), *The Iconography of Landscape* (1988), pp. 236–53.

31 See Hart (2002).

32 One of the first to recognise the importance of Hawksmoor's role at Blenheim was J. H. V. Davies in 'Nicholas Hawksmoor', *Journal of the Royal Institute of British Architects*, vol. XLIX, no. 10 (October 1962), pp. 368–76.

33 'Sir John Vanbrugh's Justification Of what he depos'd in the Duke of Marlborough's late TRYAL', transcribed in Dobrée and Webb (1928), vol. IV, Appendix 1, p. 179.

34 British Library, London, Add. MS 61353, no. 91.

35 Ibid., no. 252. See also 'Letters to Henry Joynes, 1705–13', British Library, Add. MS 19,607.

36 Dobrée and Webb (1928), vol. IV, p. 210.

37 See Green, D., *Blenheim Palace* (1951, rep. 1967), pp. 298–9, 315.

38 Shaftesbury, *Letter Concerning the art or science of Design*, in *Characteristicks*, 5th ed. (1732), pp. 401–2.

39 Aristotle, *Nicomachean Ethics*, IV.ii; see Onians, J., *Bearers of Meaning: The Classical Orders in Antiquity, the Middle Ages, and the Renaissance* (1988), pp. 123–6. See also Stevenson, C., 'Robert Hooke's Bethlem', *Journal of the Society of Architectural Historians*, vol. LV (1996), p. 268. Hart, V., and R. Tucker, '"Immaginacy set free": Aristotelian Ethics and Inigo Jones's Banqueting House at Whitehall', *Res*, vol. XXXIX (2001), pp. 151–67.

40 British Library, London, Add. MS 61353, no. 91; see Whistler, L., *Sir John Vanbrugh, Architect and Dramatist, 1664–1726* (1938), p. 237.

41 Dobrée and Webb (1928), vol. IV, pp. 45, 46.

42 See Downes (1987), p. 526. See also Ch. 2 n. 51 above.

43 Hawksmoor may well have been solely responsible for the design of this triumphalist heraldry: see ibid., pp. 287–90.

44 Discussed by Downes (1977), p. 65; Downes (1987), pp. 309–10.

45 Barbarian captives appear on Trajan's Column and on Constantine's Arch in Rome, as Hawksmoor would have seen in his copy of Desgodets, A. B., *Les Edifices antiques de Rome dessinés et mesurés tres exactement*, published in Paris in 1682; see Watkin, D. (ed.), *Sale Catalogue of*

Libraries of Eminent Persons (1975), vol. IV [Architects], pp. 45–105, lot 109. He refers to the details of this arch on a sheet of details of cornices for Worcester College chapel, Oxford: Downes (1959), p. 279 no. 264.

46   Palladio, A., *Quatro Libri* (1570), Book IV, ch. vii [see Palladio, A., *Andrea Palladio: The Four Books on Architecture*, trans. and ed. R. Tavernor and R. Schofield (1997), pp. 16, 18–19]. Wren discusses the temple in Tract IV, *Parentalia* (1750), pp. 364–6 [transcribed in Soo, L., *Wren's 'Tracts' on Architecture and Other Writings* (1998), pp. 179–84].

47   Dobrée and Webb (1928), vol. IV, p. 236. See also Downes (1959), p. 78 n. 33, 'Even the bridge at Blenheim is recognizably indebted to Palladio'.

48   Soo (1998), pp. 179–84.

49   See Downes, K., *English Baroque Architecture* (1966), p. 80.

50   Drawings in Hawksmoor's hand record the original Doric theme of this south façade. An early design is illustrated in ibid., fig. 217. See also Downes (1977), p. 62. Hawksmoor drawings of the Doric south façade are listed in Downes (1959), p. 283, nos. 412–14.

51   McCormick, F., *Sir John Vanbrugh: The Playwright as Architect* (1991), p. 116. On the bridge see Colvin, H., and A. Rowan, 'The Grand Bridge in Blenheim Park', in J. Bold and E. Chaney (eds), *English Architecture, Public and Private* (1993), pp. 159–75 [republished as 'The Grand Bridge in Blenheim Park', in Colvin, *Essays in English Architectural History* (1999), pp. 245–61].

52   Dobrée and Webb (1928), vol. IV, p. 71.

53   Ibid., p. 74.

54   Ibid., p. 35.

55   Ibid., p. 56.

56   Addison, J., *The Works of the Right Honourable Joseph Addison* (1721), vol. I, p. 83. See Ch. 3 above.

57   See Appendix One.

58   Addison (1721), vol. I, p. 46.

59   Ibid., p. 29.

60   See Appendix One.

61   Addison (1721), vol. I, p. 26.

62   Ibid., p. 64.

63   See Ridgeway, C., 'Rethinking the Picturesque', in Ridgway and Williams (2000), pp. 176–7.

CHAPTER 6

1   Dobrée, B., and G. Webb (eds), *The Complete Works of Sir John Vanbrugh* (1928), vol. I, p. 57; drawbridge reference on p. 71.

2   Van Eck, C., '"The splendid effects of architecture, and its power to affect the mind": The Workings of Picturesque Association', in J. Birksted (ed.), *Landscapes of Memory and Experience* (2000), p. 249. John Soane noted that 'the front of a building is like the prologue of a play, it prepares us for what we are to expect. If the outside promises more than we find in the inside, we are disappointed. The plot opens itself in the first act and is carried on through the remainder, through all the mazes of character, convenience of arrangement, elegance and

propriety of ornaments, and lastly produces a complete whole in distribution, decoration and construction', in Watkin, D., *Sir John Soane: Enlightenment Thought and the Royal Academy Lectures* (1996), p. 188.

3   Dobrée and Webb (1928), vol. IV, 'Letters', p. 14. On this see Anderson, C., 'Masculinity and English Architectural Classicism', in Perry, G. (ed.), *Art and its Histories: Gender and Art* (1999), pp. 148–52.

4   Dobrée and Webb (1928), vol. IV, p. 13.

5   See Downes, K., *Sir John Vanbrugh* (1987), p. 335.

6   Dobrée and Webb (1928), vol. IV, pp. 13, 19.

7   Ibid., pp. 13–14.

8   Ibid., p. 14. On this passage see Cast, D., 'Speaking of Architecture: The Evolution of a Vocabulary in Vasari, Jones and Sir John Vanbrugh', *Journal of the Society of Architectural Historians*, vol. LII, (1993), p. 187.

9   See unexecuted plan for Kimbolton in Huntingdon County Records Office, DDMIA/3/22, illustrated and discussed in Whistler, L., *The Imagination of Vanbrugh and his Fellow Artists* (1954), p. 140, fig. 48; see also Worsley, G., 'Sir John Vanbrugh and the Search for a National Style', in M. Hall (ed.), *Gothic Architecture and its Meanings, 1550–1830* (2002), pp. 111–12; Beard, G., *The Work of John Vanbrugh* (1986), pp. 51–3, 133, nos 80, 81. Vanbrugh's east entrance design, Victoria and Albert Museum, London, D. 97–91.

10   Dobrée and Webb (1928), vol. IV, p. 25. Drawing of the south façade (Fig. 219), Victoria and Albert Museum, London, D. 109–91.

11   Dobrée and Webb (1928), vol. IV, p. 15.

12   Suggested by Cast, D., 'Seeing Vanbrugh and Hawksmoor', *Journal of the Society of Architectural Historians*, vol. XLIII (1984), p. 317.

13   See Ch. 2 above; see also Anderson (1999), p. 150.

14   Dobrée and Webb (1928), vol. IV, p. 15.

15   See Vanbrugh's Accounts transcribed in Downes, K., *Vanbrugh* (1977), p. 231, n. 398.

16   See Ch. 7 below.

17   Dobrée and Webb (1928), vol. IV, p. 106.

18   Ibid., p. 138. Vitruvius, I.iii.2 [in Vitruvius, *De Architectura*, Books I–X, trans. I. D. Rowland (1999)].

19   For Jones's book on Stonehenge see Hart, V., *Art and Magic in the Court of the Stuarts* (1994).

20   Clarke, S., *C. Julii Caesaris, Quae Extant . . .* (1712). See Ch. 2 above.

21   Dobrée and Webb (1928), vol. IV, p. 20.

22   See Hart, V., *Nicholas Hawksmoor: Rebuilding Ancient Wonders* (2002), pp. 105–11.

23   See Hart, V., '"A Pretty Impudent Countenance": John Vanbrugh's Seaton Delaval', *Architectural Research Quarterly*, vol. VII, no. 3/4 (2003), pp. 311–23.

24   On the Delaval family, see Burgess, R., *Those Delavals!* (1972). On the house and its patron, see Musson, J., 'Seaton Delaval Hall Northumberland', *Country Life*, vol. CXCVII (6 November 2003), pp. 56–61.

25   Dobrée and Webb (1928), vol. IV, pp. 130, 137–8.

26   See Le Fevre, P., 'Sir Ralph Delaval' in *The Oxford Dictionary of National Biography* (2004).

27   Serlio, Book IV, fol. XXXIXv, and *Extraordinario Libro*, fol.

4*v* [in *Sebastiano Serlio on Architecture*, trans V. Hart and P. Hicks, 2 vols (1996, 2001), vol. I, p. 326; vol. II, p. 466].

28 See Serlio in Hart and Hicks (2001). Giles Worsley comments concerning the horizontal grooving on the Doric giant Order: 'Probably Vanbrugh's source was Serlio's Tuscan order, as suggested for city and fortress gates, giving it a particularly forceful, masculine, or – and this is what is probably important – almost primitive feel', see Worsley (2002), p. 117.

29 Vitruvius, III. v. 15 [in Vitruvius (1999)].

30 Worsley (2002), p. 118, suggests: 'Could Vanbrugh's symbolic use of the giant Doric and Corinthian orders have been meant to generate associations with their use in medieval buildings'. See also Worsley, G., 'Blenheim: Architecture of Albion', *Country Life*, vol. CXCVII (9 October 2003), p. 92.

31 Serlio, Book IV, fol. xvii*r* [Hart and Hicks (1996), vol. I, p. 281]. See Ch. 2 above.

32 The mason William Etty worked on both houses.

33 See Chs 1 and 2 above.

34 Dobrée and Webb (1928), vol. IV, p. 17.

35 Ibid., pp. 137–8.

36 See Beard (1986), pp. 66, 155. The ancient quadrivium and trivium had included grammar, logic and rhetoric; on the ancient Liberal Arts, esp. rhetoric, see Van Eck, C. (ed.), *British Architectural Theory 1540–1750* (2003), p. 7.

37 Serlio, Book IV, fol. XVII*r* [Hart and Hicks (1996), vol. I, p. 281].

38 On this see Musson (2003), p. 57.

39 Vanbrugh's interest in Palladio's house plans is attested by his letter to Tonson on 13 July 1703: ''Tis Palladio in French, w*th* the Plans of most of the Houses he built. there is one without the Plans, but 'tis that with 'em I would have'): Dobrée and Webb (1928), vol. IV, p. 9. Robert Williams notes that Seaton Delaval expressed a 'romantic feudal past' despite the neo-Palladian format, in 'Fortified Gardens', in Ridgway, C., and R. Williams (eds), *Sir John Vanbrugh and Landscape Architecture in Baroque England 1690–1730* (2000), p. 60.

40 See Ch. 4 above.

41 See in general Brownell, M. R., *Alexander Pope and the Arts of Georgian England* (1978).

42 Dobrée and Webb (1928), vol. II, p. 182. Later in the same Act, Leonora observes: 'but the Night confounding the Villainy of the Guilty, with the Generosity of the Innocent', p. 185.

43 Ibid., pp. 23, 24. Later Learchus observes: 'let *Oronces* be lov'd, let *Aesop* be hated; let one be a Peacock, let t'other be a Bat', p. 37.

44 On this see Serlio in Hart and Hicks (2001), pp. XXI–XXVI.

45 Hawksmoor, transcribed in Webb, G. (ed.), 'The Letters and Drawings of Nicholas Hawksmoor Relating to the Building of the Mausoleum at Castle Howard, 1726–1742', *Walpole Society*, vol. XIX (1930–31), 5 October 1732.

46 Ibid.

47 The Epilogue to *The Mistake*, written by Peter Antony Motteux, is on the inequality of Women: 'Hard Fate of Woman! Any one wou'd vex,/To think what Odds, you Men have, of our Sex./Restraint and Customs share our Inclination,/You Men can try; and run o'er half the Nation'; see Dobrée and Webb (1928), vol. III, p. 129.

48 Ibid., pp. 115, 116.

49 Ibid., p. 114.

50 Ibid., *A Short Vindication of the Relapse and the Provok'd Wife*, vol. I, pp. 212–13. In other cases fortifications are both actual and moral: in *The False Friend*, Lopez comments to his master Don John concerning Leonora, 'Will you continue the Siege of a Place, where, 'tis probable they will daily augment the Fortifications, where there are so many open Towns you may march into without the trouble of opening the Trenches.' Don John replies: 'I am going, *Lopez*, to double my Attacks: I'll beat up her Quarters six times a Night, I am now down-right in Love; the Difficulties pique me to the Attempt, and I'll conquer or I'll die', ibid., vol. II, p. 165. In *A Journey to London*, female virtue is once more alluded to as a 'Citadel . . . in Danger', vol. III, p. 161.

51 See McCormick, F., *Sir John Vanbrugh: The Playwright as Architect* (1991).

52 See Dobrée and Webb (1928), vol. I, p. 71, reference by Lord Foppington to Clumsey's moat and gate.

53 Ibid., p. 118.

54 Here, too, the interior of the dinning room (which may or may not be to Vanbrugh's designs since it was carried out after his death in 1726) had decoration of festoons of fruit and flowers which Wren would have clearly identified as 'feminine'. See Bingham, M., *Masks and Façades: Sir John Vanbrugh The Man in his Setting* (1974), p. 337; Downes (1977), p. 105.

55 See Anderson (1999), pp. 137–46; Hart, V., and R. Tucker, 'Ornament and the Work of Inigo Jones', *Architectura*, vol. XXXII (2002), pp. 36–52; Anderson, C., *Inigo Jones and the Classical Tradition* (2007), pp. 130–64.

56 See Ch. 5 above; see also Hart (2002), pp. 111–29.

57 See Anderson (1999), p. 145.

58 See Hutchinson, W., *A View of Northumberland* (1778); Musson (2003), p. 58.

59 See Public Monuments and Sculpture Association, National Recordings Project: http://vads.ahds.ac.uk/collections/PMSA.html under 'Vanbrugh'.

CHAPTER 7

1 Dobrée, B., and G. Webb (eds), *The Complete Works of Sir John Vanbrugh* (1928), vol. IV, 'Letters', p. 119.

2 In 1644, e.g., the English jurist Sir Edward Coke (1552–1634) was quoted as saying: 'For a man's house is his castle, et domus sua cuique tutissimum refugium' ('One's home is the safest refuge for all').

3 See Hussey, C., 'Kings Weston, Gloucestershire', *Country Life*, vol. LXI (30 April 1927), pp. 680–7; Hussey, C., and H. A. Tipping, *English Homes, period IV, vol. ii: The Work of Sir John Vanbrugh and his School, 1699–1736* (1928), pp. 141–56; Gotch, C., 'Mylne at Kings Weston', *Country Life*, vol. CXXIII (23 January 1953), pp. 212–15; Downes, K., 'The Kings Weston Book of Drawings', *Architectural History*, vol. X (1967), pp. 7–88. Undated drawings for

Kings Weston, catalogued as by Vanbrugh, which illustrate the built scheme, are held at the Yale Center for British Art, New Haven, basement and ground floor plan, garden and side elevation, B1977.14.1235–36, 38–39; front elevation, B1977.14.1237.

4 Dobrée and Webb (1928), vol. IV, p. 77.

5 See Hayton, D. W., 'Edward Southwell' in *The Oxford Dictionary of National Biography* (2004); Downes (1967), p. 10.

6 Victoria and Albert Museum, London, D. 123–91.

7 See Hussey (1927), p. 683.

8 The stable buildings are incorrectly attributed to Vanbrugh by Hussey and Tipping (1928), pp. 153–4; but see also Gotch (1953) and Downes (1967).

9 Campbell, C., *Vitruvius Britannicus*, vol. I (1715), p. 5.

10 The surviving proof for the engraving in an album of drawings of Kings Weston, not in Vanbrugh's hand, bought in 1973 by the Bristol Civic Trust, no. 1: Downes (1967), p. 39 cat. no. 1.

11 Campbell (1715), p. 5; see Downes (1967), p. 14 and no. 37.

12 This feature also occurs on the elevation drawing attributed to Vanbrugh via a separate backing sheet with the inscribed title 'L'elevation d'un chateau fait en Espagne par le Chevallier/vanbrugh/en son stile propre', in the Canadian Centre for Architecture, Montreal, DR1986: 0708X:002. Both elevation and associated plan have much in common with Kings Weston, in proportion, room distribution and features, and may form a preliminary astylar (i.e., pre-Corinthian) scheme for the house; see also the Preface, n. 8.

13 See Hart, V., *Nicholas Hawksmoor: Rebuilding Ancient Wonders* (2002), p. 146. See also Summerson, J., *Architecture in Britain, 1530–1830* (1991 ed.), p. 265.

14 Undated drawing for the front elevation of Kings Weston, catalogued as by Vanbrugh, Yale Center for British Art, New Haven, B1977.14.1237.

15 Transcribed in Whistler, L., *The Imagination of Vanbrugh and his Fellow Artists* (1954), p. 242. Dobrée and Webb (1928), vol. IV, p. 55.

16 Dobrée and Webb (1928), vol. IV, p. 56.

17 Du Cerceau, A., *Les plus excellents bastiments de France* (1576–79; 1988 ed.), pp. 60–1; Serlio, S., Book VII, pp. 70–1 [*Sebastiano Serlio on Architecture*, vol. II (Books VI–'VIII' of *Tutte l'opere d'architettura et prospectiva* and the *Libro Extraordinario*), trans, V. Hart and P. Hicks (2001), p. 236].

18 Girouard, M., *Robert Smythson and the Architecture of the Elizabethan Era* (1966), pp. 94, 121.

19 Dobrée and Webb (1928), vol. IV, p. 149. See the Introduction above.

20 See Beard, G., *The Work of John Vanbrugh* (1986), p. 115 no. 51.

21 Lord Carlisle served as MP for Morpeth.

22 See Ch. 6 above.

23 In an album of drawings of Kings Weston, not in Vanbrugh's hand, bought in 1973 by the Bristol Civic Trust, nos 17, 52, 66; see Downes (1967), pp. 48–9.

24 See Dobrée and Webb (1928), vol. IV, pp. 7, 9, 10–11; see also Ch. 8 below.

25 See the Conclusion below.

26 Dobrée and Webb (1928), vol. IV, p. 148.

27 See Worsley, G., 'Blenheim: Architecture of Albion', *Country Life*, vol. CXCVII (9 October 2003), p. 91.

28 Victoria and Albert Museum, London, D. 125–91; see Downes, K., *Vanbrugh* (1977), fig. 133.

29 Victoria and Albert Museum, London, D. 129–91; Beard (1986), p. 127 no. 68.

30 Downes, K., *Sir John Vanbrugh* (1987), p. 455.

31 Victoria and Albert Museum, London, D. 114–91; Beard (1986), p. 127 no. 69; see Ch. 3 above.

32 See Beard (1986), p. 127 no. 70.

33 See ibid., p. 128 no. 72; Downes (1977), fig. 138.

34 Worcester College, Oxford; see Downes (1977), fig. 134.

35 Victoria and Albert Museum, London, D. 118–91. Beard (1986), p. 128 no. 73.

36 See ibid., p. 130 no. 74.

37 See Jackson-Stops, G., 'Grimsthorpe Castle – I', *Country Life*, vol. CLXXXI (26 November 1987), pp. 72–5; 'Grimsthorpe Castle – II', ibid. (3 December 1987), pp. 140–45; Lord, J., 'Sir John Vanbrugh and the 1st Duke of Ancaster: Newly Discovered Documents', *Journal of the Society of Architectural Historians*, vol. XXXIV (1991), pp. 136–44; Longstaff-Gowan, T., 'Grimsthorpe Castle, Lincolnshire', *Country Life*, vol. CXCII (21 May 1998), pp. 50–5; Colvin, H., 'Grimsthorpe Castle, the North Front', in Colvin, H., and J. Harris (eds), *The Country Seat: Studies in the History of the British Country House* (1970), pp. 91–3.

38 See Lord (1991), p. 136.

39 Dobrée and Webb (1928), vol. IV, p. 151.

40 Lincolnshire Archives Office, 3ANC 8/2/21; see Lord (1991), p. 139.

41 Lincolnshire Archives Office, 3ANC 8/2/25; see Lord (1991), pp. 140–3. See also Downes (1977), p. 119, n. 21.

42 Dobrée and Webb (1928), vol. IV, p. 150.

43 See Pevsner, N., 'Good King James's Gothic', *Architectural Review*, vol. CVII (1950), pp. 117–22.

44 See Beard (1986), p. 159 no. 117.

45 See Ch. 4 above.

46 Vitruvius, X.xiii.1 [in Vitruvius, *De Architectura*, Books I–X, trans. I. D. Rowland (1999)].

47 Lord (1991), p. 140; see also Jackson-Stops (1987), I, p. 74.

48 Identified as Hercules and Antaeus by Jackson-Stops (1987), I, p. 74, and repeated by John Harris and Nicholas Antram in the 2002 edition of Pevsner's guide to Lincolnshire. Identified as Neptune and Amphitrite by Lord (1991), pp. 139–40.

49 Charles II acquired a drawing of Neptune and Medusa, accompanied by a dolphin, by Paolo Farinati, now in the Royal Collection.

50 Serlio, S., Book IV, fol. XVIIIv [*Sebastiano Serlio on Architecture*, vol. I (Books I–V of *Tutte l'opere d'architettura et prospectiva*), trans. V. Hart and P. Hicks (1996), p. 283].

51 See the Journal of Vanbrugh's accounts transcribed in Downes (1977), p. 231 n. 398; see also Ch. 1 above.

52 Dobrée and Webb (1928), vol. IV, p. 167.

53 See Clarke, G. B., 'Grecian Taste and Gothic Virtue: Lord Cobham's Gardening Programme and its Iconography', *Apollo*, vol. XCVII (1973), pp. 566–71; Gibbon, M., 'Stowe,

Buckinghamshire: The House and Garden Buildings and their Designs, *Architectural History*, vol. XX (1977), pp. 31–44; Mowl, T., 'Sir John Vanbrugh, Charles Bridgeman and the Rise of the Temples', in *Gentlemen and Players: Gardeners of the English Landscape* (2000), pp. 62–78; Willis, P., *Charles Bridgeman and the English Landscape Garden* (2002).

54 Transcribed in Downes (1977), 'Appendix H', p. 265.

55 Following the emblematic stage conventions depicted by Serlio; see Ch. 4 above.

56 Dobrée and Webb (1928), vol. I, p. 159 (Act IV, Sc. iv); see Downes (1987), pp. 534–5.

57 Dobrée and Webb (1928), vol. III, p. 93; see also Dixon Hunt, J., *Gardens and the Picturesque: Studies in the History of Landscape Architecture* (1992), pp. 68–9.

58 Dobrée and Webb (1928), vol. II, p. 200.

59 See Beard (1986), p. 150 no. 103; Vitruvius, IV.i.7 [see Vitruvius (1999)]; Serlio, Book IV, fol. XXXVI*v* (1996), p. 320.

60 Worsley, G., 'Stowe House Buckinghamshire', *Country Life*, vol. XCVII (27 March 2003), pp. 124–8.

61 Ibid. See also Worsley, G., 'Vanbrugh and the Spirit of Rome', *Country Life*, vol. XCVIII (16 September 2004), pp. 118–23.

62 Dobrée and Webb (1928), vol. IV, p. 112.

CHAPTER 8

1 See Downes, K., 'The Little Colony on Greenwich Hill', *Country Life*, vol. CLIX (27 May 1976), pp. 1406–8; Downes, K., *Vanbrugh* (1977), p. 95; McCormick, F., *Sir John Vanbrugh: The Playwright as Architect* (1991), pp. 121–6.

2 Dobrée, B., and G. Webb (eds), *The Complete Works of Sir John Vanbrugh* (1928), vol. IV, 'Letters', p. 46, repeated in 'A Report to the Treasury on Blenheim Palace', p. 194.

3 Beard, G., *The Work of John Vanbrugh* (1986), p. 81 nos 3–4.

4 See McCormick (1991), pp. 127, 130.

5 Downes (1977), p. 14; see also Downes, K., *Sir John Vanbrugh* (1987), pp. 232–3.

6 See Cast, D., 'Seeing Vanbrugh and Hawksmoor', *Journal of the Society of Architectural Historians*, vol. XLIII (1984), pp. 313–14.

7 On this pamphlet see Foxon, D. F., *English Verse: 1701–1750. A Catalogue of Separately Printed Poems* (1975), vol. I, pp. 518, 825.

8 See Rogers, P. (ed.), *Jonathan Swift: The Complete Poems* (1983), pp. 91–2, 96–9, 581–3.

9 Hart, V., 'Vanbrugh's Travels', *History Today*, vol. XLII (July 1992), pp. 26–32; Hart, V., *Nicholas Hawksmoor: Rebuilding Ancient Wonders* (2002), pp. 252–4.

10 'Carolini', *A Key, or Gulliver Decypher'd* (1727), p. 19, n. IV.

11 Dobrée and Webb (1928), vol. IV, p. 96.

12 Transcribed in Downes (1977), p. 192; see also Fletcher, W. E. L., 'The Maze Hill Estate of Sir John Vanbrugh', *Transactions of the Greenwich and Lewisham Antiquarian Society*, vol. VIII, no. 4 (1976), pp. 136–45; Rhind, N., *Blackheath Village and Environs, 1790–1970* (1983).

13 See Beard (1986), p. 147 no. 99.

14 On the cross see McCormick (1991), p. 123.

15 Society of Antiquaries, London, L.C.II, p. 23. Vanbrugh House drawing: Bodleian Library, Oxford, MS Top. Gen.d. 14, fol. 55.

16 Worsley, G., 'Blenheim: Architecture of Albion', *Country Life*, vol. CXCVII (9 October 2003), p. 91.

17 See Beard (1986), pp. 146–7; McCormick (1991), p. 121.

18 Victoria and Albert Museum, London, E.2124(79)-1992; see Beard (1986), p. 143 no. 93.

19 See ibid., pp. 164–5 nos 122–4; see also Ch. 2 above.

20 Dobrée and Webb (1928), vol. IV, p. 119.

21 Ovid, *Ovid's Metamorphoses* (1717), e.g., Book XI, p. 260.

22 See Rogers (1983), pp. 91–2.

23 Dobrée and Webb (1928), vol. IV, p. 149.

24 A connection made by Downes (1977), p. 13 n. 6; McCormick (1991), p. 128.

25 Downes (1976), p. 1406; Downes (1977), p. 100; Beard (1986), p. 56.

26 See the Introduction above.

27 Dobrée and Webb (1928), vol. IV, p. 163. See the Introduction above.

28 See McCormick (1991).

29 See the Introduction above.

30 Dobrée and Webb (1928), vol. IV, p. 135.

31 See Summerson, J., *Architecture in Britain, 1530–1830* (1955 ed.), p. 159; see also Whinney, M., and O. Millar, *English Art, 1625–1714* (1957), p. 340; Downes, K., *Hawksmoor* (1959), pp. 79–80. For a sketch plan and elevation (see Fig. 342) see Beard (1986), p. 135 no. 83. Elevation design by Vanbrugh (Fig. 343), Victoria and Albert Museum, London, D. 124–91.

32 Plan of Vanbrugh's garden at Chargate, c.1709–15, Bodleian Library, Oxford, Gough Drawings a. 4, fols. 80–81. See Dobrée and Webb (1928), vol. IV, p. xxxvii.

33 Sketch (possibly from Vanbrugh's Office), Victoria and Albert Museum, London, Elton Hall volume, Elton Drawings no. 177.

34 See Dobrée and Webb (1928), vol. IV, p. 105.

35 Palladio, A., *Quatro Libri* (1570), Book II, ch. xvi [see Palladio, A., *Andrea Palladio: The Four Books on Architecture*, trans. and ed. R. Tavernor and R. Schofield (1997), p. 147]. The 1738 English translation by Isaac Ware reads: 'The fore-part being thus made more eminent than the rest, is very commodious for placing the ensigns or arms of the owners, which are commonly put in the middle of the front': Palladio, A., *The Four Books of Architecture by Andrea Palladio*, trans. I. Ware (1738). See Hart, V., '"A peece rather of good Heraldry, than of Architecture": Heraldry and the Orders of Architecture as Joint Emblems of Chivalry', *Res*, vol. XXIII (1993), p. 59.

36 Victoria and Albert Museum, London, D. 121–91. See Whistler, L., 'Newly Discovered Vanbrugh Designs for Claremont', *Country Life*, vol. CV (25 February 1949), pp. 426–7.

37 Victoria and Albert Museum, London, D. 111-91.

38 Dobrée and Webb (1928), vol. IV, p. 119.

39 Green, D., *Blenheim Palace* (1951), p. 97. See Appendix One: 'finish the present Wall for the Inclosures'.

40 McCormick (1991), p. 130.

CONCLUSION

1   Serlio, S., *Libro Extraordinario* (1551), fol. 5*v* (Rustic gate VI): see Serlio, S., *Sebastiano Serlio on Architecture*, vol. II [Books VI–'VIII' of *Tutte l'opere d'architettura et prospetiva*, and the *Libro Extraordinario*, trans. V. Hart and P. Hicks], (2001), p. 468.

2   See Cunnington, C. W., *Handbook of English Costume in the Seventeenth Century* (1955), p. 192. Bingham, M., *Masks and Façades: Sir John Vanbrugh The Man in his Setting* (1974), p. 45.

3   See Ch. 2, n. 65, above. The combination of screen and staircase was one of Vanbrugh's favourite devices: see Downes, K., *Vanbrugh* (1977), p. 71.

4   Beard, G., *The Work of John Vanbrugh* (1986), p. 98 nos 26, 27. Faces were not uncommon in baroque buildings of the time: e.g., faces are carved round the west lobby window at St Philip in Birmingham by Thomas Archer.

5   Swinstead scheme in the Lincolnshire County Records Office, Anc.10/D/3. See Ch. 7 above.

6   Venturi, R., *Complexity and Contradiction in Architecture* (1966), p. 20 (here assuming that the forecourt at Grimsthorpe was the work of Vanbrugh, although it appears to be that of Edward Nutt); McCormick, F., *Sir John Vanbrugh: The Playwright as Architect* (1991), describes Vanbrugh's 'complex language, simultaneously inviting and repelling the would-be guest, the theatrical perspectives drawing his gaze and his footsteps forward, the castellar elements advising caution', p. 136.

7   See Sheppard, F. H. W. (ed.), 'The Haymarket Opera House', *Survey of London*, vols XXIX and XXX, (1960).

8   See Ch. 1 above.

9   See Bingham (1974), p. 267; Downes, K., *Sir John Vanbrugh* (1987), p. 526.

10   Vanbrugh's attempt on behalf of the Duchess of Marlborough to negotiate a marriage between her granddaughter Harriet (Henrietta) Godolphin and Lord Clare, the Duke of Newcastle: see Downes (1987), p. 369.

11   See Ch. 1 above.

12   Dobrée, B., and G. Webb (eds), *The Complete Works of Sir John Vanbrugh* (1928), vol. III, p. 127.

13   See Bingham (1974), pp. 44–5.

14   Dobrée and Webb (1928), vol. I, p. 159.

15   Farquhar, G., *Love and a Bottle, a Comedy* (1698), Act I, Sc. i.

16   MS Journal at Wilton, 1728 [see Whistler, L., *The Imagination of Vanbrugh and his Fellow Artists* (1954), p. 152]. See a plan in the Bodleian Library, Oxford, MS Gough Drawings a. 3, fol. 64.

17   E.g., Downes (1987), p. 140, comments 'for the present it is enough to make it clear that *The Country House* is still a farce in the seventeenth-century sense of a short comic play with no serious intentions or implications'.

18   Dobrée and Webb (1928), vol. II, pp. 216, 217.

19   Ibid., pp. 46–7.

20   Swift also draws on this theme in poems such as 'To Quilca, a Country House not in Good Repair' (1737) and in 'A Pastoral Dialogue between Richmond Lodge and Marble Hill' (1727) lamented that 'Marble Hill,/ Some South Sea brokers from the city,/Will Purchase me, the more's the pity, Lay all my fine plantations waste,/To fit them to his vulgar taste': see Rogers, P. (ed.), *Jonathan Swift: The Complete Poems* (1983), p. 321.

21   See Arnold, D., *Rural Urbanism: London Landscapes in the Early Nineteenth Century* (2006).

22   See Mowl, T., *Gentlemen and Players: Gardeners of the English Landscape* (2000), pp. 82–3; Ridgway, C., and R. Williams (eds), *Sir John Vanbrugh and Landscape Architecture in Baroque England 1690–1730* (2000).

23   See Pevsner, N., 'Good King James's Gothic', *Architectural Review*, vol. CVII (1950), pp. 117–22; Cast, D., 'Seeing Vanbrugh and Hawksmoor', *Journal of the Society of Architectural Historians*, vol. XLIII (1984), p. 322. On the traditional hospitality offered to the poor by the gentry see Heal, F., and C. Holmes, *The Gentry in England and Wales, 1500–1700* (1994), pp. 315–16.

24   Dobrée and Webb (1928), vol. III p. 164.

25   Ibid., vol. IV, p. 45; see Bingham (1974), p. 238.

26   Dobrée and Webb (1928), vol. IV, pp. 49, 50.

27   Ibid., vol. III, p. 159.

28   Ibid., pp. 141, 142.

29   Ibid., p. 143.

30   Ibid., p. 160.

31   Ibid., vol. IV, pp. 159–60; see also Downes (1977), p. 92 n. 40.

32   See the Introduction above; see also Downes (1987), p. 357.

33   For the scheme to reface the town hall in Oxford, see the British Library MS formally BM MS 19605, fol. 175, and Downes (1987), p. 360. Vanbrugh refers to 'Publick Work' in a letter to Carlisle of 11 February 1724.

34   See Appendix Two.

35   Dobrée and Webb (1928), vol. I, p. 206.

36   On the protective aspect of these houses, see McCormick (1991), pp. 128, 133–40.

37   Dobrée and Webb (1928), vol. I, pp. 23, 156.

38   Ibid., vol. II, p. 29. See Williams, R., *The Country and the City* (1985), esp. pp. 52–4 (Restoration comedies also acknowledge that the country has a degree of 'bumkin' about it).

39   Dobrée and Webb (1928), vol. IV, p. 167.

40   Curiously enough, despite his years working on the Crown properties Vanbrugh did not propose complete schemes for rebuilding notable national institutions in London such as the new palaces of Whitehall and Westminster, projects which preoccupied his peers. On Vanbrugh's lack of involvement in Wren's plans for Whitehall, see Downes, K., *English Baroque Architecture* (1966), p. 44. However on Vanbrugh's projects for the palaces of Hampton Court, St James's and Kensington, see the Introduction.

41   Dobrée and Webb (1928), 'The Reply of Sir John Vanbrugh on behalf of the Workmen employed in the building of Blenheim', vol. IV, p. 203.

42   See Watkin, D., *Sir John Soane: Enlightenment Thought and the Royal Academy Lectures* (1996), Lecture V, p. 563; see also p. 337.

Bibliography

PRIMARY SOURCES

Addison, J., *The Works of the Right Honorable Joseph Addison*, ed. Thomas Tickell, 4 vols, London (1721) [see Bond (1965)].

—, *Dialogues upon the Usefulness of Ancient Medals*, London (1726).

— and R. Steele et al., *The Spectator*, 6 vols, London (1712–15).

Alberti, L. B., *On the Art of Building in Ten Books*, trans. J. Rykwert, N. Leach and R. Tavernor, Cambridge, Mass. (1988).

The Annual Miscellany, for the year 1694, London: R. E. for J. Tonson (1694).

Anne, *The Blessings of Peace: Queen Anne's Speech to Parliament*, Dublin (1713).

Ashmole, E., *The Institution, Laws and Ceremonies of the Most Noble Order of the Garter*, London (1672).

Blondel, F. N., *Cours d'architecture*, 3 vols, Paris (1675–83).

Breton, N., *The Court and the Country, or A briefe discourse dialogue-wise set downe betweene a courtier and a country-man*, London (1618).

Breval, J., *Remarks on several Parts of Europe*, 2 vols, London (1726).

Browne, I., *On Design and Beauty: An Epistle*, London (1734).

Browne, J., *A Catalogue of a . . . Collection of Greek, Roman, Irish and English Coins and Medals [chiefly belonging to Joseph Browne] . . . which will be sold by auction*, London (1762).

Burnet, T., *The Sacred Theory of the Earth*, London (1684).

Burton, R., *The Anatomy of Melancholy*, London (1676 ed).

Campbell, C., *Vitruvius Britannicus, or the British Architect*, 3 vols, London (1715–25).

'Carolini', *A Key, or Gulliver Decypher'd*, London (1727).

Cave, W., *Primitive Christianity, or The Religion of the Ancient Christians in the First Ages of the Gospel*, London (6 ed., 1702).

Cibber, C., *An Apology for the Life of Colley Cibber, comedian, and late patentee of the Theatre-Royal*, vol. I, London (1740; republished 1968).

Clarke, S., *C. Julii Caesaris, Quae Extant . . .* London (1712).

Colonna, F., *Hypnerotomachia Poliphili*, Venice (1499); trans. and ed. J. Godwin, London (1999).

Davenant, C., *The True Picture of a Modern Whig, Set Forth in a Dialogue between Mr. Whiglove and Mr. Double. Two Under-Spur-Leathers to the Late Ministry*, London (1701).

Defoe, D., *A Tour Through the Whole Island of Great Britain*, London (1725).

Dennis, J., *The Select Works of Mr John Dennis*, London (1721).

Desgodets, A. B., *Les Edifices antiques de Rome dessinés et mesurés tres exactement*, Paris (1682).

Drayton, M., *Poly-Olbion*, 2 vols, London (1613–22).

Dryden, J., *The satires of Decimus Junius Juvenalis. Translated into English verse. By Mr Dryden, and several other eminent hands. Together with the satires of Aulus Persius Flaccus . . . To which is prefix'd a discourse concerning the original and progress of satire*, London (1693).

—, *The Works of John Dryden*, ed. W. Scott, 18 vols, Edinburgh (1821).

Dubreuil, J., *Perspective practical . . . also a treatise of shadows natural by the sun, torch, candle, and lamp: very useful and necessary for all painters, engravers, architects, embroiderers, carvers, goldsmiths, tapestry-workers and all others that work by design*, London (1698).

De l'Orme, P., *Le Premier tome de l'architecture*, Paris (1567).

Du Cerceau, J. A., *Les plus excellents bastiments de France*, 2 vols, Paris (1576–9).

Eachard, L., *The History of England, from the first Entrance of Julius Caesar and the Romans (to the conclusion of the reign of King James the Second, and establishment of King William and Queen Mary)*, 3 vols, London (1707–18).

Estienne, C., and J. Liebault, *Maison rustique, or, The countrey farme*, London (1616).

Evelyn, J., 'An Account of Architects and Architecture', appended to *A Parallel* (1664 and 1707 [see Fréart (1650)]; 1707 repaginated as pp. 1–57).

—, *The Diary of John Evelyn*, ed. J. Bowle, Oxford (1983).

Evens, A., *Epitaph on Sir John Vanbrugh, Architect of Blenheim Palace*, London (1726).

Farquhar, G., *Love and a Bottle, a Comedy*, London (1698).

Fischer von Erlach, J. B., *Entwurff einer historischen Architectur*, Vienna (1721).

Fréart, R. [Sieur de Chambray], *Parallèle de l'architecture antique et de la moderne*, Paris (1650) [trans. J. Evelyn, *A Parallel of the Antient Architecture with the Modern*, London (1664, 2nd ed. 1707)].

Gent, T., *Pater Patriae: Being, An Elegiac Pastoral Dialogue occasioned by the most lamented Death of the Late Rt. Honble and Illustrious Charles Howard*, York (1738).

Guillim, J., *A Display of Heraldrie*, London (1632 ed.).

Gunther, R. T. (ed.), *The Architecture of Sir Roger Pratt, Charles II's Commissioner for the Rebuilding of London after the Great Fire: Now Printed for the first time from his Note-Books*, Oxford (1928).

Hatton, E., *A New View of London*, 2 vols, London (1708).

Hawksmoor, N., *Remarks on the founding and carrying on the buildings of the Royal Hospital at Greenwich*, London (1728) [repr. (with important omissions) in *Wren Society Volumes*, vol. VI (1929), pp. 17–27].

—, *A Short Historical Account of London Bridge*, London (1736).

Haym, N., *Del Tesoro Britannico . . . overo il Museo Nummario* [with an English trans., *The British Treasury*], London (1719–20).

Hooke, R., *The Diary of Robert Hooke: 1672–80*, ed. H. W. Robinson and W. Adams, London (1935).

—, *Diary: 1688–93* in R. T. Gunther, ed., 'Life and Work of Robert Hooke (Part IV)', vol. X of *Early Science in Oxford*, Oxford (1935).

Hutchinson, W., *A View of Northumberland*, 2 vols, Newcastle-upon-Tyne (1778).

Irwin, Viscountess A., *Castle Howard*, London (1732) [transcribed in Downes (1977), Appendix J, pp. 263–6].

Kip, J., *Britannia Illustrata, or Views of several of the Queen's palaces, as also of the principal seats of the nobility and gentry of Great Britain*, 2 vols, London (1707–40).

Langley, B., *Grub Street Journal*, London (11 July 1734).

Leslie, C., *The Rehearsal of Observator*, London (1704–5).

Locke, J., *An Essay Concerning Human Understanding*, London (1690).

The London Stage, London (1707).

Morris, R., *Lectures on Architecture*, London (1734).

Osborne, P., *A Journal of the Brest-expedition*, London (1694).

Ovid, *Ovid's Metamorphosis in fifteen books, translated by the most eminent hands*, London (1717).

Palladio, A., *The Four Books of Architecture by Andrea Palladio*, trans. I. Ware, London (1738).

—, *Andrea Palladio: The Four Books on Architecture*, trans. and ed. R. Tavernor and R. Schofield, Cambridge, Mass., and London (1997).

Pepys, S., *Diary*, ed. W. Matthews and R. Latham, 11 vols, London (1970–83).

Perrault, C., *Les dix livres d'architecture de Vitruve*, Paris (1673; revised and enlarged 1684).

—, *Ordonnance des cinq espèces de colonnes selon la méthode des anciens*, Paris (1683) [trans. J. James, *A Treatise of the Five Orders of Columns in Architecture*, London (1708)].

Plot, R., *The Natural History of Oxford-shire*, Oxford and London (1677).

Pozzo, A., *Perspectiva pictorum et architectorum*, Rome (1693) [trans. J. James, *Rules and Examples of Perspective Proper for Painters and Architects etc*, London (1707)].

Pyne, J. B., *The History of the Royal Residences of Windsor Castle, St James's Palace, Carlton House and Frogmore*, 3 vols, London (1819).

Ralph, J., *A critical review of the publick buildings, statues and ornaments in, and about London and Westminster*, London (1734).

Rossi, D., *Studio d'architettura civile*, 3 vols, Rome (1702).

Rowlands, H., *Mona Antiqua Restaurata*, Dublin (1723).

Seeley, B., *Stowe: A Description of the Magnificent House and Gardens*, London (1750).

Serlio, S., *Architectura di Sebastiano Serlio Bolognese, in sei libri divisa*, Venice (1663) [Books I–V, and part of the 'Extraordinary Book of Doors'].

—, *Sebastiano Serlio on Architecture*, vol. I [Books I–V of *Tutte l'opere d'architettura et prospetiva*, trans. V. Hart and P. Hicks], London and New Haven (1996).

—, *Sebastiano Serlio on Architecture*, vol. II [Books VI–'VIII' of *Tutte l'opere d'architettura et prospetiva*, and the *Libro Extraordinario*, trans. V. Hart and P. Hicks], London and New Haven (2001).

Shaftesbury, Lord [Anthony Ashley Cooper], *Characteristicks of Men, Manners, Opinions, Times*, London (1711).

—, *Letter concerning the art or science of Design*, in *Characteristicks*, 5th ed., London (1732), pp. 401–2.

Shute, J., *The First and Chief Groundes of Architecture*, London (1563).

Stevens, J., *The History of the Antient Abbeys, Monasteries, Hospitals, Cathedrals and Collegiate Churches. Being two additional volumes to Sir William Dugdale's Monasticon Anglicanum*, 2 vols, London (1722–3).

Story, T., *A Journal of the Life of Thomas Story*, Newcastle-upon-Tyne (1747).

Swift, J., *Travels into several remote nations of the world*, London (1726) [republished as *Gulliver's Travels*, Harmondsworth (1989 ed.)].

Tavernier, J.-B., *Les six voyages de Jean-Baptiste Tavernier*, Paris (1676) [*Travels in India by Jean-Baptiste Tavernier*, trans. V. Ball, London (1925)].

Toland, J., *A Critical History of the Celtic Religion and Learning: Containing an Account of the Druids; or, the Priests and Judges . . . of the Bards, or the Poets and Heralds*, London ([1702?]).

Vanbrugh, J., *A Short Vindication of The Relapse and The Provok'd Wife, from Immorality and Profaneness*, London (1698).

—, *The Relapse, or Virtue in Danger*, ed. B. Harris, London (1971).

Vertue, G., 'Vertue Note Books', ed. K. A. Esdaile, *Walpole Society*, vol. XXII (1934), pp. 51, 77–8.

Vignola, J., *Regola delli cinque ordini d'architettura*, Rome (1562) [trans. J. Moxon, *Vignola, or, the complete architect*, London (1655)].

Vitruvius Pollio, M., *I dieci libri dell'architettura*, trans D. Barbaro, Venice (1567).

—, *De Architectura*, Books I–X, trans. I. D. Rowland, New York (1999).

Walpole, H., *Anecdotes of Painting in England, with Some Account of the Principal Artists* [collected by G. Vertue], 4 vols, Strawberry Hill (1762–71).

Ward, E., *The Secret History of Clubs, particularly the Kit-Cat, Beef-Stake, Vertuosos, Quacks, Knights of the Golden-Fleece, Florists, Beaus, & c.*, London (1709).

Wells, J., *Sciographia, or the art of shadowes*, London (1635).

Wotton, H., *The Elements of Architecture*, London (1624).

Wren, C., *Parentalia: Or, Memoirs of the Family of the Wrens*, London (1750).

Wright, J., *Historia Histrionica: An Historical Account of the English Stage*, London (1699).

MANUSCRIPTS

Carlisle, 'Essay on God and his Prophets', [n.d.], Castle Howard Archive, CH J8/35/15.

—, 'A Book of Coates & Crestes', (1699), Castle Howard Archive, CH J8/35/13.

Hawksmoor, N., 'Letters to Carlisle' [transcribed in G. Webb (ed.), 'The Letters and Drawings of Nicholas Hawksmoor Relating to the Building of the Mausoleum at Castle Howard, 1726–42', *Walpole Society*, vol. XIX (1930–1), pp. 111–63].

—, 'Letters to Henry Joynes' (1705–13), British Library, London, Additional MS 19,607.

—, 'Letters to the Duchess of Marlborough' (1722–5), British Library, London, Additional MS 61353, nos 240, 252–255b r–v.

Hickes, G., 'Observations on Mr. Van Brugg's proposals about Buildinge the new Churches', Beinecke Library, Yale University, New Haven, C Osborn/Hickes 17.363 [transcribed in Du Prey (2000), Appendix 3, pp. 139–42].

'Instructions to invest ye Electoral Prince of Brunswick', various papers, British Library, London, Additional MS 6321 fols 59r–61r.

North, R., 'Notes of Building' (1698) [transcribed in H. Colvin and J. Newman (eds), *Of Building: Roger North's Writings on Architecture*, Oxford (1981)].

—, 'Of Unity and Variety' (c.1695–6) [transcribed in Van Eck (2003), p. 39].

'Papers of the Commission for Building Fifty New Churches', Lambeth Palace Library, London, MSS 2690 (minutes) –2729, 2747–50 (MS 2750 nos 16 and 17: 'Basilica after the Primitive Christians') [repro: World Microfilm Publications, 1980].

Vanbrugh, J., 'Reasons Offer'd for Preserving some Part of the Old Manour' [at Blenheim], British Library, London, Additional MS 61353 nos 62–63 (11 June 1709) [transcribed in Appendix One].

—, 'Mr Van-Brugg's Proposals about Building ye New Churches' [c.1711], Bodleian Library, Oxford, MS Rawlinson B.376, fols 351–52; see also MS Eng. Hist. b.2. fol. 47 [transcribed in Appendix Two].

—, 'Journal of all Receipts, Payments and other Transactions, 1715–26' [transcribed in Downes (1977), pp. 180–233].

—, 'Letters' [transcribed in B. Dobrée, and G. Webb (eds), *The Complete Works of Sir John Vanbrugh*, vol. IV, London (1928)].

—, 'Plays' [transcribed in ibid., vols I–III].

Wren, C., 'Letter to a Friend on the Commission for Building Fifty New Churches', in *Parentalia: Or, Memoirs of the Family of the Wrens*, London (1750) [transcribed in A. T. Bolton and H. P. Hendry, *Wren Society Volumes*, vol. IX (1932), pp. 15–18, and in Soo (1998), pp. 112–18].

—, 'Tracts I–IV', in *Parentalia* (1750) [transcribed in A. T. Bolton and H. P. Hendry (eds), *Wren Society Volumes*, vol. XIX (1942), pp. 126–39, and in Soo (1998), pp. 153–87].

—, 'Discourse on Architecture' [Tract V], inserted in Royal Institute of British Architects, London, 'Heirloom' copy of *Parentalia*, with drawing of the elevation of the Mausoleum of Halicarnassus by Hawksmoor [transcribed in A. T. Bolton and H. P. Hendry, *Wren Society Volumes*, vol. XIX (1942), pp. 140–5, and in Soo (1998), pp. 188–95].

SECONDARY SOURCES

Allen, R. J., *The Clubs of Augustan London*, Cambridge, Mass. (1933).

Anderson, C., 'Masculinity and English Architectural Classicism', in G. Perry (ed.), *Art and its Histories: Gender and Art*, London and New Haven (1999), pp. 130–52.

—, *Inigo Jones and the Classical Tradition*, Cambridge (2007).

Arnold, D., *The Georgian Country House: Architecture, Landscape and Society*, Stroud (1998).

—, *Rural Urbanism: London Landscapes in the Early Nineteenth Century*, Manchester (2006).

Aslet, C., *The Story of Greenwich*, London (1999).

Ballantyne, A., *Architecture, Landscape and Liberty: Richard Payne Knight and the Picturesque*, Cambridge (1997).

Baridon, M., 'Ruins as a Mental Construct', *Journal of Garden History*, vol. V (1985), pp. 84–96.

Barman, C., *Sir John Vanbrugh*, London (1924).

Beal, P., *Index of English Literary Manuscripts, vol. II: 1625–1700, part 2*, London (1993), 'Sir John Vanbrugh', pp. 511–37.

Beard, G., *The Work of John Vanbrugh*, London (1986).

Beltz, G. F., *Memorials of the Most Noble Order of the Garter*, London (1841).

Bennett, J. A., 'Christopher Wren: the Natural Causes of Beauty', *Architectural History*, vol. XV (1972), pp. 5–22.

—, *The Mathematical Science of Christopher Wren*, Cambridge (1982).

Bennett, J., and S. Mandelbrote (eds), *The Garden, the Ark, the Tower, the Temple: Biblical Metaphors of Knowledge in Early Modern Europe*, Oxford (1998).

Bergdoll, B., *European Architecture, 1750–1890*, Oxford (2000).

Berger, R. W., *A Royal Passion: Louis XIV as Patron of Architecture*, Cambridge (1994).

Bernard, J., 'Sir John Vanbrugh: Two Unpublished Letters', *Huntington Library Quarterly*, vol. XXIV (1965–6), pp. 347–52.

Bernard, T., and J. Clark (eds), *Lord Burlington: Architecture, Art and Life*, London (1995).

Bill, E. G. W. (ed.), *The Queen Anne Churches: A Catalogue of the Papers in Lambeth Palace Library of the Commission for Building Fifty New Churches in London and Westminster 1711–59*, London (1979) [intro. by H. Colvin].

Bingham, M., *Masks and Façades: Sir John Vanbrugh The Man in his Setting*, London (1974).

Blunt, A., A. Laing, C. Tadgell and K. Downes (eds), *Baroque and Rococo Architecture and Decoration*, London (1978).

Bold, J., *Greenwich: An Architectural History of the Royal Hospital for Seamen and the Queen's House*, London (2000).

Bolton, A. T., 'Sir John Vanbrugh, 1664–1726', *Journal of the Royal Institute of British Architects*, 3rd Series, vol. XXXIII (10 April 1926), pp. 338–9.

—, and H. P. Hendry (eds), *Wren Society Volumes*, 20 vols, Oxford (1924–43).

Bond, D. F. (ed.), *The Spectator: By Joseph Addison, Sir Richard Steele et al.*, 4 vols, Oxford (1965).

Bond, J., and K. Tiller (eds), *Blenheim: Landscape for a Palace*, Gloucester (1987).

Bradley, S., and N. Pevsner, *The Buildings of England. London 1: The City of London*, London (1997 ed.).

Brewer, J., *The Pleasures of the Imagination: English Culture in the Eighteenth Century*, London (1997).

Brownell, M. R., *Alexander Pope and the Arts of Georgian England*, Oxford (1978).

Burgess, R., *Those Delavals!*, [Northern History Booklets, No. 19], Newcastle-upon-Tyne (1972).

Carpo, M., 'The Architectural Principles of Temperate Classicism: Merchant Dwellings in Sebastiano Serlio's Sixth Book', *Res*, vol. XXII (1992), pp. 135–51.

Cast, D., 'Seeing Vanbrugh and Hawksmoor', *Journal of the Society of Architectural Historians*, vol. XLIII (1984), pp. 310–27.

—, 'Speaking of Architecture: The Evolution of a Vocabulary in Vasari, Jones and Sir John Vanbrugh', *Journal of the Society of Architectural Historians*, vol. LII (1993), pp. 179–88.

Clark, H. F., 'Eighteenth-Century Elysiums: The Role of "Association" in the Landscape Movement', *The Journal of the Warburg and Courtauld Institutes*, vol. VI (1943), pp. 165–89.

Clarke, G. B., 'Grecian Taste and Gothic Virtue: Lord Cobham's Gardening Programme and its Iconography', *Apollo*, vol. XCVII (1973), pp. 566–71.

Colley, L., *In Defiance of Oligarchy: The Tory Party 1714–60*, Cambridge (1982).

Colvin, H., 'Fifty New Churches', *Architectural Review*, vol. CVII (1950), pp. 189–96; 'Mr. Vanbrugg's Proposals', pp. 209–10.

—, *The History of the King's Works, 1660–1782*, vol. V, London (1976).

—, *Architecture and the After-Life*, London and New Haven (1991).

—, 'Vanbrugh', in *A Biographical Dictionary of British Architects 1600–1840*, London and New Haven (1995 ed.), pp. 1003–9 [list of executed and unexecuted designs, pp. 1007–9].

—, 'Hermes, Terms and Caryatids in English Architecture', in *Essays in English Architectural History*, London and New Haven (1999), pp. 94–135.

—, and M. Craig (eds), *Architectural Drawings in the Library of Elton Hall by Sir John Vanbrugh and Sir Edward Lovett Pearce*, London (1964).

—, and J. Harris (eds), *The Country Seat: Studies in the History of the British Country House presented to Sir John Summerson on his sixty-fifth birthday together with a select bibliography of his published writings*, London (1970).

—, and J. Newman, *Of Building: Roger North's Writings on Architecture*, Oxford (1981).

—, and A. Rowan, 'The Grand Bridge in Blenheim Park', in J. Bold and E. Chaney (eds), *English Architecture, Public and Private: Essays for Kerry Downes*, London (1993), pp. 159–175 [republished as 'The Grand Bridge in Blenheim Park', in Colvin, *Essays in English Architectural History*, London and New Haven (1999), pp. 245–61].

Cottingham, J., *The Cambridge Companion to Descartes*, Cambridge (1992).

Cunnington, C. W., *Handbook of English Costumes in the Seventeenth Century*, London (1955).

Davenport-Hines, R., *Gothic: 400 Years of Excess, Horror, Evil and Ruin*, London (1998).

Davies, J. H. V., 'Nicholas Hawksmoor', *Journal of the Royal Institute of British Architects*, vol. LXIX, no. 10 (October 1962), pp. 368–76.

Dixon Hunt, J., *William Kent, Landscape Garden Designer: An Assessment and Catalogue of his Designs*, London (1987).

—, *Gardens and the Picturesque: Studies in the History of Landscape Architecture*, Cambridge, Mass., and London (1992).

—, and Willis, P. (eds), *The Genius of the Place: The English Landscape Garden 1620–1820*, London (1975).

Dobrée, B., and G. Webb (eds), *The Complete Works of Sir John Vanbrugh*, 4 vols, London (1928).

Downes, K., *Hawksmoor*, London (1959; 2nd, revised ed. 1979 [additional notes and an appendix on 'The Bow Window Room at Castle Howard']).

—, *English Baroque Architecture*, London (1966).

—, 'The Kings Weston Book of Drawings', *Architectural History*, vol. X (1967), pp. 7–88.

—, *Hawksmoor*, London (1970; rep. 1994).

—, 'The Little Colony on Greenwich Hill: Vanbrugh's Field at Blackheath', *Country Life*, vol. CLIX (27 May 1976), pp. 1406–8.

—, *Vanbrugh* [Studies in Architecture, ed. A. Blunt, J. Harris and H. Hibbard, vol. XVI], London (1977).

—, 'John Vanbrugh', *Macmillan Encyclopaedia of Architects*, London (1982), pp. 257–69.

—, 'Vanbrugh's Heslington Lady', *Burlington Magazine*, vol. CXXIV (1982), pp. 153–5.

—, *Sir John Vanbrugh, a Biography*, London (1987).

—, 'Vanbrugh', in J. Turner (ed.), *The Dictionary of Art*, London (1996), vol. XXXI, pp. 857–62.

—, 'Baroque: Historical Context', in J. Turner (ed.), *The Dictionary of Art*, vol. III (1996), pp. 266–9.

—, 'Nicholas Hawksmoor', *The Oxford Dictionary of National Biography*, Oxford (2004), pp. 950–58.

—, 'John Vanbrugh', *The Oxford Dictionary of National Biography*, Oxford (2004), pp. 71–81.

Drury, P., '"No other place in the Kingdom will compare with it": The Evolution of Audley End', *Architectural History*, vol. XXIII (1980), pp. 27–9.

—, *Audley End, Essex: HMSO Guides*, London (1984).

Du Prey, P. R., *Hawksmoor's London Churches: Architecture and Theology*, Chicago (2000).

Erskine-Hill, H., 'Heirs of Vitruvius: Pope and the Idea of Architecture', in H. Erskine-Hill and A. Smith (eds), *The Art of Alexander Pope*, New York (1979), pp. 144–56.

Evans, J., *A History of the Society of Antiquaries*, Oxford (1956).

Evans, R., *The Projective Cast: Architecture and its Three Geometries*, Cambridge, Mass. (1995).

Everett, N., *The Tory View of Landscape*, London and New Haven (1994).

Fitzgerald, P., *A New History of the English Stage*, 2 vols, London (1882).

Fletcher, W. E. L., 'The Maze Hill Estate of Sir John Vanbrugh', *Transactions of the Greenwich and Lewisham Antiquarian Society*, vol. VIII, no. 4 (1976), pp. 136–45.

Foxon, D. F., *English Verse: 1701–50. A Catalogue of Separately Printed Poems*, 2 vols, Cambridge (1975).

Geduld, H. M., *Prince of Publishers: A Study of the Work and Career of Jacob Tonson*, London (1969).

George, M. D., *London Life in the Eighteenth Century*, Harmondsworth (1966 ed.).

Geraghty, A., 'Nicholas Hawksmoor and the Wren City Church Steeples', *The Georgian Group Journal*, vol. X (2000), pp. 1–14.

Gibbon, M., 'Stowe, Buckinghamshire: The House and Garden Buildings and their Designs, *Architectural History*, vol. XX (1977), pp. 31–44.

Gill, E. J., 'Character, Plot, and the Language of Love in *The Relapse*: A Reappraisal', *Restoration*, vol. XVI (1992), pp. 110–25.

Girouard, M., *Robert Smythson and the Architecture of the Elizabethan Era*, London (1966).

—, 'Attitudes to Elizabethan Architecture 1600–1900', in J. Summerson (ed.), *Concerning Architecture: Essays on Architectural Writers and Writing presented to Nikolaus Pevsner*, London (1968), pp. 14–15.

Godwin, J., *Athanasius Kircher*, London (1979).

Goodhart-Rendel, H. S., *Hawksmoor*, London (1924).

Gotch, C., 'Mylne at Kings Weston', *Country Life*, vol. CXXIII (23 January 1953), pp. 212–15.

Grant, E., 'The Sphinx in the North: Egyptian Influence on Landscape, Architecture and Interior Design in Eighteenth- and Nineteenth-Century Scotland', in D. Cosgrove and S. Daniels (eds), *The Iconography of Landscape*, Cambridge (1988), pp. 236–53.

Green, D., 'The Vogue of Vanbrugh', *Country Life*, vol. CVII (2 June 1950), pp. 1648–53.

—, *Blenheim Palace*, London (1951; rep. 1967).

Gregg, E., *Queen Anne*, London (1980).

Hammond, P., and D. Hopkins (eds), *The Poems of John Dryden*, 5 vols, Harlow, London and Newcastle (1991–2005).

Harris, E., and N. Savage, *British Architectural Books and Writers 1556–1785*, Cambridge (1990).

Harris, J., *Catalogue of British Drawings for Architecture, Decoration, Sculpture and Landscape Gardening in American Collections, 1550–1900*, Upper Saddle River, N.J. (1971).

—, *The Artist and the Country House: A History of Country House and Garden View Painting in Britain, 1540–1870*, London (1979; revised 1985).

—, 'Diverting Labyrinths', *Country Life*, vol. CLXXXIV (11 January 1990), pp. 62–5 [on Eastbury].

—, 'The Beginnings of Claremont: Sir John Vanbrugh's Garden at Chargate in Surrey', *Apollo*, vol. CXXXVII (April 1993), pp. 223–6.

Hart, V., 'Vanbrugh's Travels', *History Today*, vol. XLII (July 1992), pp. 26–32.

—, '"A peece rather of good Heraldry, than of Architecture": Heraldry and the Orders of Architecture as Joint Emblems of Chivalry', *Res*, vol. XXIII (1993), pp. 52–66.

—, *Art and Magic in the Court of the Stuarts*, New York (1994).

—, *St Paul's Cathedral: Christopher Wren*, London (1995; republished 1999).

—, 'From Virgin to Courtesan in Early English Vitruvian Books', in V. Hart and P. Hicks (eds), *Paper Palaces: The Rise of the Renaissance Architectural Treatise*, New Haven and London (1998), pp. 297–318.

—, *Nicholas Hawksmoor: Rebuilding Ancient Wonders*, New Haven and London (2002).

—, '"A Pretty Impudent Countenance": John Vanbrugh's Seaton Delaval', *Architectural Research Quarterly*, vol. VII no. 3/4 (2003), pp. 311–23.

—, and P. Hicks (eds), *Paper Palaces: The Rise of the Renaissance Architectural Treatise*, London and New Haven (1998).

—, and R. Tucker, '"Immaginacy set free": Aristotelian Ethics and Inigo Jones's Banqueting House at Whitehall', *Res*, vol. XXXIX (2001), pp. 151–67.

—, and —, 'Ornament and the Work of Inigo Jones', *Architectura*, vol. XXXII (2002), pp. 36–52.

Hayton, D. W., 'Edward Southwell', in *The Oxford Dictionary of National Biography*, Oxford (2004).

Heal, F., and C. Holmes, *The Gentry in England and Wales, 1500–1700*, Basingstoke (1994).

Hewlings, R., 'Hawksmoor's "Brave Designs for the Police"', in J. Bold and E. Chaney (eds), *English Architecture, Public and Private: Essays for Kerry Downes*, London (1993), pp. 215–29.

Hook, J., *The Baroque Age in England*, London (1976).

Hopkins, P., 'John Vanbrugh's Imprisonment in France 1688–93', *Notes and Queries*, vol. XXVI (1979), pp. 529–34.

Hughes, D., 'Vanbrugh and Cibber: Language, Place, and Social Order in *The Relapse*', *Comparative Drama*, vol. XXI (1987), pp. 62–83.

Huseboe, A. R., 'Vanbrugh: Additions to the Correspondence', *Philological Quarterly*, vol. LIII (1975), pp. 135–40.

Hussey, C., 'Kings Weston, Gloucestershire', *Country Life*, vol. LXI (30 April 1927), pp. 680–7.

—, *English Gardens and Landscape 1700–1750*, London (1967).

—, and Tipping, H. A., *English Homes, period IV, vol. ii: The Work of Sir John Vanbrugh and his School, 1699–1736*, London (1928).

Jackson-Stops, G., 'Grimsthorpe Castle – I', *Country Life*, vol. CLXXXI (26 November 1987), pp. 72–5; 'Grimsthope Castle – II', ibid. (3 December 1987), pp. 140–5.

Jardine, L., *On a Grander Scale: The Outstanding Career of Sir Christopher Wren*, London (2002).

Johnson, A. W., *Ben Jonson: Poetry and Architecture*, Oxford (1994).

Lang, S., 'Vanbrugh's Theory and Hawksmoor's Buildings', *Journal of the Society of Architectural Historians*, vol. XXIV (1965), pp. 127–51.

Le Fevre, P., 'Sir Ralph Delaval' in *The Oxford Dictionary of National Biography*, Oxford (2004).

Leatherbarrow, D., 'Architecture and Situation: A Study of the Architecture of Robert Morris', *Journal of the Society of Architectural Historians*, vol. XLIV (1985), pp. 48–59.

Lees-Milne, J., *English Country Houses: Baroque, 1685–1715*, London (1970).

Levine, J. M., *Between the Ancients and the Moderns: Baroque Culture in Restoration England*, London and New Haven (1999).

Levine, N., 'Castle Howard and the Emergence of the Modern Architectural Subject', *Journal of the Society of Architectural Historians*, vol. LXII (2003), pp. 326–51.

Li Shiqiao, *Power and Virtue: Architecture and Intellectual Change in England 1660–1730*, London (2006).

Loach, J., 'Gallicanism in Paris, Anglicanism in London, Primitivism in Both', in N. Jackson (ed.), *Plus ça change . . . Architectural Interchange between France and Britain: Papers from the Annual Symposium of the Society of Architectural Historians of Great Britain*, Nottingham (1999), pp. 9–32.

Longstaff-Gowan, T., 'Grimsthorpe Castle, Lincolnshire', *Country Life*, vol. CXCII (21 May 1998), pp. 50–5.

Lord, J., 'Sir John Vanbrugh and the 1st Duke of Ancaster: Newly Discovered Documents', *Journal of the Society of Architectural Historians*, vol. XXXIV (1991), pp. 136–144.

Luttrell, N., *A Brief Historical Relation of State Affairs from September 1678 to April 1714*, 6 vols, Farnborough (1969 ed.).

McCormick, F., 'John Vanbrugh's Architecture: Some Sources of his Style', *Journal of the Society of Architectural Historians*, vol. XLVI (1987), pp. 135–44.

—, *Sir John Vanbrugh: The Playwright as Architect*, Pennsylvania (1991).

McEwen, I. K., 'On Claude Perrault: Modernising Vitruvius', in Hart and Hicks (1998), pp. 321–37.

McKellar, E., *The Birth of Modern London: The Development and Design of the City 1660–1720*, Manchester (1999).

Mallgrave, H. F. (ed.), *Architectural Theory: Volume 1: An Anthology from Vitruvius to 1870*, Oxford (2006).

Marsh, D., 'Aesop and the Humanist Apologue', *Renaissance Studies*, vol. XVII, no. 1 (2003), pp. 9–26.

Milhous, J., 'New Light on Vanbrugh's Haymarket Theatre Project', *Theatre Survey*, vol. XVII (1976), pp. 143–61.

—, 'Five New Letters by Sir John Vanbrugh', *Harvard Library Bulletin*, vol. XXVII (1979), pp. 434–42.

Mowl, T., *Gentlemen and Players: Gardeners of the English Landscape*, Stroud (2000).

—, and B. Earnshaw, *John Wood: Architect of Obsession*, Bath (1988).

—, *An Insular Rococo*, London (1999).

Musson, J., 'Seaton Delaval Hall Northumberland', *Country Life*, vol. CXCVII (6 November 2003), pp. 56–61.

Norberg-Schulz, C., *Late Baroque and Rococo Architecture*, New York (1985 ed.).

Norcliffe, C. B., *Genealogist*, vol. II, London (1878).

Olleson, P., 'Vanbrugh and Opera at the Queen's Theatre, Haymarket', *Theatre Notebook*, vol. XXVI (1971–2), pp. 94–101.

Onians, J., *Bearers of Meaning: The Classical Orders in Antiquity, the Middle Ages and the Renaissance*, Cambridge (1988).

Palme, P., '"Ut architectura poesis"', in *Idea and Form: Studies in the History of Art*, ed. N. G. Sandblad, Stockholm (1959).

Pérez-Gómez, A., and L. Pelletier, *Architectural Representation and the Perspective Hinge*, Cambridge, Mass. (1997).

Pevsner, N., 'Good King James's Gothic', *Architectural Review*, vol. CVII (1950), pp. 117–22.

Piggott, S., *The Druids*, London and New York (1968).

Port, M. H. (ed.), *The Commission for Building Fifty New Churches: The Minute Books, 1711–7, a Calendar*, London Record Society, vol. XXIII (1986).

Public Monuments and Sculpture Association, National Recordings Project, http://vads.ahds.ac.uk/collections/PMSA.html under 'Vanbrugh'.

Pyne, W. H., *The History of the Royal Residences of Windsor Castle, St James's Palace, Carlton House, Kensington Palace, Hampton Court, Buckingham House and Frogmore*, 3 vols, London (1819).

Randall, C., *Building Codes: The Aesthetics of Calvinism in Early Modern Europe*, Philadelphia (1999).

Rhind, N., *Blackheath Village and Environs, 1790–1970*, Blackheath (1983).

Ridgway, C., and R. Williams (eds), *Sir John Vanbrugh and Landscape Architecture in Baroque England 1690–1730*, Stroud (2000).

Rogal, S. J., 'John Vanbrugh and the Blenheim Palace Controversy', *Journal of the Society of Architectural Historians*, vol. XXXIII (1974), pp. 293–303.

Rogers, P. (ed.), *Jonathan Swift: The Complete Poems*, Harmondsworth (1983).

Roper, A., 'Language and Action in *The Way of The World*, *Love's Last Shift* and *The Relapse*', *English Literary History*, vol. XL (1973), pp. 44–69.

Rosenberg, A., 'New Light on Vanbrugh', *Philological Quarterly*, vol. XLV (1966), pp. 603–13.

Rub, T., 'A Most Solemn and Awfull Appearance: Nicholas Hawksmoor's East London Churches', *Marsyas: Studies in the History of Art*, vol. XXI (1981–2), pp. 17–26.

Rykwert, J., *The First Moderns*, Cambridge, Mass., and London (1980).

Saumarez Smith, C., *The Building of Castle Howard*, London (1990; republished 1997).

Saxl, F., and R. Wittkower, *British Art and the Mediterranean*, Oxford (1948).

Schama, S., *Landscape and Memory*, London (1996).

Scruton, R., *The Aesthetics of Architecture*, London (1979).

Sekler, E., *Wren and his Place in European Architecture*, London (1956).

Sheppard, F. H. W. (ed.), 'The Haymarket Opera House', *Survey of London*, vols XXIX and XXX (1960).

Sicca, C. M., 'Burlington', in J. Turner (ed.), *The Dictionary of Art*, vol. IV (1996), p. 609.

Smith, P., 'St Lawrence, West Woodhay: A Church by Vanbrugh?', in J. Bold and E. Chaney (eds), *English Architecture, Public and Private: Essays for Kerry Downes*, London (1993), pp. 177–87.

Smith, R., *Handel's Oratorios and Eighteenth-Century Thought*, Cambridge (1995).

Smithers, P., *The Life of Joseph Addison*, Oxford (1968).

Soo, L., *Wren's 'Tracts' on Architecture and other Writings*, Cambridge (1998).

Sowerby, R., *The Augustan Art of Poetry: Augustan Translation of the Classics*, Oxford (2006).

Speth, G. W. (ed.), *Quatuor Coronatorum Antigrapha* (Masonic reprints of the Quatuor Coronati Lodge, No. 2076), 10 vols, London (1889–1913).

Stevenson, C., 'Robert Hooke's Bethlem', *Journal of the Society of Architectural Historians*, vol. IV (1996), pp. 254–75.

—, *Medicine and Magnificence*, New Haven and London (2000).

Stevenson, D., *The Origins of Freemasonry: Scotland's Century 1590–1710*, Cambridge (1988).

Stoye, J., *English Travellers Abroad 1604–67*, New Haven and London (1989 ed.).

Strong, R., *The Renaissance Garden in England*, London (1979).

Summerson, J., *Architecture in Britain, 1530–1830*, London (1955 ed.).

Thorpe, C. de W., *The Aesthetic Theory of Thomas Hobbes*, Ann Arbor, Mich. (1940).

Thurley, S., *Hampton Court: A Social and Architectural History*, New Haven and London (2003).

Van Eck, C., '"The splendid effects of architecture, and its power to affect the mind": The Workings of Picturesque Association', in J. Birksted (ed.), *Landscapes of Memory and Experience*, London (2000), pp. 245–59.

—, (ed.), *British Architectural Theory 1540–1750*, Aldershot (2003).

Venturi, R., *Complexity and Contradiction in Architecture*, New York (1966).

Wagner, A., *Heralds of England: A History of the Office and College of Arms*, London (1967).

—, *A Herald's World*, London (1988).

Watkin, D., *The English Vision: The Picturesque in Architecture, Landscape and Garden Design*, London (1982).

—, *Sir John Soane: Enlightenment Thought and the Royal Academy Lectures*, Cambridge (1996).

—, (ed.), *Sale Catalogue of Libraries of Eminent Persons*, London (1975), vol. IV [Architects], pp. 45–105.

Whiffen, M., *Thomas Archer*, London (1950).

Whinney, M., and O, Millar, *English Art, 1625–1714*, Oxford (1957).

Whistler, L., *Sir John Vanbrugh, Architect and Dramatist, 1664–1726*, London (1938).

—, *The Imagination of Vanbrugh and his Fellow Artists*, London (1954).

—, 'Newly Discovered Vanbrugh Designs for Claremont', *Country Life*, vol. CV (25 February 1949), pp. 426–7.

—, 'Talman and Vanbrugh: Episodes in an Architectural Rivalry', *Country Life*, vol. CXII (21 November 1952), pp. 1648–52.

—, 'The Evolution of Castle Howard', *Country Life*, vol. CXIII (30 January 1953), pp. 276–9.

—, 'Vanbrugh's Smaller Houses', *Architectural Review*, vol. CXV (1954), pp. 118–22.

Wilkinson, R., *Londina Illustrata*, 2 vols, London (1825).

Williams, Ramond, *The Country and the City*, London (1985).

Williams, Robert, 'A Factor in his Success. The Missing Years: Did Vanbrugh learn from Mughal Mausolea?', *Times Literary Supplement* (3 September 1999), pp. 13–14.

Willis, P., *Charles Bridgeman and the English Landscape Garden*, Newcastle-Upon-Tyne (2002).

Willis, R., and J. W. Clark, *The Architectural History of the University of Cambridge*, 4 vols, Cambridge (1886 ed.).

Wilson Jones, M., *Principles of Roman Architecture*, London (2000).

Wind, E., 'Shaftesbury as a Patron of Art', *Journal of the Warburg and Courtauld Institutes*, vol. II (1938), pp. 182–5.

—, 'Julian the Apostate at Hampton Court', ibid., vol. III (1939), pp. 127–37.

Wittkower, R., *Architectural Principles in the Age of Humanism*, London (1948).

Woodbridge, K., *The Stourhead Landscape* [National Trust Guides], London (2002).

Worsley, G., *Classical Architecture in Britain: The Heroic Age*, London and New Haven (1995).

—, 'In the English Campagna', *Country Life*, vol. CXCV (27 September 2001), pp. 118–23.

—, 'Sir John Vanbrugh and the Search for a National Style', in *Gothic Architecture and its Meanings, 1550–1830*, ed. M. Hall, Reading (2002), pp. 97–132.

—, 'Stowe House Buckinghamshire', *Country Life*, vol. CXCVII (27 March 2003), pp. 124–8.

—, 'Blenheim: Architecture of Albion', *Country Life*, vol. CXCVII (9 October 2003), pp. 90–4.

—, 'Stowe House Buckinghamshire', *Country Life*, vol. CXCVIII (29 January 2004), pp. 52–6.

—, 'Vanbrugh and the Spirit of Rome', *Country Life*, vol. CXCVIII (16 September 2004), pp. 118–23.

—, *Inigo Jones and the European Classicist Tradition*, New Haven and London (2007).

Yolton, J. W., *Perception Acquaintance from Descartes to Reid*, Oxford (1984).

Photograph Credits

Institutions currently holding drawings, paintings and prints illustrated in this book are cited in the captions. Unless otherwise credited, the photographs of Vanbrugh's work are the author's own.

Illustrations are listed by figure number. The following sources have been used:

Ann Nutkins, 60
Bath University Library, 51, 53, 63, 99, 133, 151, 190, 201, 226, 228, 240, 242, 253, 263, 280, 281, 282, 287, 288, 291, 297, 298
Bibliothèque National de France, Paris, 48
Bodleian Library, Oxford, 8, 57, 81, 185, 210, 294, 311, 322, 345, Appendix II
British Architecture Library, R.I.B.A., London, 118
British Library, London, 5, 109, 181
British Museum, London, Department of Prints and Drawings, 34, 65, 66, 366
Conway Library, Courtauld Institute of Art, London, 116, 138, 167, 219, 256, 276, 277, 283, 284, 323, 324, 325, 329, 330, 340, 342, 343, 355
Country Life Picture Library, London, 92, 237
Crown Copyright: Historical Royal Palaces, 39
Detroit Institute of Art, 132
Devonshire Collection, Chatsworth, 85
Duke of Marlborough, 202
English Heritage Photo Library, Swindon, 100
Fitzwilliam Museum, Cambridge, 358
Greenwich Heritage Centre, Martin Collection, 320, 326, 327, 328, 331, 333
Guildhall Library, Corporation of London, 52, 80

Huntingdon Country Records, 216
Lambeth Palace Library, London, 182
Lincolnshire Archives Office, 295, 296, 362
London Metropolitan Archives, London, 33
Lord Middleton Collection, Birdsall, Yorkshire, 79
Louvre, Paris, 364
Metropolitan Museum of Art, New York, 130, 312
Municipal Archives, The Hague, 16
National Archives, Kew, 40, 115
National Maritime Museum, London, 12
National Monuments Record, Swindon, 44, 45, 47, 49
National Portrait Gallery, London, 1, 10, 30, 35
Paul Richens, 155
Ray Biggs, Grimsthorpe Castle, 6, 59, 290, 299, 300, 361
Regional Buildings Record, Bath University Library, 137, 164, 248, 251, 252, 259, 260, 261, 262, 264, 275, 364
Royal Library, Windsor, 41, 42
By courtesy of the Trustees of Sir John Soane's Museum, London, 367
Society of Antiquaries, London, 339
Staatsbibliothek, Munich, 22
Stowe School Photographic Archives, 148
Vaughan Hart [from *Nicholas Hawksmoor: Rebuilding Ancient Wonders*, 2002], 2, 29, 32, 50, 61, 71, 112, 113, 186, 192, 196, 198
Victoria and Albert Museum, London, 145, 146, 150, 154, 159, 218, 285, 304, 317, 349, 353
Wiltshire Records Office, 117
Wren Society Volumes, 103, 119, 184
Yale Center for British Art, New Haven, Paul Mellon Collection, 163

Figures in *italics* refer to illustration
  numbers

Addison, Joseph, xii, 26, 33, 36, 37, 38,
  86–109, 123, 126, 144–5, 181, 208, 230,
  231, 241, 249, 259 n. 123, 265 n. 13; *49,
  129*
Aeneas, 210
Aesop, xvi, 38, 58, 108, 116
Alberti, Leon Battista, xvi, 29–30, 137
Alexander the Great, 21–2, 36, 231; *47*
Alfred (King), 45, 259 n. 117
Amphitrite, 204
Amsterdam, 35
Anabaptists, 121
Ancaster, *see* Bertie, Robert
'Ancients', *versus* 'Moderns', 25, 214–16
Anet, château, 101, 181; *157, 160*
Angarano, Giacomo, 180, 239
Anne (Queen), 8, 18, 24, 58, 62, 121, 132,
  136, 137, 157, 162, 214, 258 n. 112; *87,
  202*
    churches of, xiv, xvi, 3, 5, 92–3, 95–109,
      111–26, 239, 250, 254–5, 267 n. 10,
      268 n. 58
Anne (Countess of Sunderland), 41
Anstis, John, 9, 67–8
Antaeus, 204
Apollo, 24, 259 n. 115, 269 n. 19
Apreece, Rhoda, 164
Arbuthnot, John, 36
Archer, Thomas, 121, 257 n. 37, 274 n. 4
Aristotle, 116, 118, 137, 267 n. 46
Arthur (King), 48, 55, 58
Ashmole, Elias, 53, 56–8, 67; *84, 86, 101, 173*
Astraea, 132, *see also* Golden Age
Aubrey, John, 59; *81*
Audley End, Essex, 65, 244, 263 n. 65; *100*
Aviler, Augustin Charles d', 30

Babylon, hanging gardens, 88
Babylon, walls, 88
Bacchus, 111
Barbaro, Daniel, 38, 267 n. 46
Barfleur, battle, 157
Barker, Thomas, 1
Bathurst, Lord, 94

Beltz, George, 53
Belvoir Castle, 80
Benson, William, 14, 16, 68
Bernini, Giovanni Lorenzo, 31, 48, 119,
  204; *56*
Bertie, Peregrine, 195
Bertie, Robert (Duke of Ancaster), xiii, 5,
  194–208, 256 n. 8
Berwick-upon-Tweed, Ravensdowne
  Barracks, 74; *116–17*
Bible, architectural wonders of, 88
Binny, Lord, 94
Blaeu, Joan, 35
Blathwayt, William, 5
Blenheim, battle at, 80, 136, 143
Blenheim Palace, Oxfordshire, xi, xii–xiii,
  xiv, xvi, 12, 13–14, 18, 30, 32, 35, 37,
  38–40, 43, 63, 72, 74, 79, 84, 91, 93, 94,
  111, 120, 129, 136–45, 159, 169, 171, 183,
  210, 216, 241, 249, 251; *3, 98, 99, 133–5,
  201–3, 205–7, 209–11, 272; see also*
  Woodstock Manor
    bridge, xvi, 12, 13, 15, 24, 142–4, 246,
      257 n. 19; *7, 8*
    estate, 248–52; *356*
    kitchen court, 53, 74, 85, 112, 138, 142,
      239; *83*
    Rosamond's Well/Bower, 51, 87, 144–5,
      164, 208; *81, 82*
    obelisk, 31–2; *57*
Blondel, François, 108, 258 n. 100; *166*
Board of Ordnance, xi, 74, 85, 220,
  264 n. 101; *see also* Chatham Dockyard,
  store and gate; Devonport, Gun Wharf;
  Woolwich Arsenal, Old Board of
  Ordnance
Board of Works, 14–22, 80–81, 136,
  258 n. 81; *see also* Vanbrugh, John,
  Comptroller
Bonduca (Boadicea), 58–9
Borromini, Francesco, 119
Boulogne, Château de ('Madrid'), 181;
  267
Boulter, Edmund (William), 9, 136
Boursault, Edmé, xiv, xvi, 38
Boyle, Henry (Lord Carleton), 268 n. 55
Brest, 7

Breval, John, 96
Bridgeman, Charles, 32, 91, 208; *63, 311*
Brown, Lancelot ('Capability'), 109, 143–4,
  263 n. 40
Browne, Isaac, 38
Browne, Joseph, 260 n. 44
Burghley House, Lincolnshire, 48, 181; *76,
  270*
Burlington, Third Earl of (Richard Boyle),
  xii, 73
Burnet, Thomas, 35
Burton, Robert, 96, 99, 108; *147*

Caesar, Julius, 22, 38, 39, 58, 59–61, 101,
  138, 156, 185, 231; *90–92*
Calais, citadel, 5, 185; *17, 18*
Calvin, John, 118
Campbell, Colen, xii–xiii, 17, 30, 63, 73,
  119, 179–80, 188, 194, 200, 249,
  266 n. 79; *51, 53, 63, 99, 133, 151, 164, 190,
  201, 228, 240, 242, 253, 263, 280–82, 287–8,
  291, 297–8*
Campen, Jacob van, 257 n. 30
Capron, William, 41; *52*
Carleton, Dudley, 1
Carlisle, First Earl of (Charles Howard),
  130
    Third Earl of (Charles Howard), xiii,
      10, 11, 12, 14, 15, 17, 24, 29, 35, 38,
      46, 53, 65, 69, 70, 91, 94, 108, 112,
      113, 116, 129–32, 134, 144, 164, 181,
      186, 225, 231, 249, 250, 258 n. 112,
      265 n. 42
Carpenter, Samuel, 244; *223*
Carya, 142
Cass, Christopher, 264 n. 101
Castle Howard, Yorkshire, xi, xii, xiv, xvi,
  7, 24, 30, 38, 39, 60, 70, 72, 74, 78, 85–6,
  89, 91, 94, 95, 99, 101, 113, 114, 120,
  129–35, 138, 154, 159, 164, 169, 205, 208,
  241, 244, 246, 249, 258 n. 112, 268 n. 5;
  *50, 93, 106–7, 128, 151, 188, 190–91, 193,
  310, 359*
    Belvedere ('Temple of the Four
      Winds'), 24, 32, 93, 112, 113, 129,
      132–5, 164, 210, 241; *168, 195–6,
      198–200*

Carrmire gate, 93, 129, 131; *136*
estate, 248–52
Mausoleum, 24, 116, 129, 164; *175*
obelisks, 38, 101, 129, 131; *153*
Pyramid Gate, 74, 88, 101, 108, 129, 131, 185; *156*
Pyramid, 24, 33, 129; *189*
Ray Wood, xvi, 91, 132
Satyr gate, 154, 244; *223*
Temple of Venus, 129, 131, 164; *192*
Wilderness, xvi, 91, 99, 132
Cave, William, 119
Cerberus, 204
Ceres, 132, 200, 204–5, 249; *310*
Chambord, Château de, 181; *269*
Charbonnier, Martin, *28*
Chargate, Surrey, 10, 46, 74, 84, 183, 213, 232–41, 262 n. 17; *342–4; see also* Claremont House
Charles II, xi, 37, 56, 60, 61, 67, 73, 150, 272 n. 49; *95*
Charlton House, 48
Chatham Dockyard, store and gate, 74, 85; *112–13,*
Chatsworth House, Derbyshire, Elizabethan house, 48
Baroque house, 24, 259 n. 118
Cheere, Henry, *2*
Chester, 1, 231, 261 n. 67; *9*
China, great wall, 88
Cholmondeley Hall, Cheshire, 30; *53*
Chrysaor, 205
Cibber, Colley, 41
Cicero, Marcus Tullius, 38, 112, 132, 267 n. 11
Civil War, 24
Claremont House, Surrey, xiii, 45, 64, 232–41, 243, 256 n. 8; *347–50, 354; see also* Chargate
Belvedere, xii, 26, 45, 64, 74, 234–6; *70, 346, 349*
Clarke, Samuel, 59, 137–8, 156, 185, 231, 263 nn. 51, 53; *90, 91*
Clayton, Thomas, 144
Clifford, Jane ('Rosamond'), 53, 144
Clitus, 36
Cobham, *see* Temple, Richard
Coke, Edward, 271 n. 2
Colbert, Jean Baptiste, 18, 48, 231
Coleman, William, 84, 148
Collier, Jeremy, 117, 119
Colvin, Howard, 22
Congreve, William, xiv, 36, 37, 39, 41, 247, 256 n. 12, 261 n. 72
Constantine, 116
arch in Rome, 269 n. 45
Constantinople, 35
Costanza, tomb of, 116; *176*
Counter-Reformation, 118
Cupid, 204

Dancourt, Florent Carton de Dancourt, xiv, 38, 101, 248
De l'Orme, Philibert, 48, 101, 181; *157*
Decker, Matthew, 248
Defoe, Daniel, 40–41, 43, 61, 112, 125, 247, 258 n. 107
Deists, 116
Delaval, Francis Blake, 157, 164, 169
Delaval, George, 108, 157–69, 231
Delaval, Ralph, 157
Denham, John, 112
Dennis, John, 36, 116
Desaguliers, John Theophilus, 36
Descartes, René, 86
Desgodets, Antoine Babuty, 269 n. 45
Devonport, Gun Wharf, 74; *115*
Devonshire, First Duke of (William Cavendish), 94, 259 n. 118
Diana, 24, 111, 132, 269 n. 19; *193*
Dido, 210
Doddington, George Bubb (Baron Melcombe), 186
Doddington, George, 108, 186–94
Dorigny, Nicholas, 35
Downes, Kerry, xii, 213
Drake, Francis, 51
Drayton, Michael, 55
Druids, 58–9; *89*
Dryden, John, xiv, 24, 36–40, 56, 59, 111, 112, 132, 144, 257 n. 12, 261 n. 72
Dugdale, William, 35, 48, 53, 228

Eachard, Laurence, 35, 56–9; *87, 88*
East India Company, 2, 35
Eastbury House, Dorset, 30, 32, 74, 85, 88, 96, 101, 171, 181, 185, 186–94, 244–6, 248; *63, 145–6, 276–88*
Easton Neston, Northamptonshire, 147, 156; *213*
Edifice des Tuteles, 181; *265*
Edward III, 55, 56, 58, 61, 200, 231
Egypt, pyramids, 88
Elizabeth I, 259 n. 117; *109*
Elton Hall, Vanbrugh Volume, xiii
Epaminondas, 259 n. 117
Erechtheum, Athens, 266 n. 2
Errard, Jean, 5, 185
Esher Old Church, Surrey, 239; *351–2*
Etty, William, 91, 113
Evelyn, John, 96, 112

Farquhar, George, 247
Fischer von Erlach, Johann Bernhard, 32–3; *62*
Fiz-Harding, Robert, 183
Fletcher, John, xiv, 38
Flitcroft, Henry, *94*
Flora, 111, 132
Fontainebleau, Grand Ferrara, *22*
Fontana, Carlo, 32, 119, 125
Fontana, Domenico, 101, 125; *158, 183*

Fort, Thomas, 258 n. 102; *39*
Francini, Alexandre, *174*
Fréart de Chambray, Roland, 2, 29, 89, 112, 113
Freemasons, 11–12, 53

Galilei, Alessandro, 156; *225*
Galileo (Galileo Galilei), 116
Garter Knights, xi, 8, 48, 53–81, 150, 225, 231, 249, 251, 263 n. 82; *103, 173*
Gent, Thomas, 132; *194*
Geoffrey of Monmouth, 59
George I (Elector of Hanover), 40, 53, 58, 62–3, 200, 201; *88*
George II, 8, 70, 263 n. 82
Gibbons, Grinling, 119
Gibbs, James, 46, 125; *68*
Gildon, Charles, 36
Girardon, François, 204
Glastonbury Abbey, 48; *75*
Glorious Revolution, xi, 20, 25–6, 45, 259 nn. 115, 123
Godolphin, Earl (Lord Treasurer), 11, 15, 63–4, 83, 108
Godolphin, Harriet (Henrietta), 274 n. 10
Golden Age, 22–6, 60, 129, 132–3, 205, 249, 252, 258 n. 108
Granville, George, 43
Great North Road, 35, 46
Greenwich, *see* London, Greenwich
Grimsthorpe Castle, Lincolnshire, xii, xiii, 30, 32, 39, 46, 78, 94, 106, 154, 171, 194–208, 246, 249; *6, 59, 165, 289–94, 299–302, 304–9, 361*
Guillim, John, 36, 71–2; *108*

Halicarnassus, mausoleum, 24
Halifax, Lord, 8, 87, 263 n. 82
Handel, George Frideric, 40, 59
Hanover Club, 12
Hanover, 8, 35, 70, 87, 263 n. 82; *27*
Herrenhausen garden, 8; *28*
Hardwick Hall, Derbyshire, 48, 186; *77*
Harley, Robert (Chancellor of the Exchequer), 137
Hastings, George (Eighth Earl of Huntingdon), 8
Hastings, Theophilus (Seventh Earl of Huntingdon), 5
Hawksmoor, Nicholas, xi, xii, 11–12, 14–15, 17, 18, 24, 29, 30, 31, 32, 33, 46, 48, 63, 67, 79, 85, 88, 89, 94, 95–6, 99, 101, 106, 108, 109, 112, 118, 120, 121, 125–6, 129, 130–34, 136–7, 147, 148, 156, 164, 181, 195, 204, 228, 244, 258 n. 100, 265 n. 61, 266 nn. 89, 91, 268 nn. 5, 64, 269 n. 45; *2, 31–3, 57, 71, 103–105, 117–18, 136, 139–41, 162, 175, 180–82, 187, 189, 192, 196, 198, 210, 213*
Cambridge plan, 125; *186*
Oxford plan, 125; *185*

Haym, Nicola, 36, 72, 159; *232*
Heidelberg, 257 n. 37
Henderskelfe Castle, *see* Castle Howard
Henry (Prince of Wales), 55, *85*
Henry I, 183
Henry II, 53, 144–5, 183, 231
Henry III, *96*
Henry V, 200
Henry VII, 200
Henry VIII, 45, 86, 152, 194, 200, 201
Heraldry, xi, 36, 48, 70–73, 114, 129, 130,
     138, 147, 169, 184, 203, 231, 264 n. 91;
     98, 102, 106–9, 234, 301–2
Hercules, 22, 72, 111, 203, 204, 264 n. 91
Hesiod, 36
Hewett, Thomas, 14, 16–17
Hill, Thomas, 11
Hogarth, William, 249–50; *65, 172, 358,
     366–7*
Hollar, Wenceslaus, 56, 67; *57, 101*
Homer, 39, 259 n. 117
Hood, Robin, 114; *see also* Skelbrooke,
     Yorkshire, Robin Hood's Well
Houghton Hall, Norfolk, 26; *51*
Hypnerotomachia Poliphili, 134; *197*

India, Taj Mahal, 208; *152; see also* Surat,
     India
Inveraray Castle, Argyll, 220, 256 n. 8; *340*
Irwin, Anne, Viscountess, 24, 36, 132, 208,
     228

James I, 24, 46, 55
James II, xi, 6, 53
James, John, 20, 24, 30; *32, 33*
Jelfe, Andrews, 264 n. 101
Jerusalem, Temple (Temple of Solomon),
     37, 55, 96
Jones, Inigo, 33, 37, 43, 55, 60, 73, 111, 114,
     119, 156, 167–9, 239, 241, 262 n. 41; *85,
     94, 178*
Jonson, Ben, 25, 37
Joseph of Arimathea, 48
Joynes, Henry, 13, 35, 121, 141
Julian the Apostate, 21, 22
Juno, 111
Jupiter, 204
Juvenal, 36, 37, 39, 260 n. 38

Katherine of Aragon (Queen), 86, 152,
     203
Kent, William, xii, 73, 81, 259 n. 117; *94,
     122–3*
Kimbolton Castle, Cambridgeshire, xii,
     xiii, 5, 29, 37, 38, 60, 64, 72, 73–4, 80,
     84, 86, 88, 94, 95, 112, 148–56, 166, 171,
     231, 244, 256 n. 8, 264 n. 102; *4, 92,
     214–16, 218–21, 225*
Kings Weston, Gloucestershire, xii, 30, 88,
     94, 101, 106, 171–85, 188, 200, 239, 244,
     246, 256 n. 8, 266 n. 79, 272 n. 12; *137,*

161, *163–4, 247–56, 259, 263–4, 266,
     274–5, 364*
   banqueting house, 179; *257–8*
   brew-house, 74, 179; *261*
   Penpole gate, 180; *262*
   stables, 179; *260*
Kip, Johannes, 183; *95, 274, 289*
Kit Cat Club, 9, 12, 24, 43, 87, 130, 148
Kiveton Hall, 48
Kneller, Godfrey, 9, 53, 136; *1, 10, 30, 35, 49,
     87, 88, 202*
Knyff, Leonard, *95, 274, 289*

La Pillonnière, François de, 36
Langley, Batty, 106–8
Le Muet, 29
Le Sage (Alain René), xiv, 38
Le Vau, Louis, 6, 7; *20, 24*
Leominster, Lord (William Fermor), 147
Leoni, James, 29
Leslie, Charles, 41
Liberal Arts, 162; *237*
Little Castle at Bolsover, Derbyshire, 48,
     220; *78*
Locke, John, 22, 86–7, 96, 108, 109
London, British Museum, 43; *66*
   Chelsea Hospital, 79; *121*
   Christ Church, Spitalfields, *121*
   Covent Garden, St Paul's church, 119;
        178
   Drury Lane, 41, 43, 114, 144
   Fire Monument, 67; *102*
   Greenwich, Hospital, 17, 30, 79, 113,
        135, 147–8, 160, 217, 231; *36–8, 55, 120*
      Queen's House, 63, 231
      The 'Nunnery', 39, 73, 166, 213,
           217–31, 239, 241; *324–8, 332*
      Vanbrugh Castle, xii, 10, 46, 73–4, 84,
           88–9, 186, 213, 217–31, 243,
           250–52; *67, 110–11, 126, 131, 315, 319,
           334–9, 341*
      Vanbrugh House ('Mince-Pie
           House'), 73, 89, 186, 213, 217–31;
           321–3
      White Towers, 73–4, 166, 213,
           217–31; *329–33*
   Hampton Court, 17, 20, 21, 36, 67, 181;
        39, 40, 44–7, 103, 271
   Haymarket, Queen's Theatre, 32, 40–43,
        64, 85, 244, 246, 247, 256 n. 12; *52, 65,
        66*
   High Holborn, Hercules Pillars
        Alehouse, 12, 72
   Kensington Palace, 20, 256 n. 8,
        258 n. 102; *42*
      Orangery, 11; *31*
   Kensington Palace Green, water tower,
        85; *127*
   New Exchange, 250
   Palace of Westminster, 196, 249–50, 274
        n. 40

Richmond Park, Merlin's Cave, 81; *123*
Royal Academy of Music, 40
St Anne, Limehouse, *139*
St George, Bloomsbury, 67, 125; *104, 141*
St George-in-the-East, 67, 106–8, 121;
     105, 162
St James's Palace, 20, 256 n. 8,
     258 n. 102; *41, 43, 181*
St John, Horselydown, 12; *33*
St Luke, Old Street, 12; *32*
St Mary Woolnoth, *140*
St Mary's in the Strand, 125
St Paul's Cathedral, 37, 112
Society of Antiquaries, 46, 217; *339*
Victoria and Albert Museum, xiii
Westminster, 125; *187*
   Abbey, 46, 258 n. 75
   Whitehall, 'Goose-Pie' House, 9, 10, 36,
        53, 71, 88, 147, 213–17, 239, 244, 251;
        29, 316–17
      Banqueting House, 43, 239, 241
      Holbein Gate, 51; *80*
      Palace, 60, 213, 274 n. 40; *94*
Longinus, 39
Louis XIV, 20, 48, 142, 231
Lowther Castle, 24, 259 n. 118
Ludwig, Karl, 257 n. 37
Lumley Castle, Durham, 154–6, 160, 184,
     196, 243–4; *224*
Lycurgus, 259 n. 117

Magna Carta, 45, 157, 252
Mahal, Mumtaz (Queen), 208
Manchester, Earl of (Charles Montague),
     xiii, xiv, 29, 43, 48, 64, 73, 84, 94, 112,
     148–56, 258 n. 108
Mansart, Jules Hardouin, *23*
Mantegna, Andrea, 60; *90, 92*
Mantua, 'Porta Cittadella', 138
Marlborough, First Duke of (John
     Churchill), xiii, 12, 18, 24, 32, 41, 59–60,
     63, 67, 74, 84, 85, 108, 118, 129, 136–45,
     157, 231, 249; *98*
   Duchess of (Sarah), xiii, xiv, xvi, 6,
        12–14, 45, 51, 83–4, 87, 91, 136–7,
        144–5, 171, 231, 247, 253; *30*
Mars, 24, 111, 129, 132; *see also* Temple of
     Mars Ultor
Matthews, William, 2
May, Hugh, 56, 60, 73, 89, 244; *95, 96*
Medusa, 94, 204–5; *306*
Merlin, 81; *see also* Richmond, Merlin's
     Cave
Michelangelo, 32, 96, 119; *58*
Middleton Park, Oxfordshire, 268 n. 55
Milton, John, 36, 101, 116, 132, 269 n. 20
Minerva, 205; *see also* Pallas Athene
Mlylne, Robert, 171
Mogul, xii, 2–3, 5, 35, 88, 101, 116, 208
Molière, xiv, 38, 256 n. 12
Morocco, 157

Morpeth, town hall, 183, 250; *273*
Morris, Roger, 186
Mowl, Tim, xii
Moxton, Joseph, 30

Nebel, river, 142
Neptune, 79, 94, 159–60, 204–5; *234, 306*
Newcastle, Dukes of, (John Holles and
    Thomas Pelham-Holles), xiii, 9, 11, 12,
    13, 15, 16, 26, 35, 45, 51, 63–4, 68, 70,
    80, 93, 116, 171, 195, 196, 220, 234–6,
    241
Nonconformists, xi, xii, 116, 121; *see also*
    Vanbrugh, John, Protestantism
Norberg-Schulz, Christian, 112
Norfolk, Dukes of, 262 n. 25
North, Roger, 25, 37
Nottingham Castle, xiii, 64, 154, 166, 243
Nottingham, Earl of, 7
Nutt, Edward, 195

Office of Works, *see* Board of Works
Order of the Garter, *see* Garter Knights
Osborne, Peregrine (Marquess of
    Carmarthen), 7
Ovid, 36, 153–4, 204–5, 208, 225; *222*
Oxford, All Souls, 46, 256 n. 8; *71*
    Bodleian Library, xiii
    Earl of, 18
    market-place and town hall, 250
    Merton College, 172
    Tom Tower, Christ Church, 46, 84; *72*
    Worcester College, 269 n. 45
Oxinden, George, 5

Palazzo Farnese, Caprarola, 30; *54*
Palladianism, xi, xii, 186
Palladio, Andrea, 2, 29, 37–8, 109, 113, 119,
    125, 141, 171, 180, 256 n. 6, 261 n. 57;
    61, 208
    Villa Rotonda, 32, 134, 239; *60*
Pallas Athene (Minerva), 24, 111, 132, 138
Pandora, 119; *179*
Paris, Académie Royale de Musique, 40
    Bastille, 6–7, 35, 231; *21*
    College of the Four Nations, 7; *24*
    Les Invalides, 7, 264 n. 106; *23*
    Louvre, 7, 20; *25*
    Tuileries, 7; *26*
    Vincennes, Château de, 6, 150, 244; *19,
        20, 217, 360*
Payne Knight, Richard, 109
Pegasus, 205
Pellegrini, Gianantonio, 24, 60, 246,
    259 n. 115; *50, 92*
Pembroke, Earl, 72
Penshurst Palace, 25
Perrault, Claude, 20, 30, 181, 203; *25, 265,
    303*
Persius, 36, 37, 39, 260 n. 38
Phaeton, 24, 70, 154, 259 n. 115; *50*
Pharos lighthouse, Alexandria, 32–3; *62*

Plato, 132
Pliny the Elder, 59
Plot, Robert, 83; *125*
Plutarch, 36
Pluto, 94, 204–5; *305*
Pope, Alexander, 25, 29, 37, 89, 164
Portugal, 157
Post, Pieter, 257 n. 30; *15, 16*
Poulet, Lord, 137, 249
Poussin, Nicolas, 144
Powell, George, 263 n. 48
Pozzo, Andrea, 24, 30, 246
Praeneste, Temple of Fortuna Primigenia,
    32, 134; *61*
Praxiteles, 210
Presbyterians, 121
Prior, Matthew, 36
Proserpine, 94, 111, 204–5; *222, 305*
Purcell, Henry, 46, 58–9

Quakers, 116, 121

Raphael (Raffaello Sanzio), 35
Ravenna, 116
Renaissance, 31, 73, 88, 109, 243
Ripa, Cesare, 114
Rocque, John, 234; *348*
Rolt, Edward, 248
Romano, Giulio, 138
Rome, Capitol, 32; *58*
    gateways, 225
    Pantheon, 31
    Piazza Navona, 31, 48; *56*
    St Peter's, 101; *158*
Romulus, 22
Rosa, Salvator, 90; *132*
Rosamond's Well/Bower, *see* Blenheim
    Palace, Rosamond's Well/Bower
Rowlands, Henry, 59; *89*
Royal Society, 22, 36, 46, 172
Rutland, Duke of, 80
Ryswick, Treaty of, 22–4; *48*

Sacombe Park, 248, 256 n. 8
St George, 53, 54, 55, 58, 61, 67, 72–3, 131,
    203, 231; *98*
St George, Henry, 55, 67, 70
St Luke, Gospel, 36
St Paul, Gospel, 36
Salinas, Maria de, 201
Salisbury Cathedral, 40
Scheemakers, Peter, 211
Seaton Delaval, Northumberland, xvi, 30,
    38, 39, 46, 60, 72–3, 74, 78–9, 106,
    157–69, 171, 194, 203, 205, 210, 243,
    246, 248, 249, 250, 252, 256 n. 9,
    261 n. 72; *64, 212, 226–9, 231, 233–45, 363*
Seneca, 39, 132
Serlio, Sebastiano, 72–3, 79, 88, 96, 101,
    111, 114, 115, 131, 134, 138, 150, 157–9,
    162, 164, 181, 203, 205, 243, 264 n. 95,
    266 n. 83, 267 n. 5, 269 n. 12, 271 n. 28;

22, 142–4, 158, 169–71, 176, 204, 230, 268,
    357
Settle, Elkanah, 36
Seward, Anna, 259 n. 117
Shaftesbury, Anthony Ashley Cooper,
    Third Earl of, 22, 26, 73, 116, 137,
    259 n. 123
Shakespeare, William, 48, 55, 252
Shute, John, 25, 119; *179*
Siberechts, John, *79*
Sixtus V, *183*
Skelbrooke, Yorkshire, Robin Hood's Well,
    6, 114; *69*
Skipwith, Thomas, 46, 262 n. 9
Sloane, Hans, 72
Smythson, Robert, *270; see also* Burghley
    House, Lincolnshire; Wollaton Hall,
    Nottinghamshire
Soane, John, 109, 213, 252, 270 n. 2; *29*
Socrates, 132, 259 n. 117
Solomon, Temple, *see* Jerusalem, Temple
Somers, John (Lord), 22, 73
South Sea Bubble, 14, 186
Southwell, Edward, 171–85, 239
    Robert, 172
Specchi, Alessandro, 32; *58*
Stairs, Lord, 94
Stanhope, Earl, 68
Stebbing, Samuel, 70
Steele, Richard, 36, 37
Stevens, John, 35, 46–8, 228; *73–5*
Stonehenge, 156
Stowe, Buckinghamshire, 29, 46, 81, 88, 91,
    99, 101, 208–11, 239, 251, 259 n. 117,
    266 n. 72; *68, 122, 124, 130, 148–9, 246,
    311–14*
Stukeley, William, 46, 217, 220, 230; *294,
    322, 339*
Sturt, John, 24
Suffolk, Earls of, 64–5, 70
Sumsion, Thomas, 106
Surat, India, xiii, 2–5, 33–5, 88; *12, 13*
    English Cemetery, xiii, 99–101, 125, 185,
    255; *5*
Swift, Jonathan, 7, 9, 25, 29, 36, 53, 70–71,
    88, 147, 213–17, 225, 226, 231, 248,
    274 n. 20, *318*
Swiney, Owen, 43
Swinstead, Lincolnshire, 195, 246; *293, 362*
Switzer, Stephen, 195; *294*
Syon House, 48

Talman, William, 8, 14, 78–9; *119*
Tate a Tate Club, 12, 72
Tavernier, Jean-Baptiste, 2–3; *11*
Temple of Aphrodite Knidos/Venus,
    Greece, 210
Temple of Mars Ultor, 141; *208*
Temple, Richard (First Viscount
    Cobham), 29, 46, 208–11, 239
The Hague, 5, 32, 194, 247, 257 n. 37
    Knights' Hall, 5; *14*

Noordeinde Palace, 5, 257 n.30; *15*
Old Town Hall, 5, 257 n. 30
Huis ten Bosch, 5, 257 n. 30; *16*
The Spectator, 87–109; *see also* Addison, Joseph
The Vine, Sevenoaks, Kent, 239; *355*
Theodoric, tomb of, 116; *177*
Thornhill, James, 15–16, 200; *299*
Tickell, Thomas, 145
Toland, John, 59
Tonson, Jacob, 2, 10, 11, 12, 13, 14, 16, 29, 35, 36, 39, 40, 41, 43, 53–4, 58, 59, 72, 87, 113, 137, 159, 208, 211, 263 n. 53, 271 n. 39; *10, 222*
Tories, xi, 25–6, 59, 121, 214, 258 n. 112, 259 n. 119, 263 n. 53, 268 n. 58
Tournai, Porte Royale, 142
Tower of Babel, 88
Townesend, George, 171
Trajan, 24
Trajan, column in Rome, 269 n. 45
Troy, 55, 225
Tynemouth Priory, 160

Valencia, 35
Van Eck, Caroline, 147
Vanbrugh, John
    Advice to Church Commission, *see* Anne (Queen), churches of
    A Short Vindication of The Relapse and The Provok'd Wife, xiv, 35, 116–18, 250
    background, xi, 1–8; *1*
    Charles (brother), 43, 217, 225
    Charles (son), 11, 36, 39, 153, 208, 217, 228, 230, 260 n. 38
    coat of arms, 1, 70, 71, 246; *91*
    Comptroller, 8, 14–22, 59, 62, 121, 136, 213, 214, 250
    Herald, xii, 9, 20, 53–81, 130, 159, 164, 217, 220, 241, 263 nn. 82, 83; *1*
    John (son), 217, 230
    Journal of Receipts (Accounts), xiv, 29–36
    marriage, 11
    Philip (brother), 217

plays by
    A Journey to London, xiv, 120, 225, 249–52, 271 n. 50
    Aesop, xiv, 7, 14, 53, 58, 118, 120, 164, 248, 249, 251
    The Confederacy, xiv, 10, 70, 118, 129, 267 n. 26
    The Country House, xiv, xvi, 101, 248, 274 n. 17
    The False Friend, xiv, 20, 35, 101, 111, 164, 205, 210, 247, 257 n. 28, 271 n. 50
    The Mistake, xiv, 12, 24, 36, 38, 39, 85, 114, 132, 165, 210, 247, 271 n. 47
    The Pilgrim, xiv, xvi, 24, 96, 111, 114, 132, 247, 257 n. 12
    The Provok'd Wife, xiv, 11, 58, 153, 166, 208, 247, 250
    The Relapse, or Virtue in Danger, xiv, 11, 35, 38, 73, 80, 114, 117–20, 147, 165–6, 210, 250, 263 n. 48
Protestantism, xi, 5, 11, 101, 111, 116–18, 132
Surveyor of Royal Gardens and Waters, 14
Vassalli, Francesco, 169
Venice, 46, 148, 262 n. 5
Venturi, Robert, 246
Venus, 24, 111, 132, 210–11; *197*
Venus and Adonis, 211
Verrio, Antonio, 21, 60, 259 n. 115, 263 n. 57; *47, 97*
Versailles, 26, 39–40, 79, 142, 167, 204, 259 n. 115
Vertue, George, 58, 59; *87, 88*
Vignola, Giacomo Barozzi da, 30; *54*
Virgil, 36, 38, 39, 132
Vitruvius, 20, 37, 38, 111–12, 113, 115, 119, 134, 159, 181, 203, 267 nn. 5, 11

Wachter, Peter, *28*
Walden, Lord, 70
Walpole, Robert, 26, 260 n. 128; *51*
Ware, Isaac, 273 n. 35
Watkins, William, 18–19, 157, 160

Webb, Geoffrey, xiv
Webb, John, *94*
Welbeck Abbey, 48, 64, 78–9, 256 n. 8; *118–19*
Whigs, xi, xii, 14, 18–26, 40–41, 45–6, 59, 70, 116, 121, 130, 132, 135, 157, 162, 194, 208, 214–16, 230, 252, 258 n. 112, 259 nn. 117, 123
Wilcocks, Joseph (Dean of Westminster), 46
William I, 200
William III (William of Orange), 5, 22, 36, 200, 231, 257 n. 30, 258 n. 112, 259 n. 117
William the Conqueror, 157
Windsor Castle, 6, 53, 56, 60, 65–7, 70, 73–81, 89, 150–52, 244, 252, 262 nn. 33, 41; *95, 96, 101*
    chapel, 55–6, 62, 231, 263 n. 57; *86*
    St George's Hall, 53, 61; *84, 96*
Wise, Henry, 91
Wollaton Hall, Nottinghamshire, 48, 181, 186, 220; *79*
Woodstock Manor, Blenheim Park, 13, 32, 35, 45, 51–3, 83–4, 87, 89–91, 95, 109, 144, 164, 166, 183–4, 208, 230, 241, 252, 253; *34, 125*
Woolwich Arsenal, Old Board of Ordnance, 74, 85; *114*
Worksop Manor, 48, 220
Worsley, Giles, 210, 271 nn. 28, 30
Wotton, Henry, 72, 79, 119, 130
Wren, Christopher, 11, 14–17, 18, 24, 29, 30, 33, 36, 37, 40, 43, 46, 65–7, 73, 79, 92, 106, 109, 112, 118, 120, 121, 125, 141, 152, 167–9, 213, 257 n. 37, 259 n. 123, 267 n. 46; *35, 72, 101, 102, 120–21, 184*
    Christopher (son), 16, 72, 121

Yarburgh, Henrietta Maria (Lady Vanbrugh), xiv, 11, 116
York, 160

Zorrilla, Franciscode Rojas, xiv